Marxism and Realism

This book rethinks Marx's sociology as a form of realist social theory, extending Roy Bhaskar's philosophical realism into the social sciences. The book puts forward an anti-reductive ontology of society, identifying a stratified social world in which individuals, practices and structures are the key levels. Within this framework, the key task of realist social theory is to investigate the dialectical interplay between these key levels in shaping historical processes and systemic outcomes.

By constructing historical materialism as realist social theory, it becomes possible to resolve many long-standing dilemmas in Marxist discourse, such as voluntarism versus determinism, humanism versus economism and agency versus structure. Social realism provides the means to theorise the interface between subject and system, or individual and society, which reveals the emergent nature of social systems.

The book also argues that realism requires a thoroughgoing materialistic application in order to avoid the residual idealism and empiricist pluralism in social analysis of most major schools of sociological thought. In contrast, this book argues that social systems are best grasped as being shaped at the interface between specific kinds of structural and interactional mechanisms, namely between the forces and relations of production, base and superstructure, and social labour and class struggle.

Sean Creaven has taught sociology and social policy at the University of Plymouth and completed a doctorate at the University of Warwick.

Routledge Studies in Critical Realism

Critical realism is one of the most influential new developments in the philosophy of science and in the social sciences, providing a powerful alternative to positivism and post-modernism. This series will explore the critical realist position in philosophy and across the social sciences.

1 **Marxism and Realism**
A materialistic application of realism in the social sciences
Sean Creaven

Also published by Routledge:

CRITICAL REALISM: INTERVENTIONS
A series edited by Margaret Archer, Roy Bhaskar, Andres Collier, Tony Lawson and Alan Norrie

Critical Realism
Essential readings
Edited by Margaret Archer, Roy Bhaskar, Andres Collier, Tony Lawson and Alan Norrie

The Possibility of Naturalism
A philosophical critique of the contemporary human sciences
Roy Bhaskar

Being & Worth
Andrew Collier

Quantum Theory and the Flight from Realism
Christopher Norris

From East to West
Odyssesy of a Soul
Roy Bhaskar

Realism and Racism
Concepts of race in sociological research
Bob Carter

Marxism and Realism

A materialistic application of realism in the social sciences

Sean Creaven

London and New York

First published 2000
by Routledge
11 New Fetter Lane, London EC4P 4EE

Simultaneously published in the USA and Canada
by Routledge
29 West 35th Street, New York, NY 10001

Routledge is an imprint of the Taylor & Francis Group

Typeset in Garamond by Taylor & Francis Books Ltd
Printed and bound in Great Britain by MPG Books Ltd, Bodmin

British Library Cataloguing in Publication Data
A catalogue record for this book is available from the British Library

Library of Congress Cataloging in Publication Data
Creaven, Sean, 1963–
Marxism and realism: a materialistic application of realism in the social sciences / Sean Creaven.
(Routledge studies in critical realism)
Includes bibliographical references and index.
1. Marxian school of sociology. 2. Realism. I. Title. II. Series.
HM471 .C74 2001
301–dc21 00–055230

ISBN 0–415–23622–3

This is for Patricia, with love

Contents

Preface

This thesis will be concerned with articulating and defending a form of realist social theory I have entitled 'emergentist Marxism'. As such, its principal objective is less to investigate the voluminous literature on 'social realism' and more to show the ways in which Marxist theory can be legitimately 'constructed' as a specific 'materialistic' application of ontological and methodological realism in the human sciences.

The significance of this research is that it functions simultaneously as a contribution to the social science component of Roy Bhaskar's philosophical realism, and as a Marxist commentary upon and perhaps intervention against it. The latter is less certain, however, because Bhaskar's depth realism appears to be consistent with the version of anti-reductive materialism defended here.

'Realism' or 'emergentism' refers to an ontological position denoting a stratified social world of irreducible levels, of which persons, practices and structures are the most fundamental, all of which are efficacious by virtue of the properties and powers which pertain to each of them. 'Materialism' denotes the ontological position where the material structures of social systems vertically explain social and cultural structures without 'explaining them away'. Thus 'emergentist Marxism' is an anti-reductive socio-historical materialism and attendant dialectical realist method. Translated into practical social research, it is applied concretely here to the task of theorising the interface between the properties and powers which pertain to human agents, and those which pertain to social structures, in shaping the constitution and dynamics of social systems.

Acknowledgements

Several people have provided me with invaluable support and assistance during the writing of this book. First and foremost, thanks to Patricia for all her emotional support and encouragement over the past four years. I also owe an enormous debt of gratitude to my parents, Linda and Kevin, for providing me with much needed financial support, without which I would not have been able to complete the project. And, of course, the same is true of Patricia's parents, Joy and Ray, who generously allowed me to colonise their front sitting room as an office, and who supplied me with a steady flow of tea over the past four years.

Special thanks are due to Professor Margaret Archer, who has allowed me to draw on her work with impunity, and whose advice on theoretical matters and on editing the final manuscript has been much appreciated. It was Professor Archer who made the suggestion that I investigate the relationship between realism, Marxism and explanatory theory, which forms the core of this book. And the reader will notice that her work on the sociology of agency, and on the nature of the structural conditioning of human interaction, has been very influential in the formation of my own account of the interface between structure and subject in social systems contained herein.

Last but not least, I would like to acknowledge the invaluable contribution made to the theoretical development of this work by certain leading comrades of the Socialist Workers' Party, including and especially Alex Callinicos, Chris Harman, John Molyneux and John Rees, whose understanding of Marxism and social theory has considerably informed and enriched my own. This is particularly true of Alex Callinicos. His work on the interface between structure and agency in historical materialism has had considerable input into this book, and has been its inspiration and starting point.

Introduction

The task of this thesis is an ambitious one: to outline and defend a Marxist understanding of the relationship between human agency, social interaction and social structure in social systems. To these ends I have 'reconstructed' Marx's socio-historical materialism as a radicalised form of realist or 'emergentist' social theory: 'emergentist Marxism'.

Theory and method

By 'emergentism' I mean a philosophical ontology which specifies a stratified material world, comprised of irreducible levels (many of which are unobservables), extending from the most basic structures of inorganic matter to the higher strata of mind, self and society. Each of these levels is defined as such by its possession of discrete autonomous causal properties and conditional effects, and each arises once a given complexity of interaction at an anterior or underlying level of organisation is reached. By social realism I mean an emergentist ontology of society. This specifies a stratified social world, comprised of distinct levels of necessarily and internally related phenomena (of which 'individuals', 'interaction' and 'structure' are the most basic), each of which is irreducible to the others 'precisely because of the properties and powers which only belong to ... them and whose emergence from one another justifies their differentiation as strata at all'.[1]

The methodological task of realist social theory is to investigate the dialectical interplay between these distinct 'domains' of the social world in shaping structural or systemic outcomes. 'Emergentist Marxism' accepts this philosophical argument, and the practical analytical conclusions which are drawn from it. But this form of realist social theory is committed to defending the controversial but central claim of classical Marxism, that specific forms of human agency (social labour and class struggle) and social structure (the forces and relations of production) have explanatory primacy in shaping the constitution and dynamics of social systems.

My reason for constructing socio-historical materialism as realist social theory is a straightforward one. Only by doing so can the long-standing dilemma of voluntarism versus determinism, structure versus agency be resolved. An emergentist ontology of the social world, together with those 'analytical logics' consistent with it, is a necessity for Marxist theory because it provides the researcher with an invaluable redoubt against the various reductive forms of contemporary social theory which have bedevilled attempts to grasp the nature of the individual-society or micro-macro connection. What such approaches have in common is a commitment to treating one or other of the constitutive strata of social reality (whether individuals, practices or structures) as alone providing the 'master key' by which it should be analysed or explained. By contrast, emergentist Marxism is resolutely anti-reductive, by virtue of its advancement of a realist 'stratified model' of reality.

Now, the advantages of endorsing emergentism and attendant methodological realism in social analysis are best demonstrated by considering in a little more detail the unhappy fate of those sociological approaches (namely holism, atomism and elisionism) which reject it. Consider, first of all, the competing claims of both sides of the long-standing debate between exponents of holism and individualism in the philosophy of social science.

Holism versus individualism revisited

This debate has been kept alive to a large extent beyond its sell-by date by the fact that both sides have contributed something of value to sociology. From the atomist camp (or at least that part of it which rejects psychologism and biologism) has come the insight, in opposition to holism, that people are *sui generis*, that it is they and not societies who make history, and that social interaction between individuals, not 'structural laws' or 'system imperatives', are responsible for societal reproduction or elaboration. From the holist camp has come the insight, in opposition to atomism, that the interaction of human agents and much of their disposition-set is explainable in terms of the socio-cultural structures and 'situations' within these structures into which they enter involuntarily at birth.

Both kinds of perspective thus capture something of importance about the experience of people in society. Individualists (though not atomists generally) rightly emphasise the fact that people are 'sovereign artificers', possessing powers of subjectivity and agency irreducible to the facts of their society's structural organisation and their biological constitution, and argue with equal veracity that society and culture are dependent for their existence and persistence upon the ideas and activity of people. Holists rightly emphasise the fact that individuals are inserted involuntarily into patterned and enduring social relationships which exist independently of their will, which shape their actions and consciousness in determinate ways, and which offer resistance even to concerted collective efforts to alter or transform them.

Where atomism and holism go wrong, however, is in building up their respective partial insights into the nature of society into full-blown philosophical ontologies of social being. By doing so they each, in their own way, ride roughshod over the 'vexatious fact of society',[2] which is definable as such by its complex articulation of powers and properties pertaining to structures and individuals respectively. For atomists (including exponents of biological or psychological reductionism), the necessity and desirability of their ontology and methodology is given by the logical absurdity (as they see it) of attributing existential status to unobservable 'societal facts' (i.e. socio-cultural structures) which nonetheless are dependent for their existence and development upon human beings, their dispositions and activities. The activity-dependence of structures is, for them, suggestive of an underlying identity between individuals and their 'relational properties', the latter being merely an aggregation of the behaviours (derived from pre-social impulses) of the former.

For holists, by contrast, the fact that atomists are not able to reduce social facts to facts about individuals (or human nature), is itself indicative of the need for social analysis to embrace an ontology and method which deals only with the relations between 'holistic' entities and which infers sociological 'laws' (e.g. of integration or adaptation) irreducible to individual beliefs, desires or dispositions on this basis. The necessity of socio-cultural entities to describe and explain the social behaviour and attitudes of individuals is, for them, proof of their independent and irreducible ontological status *vis-à-vis* individuals, and of the methodological dispensability of reference to individuals and their activities in explaining social structure.

For both parties, then, a dogmatic refusal to acknowledge the valid insights of the other side, and to assume their own insights must be exhaustive of social reality, has generated the pernicious long-term consequence of denying sociological analysis the theoretical tools to conceptualise the relationship between structure and interaction, human nature and social order. For it is only by abandoning the either/or polarity of the atomism versus holism debate that the social analyst can begin to get to grips with the problem of theorising how structures can be dependent upon the activities and attitudes (or dispositions) of human beings and yet enjoy existential (and hence explanatory) autonomy from them. This has been (until recently) the outstanding unresolved theoretical problem of sociology.

But how can this mutual wilful disregard by practitioners of atomism and holism of the insights and arguments of each other (which has discouraged for so long the articulation of an emergentist alternative to both) be explained? Undoubtedly, an important explanation of why many social analysts have found themselves drawn to ontological atomism and methodological micro-reductionism is to be found in their acceptance of empiricist epistemology.

For instance, atomists of a 'subjectivist orientation' have managed to turn a blind eye to the explanatory autonomy and causal efficacy of structures by dismissing anything that is unobservable from social analysis (without noticing that the 'personal dispositions' of individuals which they hold to be 'ultimate' are also unobservable!). By contrast, the ontological warranty of holism appears rather more ambiguous and uncertain than that which underwrites atomism, motivated as it has been by both empiricist assumptions (in the work of the functionalists) and their mirror-opposite (in the work of the structuralists).

For the functionalists, adherence to sociological holism does not seem consistent with a genuinely scientific empiricism (given that all 'social facts' other than those specifying small groups are not amenable to 'sense data'). Doubtless it is this fact which explains Durkheim's resort to positivism, a move which allowed him to treat social facts as empirically specifiable things, operating in a law-like manner and manifesting observable regularities at the level of events.

For the structuralists, rejection of Humean causality, though entirely defensible, has inevitably underwritten forms of social theory which are emancipated from the disciplines of any kind of empirical checking and which function to assimilate the tangible to the intangible (the abolition of the subject and the postulation of an 'indeterminate' human nature). Here holist ontology and method is defended by means of theoretical fiat: unobservable properties of society are asserted to be real, autonomous of people, and alone causally efficacious in explaining interaction, even where no empirical data can substantiate or otherwise suggest their existence. Thus, whereas for atomists the baneful shadow of empiricism has been the chief culprit in fostering an uncritical and unreflective refusal on their part to countenance the disconfirming arguments of collectivists, for holists opposition to individualism (where it has not itself been undermined by adherence to empiricism) has been justified in the name of an anti-empiricism which blinds itself to the fact that some empirical means of validating emergent entities is necessary and that tangible flesh-and-blood individuals are also causally efficacious and are hence irreducible to the unobservable structures they inhabit.

The fundamental problem with holism, on the one hand, is that reference to individuals and their social interaction is indispensable to specifying what 'societal entities' are and what they do. 'Structures' and 'systems of structures' are not self-regulating or self-determining, and they cannot be explained in abstraction from people, their powers and doings, since they depend for their existence and persistence on the activities and attitudes of individuals.

The fundamental problem with atomism, on the other hand, is that reference to the existential reality and explanatory autonomy of structures is necessary to account for much of the 'attitudes' and 'actions' of individuals. Structures are real because they pre-exist the individuals who animate them, and because they generate or define causal powers or conditional effects which are not explainable in terms of individual human organisms or subjects, their dispositions or interaction in the present tense. At the same time, however, structures are not explainable 'in their own terms', and nor do they operate as hydraulic determinants of human agency and social interaction. They are, in fact, 'emergent' from the activities and attitudes of previous generations of human beings. Yet the properties or powers they possess in their own right are not those specifying how individuals must think and act, but are rather those defining their 'situational logics' (and their objective social interests) and the cultural resources which constrain and enable their thinking.

The new sociologies of praxis

Consider now the theoretical logic of the new 'elisionist' sociologies (i.e. symbolic interactionism, social constructionism, structuration theory and post-structuralism). Practitioners of these all have claimed to offer a viable solution to the either/or polarities of structure or agency, macro or micro, system or subject (and related divides such as determinism/voluntarism, objectivism/subjectivism, etc.) represented traditionally by both sides of the holism versus atomism dispute. But, whereas holism and atomism have opted for different sides of the dualism of structure and subject, the elisionist theorists have sought to deny the relevance of the old dispute, replacing it with theoretical perspectives which treat subjects and their social 'environment' or 'circumstances' as twin aspects of the duality of social interaction, cultural praxis or social or signifying practices. From this point of view, neither subject nor structure is the 'basic constituent' of social reality, since both social organisation and self-identity emerge from the immersion of human beings in ongoing social practices or processes of interaction, meaning that neither have any autonomy or efficacy apart from inter-subjective relations.

In embracing central conflation in theory and mesoreduction in method, however, the elisionist sociologists have surrendered important insights of both the earlier approaches they have sought to synthesise or transcend – most notably individualism's emphasis on the irreducibility of the subject, and holism's opposite stress on the irreducibility of structure and system, both of which are entirely respectable. That neither subjects nor structures of social relations can be reduced 'without remainder' to social practices or interaction, is indicated by the fact that explanation in terms of the latter always presupposes properties and powers pertaining to the former.[3] But this means that social analysis must proceed by examining the interface of at least three distinct levels of reality: subjects, interaction and structure. To put the matter economically: structure cannot be an aspect of current or ongoing social practices because interactants always find it 'already made', the ineluctable environment of their conduct, meaning that social interaction modifies or replicates but never creates structure.

Realism and analytical dualism

The failings of holism, atomism and elisionism indicate the advantages to the theorist of endorsing sociological emergentism. For only a realist ontology, which specifies a stratified social world comprised of irreducible levels embodying 'real' yet unobservable emergent entities, is capable of coming to grips with the dualistic nature of social reality, and hence of providing a plausible explanation of why statements pertaining to structure, interaction and subject are ineliminable from social description and explanation. Moreover, only sociological emergentism can unravel the problem of empiricist sociology of specifying how structures can be different in kind from people and their interaction yet be dependent upon them.

This is because structures are theorised by realists in a way which preserves their activity-dependence (and hence protects them against charges of reification) and which secures their real existential status *vis-à-vis* individuals. On this view, structures are the unobservable resultants of the interaction of past generations of human agents which, though activity-dependent upon contemporary individuals in the sense that these can be reproduced or transformed only through the doings of the living, nonetheless confront flesh-and-blood people as an inherited social environment of independent powers and effects (of objective constraint, enablement and impulse).

Now, an acceptance of the necessity of an emergentist or realist social ontology immediately furnishes the sociologist with stringent guidelines as to which forms of explanatory methodology and modes of practical theorising are appropriate to the task of analysing society. I have suggested that the autonomy of structures from flesh-and-blood human agents and their social interaction is revealed by their pre-existence: every generation of individuals is born into an already functioning societal organisation which is constraining and enabling of its activity and ideas. This is in itself a practical demonstration of the factual separability of structure and interaction in social systems, since it is indicative that these two key strata of society are not co-existent in time. Because structure always predates the interactions which reproduce or elaborate it, and because interaction always predates the elaborated or reproduced structure which results from it (structural elaboration necessarily post-dating social interaction), it follows that the two cannot be identical and hence must be treated as analytically separable for purposes of social theorising.

It is, in other words, the temporal disjunction between structure and interaction which evidences their existential independence, and which thereby justifies their analytical separability in social research. It follows from these observations that the methodological task of social analysis is to examine the manner in which the powers and properties which belong to the 'people' of a society interact over time with the properties and powers which belong to the 'parts' which compose its social structure. For any 'inert' or 'static' conception of society which neglects the temporal dimension must render either structure or individuals as epiphenomena of the other.

Another way of making this argument is to point out that a realist ontology of society requires both 'analytical dualism' and the 'morphogenetic/static' theoretical approach.[4] A useful specification of the warranty of methodological dualism in social research has recently been provided by Nicos Mouzelis:

> [T]he utility of the agency-institutional distinction is that it helps us to realise that for a full explanation of social stability or change one must look at social phenomena from both an institutional [i.e. structural] and an agency perspective. Parsons does not do this, with his emphasis on institutional compatibilities, but Marx does, with his emphasis on structural contradictions and social conflict. ... The crucial point here is that although the system-social integration distinction ... is an analytic one, it refers to aspects of social reality that can vary in relatively independent fashion – given that growing institutional incompatibilities do not automatically generate social conflict or a certain type of strategic conduct. Situations can be envisaged in which, for example, specific institutional incompatibilities, on the level of agency, lead to revolutionary, reformist or 'apathetic' conduct. ... [This] makes it clear that the distinction between institutions and actors (between system and social integration in Lockwood's formulation ...) becomes useful when one allows for agents to react in a non-fixed, not predetermined manner to ... [structural] incompatibilities. That is to say, it becomes useful for asking questions about how actors perceive institutional incompatibilities (if at all), and what they do about them. Who, for instance, is aware of such incompatibilities and how? Who is trying to maintain, and who to transform them, and why? Such ... questions are absolutely indispensable for understanding how institutional analysis is related to an analysis in terms of strategic conduct, and they can be asked only if one introduces the concept of 'dualism' at levels of 'structure' and 'system'.[5]

The morphogenetic-static approach to social analysis is the practical application of methodological dualism in social analysis. Its warranty is a function of the necessity of social analysis to approach the study of the dialectical interface between structure and interaction in a way which allows the theorist to grasp the manner of their mutual interplay across time and space in the reconstitution and elaboration/ transformation of social systems. From this perspective, since structure always predates and preconditions the social interaction which replicates, modifies or transforms it, and since structural replication/elaboration/transformation always postdates the activities which have given rise to it, it follows that social theory must conceptualise and study the dynamics of social systems accordingly. In practice, this means endorsing a diachronic and sequential mode of analysis, whereby structural conditioning (*p1*) is 'present' in the social interaction of agents, in which structurally conditioned social interaction (*p2*) then gives rise to an elaborated or reproduced structure (*p3*), which in turn preconditions subsequent interaction (*p1*), hence marking the start of a new morphogenetic/static cycle of societal dynamics.

Thus, grasped concretely from this realist perspective, structural contradictions and compatibilities (conceived as emergent entities constraining and facilitating action) operate to distribute differential life-chances, vested interests and causal powers to differently situated collectivities of agents and institutional functions, and by doing so exert a directional pressure upon agents to act in ways which protect or further their interests. These are the antecedent conditions for social malintegration (i.e. inter-agential antagonisms and conflicts), and these correspond to the first phase of the morphogenetic cycle. The actuality and outcome of social malintegration (*p2* and *p3* respectively) is then subsequently resolved either in terms of system replication or elaboration or in terms of system transformation, depending crucially on the success or otherwise of agential groupings in articulating their common interests in stability or change, and mobilising their structural and institutional capacities (of organisation, political leadership, ideology, etc.) towards the realisation of these ends.

Realism and morphogenesis thus provide the sociologist with the analytical tools to reconcile the 'structuralist' and 'activist' dimensions of sociological thought within a unitary theoretical research programme. For the first time, coherent philosophical and methodological grounds can be given to justify Percy Cohen's famous assertion that

> in all sociological inquiry it is assumed that some features of social structure and culture are strategically important and enduring and that they provide limitations within which particular social situations can occur. On this assumption the action approach can help explain the nature of the situations and how they affect conduct. It does not explain the social structure and culture as such, except by lending itself to a developmental inquiry which must start from some previous point at which structural and cultural elements are treated as given.[6]

Realism and Marxism

This realist method and social ontology informs and enters into all of the explanatory hypotheses advanced in the forthcoming analysis. But why should a realist theory of the social world be reconstructed or redefined as 'emergentist Marxism'? Or to put it more bluntly: why does realism need materialism?

My point of departure from philosophical realism is that only by grasping social realism as a kind of anti-reductive materialism can two unacceptable theoretical-methodological positions in the social sciences be avoided. The first of these is a residual idealism, which can be justified on the grounds that 'cultural elements', because irreducible, are *autonomous* of social and material structures. The second is 'pluralism', or what Althusser once (rightly) dismissed as a 'theory of factors'.

One major conceptual difficulty with the latter approach is that it sanctions an understanding of society which disassembles it into autonomous institutional spheres or 'modes of social power', and in doing so abstracts away from its relational nature. Little wonder that practitioners of 'multi-factoral' social theory (notably postmodernists and neo-Weberians) often find themselves denying the reality of social systems. A second major conceptual difficulty of pluralist social theory is that it cannot support an understanding of societal change as development or evolution, which I consider to sit uneasily with the historical facts of the matter. Instead, history has to be grasped as just-so empirical narrative, which in practice reduces it to Weber's 'chaotic flux' or 'meaningless multiplicity'.

Emergentist Marxism offers a solution to each of these difficulties. First, the 'ideal elements' of social systems are explainable, in terms of material structures which are 'basic' to them, yet are not 'explained away' by them, or denied emergent powers or real-world effects in their own right. They remain real and efficacious apart from their 'causes' or 'conditions'. Second, the idea of 'structure' or 'system' is preserved, because sets of social relations constitute a 'unity in difference' by virtue of their common locus or anchorage in relations of production and/or modes of class power.

Finally, so too is the 'problem of history' (i.e. the fact that social change evidently is not a directionless flow of events) offered a solution of sorts. For the 'dominance' of the mode of production, in shaping structural dynamics, allows one to account for the fact of 'directionality' in historical process, by virtue of its unique generative powers in enabling and stimulating overall societal evolution and/or transformation, and its 'tendency to assert its own movement as necessary', even against obstruction from the 'non-economic' structures and practices of social systems.

Structure of thesis

These in a summary form are the central arguments of the present undertaking. I have organised them as follows. Chapter 1 is an introductory chapter. Its purpose is to investigate the relationship between philosophical realism and emergentist materialism and to investigate the ways in which Marxism is a 'materialism' and what kind of materialism it is. I am also concerned here with identifying and defending the main explanatory claims of Marx's philosophy and social theory (prior to their more substantial treatment in later chapters), showing their compatibility with ontological and methodological realism, yet showing also the ways in which they can be legitimately said to enrich or deepen the realist approach.

Chapter 2 addresses the 'micro-foundations' of social systems: individuals as the bearers of organismic and subjective properties and powers. Here I am concerned with theorising the relationship between 'species-being' and 'social being'. My argument is that specifying the relative autonomy of the subjectivist and organismic properties of human agents from socio-cultural conditioning is indispensable to any adequate explanation of societal organisation and societal change.

Chapter 3 addresses the 'interaction order' which rests upon and is emergent from the organismic and subjectivist strata of individuals. My objective here is to obtain a purchase on the question of the relationship between the 'macroscopic' (structural) and microscopic (psycho-organic) properties or levels which are constitutive of social systems. My argument is that 'interaction' is the mechanism of system elaboration or statics, as this is forged in the interface between structural and organismic conditioning (human needs mediated by vested social interests).

Finally Chapter 4 is concerned with theorising the structural properties of social systems. Its primary aim is to show how a realist 'stratified model' of society can sustain a Marxian understanding of 'structural causality' (the vertical determination of superstructure by structure) which does not 'decentre' human agency or collapse into economic reductionism. My argument is twofold. First, that structural conditioning operates on agents by defining the situations they confront, the vested interests attached to situations, and the costs or benefits which follow from the neglect or pursuit of these vested interests determined by 'situational logics', this explaining the 'regularities' of social interaction which reproduce and elaborate social systems. Second, that the 'situational logics' and vested social interests determined by class positions within social relations have explanatory primacy in explaining the socio-political consciousness and agency of interactants (because these are decisive in determining the access of agents to material and cultural goods), this accounting for why superstructural forms have a tendency to 'correspond' with relations of production and systems of class power.

This, I conclude, leaves us with as much of Marx's social theory as is reasonable to hope for: a defensible, materialist account of the constitution and dynamics of social systems.

1 Critical realism and Marxism

The tasks of Marxism in philosophy and social analysis

In the Introduction to this book I have briefly set out the case for a realist (or emergentist) ontology of the social world and those theoretical and methodological perspectives which are consistent with it. This has been accomplished by presenting the conceptual and methodological defects of the more influential misadventures in social theory of recent years (i.e. individualism, holism and elisionism in their various guises) and by showing how analytical models rooted in sociological emergentism overcome these.

So it is that individualism fetishises the subject by placing him or her prior to the ensemble of social relations which are necessary to explain his or her thinking and conduct (e.g. Weber's attempt to grasp social institutions in accordance with his typology of the value-orientations and ends of social action). So it is that holism reifies social relations by endowing these with powers of reason, intentionality and agency by virtue of which individuals are mere 'bearers' of their teleological or functional 'needs' (e.g. Parsons' 'system imperatives' of adaptation, pattern-maintenance, goal attainment and integration). And so it is that elisionism de-centres both the social-structural and organismic-subjective properties of society – by treating these as 'two sides of the same coin' of social practices or routinised interaction – and in so doing locates the 'over-plastic self' in a world devoid of objective material constraints (e.g. Blumer's and Giddens' collapse of subject, society and nature into inter-subjective relations). Thus the burden of my critique so far has been to demonstrate that reductive-conflationary social theory in all its forms is inadequate, because it is an abstraction from the multi-layered complexity of social reality and from the irreducibility and causal efficacy of its constitutive emergent strata.

In contrast to these 'simplifying manoeuvres', which seek to render social analysis less daunting by squeezing its object into a uni-dimensional space, the task of sociological emergentism is to grasp society as a 'differentiated totality', as the resultant of a plurality of generative mechanisms operative at different levels of the social and natural worlds. This implies a definite form of theory and method. Structural analysis will not alone suffice, because structural properties are reproduced and elaborated only by virtue of social interaction, and these systemic outcomes are by no means determined in advance of interaction. The problematic of 'interaction' or 'praxis' will not do either because the doings of agents are precisely 'routinised' or 'structured' in various ways by virtue of the existence of an objective social world, which from the point of view of every generation of people is 'already made'. Nor can social theory make its appeal to subjects as its 'ultimate constituents', for although the individual is 'author' of his or her social behaviour, he or she is also forged in the space between physical, biological and social reality, and in this sense is the product of 'a rich totality of many determinations and relations'.[1]

It is this 'Janus-faced' nature of human-social reality which necessitates a methodological-theoretical approach which neither dissolves its hierarchically structured complexity nor simply reproduces a 'chaotic conception of the whole'[2] in thought. For this reason I have argued that methodological dualism (the analytic abstraction of structure from interaction, and the analysis of the reciprocal effectivity of these strata over time in shaping systemic outcomes) and morphogenetic theorising (the activation or contextualisation of analytical dualism within a diachronic cyclical model of society, whereby anterior structural properties condition social interactions which in turn give rise to structural elaboration or reproduction) provide the sociologist with indispensable tools for the practical business of 'doing' research.

Yet realist social science is not fully adequate to the task its practitioners have set for it, of providing the theoretical and methodological tools for grasping the interface between the different strata which comprise the subject-matter of the human and social sciences. This is because scientific realism can only benefit from the incorporation of dialectical methodology into its analytical framework, in the absence of which it is necessarily incomplete or partial. Methodological realism investigates the 'real object' as follows. First, by moving from the concrete to the abstract (through finer and finer conceptual abstractions), proceeding in this way until its constituent elements or relations (which generate its manifold causal powers and empirical effects) are identified and delineated. Then, by retracing its steps until the 'chaotic whole' (concrete reality) is reconstructed in thought as a systematically ordered totality which distinguishes between its essential and inessential aspects and between its contingent and necessary relations with other objects.

Andrew Sayer summarises the approach as follows:

> As a concrete entity, a particular person, institution or whatever combines influences and properties from a wide range of sources, each of which (e.g. physique, personality, intelligence, attitudes, etc.) might be

> isolated in thought by means of abstraction, as a first step towards conceptualising their combined effect. In other words, the understanding of concrete events or objects involves a double movement: concrete ⇒ abstract, abstract ⇒ concrete. At the outset our concepts of concrete objects are likely to be superficial or chaotic. In order to understand them we must first abstract them systematically. When each of the abstracted aspects has been examined it is possible to combine the abstractions so as to form concepts which grasp the concreteness of their objects.[3]

This is basically Marx's method in *Capital*. Marx's purpose here is to outline 'a hierarchy of theoretical models, ascending by successive approximation from very abstract models representing the basic social forms present in modern bourgeois society up to fuller, more detailed models of this society'.[4] Such an analytical approach is necessary for two reasons. First, because 'concrete objects' (and the structures which comprise them) are often unobservables. Second, because the empirical world (which is directly amenable to the senses) is the chaotic resultant of a plurality of generative mechanisms derived from various underlying structures, together with the multiple contingencies of their functioning in the open social system, and hence is a poor guide to the determinate causal powers of any of these structures.

Now, this method is already dialectical in the sense that it does not seek to decompose its objects of knowledge (unobservable structures or systems of structures) into 'a chaotic collection of fragments ... or a mere aggregate of unconnected happenings',[5] but instead attempts to grasp these as wholes of interconnected parts. 'The true is the whole',[6] as Hegel put it. And the whole can be grasped only by means of an analysis of the dynamic interplay of its parts, just as the parts can be understood only by examining their interplay with the whole, not least because the powers and characteristics of both are modified or even transformed by the interaction between them.

This method is also dialectical in the sense that it attempts to grasp objects or structures by differentiating between those elements or relations which define their essence and those which are simply contingent or phenomenal aspects of their organisation or functioning. Wholes have to be grasped as *organic* totalities, as Marx and Hegel both insisted, since this allows us to understand dynamic processes in terms of *internally generated development*. For example, it does not make any sense to define 'value' in abstraction from the relations between 'many capitals' and between employers and wage-labourers. The law of value can exist only by virtue of the internal and necessary social relations of commodity production, which in its turn gives rise to a specific pattern of economic motion (the boom-slump cycle, organic crisis, concentration-centralisation of production, etc.).

Finally, methodological realism is dialectical because its mode of operation is based foursquare upon 'a dialectic between *concept* and *fact*'[7] operative at each level of scientific inquiry. This is for the simple reason that the concepts which are applied to each aspect of a 'unity-in-difference' (the natural and social worlds) cannot be ahistorical givens or the product of a universal method, but must 'be carefully scrutinised and grounded in the particular subject matter under investigation',[8] as the understanding of this is developed through the ongoing process of practical scientific activity, and the theoretical abstractions and methodological innovations which are derived from it. In other words, scientific realists, in common with Marx, recognise that science is 'a dialectical process in the sense that its methods and concepts, as well as its theories, develop over time in dynamic interaction with one another and with the material world, allowing progressively more accurate descriptions of reality to emerge'.[9] So, for example, the

> various concepts of physics – such as mass, velocity and energy ... did not arise automatically from experience, but were developed by a long and complex process of abstraction, and the same holds true for the very different concepts employed in cell biology or in meteorology or in any other area of science.[10]

Nonetheless there is one important way in which realist methodology neglects dialectics, and is the poorer for it. I refer to the failure of many contemporary scientific realists to acknowledge explicitly that dialectical thinking is necessary to scientific inquiry for the simple reason that the nature of reality demands it. Marx argues that dialectical thinking

> includes in its comprehension and affirmative recognition of the existing state of affairs, at the same time also, the recognition of the negation of that state, of its inevitable breaking up; because it regards every historical developed ... form as in fluid movement, and therefore takes into account its transient nature not less than its momentary existence.[11]

The basis for this view is Marx's understanding, in common with Hegel, that objects or systems are often contradictory in themselves, invariably exist in relations of tension as well as compatibility with other objects or systems, and that it is this fact which makes historical change a possibility, whether in nature or society.[12]

As Hegel himself puts it, 'contradiction is at the root of all movement and life, and it is only in so far as it contains a contradiction that anything moves'.[13] The reason for this is simply that all processes of internal change or development to which structures or objects are subject are necessarily and simultaneously processes of self-cancellation and self-affirmation.[14] This means that in order to understand the nature of concrete objects, one cannot simply examine the whole, nor its separate parts, but must instead study '*the process of development* through which the parts come to constitute the whole and, in doing so, become different than they were in their pre-existing form'.[15]

A dialectical method is therefore appropriate in scientific research because reality *is* dialectical.[16] The basic idea is that if thought objects are to correspond to real objects which are dialectical they too must have a dialectical structure. Such a view is not in the least bit difficult to fathom and is entirely defensible. Consider the alternative. If reality is not dialectical there can be no impulse towards change in either nature or society; without contradictions as well as complementarities built into the structures of reality there can only be cyclical processes of simple reproduction or repetition at work in the world, not processes of molecular development interspersed by novel transformations.

Thus a non-dialectical worldview and method of cognition reduces the world to a dead collection of facts, devoid of life or movement; and it is this which is the basis of empiricist and theological views of unchanging 'things-in-themselves' as constitutive of the universe. Yet the proof of the necessity of a dialectical approach is precisely to be found in the historical development of scientific inquiry itself. For it can hardly be doubted that empirical science has uncovered 'a world of dynamic, interconnected processes – processes which frequently involve elements which not only interact but are in conflict with one another, and thus give the system to which they belong an inherent tendency to develop', and leading over time 'to sudden radical changes in the system as a whole'.[17] To admit of this however is to do no more than concede Engels' basic argument: 'Nature is the proof of dialectics, and it must be said for modern science that it has furnished the proof with very rich materials, daily increasing'.[18]

By way of demonstration of the efficacy of dialectical method, I will consider a single example: the question of the appropriate analytical and theoretical tools for conducting sociological research. I have suggested that methodological dualism and morphogenetic theorising are indispensable for this purpose. This is true enough as far as it goes. But it does not go far enough. The basic morphogenetic model (of: structural conditioning ⇒ social interaction ⇒ structural elaboration/reproduction) is non-propositional as to why social systems 'as a rule' undergo continual change, even if the change is for the most part merely quantitative. Nor does it provide any overall guidance as to why social systems are sometimes transformed into different kinds of social systems with novel properties. This becomes a merely empirical question, contingent upon the precise characteristics of any given structure at any given point in time. Yet a voluminous output of historical research since the last war has revealed that specific kinds of structural mechanisms (specifically the interface between forces and relations of production and between social classes) have been deeply implicated in every major epochal transformation of social relations since the demise of the earliest pre-class communities.[19] Any collapse of social analysis, into the immediate process by which specific structural properties enter into and are reproduced or elaborated in a given society, is likely to lose sight of this elementary process.

In order to address issues such as these, it is necessary to grasp processes of societal change (whether molecular or macroscopic) as being animated by contradictions internal and necessary to social systems as preliminary to the empirical investigation of specific historical episodes or events. Dialectical thinking draws our attention to the fact that ongoing and thoroughgoing systemic change is a function of structural contradictions, which it is then the task of social analysis to identify and investigate. As John Rees puts it:

> A dialectical approach seeks to find the cause of change within the system. And if the explanation of change lies within the system, it cannot be conceived on the model of linear cause and effect, because this will simply reproduce the problem we are trying to solve. If change is internally generated, it must be a result of contradiction, of instability and development as inherent properties of the system itself. Contradiction is, therefore, the *form* of explanation of how one type of ... society succeeds another. ... [But] it is only the *form* of an explanation, because the explanation itself will depend on the concrete, empirical conditions that obtain in each society. The exact contradictions and working out of these contradictions will vary accordingly.[20]

By contrast, in the absence of a dialectical approach to structural dynamics, an account of social change can only be a theory of *external causality* (such as Parsons' understanding of 'structural differentiation' as an adaptive strategy animated by extraneous 'disturbances' to the stable equilibrium of societies), or else a simple 'just so' narrative (which in effect collapses historical explanation into historical description).

A second ambiguity of the morphogenetic-static approach to socio-historical analysis is that, in insensitive hands, it can lend legitimacy to the peculiar idea that societies are static 'moments' or 'points' (of structural conditioning and structural elaboration/reproduction), interspersed by 'processes' of social interaction leading from one to the other. But this is simply not dynamic enough, even as methodology. For what is lost in this construction is the simple point that even at *p1* and *p3* (the 'moments' of structural conditioning and structural remodelling) the structures are themselves fluid rather than static (as for instance any physical object is undergoing 'incessant molecular changes'[21] from one moment to the next). By this I mean that both the antecedent societal 'conditions' of interaction and its 'resultants' are in the moment of their becoming already being reshaped by interactants, and that this reshaping is unavoidable and continuous. Thus even where the outcome of structurally conditioned social interaction is structural replication, this replicated structure is never identical to that which went before. On the contrary, the replicated structure is in this case a 'dynamic equilibrium', in the sense that it is the outcome of a series of quantitative changes which have not yet brought about a qualitative effect. Dialectical logic, with its emphasis on movement and change as fundamental to the mode of existence of all things, is well equipped to avoid the fallacy of 'misplaced concreteness' which has tended to characterise macroscopic sociological theorising of all hues.

Enough said about method. Let us now consider the adequacy of realism as ontology. Is 'depth realism'[22] by itself sufficient to 'under-labour' the human sciences? Not without conceptual modification, or so I would contend. This is for the simple reason that 'realism' as such is non-commital in relation to the fundamental question of which strata of reality are basic to or emergent from which (and this applies as much to the stratification of nature as to that of society). Instead this becomes a matter for individuals to decide on other grounds – specifically on the basis of whether they are materialists or idealists, or have conceived some kind of uneasy or unstable compromise between these unmixables.[23]

After all, it can scarcely be doubted that many philosophers, social theorists and even natural scientists who would endorse a strong realist view of the world (as enmattered, independent of human consciousness, differentiated, even stratified), might as easily insist that the universe is the product of a spiritual 'first cause' than claim that it is nothing but cause and consequence of the law-governed interactive movement of matter through ascending levels of complexity of organisation. Indeed, it is far from uncommon for working scientists to accept that, say, physical structures explain chemical structures, or that biological structures explain psychological structures, or whatever, and yet still make their appeal to some kind of cosmic super-subject (i.e. God) to furnish the 'basic constituents' of nature and the laws governing their interaction from which more complex strata are emergent over time.[24] In this case, of course, the theorist or analyst remains a materialist in their science but an idealist in their philosophy.

This 'conventionalist stratagem' is a case of what Engels once described as 'shamefaced materialism'. For it is the *practical* refutation of idealism during the history of scientific advance and investigation (in the sense that God has been shown to be superfluous to a rational and empirically testable knowledge of natural processes or laws) which has forced its allegiants to make their appeal to a 'final instance' of undetermined creation beyond current knowledge and therefore outside the reach of rational criticism.[25] Now, one should always be suspicious of 'final instances' which base their authority not on firm scientific knowledge (albeit provisional and incomplete) but on its uncertainty or even absence. The possibility that physical scientists may never develop a satisfactory theory of the 'origins' of the universe should not be allowed to give comfort to those idealists whose own belief in a spiritualist 'first cause' of nature is entirely speculative and intuitive.

But it is important to be clear that the realist emphasis on stratification and emergence, and the externality of the world to the knowing subject, provides no redoubt against this kind of manoeuvre. For it is 'equally possible' that materialist or idealist philosophy be either emergentist or conflationist in terms of ontology, either reductive or anti-reductive in terms of methodology. Indeed, it is undoubtedly the case that a failure to recognise this elementary fact has, more often than not, led philosophers and social theorists headlong into the disastrous error of postulating the Cartesian mind/body dualism as an alternative to the competing claims of each.

The above exposition shows that the dispute between realist social theory (sociological emergentism) and the various modes of conflationary social theorising is quite distinct from, and no less vital than, that older debate which trades under the label of materialism versus idealism. This is despite the fact that the conflict between holism and atomism is often treated as closely related to that between idealism and materialism, and despite the fact that elisionism is often erroneously portrayed as 'transcending' the terms of the latter as well as the former.[26] But idealist ontologies of society can be either atomistic or holistic, either voluntarist or determinist, either subjectivist or objectivist (so long as the 'objectivism' in question is understood as something other than human inter-subjectivity – the Mind of God, etc. – which confronts human beings as an external and hence objective power). Materialist theories of society, by contrast, can never be subjectivist or voluntarist. However, they can be either atomistic or holistic. And in insensitive hands they are always reductive and mechanical.

Comtean and Durkheimian perspectives, for instance, are undoubtedly holistic inasmuch as both regard 'society' or 'social facts' as the basic unit of sociological analysis. Yet these approaches are also idealist (though neither voluntarist or subjectivist) insofar as they postulate social ideas (Comte) or cultural norms and values (Durkheim) as the building blocks of social structure and as the locomotive of societal development. Biologistic, behaviourist and 'orthodox' Marxist approaches, on the other hand, are obviously materialist accounts of society, although the former are as atomistic as the latter are (normally) holistic.

The same indeterminate relationship holds true between the philosophical claims of idealism and materialism and most forms of social theory anchored in an elisionist ontology. Few would doubt that the theoretical traditions of symbolic interactionism, social phenomenology, social constructionism and post-structuralism, to offer a random sample, are species of sociological idealism. Such approaches are idealist because they treat 'real objects' (cultural and social structures) as products of thought or discourse, as 'unknowable in themselves', and hence as indistinguishable from the nebulous realm of 'general meanings'. Yet they are obviously radically anti-individualist *and* anti-holist inasmuch as they both reduce human subjects to social selves (forged in social interaction) and 'bracket' or otherwise 'de-centre' overall *systems* of structural social relations.

The debate between idealism and materialism is, strictly speaking, less 'internal' to sociology than that which has taken place between rival forms of conflationary theorising. It has arisen, not so much from ontological and methodological problems which have emerged within the discipline, but rather as a kind of by-product of the broader ideological collision and subsequent accommodation between religion and science (or between theology and secular rationalist philosophy) which characterised the seventeenth-century Enlightenment and its aftermath. The respective ontological claims of idealism and materialism in philosophy are well enough known to require little detailed treatment here. Idealism regards 'matter' as either produced by or dependent upon 'mind' or 'consciousness' or (less radically) postulates the mutual existential independence of the immaterial and the material. Materialism asserts precisely the opposite state of affairs – namely the reducibility of mind to matter, or at the very least, the existential dependence of the former upon the latter.

Ultimately, all idealist philosophy, irrespective of self-conceptions to the contrary, is dependent upon a theological view of the universe. As we have seen, the claim that the material world is the product of ideas, or that the immaterial and the material are autonomous factors of existence, has to discover the origins of the universe in an initial act of 'undetermined' creation, in a 'final cause' traceable to an incorporeal being. In other words, for idealism to be philosophically respectable, 'matter' has to be either reducible to mind or 'emergent' from it and not vice-versa. Materialist philosophy, by contrast, because it insists that mind is reducible to or emergent from matter, cannot but avoid being resolutely atheistic (which is not to say that all materialists are consistent on this basic point!).[27] Thus materialism as philosophical ontology is to a large extent defined by its denial of such entities as the metaphysical Cartesian 'mind stuff', spirits, angels, deities or other assorted phantoms, and by its insistence that 'mind' or 'consciousness', and the products of consciousness, are necessarily embodied or enmattered.

Translated into the subject-matter of sociology and social anthropology, of course, the concepts of idealism and materialism have inevitably become considerably modified, albeit in ways shaped or influenced by the conceptual presuppositions of their 'parent' philosophical outlooks. Idealism in the social sciences, for instance, is not about furnishing an ontological justification of the existential reduction of matter to mind, or the lesser view that the material universe is 'real' but nonetheless presupposes a conscious 'law-giver' (stronger and weaker versions of objective idealism). Nor is such an approach concerned with arguing the philosophical case for treating 'things-in-themselves' as mind-dependent in the sense that material objects have form and content forced upon them arbitrarily by human consciousness (or language) and are hence 'unknowable' and inefficacious until constructed as meaningful objects of cognition (subjective idealism). Rather, the purpose of social idealism is to seek out the explanation (or interpretation) of society and social change in terms of the ideational products of human consciousness or language. But this is a focus which nonetheless always has a certain affinity with the broader philosophical assumptions of ontological idealism in one or other of its guises, and it can scarcely be doubted that most social idealists have been motivated to embark upon their theoretical and other work in the light of these ontological presuppositions.[28]

The same basic point applies to materialism in the human sciences. Social materialism, like social idealism, is not concerned with justifying its own ontological grounds (this is the task of philosophical materialism), but is instead concerned with articulating a theory of society and social process which offers a causal explanation of the contents of human thinking and of the products of social interaction in terms of material structures *immediately* relevant to the human life-process. The crux of the debate between idealism and materialism in the social sciences thus centres on the question of whether it is 'ideal elements' (i.e. the attitudes, norms, values, beliefs, etc. of individuals or communities of individuals) or 'material elements' (i.e. the structures of the sensuous environment, human biology or 'species-being', and socio-economic relations) which should rightly enjoy explanatory primacy in social analysis. This is obviously a quite separate matter to those concerns which are dealt with under the terms of the atomism-holism-elisionism debate.

Now, it seems to me uncontentious that sociology and social anthropology have for the most part been influenced far more profoundly and directly by philosophical idealism than its opposite, notwithstanding notable exceptions to the contrary. Whereas most sociologists of a 'reductive-conflationary' theoretical orientation have been divided on the question of whether to endorse atomist, holist or elisionist social ontologies, nearly all have tended towards idealism in one form or another. For example, it is a commonplace that Max Weber's social theory and method recommends that the explanation of 'social facts' has to be sought in the subjective ends and values of individuals, and modes of society are accordingly held to be defined and organised on the basis of the typical value-orientations and goals which motivate their characteristic patterns of social action. The same is true of the 'objectivist' sociologies of Durkheim and Parsons. These too recommend the analysis of social systems in terms of their characteristic 'collective sentiments' or 'central value-systems', albeit 'sentiments' or 'values' conceived holistically as those corresponding to the 'needs' or 'functional imperatives' of society.

Nor is this the end of the story. I have pointed out that most of the elisionist perspectives have been quite explicitly idealist. And even those versions of the approach (e.g. Giddens' structuration theory) which have claimed to be searching for a balance between the two (structures as 'rules *and* resources') have in practice veered towards idealism (i.e. by rendering resources 'virtual' rather than 'real' until instantiated by conscious human agency and as having no determinate impact upon agents until translated into praxis).

But perhaps the one great exception to this general picture (aside from Marxian philosophy and social theory) is to be found in that (highly ambiguous and not consistently followed) aspect of Weber's substantive historical work which embarks upon a 'pluralist' or 'multi-factoral' analysis of social structure and social change? There is an element of truth to this. But Weber's substantive conceptual-analytical pluralism is never reconciled with his philosophical and methodological writings, and furthermore appears to move away from the 'either/or' polarities of voluntarist idealism versus vulgar materialism, only at the heavy cost of endorsing the opposite fallacy. I refer, of course, to his autonomisation, or fragmentation, of the social system into its individual elements (culture, economy, polity, etc.), and the analysis of these elements (and sub-elements which compose them) in their own terms, in abstraction from the social relations which constitute them.

No doubt a major reason why academics (sociologists included) have tended to endorse an implicit, taken-for-granted idealism is explainable in terms of the peculiarity of their institutional role as agents of 'knowledge production', or as 'bearers of discourse' in capitalist society. After all, who would doubt that those who spend their working lives dealing with abstract problems in theory, assessing the validity of concepts by means of other concepts, do tend to overstate the efficacy of ideas or language in constructing reality. As Andrew Collier sardonically remarks, 'academics, at least in the arts, are mainly engaged in meta-discourse – that is, talking about talking – and do not, in their professional capacity, interact much with extra-linguistic realities. They are therefore prone to non-realism about such things'.[29] Professional intellectuals also naturally tend to overestimate their own role as the purveyors of socially efficacious ideas: elitism and idealism are natural bedfellows in the ivory towers of academe.

A second important explanation of the dominance of idealism in philosophy and sociology, aside from the 'religious yearnings' of many intellectuals or academics, refers us simultaneously to the popularity (in a lesser key) of the most crude forms of reductive-conflationary materialism elsewhere in the human sciences (e.g. behaviourism and sociobiology). It has always been a characteristic of the human sciences to oscillate between the wildest forms of idealism (especially in philosophy and sociology) on the one hand, and the most vulgar and deterministic modes of materialism on the other (e.g. in human sociobiology and psychology).

Once again, this intellectual polarisation is comprehensible, I would contend, in terms of the dual experience of people in society of being simultaneously free yet unfree, especially inasmuch as this experience is shaped by class relations and class ideology. On the one hand, the 'laws of capital' appear, in the eyes of the elite, to reduce the propertyless to the status of mere 'things' (whether hands or stomachs) shaped by outside pressures. Thus the members of the proletariat, in common with all material things, appear to the rich and powerful as mere use-values who are swept along by historical forces beyond their control. This is the social basis of reductive materialist outlooks in the lower-order human sciences, then transmitted to the non-social world. On the other hand, the self-perception of the members of the bourgeoisie is not at all conducive to vulgar materialism, since their class location allows not only a diminution of punishing social constraints and a widening of social horizons, but also the capacity of individuals to function as 'macro actors' who are capable of shaping the lives of millions through their decisions. This is the social basis of voluntarist-idealist outlooks in sociology and philosophy.

It was out of this dual reality of class society that the classical compromise to the dichotomies of voluntarist idealism and mechanical materialism was forged: namely Cartesian dualism. This rigid abstraction of 'mind' and 'self' from the law-governed world of biological and physical nature allowed human beings to be treated as machine-organisms governed by the 'natural laws' of biological and economic necessity for six days a week and then gifted the powers of reflection, intentionality and 'soul' in time for 'moral education' on the Sunday! On top of this, Cartesian (and later Kantian) dualism sanctioned or lent legitimacy to the mutual alienation of the physical and human sciences, served to polarise the social sciences between 'material' and 'cultural' specialisms, and furnished philosophical justification for the subsequent development of a tradition of run-of-the-mill pluralist or 'multi-factoral' sociological theory which has been with us ever since.

The classical example of pluralist sociology (though in this case it is far from 'run-of-the-mill'), i.e. Weber's historical and comparative work into the origins and trajectory of modernity, is of course rooted foursquare in this abstract materialism-idealism dualism first made respectable by Descartes (and developed subsequently by Kant). Weber's claim that social structures are composed at root of 'ideal elements' and 'material elements' (the basis of his abstraction of 'society' from 'economy'), which are autonomous or self-governing properties of the social world, was obviously an attempt to reconcile the 'warring gods' of neo-Kantian and Nietzschean idealism with the atomistic materialism of 'marginalist' political economy within the social sciences. Thus Weber recommends, first, that social structures be analytically de-composed into distinct 'spheres' (the *realfaktoren* of economic and political institutions or forms of social action on the one hand, and the *idealfaktoren* of cultural institutions or practices on the other), and second, that social explanation proceed on the assumption that the 'autonomous' spheres operate in the long run as equivalent causal 'factors' of macroscopic historical change.

My own reasons for rejecting Weber's analytical pluralism (and the social ontology in which it is rooted) will become apparent from some of the arguments to be elaborated in this chapter. For now it is important to note only that pluralist sociology is rooted in a compromise between the claims of *subjective* idealism (with its emphasis on the independent power of human consciousness to 'order' or 'construct' an essentially formless world) and *reductive* materialism (with its emphasis on the objective determination of human consciousness by biological and environmental facts). That is, in its treatment of 'ideal factors' and 'material factors' as autonomous yet mutually efficacious factors of society and history.

To recap. In my Introduction I have sought to define the 'problem of sociology' as one of developing appropriate conceptual and methodological tools for describing and analysing a multi-faceted 'object' of knowledge – society. The purpose of my exposition here so far has been to show that the same is true of social theory more generally – though the 'object' in question here is the interface between the human-social and natural worlds. The failure of social philosophers and sociologists to deal adequately with their objects of knowledge (as stratified totalities comprised of internal and necessary relations of 'unity-in-difference') has generated two central weaknesses of philosophy and social theory: the fallacy of reductive-conflationary social analysis, and the unresolved debate between materialism and idealism (and pluralist or 'dualist' compromises between the two) in the human sciences.

I have argued that sociological emergentism and attendant methodological dualism offer a solution to the first of these difficulties. The objective of this chapter is to indicate a solution to the second difficulty. Thus I propose here to reconstruct sociological emergentism as Marxist social theory rooted in a broader anti-reductive materialist philosophy of nature. My purpose in doing so is to offer a practical alternative to the ontological and analytical positions of idealism and dualism, which I hold to be no more acceptable than those of holism, atomism or elisionism.

To these ends I will organise the work on the basis of an exposition and defence of two kinds of materialism – ontological (or philosophical) and analytical-explanatory (i.e. anthropological and sociological) – which I hold to be consistent with one another.[30] This will entail the following procedure. First I will defend the ontological position of transcendental realism, which will be shown to offer a persuasive alternative to reductionism. Then I will show how transcendental realism is enormously enriched by engaging with Engels' *natural-philosophie* (otherwise known as 'dialectical materialism').[31] My contention here is that the core concepts of realist ontology (i.e. 'stratification' and 'emergence') have their precursors in dialectical materialism, and that the former will benefit from the incorporation of the latter's emphasis on dialectical motion in governing the formation of each of the 'emergent' levels (and attendant generative mechanisms) which comprise natural and social reality. Thus a fusion of depth realism and Engels' philosophy of nature not only preserves the 'rational kernel' of materialism in the human sciences – namely that 'mind' is always embodied and necessarily anchored in 'matter' (and never vice-versa) – but also supports a dynamic understanding of system dynamics in nature more generally, whereby the motion of matter through ascending forms of complexity is governed by processes of dialectical interaction internal and specific to its different levels of organisation.

Next, the product of this 'synthesis' between depth realism and dialectical materialism at the level of the social sciences (namely a social ontology I shall dub 'critical materialism'), will be shown to support an account of society and social process which is both anti-reductive in method and non-conflationary in theoretical practice. Critical materialism is grasped as the human and social science component of emergentist materialism, and is therefore treated as a radicalised form of critical naturalism (i.e. the specific application of materialism to the study of human beings and human society).[32] Just as emergentist materialism overcomes the ambiguities of philosophical realism (which fudges the question of whether matter is 'basic' to mind or vice-versa, and hence leaves open the possibility of a world populated by disembodied entities and of an immaterial 'first cause' of the universe), so critical materialism is precisely a social ontology which grasps the 'ideal elements' and other 'superstructural properties' of social systems as emergent from and anchored in underlying material structures (the forces and relations of production and 'deeper structures' immediately 'basic' to these). This critical materialism is, as I have suggested beforehand, consistent with two distinct but compatible methodologies (dialectical logic and analytical dualism).

Thus 'emergentist Marxism' is a radicalised version of the realist social theory outlined in the Introduction. Its point of departure from 'orthodox' sociological emergentism is its acknowledgement that the socio-cultural emergents which predate social interaction, and which condition it in specific ways, are hierarchically structured in terms of their explanatory function in determining social systems and their developmental dynamics and possibilities. From this perspective, socio-economic emergents (and those 'substructural' levels they presuppose) *vertically* explain other social and cultural emergents as well as exercising a disproportionate weight in the *horizontal* conditioning of social interaction and its structural resultants.[33] In this way, critical materialism, as a particular form of emergentist sociology and social anthropology, not only avoids the fallacy of reductive-conflationary social theorising, but does so without risking any kind of 'realist' or 'dualist' compromise with idealism, and without collapsing social analysis into the historical indeterminacy which flows naturally from a pluralist (i.e. empiricist) 'theory of factors'.

Ontology and science: depth realism and dialectical materialism

Roy Bhaskar defines 'transcendental realism' as a 'tradition' in the philosophy of science which regards

> the objects of knowledge as the structures and mechanisms that generate phenomena; and the knowledge as produced in the social activity of science. These objects are neither phenomena (empiricism) nor human constructs imposed upon the phenomena (idealism), but real structures which endure and operate independently of our knowledge, our experience and the conditions which allow us access to them. Against empiricism, the objects of knowledge are structures, not events; against idealism, they are intransitive [i.e. existing independently of consciousness or human activity]. ... On this conception, a constant conjunction of events is no more a necessary than it is a sufficient condition for the assumption of the operation of a causal law. According to this view, both knowledge and the world are structured, both are differentiated and changing; the latter exists independently of the former (though not our knowledge of this fact); and experiences and the things and causal laws to which it affords us access are normally out of phase with one another. On this view, science is not an epiphenomenon of nature, nor is nature a product of man.[34]

An important function of Bhaskar's philosophy of science is to establish the case for endorsing a 'depth model' of reality in opposition to the claims of classical empiricism (the view that only 'impressions' or 'sense data' can be said to comprise the 'real') and 'empirical realism' or 'actualism' (the view that the 'real' is comprised of both 'impressions' and 'events', the former being experiences of the latter). This is achieved by drawing upon transcendental arguments. By this method, Bhaskar has little difficulty disposing of the pretensions of classical empiricism:

> The intelligibility of sense-perception presupposes the intransitivity of the objects perceived. For it is in the independent occurrence or existence of such objects that the meaning of 'perception', and the epistemic significance of perception, lies. Among such objects are events, which thus must be categorically independent of experiences. ... If changing experience of objects is to be possible, objects must have a distinct being in time and space from the experiences of which they are the objects. For Kepler to see the rim of the earth drop away, while Tycho Brahe watches the sun rise, we must suppose that there is something that they both see (in different ways). Similarly when modern sailors refer to what ancient mariners called a sea serpent as a school of porpoises, we must suppose that there is something which they are describing in different ways. The intelligibility of scientific change (and criticism) and scientific education thus presupposes the ontological independence of the objects of experience from the objects of which they are the experience. ... Events then are categorically independent of experiences.[35]

Bhaskar thus establishes that the basic problem with an ontology (such as that of classical empiricism) which reduces reality to sense impressions is that it leaves the 'experiences' which compose sense-data unexplained. This approach also rides roughshod over the obvious fact that not all events are the subject of experience. For these reasons most empiricists are prepared to endorse actualism. Actualists introduce a second level or dimension into their explanatory models. This is, of course, the level of 'events', which experiences are about, and which may often occur unexperienced, but whose reality can nonetheless be established by observing their empirical effects (i.e. the 'happenings' which are caused by other 'happenings').

Whereas Bhaskar's transcendental argument disposes of the warranty of classical empiricism (in its Berkeleian and Humean forms), by demonstrating that 'experience' presupposes the *intransitivity* of the object world, it is not by itself sufficient to refute actualism. In order to achieve this purpose Bhaskar has to be able to show that the objects of science are not only intransitive but also *structured*. In other words, if depth realism is to be defensible, Bhaskar has to find some means of demonstrating that real-world events are comprehensible in terms of underlying structures and attendant generative mechanisms and not simply in terms of 'other events'.

To these ends Bhaskar introduces another transcendental argument.

> It is not necessary that science exists. But given that it does, it is necessary that the world is a certain way ... [G]iven that science does or could occur, the world *must* be a certain way. Thus ... that the world is structured and differentiated can be established by philosophical argument.[36]

Bhaskar goes about this task by considering the question of what the actuality of experimental science tells us about the nature of its objects: 'The intelligibility of experimental activity presupposes not just the intransitivity but the structured character of the objects investigated under experimental conditions'.[37]

Bhaskar points out that the practice of experimental science involves setting up an 'artificial closure' under laboratory conditions in order to establish the existence of those real structures responsible for the causal mechanisms which account for observable events. By means of experimental closure, the scientist 'triggers' or 'activates' a 'single kind of mechanism or process in relative isolation, free from the interfering flux of the open world, so as to observe its detailed workings or record its characteristic mode of effect and/or test some hypothesis about them'.[38] In this way the scientist identifies the specificity of causal mechanisms pertaining to particular structures and the kinds of events or effects which (in closed systems) must necessarily follow from their activation.

But if causal laws are simply 'constant conjunctures'[39] between events in the realm of the actual (which they must be if underlying mechanisms do not explain events), this kind of painstaking scientific endeavour must be both pointless and impossible. Pointless because one does not need experimental closure to observe sequences of events at the level of the actual, since closure would already exist in this uni-dimensional world, of which 'constant conjunctures' would be the inevitable expression. Pointless because 'experimental activity can only be given a satisfactory rationale if the causal law it enables us to identify is held to prevail outside the contexts under which the sequence of events is generated', this suggesting 'there must be an ontological distinction'[40] between causal laws and sequences of events.[41] Pointless because if experimental science is simply about engineering events so as to bring about other events, it must be a process which 'constructs' causal laws, not one which discovers pre-existing laws (by activating them in isolation from other variables), and is thus scientifically uninteresting.[42] (Indeed, in this sense rather absurd also, for in the absence of this distinction between causal laws and patterns of events, how do we avoid interpreting certain chance happenings, for example those which might disrupt a particular scientific experiment, as anything other than a contravention of certain of nature's laws?) Impossible because one can establish a closed system by means of scientific procedure (in which a generative mechanism, the events it governs, and the observation of these processes by a knowing subject are brought into correspondence) only on the assumption that nature *is* an open system, comprised of a plurality of causal mechanisms, each of which can be rationally apprehended only by means of experimental closure.[43]

Bhaskar's transcendental realism therefore provides a philosophical rationale for holding to a conception of reality as 'ontological depth'. But does his approach allow us to take the further step of grasping nature as stratified? My belief is that it does succeed in doing this, though it is not the only acceptable way of doing so, or even necessarily the best.[44] Bhaskar bases his argument for the stratification of nature on the explanatory logic of scientific inquiry itself as this has unfolded historically. He makes the legitimate point that science proceeds by uncovering specific generative mechanisms, before then going on to seek out a causal explanation of these mechanisms in terms of others which are necessarily more 'basic' or 'fundamental' (such as the explanation of psychological mechanisms in terms of biological mechanisms,[45] or of chemical mechanisms in terms of physical mechanisms).

One important feature of this process of scientific work is that, having established a 'tree' of sciences, each relating to real aspects of the world, it has been unable to establish the redundancy of the higher in favour of the lower. For example, despite the best efforts of many generations of practising philosophers of social science to argue the case for treating the 'real objects' of sociology (i.e. social structures and attendant generative mechanisms) as epiphenomena of the 'real objects' of cognitive psychology and/or human biology (i.e. the psycho-organic structures and attendant causal powers of individuals), no practical results have been forthcoming, and nor are they expected. But this stratification of the sciences, which has proven highly resistant to attempts by 'greedy reductionists'[46] to dissolve, is precisely good evidence of the relative autonomy and hierarchical layering of their respective objects of knowledge in the real world, that is, of the stratification of nature.

In any case, such 'translations' (of the concepts of one science into those of a more basic one) are logically impossible, as Bhaskar himself demonstrates, and this is additional evidence for the stratification of nature. Thus, against Richard Rorty's claim that '[p]hysicalism is probably right in saying that we shall someday be able, "in principle", to predict every movement of a person's body (including those of his larynx and writing hand) by reference to microstructures within his body',[47] Bhaskar offers the following acute counter-argument:

> Suppose A goes into a newsagent's and says to the proprietor B, 'The *Guardian*, please', and B hands him a copy of it. Now if physicalism is correct in its basic claim that an individual's actions (including speech-acts) are 'in principle' deducible from the micro-constituents of his or her body, it must follow that B would have handed A the *Guardian* even if A had performed some quite different action, such as asking for the *Independent* or for a packet of chewing gum or B to marry him or dancing a jig, and even if A had not been there at all'.[48]

Bhaskar's basic point is that no statements about the 'microstructures' of A or B explain why this particular passage of interaction is enacted or how it unfolds. It is not A's neurobiology which explains A's preference for this particular newspaper or newspapers in general. This is accountable in terms of social biography and social positioning within specific socio-cultural relations (the *Guardian* is produced only in UK society, its readership and outlook is overwhelmingly liberal middle-class professional, not all historical social relations have enabled the manufacture of paper, etc.). Nor is B's action in handing this particular newspaper to A explainable in terms of B's neurophysiology. For a start, B responds not to 'sound waves' issuing forth from A, but to the concepts these sounds express, which are meaningful only because they are derived from a linguistic structure (external to the interactants) and applied concretely in a particular interactional setting. Moreover, B acts on A's request for the simple reason that it is in B's vested interests to do so (i.e. to make a livelihood by exchanging goods for money), and of course these vested interests are determined by B's social role as proprietor within the social relations of commodity production.

Stratification, rootedness and emergence in depth realism

Bhaskar's philosophical ontology identifies a hierarchically ordered world of distinct strata and attendant generative mechanisms governed by causal relations of vertical determination. Such a worldview need not rest upon Bhaskar's philosophical arguments, however. In fact, it can instead be legitimately derived 'from the *results* of the sciences', from the development of scientific knowledge itself. From this it appears reasonable to draw two conclusions. First, that a materialistic view of nature (including human nature) is altogether appropriate, on the grounds that

> the material universe existed before there was organic life, and ... living organisms can only exist as composed of and surrounded by matter. In this sense, matter may be said to be more 'basic' than life; life in turn may be said to be more basic than rationality (in the sense that we are rational animals), and hence than human society and its history. This suggests that the sciences that explain a more basic layer may have some explanatory primacy over those explaining a less basic layer. Laws of physics and chemistry may *in some sense* explain the laws of biology.[49]

Second, that a naturalistic approach to the human and social sciences (which stress a fundamental methodological unity between these and the natural sciences) is at least possible, for the simple reason that it is now philosophically defensible to view the world

> historically, as a complex of processes of development ... in which there are no sharp distinctions, on the one hand, between the various domains of the physical world ... and, on the other hand, between the physical world as a whole and the human, social world.[50]

In this sense, Bhaskar's philosophy of nature is entirely consistent with that form of ontological materialism (defended by Marx and Engels) which postulates the unilateral existential dependence of the objects of knowledge of the human and social sciences upon those of the natural sciences, and the historical development of the former out of the latter. From this point of view, the stratification of nature must be grasped from the 'bottom up' (so to speak), as running from the physico-chemical to the human and socio-cultural (via the intermediary of the biological). This is for the simple reason that it is impossible to conceive of social or cultural mechanisms existing in the absence of biological ones, or of biological mechanisms existing in the absence of physico-chemical ones, but perfectly possible to conceive of the converse arrangements.

Nonetheless it is important to be clear that this vertical explanation of higher mechanisms by lower ones does not 'explain away' the former. The higher are as real as the lower by virtue of the distinct causal powers and properties which pertain uniquely to them. Chemical structures explain biological structures, for example, in the sense that the latter arise from the former and could not exist without them, the reverse never being the case. But the generative mechanisms of organic structures are nonetheless irreducible to those of chemical structures, since nothing about the organisational and behavioural properties of the first will tell us anything about those of the second.

Yet this 'stratified model' of nature in no way implies that more basic mechanisms or strata pack a greater causal punch than higher-level ones, in accounting for the constitution of objects or entities. This point is well made by Steven Rose:

> A living organism – a human, say – is an assemblage of subatomic particles, an assemblage of atoms, an assemblage of molecules, an assemblage of tissues and organs. But it is not first a set of atoms, then molecules, then cells; it is all of these things at the same time.[51]

Nor does Bhaskar's ontology commit us to the peculiar idea that more basic strata or mechanisms have explanatory priority over higher-level ones in shaping the pattern of events in the phenomenal world:

> Being a more basic stratum does not necessarily mean being a stratum whose effects are more widespread. For though animals are *governed* by zoological laws while inanimate things are not, anything and everything may be *effected* by zoological laws, since animals have effects on the inanimate world.[52]

Clearly, there is a necessary distinction being made here between relations of vertical determination between strata, and relations of horizontal causality between mechanisms and events/or objects. Events and things are determined conjointly by the plurality of mechanisms operative at different levels of reality.[53] So, for instance, zoological laws presuppose chemical laws, which in turn presuppose physical laws, living creatures being a combinatory of physico-chemical and organic structures. This means that relations of vertical causality between strata, aside from being relations of 'ontological presupposition', are also often 'one-way relations of inclusion'[54] *of* the various strata. Thus organic entities (such as animals) will be necessarily subject to a broader range of causal mechanisms than inorganic entities (such as rocks), just as cultural entities (e.g. individual speakers) will necessarily be subject to a wider range of causal mechanisms (those of society, mind, biology, chemistry and physics) than biological entities (to which only the last three apply).

But how is it that higher-order mechanisms and structures are explainable by, yet irreducible to, lower-order ones? Bhaskar's solution to this problem is to grasp the interface between the two in terms of rootedness and emergence: higher-order strata are rooted in and emergent from lower-order strata. 'Rootedness' simply denotes the elementary fact that 'the more complex aspects of reality (e.g. life, mind) presuppose the less complex (e.g. matter)'.[55] The idea here is 'of some lower-order or microscopic domain providing a *basis* for the existence of some higher-order property or power; as for example the neuro-physiological organisation of human beings may be said to provide a basis for their power of speech'.[56]

'Emergence' is a more difficult idea to grasp, not least because it has a complicated intellectual history. For realists, however, it has two basic meanings and functions. First, as simply another way of describing and defending their thesis of the irreducibility of the constituent levels of reality:

> We would not try to explain the power of people to think by reference to the cells that constitute them, as if cells possessed this power too. Nor would we explain the power of water to extinguish fire by deriving it from the powers of its constituents, for oxygen and hydrogen are highly inflammable. In such cases objects are said to have *emergent powers*, that is, powers or liabilities which cannot be reduced to those of their constituents.[57]

Second, as an explanatory thesis, which locates the emergence of a higher-order stratum in a specific interaction or combination of generative mechanisms internal to those objects or structures which exist at a stratum immediately 'basic' to it. In this sense, 'emergent properties' are a function of internally related objects or structures, because the relations which define or comprise them as such grant their constituents powers and capacities they would not possess, apart from their interaction or combination as parts of a whole:

> The nature or constitution of an object and its causal powers are internally or necessarily related: a plane can fly by virtue of its aerodynamic form, engines, etc.; gunpowder can explode by virtue of its unstable chemical structure; multinational firms can sell their products dear and buy their labour power cheap by virtue of operating in several different countries with different levels of development; people can change their behaviour by virtue of their ability to monitor their own monitorings, and so on.[58]

Biological reality, for instance, is 'emergent' from a specific combination of generative mechanisms internal to the chemical level, just as socio-cultural reality is 'emergent' from a specific interaction of causal powers internal to the biological level.

Emergent properties are also to be found *within* particular domains of reality. Thus the 'physical', the 'chemical', the 'biological', and the 'human-social' levels each give rise to higher and lower strata. For example, totally novel powers arise within the socio-cultural domain as a result of social interaction. 'Even though social structures exist only where people reproduce them, they have powers irreducible to those of individuals (you can't pay rent to yourself)'[59] or sell goods or pay wages to yourself or accumulate capital by yourself. Nor can any of us 'fly by flapping our arms either singly or in a crowd. Yet we do fly as a result of technology, airplanes, ground crew, all *de novo* products of social activity, qualitatively different from our individual acts'.[60]

In all these cases, individuals obtain novel characteristics by virtue of their insertion within specific kinds of social relations, not simply by pooling their individual capacities or powers. Because such properties and powers of individuals are not merely 'aggregative' products of their interaction, they must instead be recognised as 'emergent properties' of the societal organisation in which their interactions are situated. Such is what renders meaningful the idea that society is more than the sum of its parts and that its 'parts' (i.e. people and their interpersonal relations) are transformed by being parts of the social whole.

Ontological materialism and the dialectics of nature

I have made the assertion that depth realism would be substantially enriched by engaging with (and learning from) the basic concepts of dialectical materialism (as this has been understood in the classical Marxist tradition). It is now time to add a little substance to this argument. Clearly I do not mean that Marx, Engels and one or two others are alone in possession of the 'master key' (i.e. the 'materialist dialectic') to unlock the secrets of nature and society. My purpose is not to rehabilitate Stalinist dogmatics or to lend legitimation to any kind of mysticism. Nor am I arguing that Marxian materialism has nothing to learn from other philosophical traditions, including and especially Bhaskar's depth realism. This should be clear enough from what I have said so far in this section. After all, my contention in the foregoing has been that the core concepts of Bhaskar's philosophical realism (i.e. stratification, rootedness and emergence), plus the logico-theoretical arguments by which he demonstrates their authenticity and efficacy, are indispensable to the articulation of a defensible anti-reductive materialist or naturalist ontology of being. In view of this, what I am proposing is not that dialectical materialism supplant depth realism, or obviously that depth realism supplant dialectical materialism, but rather that the best elements of each be combined in a new synthesis.

I have already made the point that a consistent stratified model of reality is in fact a particular form of ontological materialism – namely an anti-reductive or 'emergentist' materialism. This being the case, it is mysterious that most leading figures of the realist movement do not describe their ontology in these terms. Of course, it is true that Bhaskar dubs his view of the mind-body relation 'synchronic emergent powers materialism'. But he does not describe his overall philosophical outlook as such. He also leaves 'open' the question of whether a materialistic explanation is 'in principle' possible for mind, on the grounds that it is 'equally possible' that 'mindedness' is the property of an immaterial substance, which does not seem to me to be consistent with any form of materialism, emergentist or otherwise.[61]

Perhaps part of the explanation for this preference for the term 'realism' over 'materialism' in the contemporary philosophy of science is that the latter has traditionally been associated with reductive-mechanical outlooks in both the physical and human-social sciences, and obviously critical realists do not wish to be found guilty of the same errors by terminological association. Yet an emergentist materialism, such as that endorsed in practice by realists such as Bhaskar and Collier, is not in the least bit vulnerable to a micro-regress of higher-order strata and attendant sciences to lower-order ones. Indeed, as I have suggested beforehand, identifying depth realism *as* 'emergent powers materialism' has the positive advantage of undermining the rational basis of both vulgar materialism (the view that the objects of the human and social sciences are 'translatable' into the objects of the biological and physico-chemical sciences) and 'shamefaced' idealism (the postulation of a spiritualist 'prime cause' in accounting for the universe). This is one of the great virtues of dialectical materialism. From its inception in the work of Engels, this has been an ontological approach which has explicitly acknowledged the falsity of these abstract dualisms. In this sense, dialectical materialism is important because it is precisely an anti-reductive materialism, and as such suffers from none of the ambiguities associated with philosophical realism.

I take it that the lack of scientific support for any 'mind-first' understanding of the universe is sufficient proof of the necessity of a materialist ontology of being against those who take a 'compromise' position (i.e. ontological realism) on this question. There are no good reasons why an ontology of existence should make any compromise whatsoever with the idea that 'the ideal' or 'mind' has any kind of existential autonomy or explanatory primacy over 'matter'. But perhaps those allegiants of philosophical realism who accept that their approach is indeed 'materialistic' or 'naturalistic' might still object to my critique on other grounds. Two possibilities spring to mind. First, that my 'anti-realist' argument reveals only a semantic ambiguity rather than a substantive conceptual weakness in the realist ontology. Second, that dialectical materialism is not an emergentist ontology at all, or at least not a successful one, hamstrung as it is by concepts which are either vague, misleading or plain wrong. From this point of view, depth realism has no need of any kind of dialogue or encounter with dialectical materialism, only of a change of title to something less neutral and more appropriate.

My first response to these (hypothetical) arguments is to freely concede that a large measure of my critique of depth realism (at least as this is articulated by Bhaskar) is indeed a quibble over terminology. But I do not find this an uncomfortable admission. After all, I have already said that my intention is not to replace Bhaskar's depth realism (or emergentist materialism) with Engels' dialectical materialism. Nonetheless, this 'semantic quibble' is an important one, for reasons I have already discussed. My second response is simply to suggest that certain of the basic concepts of dialectical Marxist philosophy are neither misleading or false (though some of them are difficult by necessity, because they are designed to capture a reality which is itself ambiguous because fluid and contradictory rather than static and functional). On the contrary, these concepts remain valid and necessary. There are three basic reasons for this.

First, dialectical concepts are in fact explicit descriptions of the reality of stratification and emergence, though expressed in a different philosophical vocabulary to that favoured by contemporary critical realists. As Ted Benton rightly points out: 'Engels proposes a hierarchy of 'forms of motion' with transitions one to the other. ... The different domains of the universe are constituted by levels in the hierarchy of complexity of laws of motion'.[62] This stratification of the world ensures that the sciences must also be arranged hierarchically and treated as irreducible to each other. This is for the simple reason that at each level of organisation or interaction of matter, those laws operative at lower levels are 'subsumed' or 'pushed into the background by other, higher laws', which themselves constitute 'a leap, a decisive change'.[63] As Engels himself puts it:

> If I term physics the mechanics of molecules, chemistry the physics of atoms, and furthermore biology the chemistry of albumens, I wish thereby to express the passing of any of these sciences into one of the others, hence both the connection, the continuity, and the distinction, the discrete separation.[64]

Such a conception of nature as comprised of irreducible levels of interaction and organisation, and hence of the necessary 'unity-in-difference' of the different branches of science, is clearly compatible with 'transcendental' realism. But it is Engels' utilisation of dialectical-materialist concepts which has allowed him to obtain this insight nearly one hundred years ahead of his time.

Second, and more importantly, such concepts are as reasonable a way as any of capturing in the most general terms the reality of the world as a 'differentiated totality':

> What is involved here is a kind of natural scientific ontology of nature as a unified, though internally structured and differentiated whole, which Engels regards as preferable to the ontology implicit in mechanical reductionism. ... Engels' ontology is the product of philosophical reflection on what is presupposed by the recent development of the sciences. The convergence, the realignment of whole fields of theory

which had previously developed separately (organic/inorganic chemistry, mechanics/theory of heat, etc.) is unintelligible, as is the replacement of one theory by another within the same specialism, unless these different fields of theoretical discourse are apprehended as so many attempts at knowledge of a unitary, though internally differentiated, natural universe. This unity of nature is an essential precondition for convergence of the sciences, for the repeated discovery of 'interconnections', whilst the differentiation of nature is implied by the discreteness and uneven historical development of the different sciences.[65]

Benton thus notes the 'points of contact' between Engels' ontology of nature and Bhaskar's transcendental realism. But he makes the further point that the latter legitimately transcends the former in one important respect:

> Bhaskar's 'transcendental' realism argues for the philosophical legitimacy of arguments from the character of rational procedures in science (for example experimentation) to conclusions of a very general kind about the nature of the world as presupposed in the rationality of those procedures. ... Engels' scientific metaphysics includes arguments and conclusions of this general type, but it goes beyond this to represent in a unified and more-or-less coherent form a detailed ontology based on current substantive knowledge in the different sciences. Engels is here doing no more than generalising from procedures employed by scientists themselves in bringing to bear discoveries in one discipline upon controversies in an adjacent one, but this generalisation of the procedure results in a quite distinct type of theoretical structure (a 'world-view') and discourse.[66]

Finally, and most importantly of all, Engels' dialectical concepts are successful in *historicising* stratification and emergence. That is to say, they allow us to grasp the dynamics or processes through which higher-order levels of the material world develop out of lower-order levels not as 'radical contingencies'[67] but as integral aspects of a continually evolving totality of interrelated systems:

> The great basic thought is that the world is not to be comprehended as a complex of ready-made things, but as a complex of processes, in which the things apparently stable ... go through an uninterrupted process of becoming and passing away. ... For dialectical philosophy nothing is final, absolute, sacred. It reveals the transitory nature of everything and in everything; nothing can endure before it except the uninterrupted process of becoming and passing away, of endless ascendancy from the lower to the higher. ... The motion of matter is not merely crude mechanical motion, mere change of place, it is heat and light, electric and

> magnetic tension, chemical combination and dissociation, life, and finally, consciousness.[68]

This is the most controversial aspect of Engels' 'dialectics of nature'. For he is often taxed with endorsing an evolutionary teleology of higher forms from lower forms, according to which the latter inevitably or necessarily give rise to the former in a linear fashion, governed by an all-encompassing 'dialectical law' uniformly operative at all levels of reality. This, for example, seems to be Benton's view, notwithstanding his acknowledgement of and high praise for Engels' 'first approximation' to 'a concept of emergent qualities and laws'.[69] He accuses Engels of mixing with his legitimate 'attempt to confront the problem of the emergence of new forms and structures as a specifically historical problem ... a dubious ... notion of historicity as progressive development'.[70] The reader will be unsurprised to learn that Engels' 'external' and 'inessential' use of Hegelian categories is held by Benton to be responsible for the alleged tendency of his philosophy to sometimes veer towards teleological historicism:

> That Engels suggests, by his indifferent application of the dialectical laws of the transition of quantity into quality, and negation of the negation, to all of these histories [natural-inorganic, natural-organic, and human-social], that they ... share a *common* historicity is, to say the least, unfortunate ... the indifferent application of categories of the 'dialectic' to different domains in nature can give the impression that human history and the history of ... nature can be understood through identical philosophical ... categories.[71]

But such an interpretation fails on a number of counts. First, Benton provides no solid evidence that Engels does in fact hold that development in nature and society is part of a uniform evolutionary process governed by a universal dialectical law, or that this development is inevitably progressive or linear. Benton's only substantive argument against Engels' use of dialectical concepts is that he does not always apply these appropriately or successfully when dealing with emergent properties and laws, which is hardly proof of any dalliance on his part with the Hegelian notion of an identity of development in nature and society.[72] Indeed, Benton admits that 'surprisingly enough, Engels does recognise that nature and human society do not share a common historicity, the looseness of his appropriation of the dialectic notwithstanding'.[73]

Second, Benton appears to believe that a historical account of nature is teleological (or 'quasi-teleological' – whatever that means)[74] simply by virtue of the fact it postulates a certain directionality or evolutionary movement 'from the simple to the complex'[75] in structural forms. Not only is such a conception manifestly non-teleological (by any reasonable definition of the term),[76] it is also far from being indefensible. Such a pattern of development is certainly discernible at the biological level (the 'ratchet' of natural selection generating cumulative organismic specialisation and enhanced survival-value).[77] It is also discernible at the societal level (the cumulative development of the productive forces under the stimulus of meeting and developing human needs). Indeed, so too at the physico-chemical level, since the 'consensus view' of physical scientists today is one of 'the inevitability and probable universality of life', on the grounds that 'life is a logical consequence of known chemical principles operating on the atomic composition of the universe'.[78]

In a sense, then, Engels is right to suggest that the differentiated elements of nature (physico-chemical, biological, human-social, etc.) have a common historicity. For all are 'phases' in the development of matter through ascending levels of complexity, and all are composed of those 'basic' elements which ontologically and historically presuppose their existence. Yet it is important to be clear that there is nothing in this conception which implies that this 'common historicity' of nature is an undifferentiated or unstratified one, or that the evolutionary emergence of higher from lower domains of nature was necessary or preordained.

Finally Benton's 'surprise' at not discovering a materialist 'inversion' of Hegel's logic in Engels' writings is a function of his own arbitrary imposition of the Hegelian 'system' upon Engels' philosophy. For he simply assumes that Engels' dialectical concepts must logically commit him to a monistic and teleological view of the universe, on the grounds that these are borrowed from a philosophical system which is itself teleological and monistic. Benton does not see that the content of concepts is determined by their function within a theoretical discourse. Transposed into a different theoretical system, their meaning can be, and often is, transformed.

This is clear enough if we consider what Engels himself has to say about his own application of the dialectical method to the different domains of society and nature. For a start, in opposition to Hegel, Engels insists that dialectics is no 'proof producing instrument',[79] a formula into which the real world has to be fitted, but must instead be discovered by means of empirical-scientific investigation into the different facets of the world. For him, in other words, there is 'no question of building the laws of dialectics into nature, but of discovering them in it and evolving them from it'.[80] Of equal importance, Engels also recognises that dialectical processes function differently for each distinct stratum of reality. 'Every kind of thing ... has a peculiar way of being negated in such a way that it gives rise to development, and it is just the same with every kind of conception or idea'.[81]

That Engels is especially insistent that the dialectic of human-social development is a radical departure from the dialectic of unreflective nature is revealed in a key passage from his *Ludwig Feuerbach and the End of Classical German Philosophy*:

> In one point, however development of society proves to be essentially different from that of nature. In the history of nature – insofar as we ignore man's reaction on nature – there are only blind, unconscious agencies acting on one another, out of whose interplay the general law comes into operation. Whatever happens … does not happen as a consciously desired aim. On the other hand, in the history of society the actors are all endowed with consciousness, are men acting with deliberation and passion, working towards definite goals; nothing happens without conscious purpose, without intended aim.[82]

Engels is grappling with the idea that 'the structure of the dialectic in society is different to that in nature – the former must take account of the development of consciousness in a way that the latter need not'.[83] In keeping with this broad philosophical conception, he goes to some pains to show that the 'negation of the negation', as this concept is utilised by Marx in *Capital* to demonstrate the cancelling out of bourgeois property relations by socialist common ownership, is not designed to 'prove' the historical necessity of socialism or the inevitable demise of capitalism, but is instead meant to highlight the structural contradictions of the system, which generate pressures or tendencies towards crises and revolutionary change.[84] But Engels' careful handling of dialectical categories might as well not exist for all the attention Benton pays it. Because of his own misconception as to the manner of Engels' appropriation of Hegel's legacy, i.e. his unsubstantiated assumption that any resort to dialectics is tantamount to teleological and monistic backsliding, Benton can find only incoherence in Engels' explication of the historicity of stratification and emergence. Benton makes this error because he has failed to address the meaning and function of dialectical concepts within *Engels'* philosophy.

I have suggested that dialectical concepts are appropriate and indispensable to the analysis of nature, for the simple reason that natural evolution is governed by processes of dialectical interaction, from which higher-order structures develop out of lower-order structures over time. There are, however, at least two other good reasons for endorsing a 'dialectics of nature'. First, dialectical materialism, like depth realism, provides a philosophical rationale or resource for countering reductionism and anti-scientific irrationalism or romanticism. Lacking this kind of outlook, natural scientists and philosophers of science have traditionally found themselves drawn towards reductionist worldviews, where science is making rapid progress and is confident (for want of a sophisticated alternative), and back towards 'the mystical path' where the contradictions of old established theories are becoming glaringly apparent and where the suspicion dawns that growing scientific knowledge of the world does not always translate into a more rational world.[85]

Second, the dialectical perspective equips practising scientists and philosophers of science with the requisite flexibility of thought or 'open-mindedness' to view far-reaching transformations of scientific knowledge as a natural aspect of its internal development, not as threats to the rationality or stability of the enterprise.[86] This is because a dialectical understanding of nature is an explicit acknowledgement of its complexity, its fluidity, its capacity for endless innovation and development, of the challenge it poses to static common-sense, and so of the approximate and provisional nature of scientific discoveries. Indeed, there can be no doubt that endorsing a dialectical worldview has greatly assisted many scientists in making important contributions to scientific knowledge.[87]

Now, my contention is that processes of natural development (the dynamic structuring and restructuring of nature) are better understood by interpreting them in the light of Engels' so-called 'laws of the dialectic': the 'unity of opposites', the 'interaction and interpenetration of opposites', the 'transformation of quantity into quality', and the 'negation of the negation'.[88] The basic idea is that these provide us with 'the general formula of all evolutionary processes – of nature as well as of society ... insofar as we view the whole universe – without any exception – as a product of formation and transformation and not as the fruit of a conscious creator'.[89] Is such a claim a 'totalitarian' or 'metaphysical'[90] one? Not if a dialectical conception of nature can be derived from the practice and results of the various sciences. If practising natural scientists of whatever persuasion find themselves drawn to dialectical method in conducting their researches, or cannot avoid drawing dialectical conclusions from their scientific endeavours, it is entirely appropriate to conclude that, to the best of our rational knowledge, nature is dialectically structured. In fact, the results and activity of science do indeed support this conclusion.[91]

A final observation. There is one important ambiguity of Engels' dialectics which requires attention. Engels says that 'dialectics [is] ... the science of the general laws of motion, both of the external world and of human thought ... two sets of laws which are identical in substance'.[92] Now I do not think this view is defensible, although I see no good reason why endorsing it commits Engels (against his best intentions) to either reductionism or determinism.[93] The problem is that dialectical concepts are not 'laws' at all in a strict scientific sense, since their purpose is not to denote the discrete generative mechanisms responsible for specific phenomena in the world. Rather, 'dialectical laws' are an abstraction from 'the features common to physical and social processes ... produced by a wide variety of different mechanisms',[94] which are then utilised to illuminate particular forms of dialectical motion. As such, their function is to reveal the dialectical pattern of interaction at work at each level (or between levels) of reality, as this is generated by the collision of various generative mechanisms which stimulate development and emergence.

But since the dialectical process specific to each stratum, or to the interface between strata, is the product of the generative mechanisms operative at these levels, it is clear enough that the 'dialectic of nature' cannot always and everywhere be identical in substance. This point is well made by John Rees: 'The dialectic cannot remain some immutable stratum on top of which everything else changes but which itself is immune to change. The dialectic itself is transformed as the natural world and the social world develop'.[95] However, as Alex Callinicos points out,

> this line of thought suggests that we should see the dialectic of nature as a broad philosophical conception of nature rather than a set of general laws from which more specific ones applicable to particular aspects of the world can be deduced.

This interpretation of the dialectic of nature

> has the advantage that it rules out the kind of dogmatic dictation to working scientists which gave the idea a bad name under Stalinism, but it implies a fairly loose and open relationship between dialectical philosophy and scientific research which ought to be explicitly recognised.[96]

Critical materialism and social science theory

As we have seen, philosophical materialism, as an emergentist ontology of nature, postulates the existential dependence of the objects of the human and social sciences upon the objects of the eco-biological sciences, which in turn presuppose the objects of the physico-chemical sciences. So the relations between the various strata of nature are those of ontological presupposition and vertical determination. This does not mean that objects which are comprised of a variety of different strata are as a rule 'determined' more by the lower than the higher. Organisms, for instance, are governed by zoological laws, not the laws of chemistry or physics, although the reverse is true of the parts from which they are composed. Nor does it mean that objects are shaped or conditioned more by those lower-order *vis-à-vis* higher-order mechanisms which constitute their 'external' life-world. Organisms, for instance, are conditioned (in terms of their physical organisation and behavioural tendencies) by the multiplicity of generative mechanisms (organismic, physical, chemical and sometimes social) which have fashioned the sensuous environment which they inhabit. Still less does this perspective necessarily entail that lower-order strata historically predate those higher-order strata which they immediately 'found' or explain. Certainly this is often the case: few would doubt that inorganic matter existed long before the emergence of life on earth, or that non-conscious life existed long before the emergence of conscious life. But this is not always so: human psychology (including its causal powers of mind and self) is undoubtedly dependent upon and explainable in terms of the physical architecture of the human brain and nervous system, yet the biological and psychological aspects of human development are not detachable in either a synchronic or diachronic sense.

Translated into the domain of the human-social sciences, ontological materialism can be compressed into three basic propositions. First, that humanity's 'being' or 'existence' (including social being) determines in some sense its 'consciousness' and 'culture' (Thesis 1). Second, that a particular dimension of 'social being' – namely the 'material' element of social production to procure a livelihood from the material environment – has explanatory primacy in accounting for the evolutionary emergence of the human species and hence of the origins of human culture (Thesis 2). Third, that this same dimension of social being, i.e. social labour and the economic relations emergent from it, including (where appropriate) relations of economic exploitation, has explanatory primacy in accounting for the wider socio-cultural structures of a society and the directional logic of overall socio-historical development (Thesis 3). I will now offer an explanation and defence of each of these positions.

The determination of consciousness and culture by social and material existence

The Marxist thesis of the determination of consciousness and culture by 'being', 'existence' or simply 'life' is the most simple of those cited above and can be summarised as three distinct proposals. First there is the claim that mind is an emergent property of a certain combination of organic matter (i.e. the human brain and nervous system) and can develop only in active interchange with the external world (Thesis 1a). Next there is the claim that it is the biological nature (i.e. psycho-organic needs and capacities) of human beings and the 'naturalistic self' which provide the most basic form of explanation of how society and culture are possible, and of why these have a history (Thesis 1b). Finally there is the claim that the contents or products (ideas, concepts, etc.) of human consciousness are necessarily enmattered, in the sense they are always derived (in the final analysis) from the material reality of nature and society (Thesis 1c).

I take it that enough has already been said in this chapter to render Thesis 1a defensible. Not even the most naive of ontological idealists deny that humanity's natural powers of mind, self and rationality have a biological basis, or that these same capacities are developed and greatly enriched through processes of social learning and enculturation. Although there are cultural imperialists who would deny that non-social interaction with the physical environment is efficacious in shaping human development in these crucial respects, this is not the perspective of those outside this charmed circle, and I have demonstrated the falsity of this view elsewhere in the present undertaking.[97] Thesis 1b is more controversial and unpopular than 1a, especially among social scientists, not least because it is seen as leading inevitably to the micro-reductionism of sociobiology. However, properly understood, it entails no such thing, and is beyond rational dispute, as I have again tried to show elsewhere.[98]

Yet it is important to be clear that one important reason why naive biologism has secured for itself any kind of following amongst philosophers and scientists outside sociology, is that successive forms of sociological theorising (functionalism, hermeneutics, constructionism, structuralism, postmodernism, etc.) have sought to demonstrate the 'autonomy' of their subject-matter (socio-cultural reality) by implausibly denying the relevance or even existence of a human nature. To their eternal discredit, in their efforts to stay abreast of the latest fads in social philosophy, a great many Marxists have been to the forefront of this tendency, and in so doing have fallen into a thoroughgoing humanism where they have avoided cultural or linguistic reductionism.

This point has been brilliantly made by Sebastiano Timpanaro:

> The position of the contemporary Marxist seems at time like that of a person living on the first floor of a house, who turns to the tenant of the second floor and says: 'You think you're independent, that you support yourself by yourself? You're wrong! Your apartment stands only because it is supported on mine, and if mine collapses, yours will too'; and on the other hand to the ground floor tenant: 'What are you pretending? That you support and condition me? What a wretched illusion! The ground floor exists only insofar as it is the ground floor to the first floor. Or rather, strictly speaking, the real ground floor is the first floor, and your apartment is only a sort of cellar, to which no real existence can be assigned'. To tell the truth, the relations between the Marxist and the second floor tenant have been perceptibly improved for some time, not because the second floor tenant has recognised his own 'dependence', but because the Marxist has reduced his pretensions considerably, and has come to admit that the second floor is very largely autonomous from the first, or else that the two apartments 'support each other'. But the contempt for the inhabitant of the ground floor has become increasingly pronounced.[99]

However, since cultural determinism (or alternatively the humanist emphasis on a kind of 'undetermined' praxis in shaping the social and natural worlds) is so manifestly contradicted by the elementary facts of human experience, and is generally identified as the only alternative to biological reductionism, it is hardly surprising that sociobiology remains a force to be reckoned with, despite the devastating criticism to which it has been subjected. After all, all parents know their children are not born *tabula rasa*. Indeed, most people would have no difficulty endorsing Timpanaro's justifiable stress on

> the passive element of human experience ... the fact that man as a biological being, endowed with a certain (not unlimited) adaptability to his external environment, and with certain impulses towards activity and

> the pursuit of happiness, subject to old age and death, is not an abstract construction, nor one of our prehistoric ancestors ... now superseded by historical and social man, but still exists in each of us and in all probability will still exist in the future.[100]

But so long as social theory counterposes culturalism to naturalism, failing to articulate an understanding of the interface between biology and society, crude reductive modes of naturalistic social theory remain enormously appealing to academics and lay persons alike, for lack of serious competitors.

Grasping the relationship between human society and human nature in a way which avoids biological and cultural reductionism is exactly what Timpanaro is about. His point is not to affirm that 'certain historical and social forms such as private property or class divisions are inherent in humanity in general', or to deny that 'there is hardly anything that is "purely natural" left in contemporary man ... that has not been enriched and remoulded by the social and cultural environment'. Rather, his purpose is to warn of the 'idealist sophistry' of those 'historicist polemics' against 'man in general' which 'maintain that, since the "biological" is always presented to us as mediated by the "social", the "biological" is nothing and the "social" is everything'. In a brilliant anticipation of the forthcoming 'postmodern turn' of contemporary academic culture, he asks of his contemporaries:

> If we make it [anti-naturalism] ours, how are we to defend ourselves from those who will in turn maintain that, since all reality (including economic and social reality) is knowable through language (or through the thinking mind), language (or the thinking mind) is the sole reality and all the rest is abstraction?[101]

If his warning had been heeded, and naive anti-naturalism had not become the new orthodoxy in the social sciences, most likely we would not have had to endure the reinvigoration of its destructive antithesis of crude biological determinism, with its treatment of human beings as 'selfish replicators' or 'machine-organisms', competing over territory and for access to mates.

Yet Timpanaro's emphasis on 'the passive side of experience' is a one-sided view of human nature, which neglects the 'active' side of self-conscious redirective labour and over-amplifies biological constraints *vis-à-vis* biological enablements in the human condition.[102] This is an understandable weakness, given that Timpanaro is concerned with countering the humanist fetishisation of 'praxis', which is accorded magical properties of making of the world whatever it would like. Nonetheless it is necessary to point out, in modification of Timpanaro's position, that our biological nature also allows, and perhaps impels, us to construct and elaborate complex socio-cultural relations, and to socialise and modify nature in service of our interests and needs (biological and cultural).

Certainly, it is hard to see how anyone can sensibly deny that processes of socialisation and enculturation and the reproduction and development of society and culture presuppose the existence of organisms in secure possession of certain natural capacities (mind, self, intentionality, rationality, etc.).[103] And nor is it possible to conceive of self or personal identity as socially dependent.[104] Of equal significance, every sensible person knows that, just as every individual must live in order to think, so too must 'mankind ... first of all eat and drink, have shelter and clothing, before it can pursue politics, science, religion, art, etc.'.[105] But it is this which ensures that scientific analysis of society and societal history must always start from the biological 'givens' (in this case needs and interests) of the human species, and the natural environment which supplies the means of human needs-satisfaction. It should go without saying, of course, that the sciences of evolutionary ecology and biology have shown us that these human capacities and needs, the exercise and satisfaction of which makes possible society and social history, are the historical product of a specific law-governed pattern of adaptive evolution, itself forged in the interface between organismic needs-satisfaction and the object-world.

The fundamental point of contact between ontological materialism and explanatory (anthropological and sociological) materialism is thus to be found in the simple fact that the laws or tendencies of humanity's biological nature are basic to the laws of socio-cultural and socio-historical reality. There is, in short, a 'chain of being'[106] extending from physico-chemical reality to biological reality and then to socio-cultural reality. This does not mean that the relationship between human biology and psychology, on the one hand, and socio-cultural relations, on the other hand, is one in which the former is ontologically independent of and historically prior to the latter. Humanity's nature or 'species-being' is an indissolubly social one, and natural and socio-cultural evolution, as this has led from the hominids to fully modern *homo sapiens*, have proceeded hand-in-hand as integral and mutually reinforcing aspects of a totality. Yet despite this, it is still valid to say that humanity's psycho-organic nature 'founds' socio-cultural reality. There are two important reasons for this.

Most obviously, of course, our conscious 'species-being' is an emergent property of unreflective organic nature, and it is therefore reasonable to say that biological mechanisms underpin and explain socio-cultural mechanisms, albeit via the intermediary of social-psychological mechanisms in this case. More importantly, though, we have already seen that relations of vertical causality between strata are not necessarily those in which the more basic strata enjoy an ontologically separate existence to those which it 'founds'. On the contrary, one-way relations of ontological presupposition and vertical causation can exist between strata, even where they have a simultaneous historical origin and where the higher has integral effects on the lower. So our species-being is the historical product of biological and social mechanisms combined, but at the same time our biological and psychological capacities and needs, as these are the historical products of natural selection, are always prior to the specific or actual socio-cultural relations which we inhabit. The species-being of individuals is thus always and everywhere an *antecedent condition* of their socio-cultural interaction and learning, of any *particular* social structure into which they are born, and therefore of the reproduction or elaboration of all historical socio-cultural systems.

Turning now to Thesis 1c. In what sense are the products or contents of human consciousness 'determined' by the facts of the material and social environments which individuals inhabit? At times Marx seems to suggest that the relationship between 'thought' and 'life', or between ideas and reality, is one in which the former passively 'mirrors' or 'records' the latter:

> My dialectical method is, in its foundations, not only different from the Hegelian, but exactly opposite to it. For Hegel the process of thinking, which he even transforms into an independent subject, under the name of 'the Idea', is the creator of the real world, and the real world is only the external appearance of the idea. With me the reverse is true: the ideal is nothing but the material world reflected in the mind of man, and translated into forms of thought.[107]

Yet such an interpretation of Marx's meaning sits uneasily with key tenets of his philosophy. First, with his theory of knowledge, which holds that the phenomenal forms of reality are often poor guides to its underlying structures, this necessitating scientific analyses of the world. Second, with his theory of alienation, which is designed to show that 'in a society where human beings [cannot] control either their natural environment or the social and economic mechanism it [is] inevitable that they ... fail to ... comprehend their world'.[108] Furthermore, it is clear that both Marx and Engels use the language of 'reflection' as a polemical device to distinguish their own position in the most general way from that of the Hegelian school, which insisted upon the construction of the material world by and through thought. It has no other function in their writings. For wherever Marx or Engels go beyond general formulas, when specifying the relationship between thought and existence, their analysis immediately becomes more subtle and qualified.

Engels, for instance, makes the point that

> [o]nce it has arisen ... every ideology develops in conjunction with the given conceptual material and elaborates on it; otherwise it would not be an ideology, that is, dealing with ideas as autonomous entities which develop independently and are subject to their own laws.[109]

Elsewhere he makes the more general point that thought can never simply mirror reality because reality is itself in continual motion and change:

> The concept of a thing and its reality … run side by side like two asymptotes, always approaching each other yet never meeting. The difference between the two is the very difference which prevents the concept from being directly and immediately reality and reality from being immediately its own concept … the concept … does not therefore prima facie directly coincide with reality, from which it had to be abstracted in the first place, it is nevertheless more than a fiction, unless you declare that all the results of thought are fictions because reality only corresponds to them only very circuitously, and even then approaching it only asympomatically. … From the moment we accept the theory of evolution all our concepts of organic life correspond only approximately to reality. Otherwise there could be no change. On the day when concepts and reality completely coincide in the organic world development comes to an end. The concept fish includes life in water and breathing through gills: how are you going to get from fish to amphibian without breaking through this concept?[110]

Nonetheless, Marx and Engels are right to suggest that material reality 'determines' the products or contents of human consciousness, and not vice-versa, even if the 'determination' of the latter by the former is neither mechanical nor absolute. Two points are relevant to this issue. For one thing, as Engels points out,

> if the … question is raised [of] what thought and consciousness are and where they come from, it becomes apparent that they are products of the human brain and that man himself is a product of nature, which has developed in and along with its environment; hence it is self-evident that the products of the human brain, being in the last analysis also products of nature, do not contradict the rest of nature's interconnections but are in correspondence with them.[111]

For another thing, it is clear that human thought always has a context, an external referent, to which it is related or oriented: ideas are always about *something*. This 'something' is, for lack of plausible other candidates, nothing other than the social and natural worlds in which individuals are situated, which forms the medium and focus of their interactions. As Antonio Labriola famously puts it: 'Ideas do not fall from heaven, and nothing comes to us in a dream'.[112]

The point Labriola is making is this. The linguistic signs we use to communicate with others, the resources which we draw upon to act socially, the norms or rules which regulate our social conduct, the technical knowledge which we use to produce our livelihood – none of these are ever spontaneous creations of the human mind, but are always appropriated (albeit creatively) from a socio-cultural environment which we find in existence at birth. None of us, for instance, have any real choice over whether or not we learn or make use of the linguistic concepts native to our culture. This we must do if we are to communicate with others, and communication is not simply an objective capacity of human beings but also an objective need of our species' sociality. Equally, not even the greatest of geniuses pluck their ideas out of thin air. These are always the product of painstaking conceptual labours, and are developed in response to an existing cultural context which defines the problems to be dealt with and the intellectual materials from which a novel solution to these might be fashioned: there could not be an Einstein before a Newton or a Marx before a Ricardo. Further, nor do any of us have a real choice over whether or not we utilise the stock of tools, technology and technical know-how at our disposal, or enter into definite kinds of economic relations in doing so, all of which are products of social activity. This we must do if we are to ensure our own physical survival or well-being and that of our dependants. All of this is indicative of the fact that socio-cultural productions are developed historically, not by means of the relentless unfolding of human reason as a force standing apart from nature or society, but by means of the dynamic 'lived relation' between social labour and the material environment, the latter of which is always the 'inorganic body'[113] of human thought and interaction.

The upshot of all this is that individuals *must* reflect upon the social and material worlds they inhabit with others, because these constitute the *given* circumstances which frame their lives, defining the possibilities and limitations of their activity at any given point in time. These 'circumstances' are always the starting point of any analysis of ideology or consciousness, because thought is always a response to existential problems, to real-world processes, even where it is an 'active' or 'creative' response which seeks to understand the world in order to change it. Yet analysis of the material conditions of human thinking and action is only the starting point of the analysis, because it must also be recognised that 'men are the producers of their conceptions, ideas, etc.',[114] and that these ideas are often interventions against existing conditions. Translated into practical activity, these ideas can sometimes bring into being a modified or even transformed set of circumstances and relations, which then confront individuals with a new range of existential problems which have to be dealt with in thought and deed, and which therefore condition consciousness and interaction rather differently than previously.

This seems to me what Marx is getting at when he argues: 'Men, developing their material production and their material intercourse, alter, along with this their actual world, also their thinking and the products of their thinking. It is not consciousness that determines life, but life that determines consciousness'.[115] This emphasis on the dynamic interplay between 'conditions' and 'consciousness', though always starting out from the 'conditions' in which 'consciousness' is situated, is what distinguishes a dialectical materialist analysis of reality from a reductive or mechanical one, the latter of which sees 'consciousness' as mere adaptation to or passive reflection of antecedent circumstances or relations.

Anthropological materialism: social labour and the origins of human beings and human culture

Turning now to Thesis 2. In Chapter 2 I argue that Marx and Engels furnish an account of human nature or 'species-being' which in effect provides a naturalistic foundation or anchorage point for their theory of society and history. This is one important sense in which sociological and historical materialism can be said to be 'materialistic'. In Chapter 2 I also argue that Marx and Engels grasp human nature as a 'stratified totality', that is, as a unitary psycho-organic system of distinct properties and powers (including sociality, consciousness, self, rationality, labour and language). From this perspective, human nature (i.e. the nature of modern *homo sapiens*) is the evolutionary end-product of a process by and through which certain 'core' properties of our earliest non-human ancestors (elementary sociality, tool-use and cooperative labour) provided a foundation for the subsequent physiological restructuring and corresponding elaboration of the wider and richer range of properties outlined above, which precisely define us as a species qualitatively distinct from the hominoid apes.

Now, this stratified conception of human nature is articulated on a philosophical level by Marx, who takes these properties and capacities of human nature 'as given', as founding the socio-cultural laws which his social theory is designed to unravel. By contrast, the task of investigating their historical origins and development fell to Engels, whose purpose is to provide a scientific basis for Marx's speculative anthropology. In his *The Part Played by Labour in the Transition from Ape to Man*, Engels offers an historical account of the formation of modern humans, and of society and culture, which stresses the role of both purely natural-evolutionary processes, and of the historical interface between social labour for material subsistence and the physical environment, in bringing about these outcomes. What is distinctive about Engels' approach? How does it fare in the light of our greater scientific knowledge of human evolution in the years since his death? I will address both of these questions in turn.

Here, in a compressed form, is Engels' account of human origins:

> Many hundreds of thousands of years ago, during an epoch not yet definitely determinable … a race of anthropoid apes lived in the tropical zone … in bands in the trees. … These apes began to lose the habit of using their hands to walk and adopted a more and more erect posture. This was *the first decisive step in the transition from ape to man*. Other diverse functions must have devolved upon the hands. The first operations for which our ancestors gradually learned to adapt their hands … could have been only simple ones. … But the decisive step had been taken,

> the hand had become free and could henceforth attain ever greater dexterity and skill, and the greater flexibility thus acquired was inherited and increased from generation to generation. Thus the hand is not only the organ of labour, *it is also the product of labour.* ... But the hand did not exist by itself. ... Much more important is the direct ... reaction of the hand on the rest of the organism. ... [O]ur simian ancestors were gregarious ... the development of labour necessarily helped to bring the members of society together by increasing the cases of mutual support and joint activity, and by making clear the advantages of this joint activity to every individual. Men-in-the-making arrived at the point where *they had something to say* to each other. Necessity created the organ; the undeveloped larynx of the ape was slowly but surely transformed by modulation to produce constantly more developed modulation, and the organs of the mouth gradually learned to produce one articulate sound after another. ... The reaction of labour and speech on the development of the brain and its attendant senses, of the increasing clarity of consciousness, power of abstraction and of conclusion, gave both labour and speech an ever renewed impulse to further development.[116]

As Chris Harman points out, in a nutshell, 'Engels' position ... sees human evolution as going through a number of interlinked stages: two-legged walking, tool-making and use, development of the hand, sociability, brain and speech development, more control over nature, more sociability, more brain and speech development'.[117] His ideas on evolution are normally assumed to be a mere 'materialist' restatement of Darwin's theory. But, although dependent upon the research of his illustrious contemporary, in fact Engels modifies Darwin's evolutionary sequence (of stages leading from ape to human) in one important respect. Darwin and his successors argued that the development of the brain and its attendant intellectual powers must have happened *prior* to the transition to bipedalism and tool-use and manufacture, on the grounds that only an increase in brain-power would allow these latter developments to take place. Engels, by contrast, claimed that the reverse must be true. His argument was that two-legged walking and the resultant freeing of the hands for tool-use, tool-making and attendant cooperative labour occurred *before* the reorganisation of the brain and increase in intellect, this providing the initial impetus for subsequent developments. The archaeologist Bruce Trigger explains:

> Engels argued that an increasingly terrestrial life-style had encouraged ... increasing use of tools. This caused natural selection in favour of bipedalism and manual dexterity as well as ... a more complex division of labour. Tool making and the development of a capacity for language the better to co-ordinate productive activities led to the gradual transformation of the brain of an ape into that of a modern human being.[118]

What is remarkable about Engels' account is the extent to which it has been vindicated in basic essentials by developments in archaeology, palaeontology and palaeoanthropology in recent years. Consider the question of the 'first impulse' behind the evolution of the human brain and consciousness. Was it the freeing of the hands for tool-making and cooperative labour which stimulated brain development (Engels) or was it brain development which provided an impulse towards bipedalism and social labour (Darwin)? Harman makes the point that, up until the 1950s, Darwin's 'idealist' view of human evolution was virtual orthodoxy, and Engels' alternative either unknown or rejected out of hand. Indeed, as Harman also says, such was the dominance of the Darwinian orthodoxy, that for more than forty years (from 1912 to 1955) it blew off course the whole study of human origins. This it did by encouraging the uncritical acceptance by scientists of one of the greatest scientific frauds ever perpetrated – the so-called 'Piltdown Affair'. The Piltdown skull (an ape-like jaw plus large modern-looking cranium) was 'discovered' in a gravel pit in southern England by amateur archaeologist Charles Dawson. The entire British scientific establishment (with one or two notable exceptions) accepted the Piltdown skull as the 'missing link' separating humans from the apes. As Richard Leakey points out, this was not because the skull 'was demonstrably old and genuine, but because it matched powerful preconceptions of what our ancestors were like ... the first man was clearly intelligent ... and an Englishman'.[119]

Eventually the 'fossil' was revealed as a blatant forgery: a human skull grafted to the jaw of an orang-utan and treated to give the impression of age. But its near-universal acceptance as the genuine article meant that authentic finds (which indicated that bipedalism and cooperative labour predated brain development) were ignored or ridiculed for decades.[120] In fact, Darwin's sequence was not completely abandoned by the scientific community until 1974, following the discovery by Donald Johanson 'of a complete three and half million year old skeleton with an ape sized brain and an erect posture'.[121] More than a hundred years after the publication of *The Descent of Man*, Engels had finally been proven right against Darwin on the question of the first impulse behind human evolution. Here, as in other areas of scientific research, it is clear that our knowledge would have developed far more rapidly and smoothly if those entrusted with its development had held from the outset a thoroughgoing materialist understanding of nature (in this case of human nature).

But I have suggested that the whole of Engels' account, not just 'this or that' aspect of his argument, is broadly consistent with contemporary scientific knowledge of human origins and prehistory. It is time to add a little substance to this claim. Obviously I am not saying that every detail of Engels' understanding is correct (this would be remarkable indeed, and if true a negation of dialectics!) or that there are not substantial gaps in his explanation. One important weakness of Engels' account is that it does not specify those material circumstances, external to biological selective mechanisms, which ensured that evolution in the direction of bipedalism was a viable and useful adaptive strategy. Instead, Engels simply states that our distant hominoid ancestors 'lost the habit' of quadrupedalism, which of course has voluntarist connotations. Engels also overstates the role of tool-use and tool-making in stimulating evolution in the direction of sociality, consciousness and culture (and attendant physiological restructuring). A broader range of factors were of crucial importance in this respect, as we shall soon see.

Yet neither of these weaknesses is especially damaging to Engels' enterprise. After all, Marx and Engels do recommend in *The German Ideology* that materialist analysis of society and history proceed from the anterior biological *and* environmental facts of human existence. Therefore, any specification of the physical circumstances conducive to human evolution can only deepen and enrich a materialist understanding of our origins. And, of course, Engels' 'failure' to follow through his own (and Marx's) recommendation in *The Part Played by Labour in the Transition from Ape to Man* is largely explainable in terms of the absence in his own day of knowledge of those geological and ecological circumstances which prevailed in human prehistory, for which he can hardly be faulted. More significantly, although Engels' unilateral emphasis on the role of tool-making and use in stimulating selection in the direction of brain development, intellect and language has been shown to be over-simple, at the same time the new archaeology and palaeoanthropology has shown that the primary impulse behind the evolution from hominoid to modern human being was nothing other than *social labour to procure material subsistence*, that is, cooperative economic activity in general (of which tool-making was nonetheless a crucial ingredient). This can hardly be seen as contradicting the fundamental point of Marxian materialism in historical social anthropology: the explication of human and cultural origins in terms of socio-economic relationships and technology.

In any case, the 'gap' in Engels' account can be filled now in a way which does not in the least compromise it. Modern archaeology and palaeontology have shown that it was the formation of the East African Rift Valley ten million years ago, resulting in dramatic changes in climate and drainage, and with this the development of 'far more complex and varied mosaic of habitats', which most likely was 'instrumental in the evolutionary origin of the first upright hominoid'.[122] The reason for this is that these geological-climatic changes resulted in the gradual fragmentation of the formerly dense forest cover east of the Rift Valley (which provided the habitat of the earliest hominoid bands). This in turn forced many of the hominoids to struggle for subsistence upon a new open savannah terrain where escape to the safety of the trees was not always an option and where foodstuffs were less plentiful, more dispersed, and hence harder to come by.

To understand why these environmental changes triggered selection in the direction of bipedalism for certain of the hominoid species it is important to grasp two points. First, as David Pilbeam points out, since 'the contexts in which … primates … stand or walk upright are for the most part when they are feeding … on the ground', it is reasonable to conclude that the first hominids (which were much smaller than modern gorillas and chimpanzees) 'would have walked upright readily when … on the ground'.[123] Second, as Peter Rodman and Henry McHenry point out, bipedalism in humans is a far more efficient mode of locomotion than quadrupedalism in the modern great apes, because the latter is a compromise between walking on the ground and climbing in the trees. 'If you're an ape, and you find yourself in ecological circumstances where a more efficient mode of locomotion would be advantageous, the evolution of bipedalism is a likely outcome'.[124]

Of course, the dispersal of food sources in the new savannah terrain provided exactly these kinds of circumstances. 'Bipedalism provided the possibility of improved efficiency of travel with modification only of hind limbs while leaving the [ape] structure of the limbs free for … feeding'.[125] Therefore, the habitual behavioural tendency of the hominoid apes to stand and walk when feeding on the ground became genetically enhanced by selection, because they were placed in a situation where they were forced to move from place to place in search of food, 'taking fruit, berries and nuts from low bushes'.[126] It was this development, marking the transition from hominoid to hominid, which freed the hand from its primary function of tree-climbing and made possible the development of tool-use and cooperative labour on a scale and intensity not seen among the modern great apes (whose ancestors did not leave their traditional arboreal haunts). And from this followed the beginnings of tool-making, the reorganisation of the brain, the birth of consciousness and eventually language, culminating in the cultural mode of modern *homo sapiens*, over a period of about 2.5 million years.

Yet it is important to stress that there was nothing inevitable in the subsequent pattern of evolution from small-brained bipedal ape to large-brained modern human being. Again, this adaptive strategy depended on a new host of environmental changes coming into being, as Richard Leakey explains:

> The initial appearance of the hominid family 7.5 million years ago coincided with global cooling and local geological events that fragmented and thinned the previously carpet-like forest cover in East Africa. What of the origin of the genus *Homo*? Does it 'coincide' with anything significant? Yes it does: another global cooling event, much bigger than before. Huge ice mountains built up in Antarctica close to 2.6 million years ago, and for the first time significant amounts of ice formed in the Arctic. The frigid grip produced cooler, drier climates in

> the rest of the globe, including the varied highland terrain of eastern Africa. Such climatic changes break up habitats, and may drive pulses of extinction throughout the plant and animal worlds. But they may also cause speciation, the development of new species from isolated populations, adapting to new conditions. Among the African antelopes, whose fossil record is as good as any terrestrial vertebrates, can be, this pulse of extinction and speciation at around 2.6 million years ago is clearly seen. Suddenly, a range of existing species vanished and a crop of new ones appeared. Glimpses of this pattern are also seen, albeit less clearly, in other grazing and browsing animals of Africa. I suggest that it is to be found in the hominids, with the evolution of australopithecines and of *Homo*.[127]

In these circumstances, the biological evolution of the hominids (upright apes) moved in at least two different directions.

> One was a further exaggeration of the basic hominid form. This resulted in the robust australopithecines. ... These creatures were able to process large amounts of tough plant foods, the kind found in arid environments. The second ... was something of a breakthrough, one that is recognised by the appellation *Homo*. Because the traditional hominid diet became more difficult to subsist on, there was the potential for expanding the diet, not specialising it, as the robust australopithecines did. The expansion involved making meat an important food source, not just an occasional item, as it was with earlier hominids and is still for baboons and chimpanzees.[128]

What was the significance of this development?

Every biological species will have as big a brain as it can afford to build (in energy terms), for the simple reason that intelligence greatly enhances adaptive survival value. This is why 'throughout evolutionary history ... animals have become brainier: mammals are brainier than reptiles and amphibians ... [a]nd within mammals ... primates are the best endowed of all'.[129] But those primates, already better endowed in terms of brain size and intellect than any other species, who are able to adapt their diet in such a way as to greatly increase their capacity to generate and conserve energy, will obviously have far more scope to undergo brain reorganisation and development in the direction of enhanced intellect. This is exactly what did happen to our hominid ancestors. The addition of meat to the previous mostly herbivorous diet of those hominids destined to become the first of the *homo* line provided them with far higher levels of energy than those hominids who adapted in the direction of dietary specialisation in plant foods alone (because meat is far richer in calories, fat and protein than vegetation). Over countless generations – from *homo habilis* to *homo erectus* and on to *homo sapiens* – the 'surplus' of bodily energy was 'reinvested' in brain and intellectual growth under the aegis of natural selection, a process culminating in the formation of the brain of modern humans (which constitutes just 2 per cent of total body weight yet uses up 20 per cent of total energy).[130]

But none of this could have occurred unless our hominid ancestors had discovered a means of stabilising the food supply upon which their new mixed diet depended. This means was precisely the innovation of tool-making within the hunter-gatherer mode of economic subsistence in its earliest or crudest form:

> The initial expansion of brain size in the hominids, which established the genus *Homo* ... required an adaptation that required more complex behaviour: the hunting-and-gathering way of life in embryo. But it also fuelled itself, in a kind of positive feedback. ... The dietary shift in *Homo* drove the change in pattern of tooth development and facial shape. ... Our ancestors achieved this dietary shift through *technology*, and thus opened the road to the potential – but not ... not inevitable – development of yet bigger brains. Primates have great difficulty in getting at the meat of large, tough-skinned animals. With a sharp stone flake, however, even the toughest hide can be sliced through, literally opening up a new nutritional world. In a very real sense, by taking a crude hammer stone and striking it against a pebble to produce a small, sharp flake, our earliest *Homo* ancestors began to control their world in a way that no other creature has done before or since. ... Here, we have the fruits of ingenuity, part of the evolutionary package. Our ancestors made these tools, but in a real sense, these tools made our ancestors. By the same token, they made us what we are today. ... In the enlarged brain, the newly emerging tool-making ability, ... the beginnings of a hunting-and-gathering subsistence, the interconnectedness of things, we recognise hints of ourselves, our humanity.[131]

Such social labour and cooperative tool-making was also efficacious in reshaping the physical organisation of our hominid and *homo* ancestors in a wide range of ways, which are only just beginning to be understood by evolutionary biologists. The development by *homo habilis* of an embryonic form of the hunter-gatherer mode of subsistence itself gave a boost towards the further evolution of a more efficient bipedal body plan. In particular, as Dean Falk has pointed out, the demands of cooperative hunting required improved modes of locomotion (as a rule animals are less static than plant foods!), which in turn required a reorganisation of the blood vessels (to prevent overheating of the brain during strenuous physical activity). Natural selection then operated along this pathway: more efficient bipedalism giving rise to an increasingly complex drainage and circulatory system, which in turn stimulated the further development of our ancestors' capacity to run an efficient hunting economy.[132] At the same time, research by Ralph Holloway has shown that tool-making skills and cognitive skills have marched forward in concert as part of an 'evolutionary package'. Holloway observes that tool-making and cognitive skills have a close proximity in the brain, which indicates a common origin.[133] This being the case, it does seem reasonable to hypothesise that, since the fossil record suggests that tool-making considerably predated the process of brain enlargement, it is most likely that the initial spur for the latter was provided by the former.

But I have suggested that, whatever the initial impetus for the growth of the brain and attendant intellectual development, its subsequent cumulative expansion and development cannot be attributed simply to the evolution of the increasing manual skills of tool-making. Of greater importance in this process was the emergence of new socio-economic relations alongside this technology of subsistence. Glynn Isaac and his colleagues have provided persuasive evidence for supposing that the development of the hunter-gatherer mode of economic activity (involving 'home bases' and a sexual division of labour whereby females did most of the gathering of plant foods and men most of the hunting and scavenging) went hand-in-hand with a new adaptive strategy of egalitarian food-sharing (whereby food was transported to the home base and distributed according to need and consumed socially).[134] The move towards a food-sharing economy made good sense in adaptive terms because it reinforced social solidarity and communal ties (necessary for integrated hunting and gathering), and ensured a stable environment for the reproduction of the band and the rearing of the young.

The significance of this development in evolutionary terms was that it encouraged selection in favour of increased sociality, which in turn allowed the construction of increasingly complex social relations and rich social interactions, this allowing the emergence and cumulative enrichment of 'social chess' among members of the band. Yet learning to cope with greater societal complexity (the formation of alliances, the interpretation of and orientation towards the behaviour of others, mastering the intricacies of reciprocity, the understanding of rituals, etc.), on top of the demands of the material environment and of tool-making, itself required an enormous expansion in intellect or consciousness. Because of this, the dialectic of tool-making, cooperative hunting and gathering and food-sharing drove the 'evolutionary ratchet' in the direction of brain development and growing intellectual powers of mind and abstraction.

Again, the logic of this particular evolutionary sequence is brilliantly summarised by Richard Leakey:

> With the advent of *Homo* and the appearance of the hunting-and-gathering way of life, the game of social chess would have become more demanding. There would indeed have been reproductive advantages to the possession of a more acute mental model, one that would have been

> aided by a sharper consciousness. Natural selection would have worked with this, moving consciousness to higher and higher levels. This gradual unfolding consciousness not only fashioned a new kind of reality in our heads, it also changed us into a new kind of animal. The two million year heritage of a hunting-and-gathering life, rudimentary at first but ultimately superbly refined, left its mark on our minds as much as it did on our bodies. On top of the technical skills of planning, co-ordination and technology there was, equally importantly, the social skill of co-operation. A sense of common goals and values, a desire to further the common good, co-operation was more than simply individuals working together. It became a set of rules of conduct, of morals, an understanding of right and wrong in a complex social system. Without co-operation – within bands, among bands, through tribal groups – our technical skills would have been severely blunted.[135]

These same socio-economic mechanisms also provide the most plausible explanation of why language and dialogic self-consciousness evolved. For most anthropologists and archaeologists, the acquisition of language marks the point of no return in the development from upright ape to modern human being. Certainly, language was the crucial breakthrough in terms of allowing our ancestors to develop a sense of self far denser and richer than anything to be found in the modern great apes, and in allowing a further enormous expansion in technical know-how, plus a further giant hike in the complexity and density of social life, all of which were undoubtedly beneficial to the reproductive success of the *homo* line. Indeed, it is quite possible that the formation of the brain of modern *homo sapiens* (itself substantially larger than the brain of *homo erectus*) was itself stimulated primarily by the development of language. As Harry Jerrison points out:

> Technology has long since been regarded as the driving force behind human brain expansion. [This] ... seems to me to be an inadequate explanation, not least because tool-making can be accomplished with very little brain tissue. The production of simple, useful speech, on the other hand, requires a substantial amount of brain tissue.[136]

Yet language and the dialogic self, which together constitute the foundations of human culture, would not have arisen in the absence of the denser social networks which formed around the hunter-gatherer and food-sharing modes of the new cooperative economy. In such communities, communication is necessarily more intense and sophisticated than the vocalisation which goes on in even the most social of primate bands. This is because abstract communication greatly enhances the planning and coordination of cooperative labour and tool-making in a complex social economy.

> With a shift towards a mixed economy of hunting and gathering, in which daily divisions of troops are routine in the separate food quests, the need for organisation and agreement becomes yet more intensified. A sophisticated degree of communication is important, as it is for overall increased sociality.[137]

And so, given the socio-economic mode of the *homo* species, the development of a spoken language and appropriate reorganisation of the larynx, the pharynx, the tongue and lips hardly constitutes a surprising adaptive move or evolutionary 'good trick':

> In all likelihood, a rudimentary form of verbal communication arose as long ago as two million years …, at the time of *Homo habilis*, and there may even have been language of some sort among the australopithecines. The emergence of *Homo erectus* was probably marked by a further development of this ability, with perhaps a greater vocabulary and a capacity for basic sentence structure. The evidence suggesting ritual acts in later *Homo erectus* populations might well indicate that there had been a further refinement of language to convey more subtle concepts. Finally the symbolism and imagery embodied in the art that flourished from 30,000 years ago onwards surely signals the origins of modern language capacity, including the capacity to articulate complex abstract ideas.[138]

But of all this means that *social labour* within a cooperative food-sharing economy is the 'missing link' which explains the emergence of modern human beings and the subsequent flowering of human culture, as Engels rightly insisted. For, in summary, the dominant view in contemporary evolutionary biology, palaeontology and archaeology, locates the successive enlargements of the brain over 2.5 million or so years in the growing dependence of our ancestors

> on communicative and cognitive skills, which in turn were necessary for the transmission of knowledge about increased tool-making, for cooperative gathering and hunting, and for coping with the much denser networks of social interaction which grew out of both these activities.[139]

This perspective, though not universally accepted,[140] is the dominant one because backed up by the archaeological record: the evidence of 'home bases' and tool-making among *homo habilis*, the expansion of the *habilis* and *erectus* populations beyond their African homelands into cooler and less hospitable climes (which suggests a greater reliance on technology and culture); the decline of the relative size differences between male and female during the same period (which is suggestive of the growing importance of society and culture in providing a defence against predators); the evidence of 'fire use by *homo erectus*', of 'ritual burial sites', 'ochre skin painting' and 'hut building' among archaic *homo sapiens*.[141] Such archaeological data is, as Charles Woolfson has said, strongly indicative that 'the broad outlines of Engels' theory are, by and large, confirmed ... and that, in this respect, Engels' essay is a brilliant scientific anticipation of what is now thought to be the likely pattern of human evolution'.[142]

Socio-historical materialism: base, superstructure and social change

My exposition so far has outlined and defended two key explanatory hypotheses of critical materialism:

(i) the determination of 'consciousness' (including social consciousness) and 'culture' by 'being' (including social being) or 'nature' (Thesis 1);
(ii) the explanatory primacy of cooperative economic activity in determining the evolutionary emergence of human nature and the origins of human culture (Thesis 2).

All of this brings me on to the third component of critical materialism: the explanatory primacy of the mode of economic production in determining social systems and overall trajectories of socio-historical development (Thesis 3). For convenience this thesis can be divided into two parts. First, into the claim that the political, ideological and ideational 'superstructure' of a society is determined by its economic 'base' or 'basis' (Thesis 3a). This is a statement of *vertical causality* in social systems. Second, into the claim that societal evolution (together with the revolutionary movement from one type of social system to another) is governed primarily by the interface between the forces and relations of production, and by the dynamic of class conflict fixed by the economic base (Thesis 3b). This is a statement of *horizontal causality* in societal development, which renders meaningful a materialist theory of history. Since I address the vexed question of the relationship between base, superstructure and social change in greater detail in Chapter 4, I will here content myself with a summary treatment of the relevant issues, in effect 'setting the scene' for the later discussions.

Base and superstructure

The first point to make is that the Marxist distinction of base from superstructure does not correspond to a simple contrast between 'economy' and 'society'. There are two reasons for this. First, Marx, unlike for instance Max Weber, is fully alive to the fact that economic relations are not simply technico-natural relations between individuals and scarce objects of utility, but are also *social* relations between people and between the class 'positions' which people occupy in society *vis-à-vis* the means of production and subsistence. Because of this there can be no legitimate abstraction of society from economy, or of the science of economics from the science of sociology, of the kind recommended by Weber. Second, the Marxist application of the base-superstructure model is not simply restricted to outlining a hierarchy of structural causality in *society* (the determination of politico-ideological forms by the forces and relations of production) – although of course this is one of its most important functions – but extends much deeper and wider than this.

More broadly, in fact, the base-superstructure model is designed to illuminate the 'rootedness' of the social and cultural structures constitutive of social systems in those deeper *non*-social structures 'basic' to these which have direct relevance in explaining society and history. From this point of view, superstructural social forms have their roots in the socio-structural 'level', and structural social forms have their roots in non-social substructural levels or strata. Base-superstructure, in its wider application, is thus theoretical shorthand for a tripartite model of hierarchically ordered structures: *substructure* (human biology and its natural powers), *structure* (the mode of production and surplus extraction of a society) and *superstructure* (those social relations and ideological forms which are not themselves integral aspects of the structure).[143]

Now I would say that it is reasonable to 'reconstruct' the base-superstructure model, in the light of the realist philosophy of science, as one in which the higher-order strata are 'emergent' from the lower-order strata. Certainly this kind of interpretation is consistent with Marx and Engels' commitment to an anti-reductive form of materialism in both philosophy and social theory. But this means that the relations between structures in this 'chain of being' are best grasped as those of *ontological presupposition* (the higher existing only by virtue of the lower and not vice-versa) and *vertical determination* (the lower explaining the higher without explaining them away).

I have addressed the ways in which a society's (or social system's) mode of production is efficacious in vertically determining certain of its (their) non-economic institutions and ideologies, in Chapter 4.[144] Therefore I will give this matter no consideration here. Instead I will address the more contentious issue, of whether economic structure can plausibly be seen as ontologically basic to politico-ideological and ideational superstructure in social analysis.

My argument is that this is indeed the case. However, the unilateral ontological dependence of superstructure upon structure is plausible only if grasped *diachronically*, as specifying the *historical* origins of distinct cultural and political institutions in the development of the forces and relations of production. As a matter of historical record, the first human social relations were cooperative economic relations, and it was the development of these economic relations which provided a basis for a more diversified social and cultural existence. These economic relations (the hunter-gatherer mode of economic subsistence of *homo habilis*, *homo erectus*, archaic humans, and finally fully modern *homo sapiens*) were themselves in turn the historical product of a dialectic of economic labour and biological elaboration, and it is this which provides the link between a materialist anthropology of humanity and society and a materialist sociology of politics, culture and history, the former founding the latter. By contrast, if grasped *synchronically*, as specifying the one-way ontological dependence of superstructure upon structure in a specific society or at a given point in time, this argument is for the most part unsuccessful (because superstructural forms, especially politico-military relations, where these are not directly relations of production, often function to 'fix' or stabilise the relations of production which vertically explain them).

The second point to make is that Marx's base-superstructure model, in its narrower application (as a thesis of the relationship between mode of production and non-economic social structures) does not map neatly on to a distinction between 'structure' and 'culture', as is often imagined. The distinction between 'structure' and 'culture' is a broader one, and one rooted in the simple recognition that the social world is populated by both material and cultural structures, both of which are aspects of a social world which (from the point of view of every generation of individuals) is 'already made'. Realists quite rightly argue that material and cultural structures are both emergent properties of the social activities of the dead generations, which confront the living as a set of constraints, enablements and impulses upon their thinking and conduct. Both are 'basic' to social interaction and human agency in this sense. But having said this, it is nonetheless necessary to draw a distinction between structure and culture, for the obvious reason that these terms refer us to 'societal emergents' which are *different in kind*. 'Structure', for instance, refers us to relations governing the production of use-values and the appropriation-distribution of allocative and authoritative resources in a society. 'Culture', by contrast, refers us to the ensemble of ideological and ideational structures of a society (i.e. systems of communication, meaning, legitimation and knowledge).

Now, because the base-superstructure model, in its narrower application, does not correspond exactly to a simple contrast between 'economic emergents' and 'cultural emergents', it can hardly be construed as logically excluding the possibility that the 'economic structure' of society is itself comprised of 'material' and 'cultural' elements. Furthermore, because the superstructure of any society is determined not simply by the economic structure upon which it rests, but also by the substructure basic to the economic level (humanity's biologically-given needs and capacities), nor can it be plausibly affirmed that Marx wishes to categorise all superstructural spheres or properties as 'reflexes' of economic conditions or class interests. In fact, Marx is committed to neither of these positions often attributed to him. He does not affirm the unilateral determination of superstructure by structure, nor the purely 'material' nature of structure.[145]

Whatever Marx's own view, however, what cannot be doubted is that certain cultural structures are an integral part of the material basis of a society (broadly defined); that others are neither base nor superstructure but are interwoven with and essential to both; and that still others are shaped as much by substructural levels as by the structural level of economic and class relations. Into the first category fall cultural emergents such as scientific knowledge of natural laws, 'recipe knowledge' of the material world, and the technical know-how derived from scientific and practical knowledges of nature combined. These are an indispensable part of the base for two simple reasons.

First, because they are the emergent products of modes of constitutive social labour which immerse human agents most immediately and directly in the 'natural terrain' upon which their social relations and interactions are based (i.e. practical labour on the material world to procure a livelihood, and scientific labour designed to reveal the underlying structures of nature by rational procedures of experiment and empirical checking). This renders these cultural emergents 'material' in a way that political and ideological structures are not (the latter of which are emergent from the 'artificial terrain'[146] of society, and express the vested interests and outlooks of specific agential groupings in social relations). Second, because the primary function of both scientific and recipe knowledge is to extend practical human control over nature so as to develop material production in the service of human needs and social interests.

Into the second category fall the linguistic structures of a society. These are simultaneously base and superstructure because indispensable to every complex form of social activity (and hence social structure), all of which are dependent upon the communication of meaning in interaction. This does not free them from an 'ultimate' material determination, of course. But the material basis of linguistic structures nonetheless lies outside society itself, in the biological needs and capacities of humanity's species-being, as these were generated historically in the interface between cooperative labour and physical reality.

Finally, into the third category falls a whole range of cultural forms (religious, artistic, philosophic, etc.). Certainly these are, for the most part, shaped in terms of their content and function by economic conditions and class relations and positioning, though often indirectly via intermediate superstructural mechanisms. But since 'men, while living in society, do not thereby cease to live in nature, and to receive from it occasion and material for their curiosity and for their imagination',[147] it is hardly a matter of contention that certain cultural structures will inevitably embody some-or-other expression of the 'general human condition'.

This is clearest of all in the case of artistic and religious productions. These are never straightforward articulations of economic or class mechanisms, though of course we can be sure that these will be present, not least because people living naturally do not cease to live socially. In fact, they are also expressive of general human emotions, aspirations and needs (for fellowship, community, meaning, order, love, sexual relations, aesthetic expression, or of the pain and anger of their absence or frustration, of fear and lament of old age, sickness and death, etc.), which are themselves comprehensible only in terms of the biological constitution of human beings.[148]

A final point of clarification before proceeding. A common mistake of Marxist and non-Marxist interpreters of Marx is to treat his couplet of base and superstructure as pretty much the same thing as his distinction between 'being' and 'consciousness'. This is not the case. The couplet of being (including social being) and consciousness (including social consciousness) is the most general concept of all in Marxist theory, and as such it corresponds neither to the broader or narrower applications of the base-superstructure model (though obviously it is closer to the first than the second). On the contrary, it refers not only to vertical relations between those emergent structures (biological, psychological, socio-economic, socio-cultural, etc.) which 'bound' and 'found' human agency and interaction in determinate ways, but to the totality of social and material relationships (anterior and adjacent) into which individuals are inserted at birth or enter into during their life-cycle. Thus, whereas Marx's base-superstructure model establishes the case for a materialist account of the emergent entities which constitute and which immediately found a social system, his couplet of being-consciousness establishes the case for a materialist ontology and method in the human sciences generally. This it does on the grounds that human beings are not born with concepts, values, beliefs or properties of self-consciousness 'ready-made' (the human 'spirit' or 'essence', etc.), but instead acquire these through active ongoing interaction with subjects and the sensuous object-world (the 'inorganic body' of human thought and conduct) within an inherited social and material environment shaped by both natural laws and by a history of human manipulation of these laws.

By grasping the determination of consciousness by being in this sense (and not under the narrower terms of base-superstructure), it becomes possible to avoid the dilemma that Marx's materialism is suggestive of an implausible abstraction of thought from action, or of ideas (superstructure) from social practices such as economic production (base).[149] Of course, when analysing social practices, the theorist cannot dispense with the ideas or beliefs (i.e. forms of consciousness) which energise or motivate them. But this is beside the point, for such an analysis pertains to the 'life-world' of human social and physiological interaction, not to the properties of a social and physical environment which is 'already made'. To repeat it once more: base-superstructure is about the emergent properties of human biology and social interaction and their hierarchical ordering in a social system. By contrast, being-consciousness is a thesis of the 'determination' of the consciousness of living individuals by the totality of material and social circumstances and relations (physical, social-structural, social-interactional) in which they are placed or enter into during their life-process.

Structure, superstructure and history

I have said that Marxian materialism is also committed to a theory of history (Thesis 3b). According to this, socio-historical processes are governed by the motion of the forces of production, the contradiction between forces and relations of production, and the dynamic of class conflict emergent from these structural contradictions of the mode of production. These are universal mechanisms of societal motion (in class societies), though the precise form which they take is determined by the nature of the relations of production which prevail in a particular social system. Yet it is important to grasp that this historical materialism is not a theory of social change as such, but rather of a particular form of social change. That is to say, historical materialism is an attempt to theorise societal evolution, the developmental tendencies or 'logics' which impart to societal change a certain directionality towards more developed social forms out of less developed social forms, and the mechanisms (structural contradictions and attendant class struggle) which bring about the revolutionary overthrow of one form of social system by another. This being the case, a mere postulation of momentous historical events which have no apparent economic locus or cause is not sufficient to refute historical materialism, despite the contrary belief of most anti-Marxist scholars. In a nutshell, then, Thesis 3b is a theory of horizontal causality in social systems, and it is only by virtue of its status as such that it is possible to speak of a 'materialist conception of history' as opposed to a 'pluralist' or 'multi-factoral' one.

My purpose here is not to enter into an exposition or defence of Marx's theory of history. Instead I would like to briefly address one issue. This is the question of whether privileging the 'economic base' *vis-à-vis* the politico-ideological and ideational superstructures of society in a causal explanation of historical process is inherently disreputable in the sense of being logically unsustainable. For most philosophers and social theorists the answer to this is a definite yes. For them it makes no sense to postulate the primacy of socio-economic mechanisms (i.e. the mode of production and attendant class relations) in imparting directionality to systemic evolution and transformation, for the simple reason that all historical events are determined conjointly by the plurality of generative mechanisms (economic, political, linguistic, ideological, etc.) at work in society. None of these mechanisms can be attributed any kind of explanatory primacy in governing societal dynamics because all are necessary and indispensable to any passage of social interaction leading to any determinate socio-historical outcome. There cannot be a development of the productive forces, for example, unless individuals draw upon a linguistic and cultural structure to communicate meaning during economic production. There cannot be a social revolution, to offer another example, unless merely economic conflicts are generalised into political and ideological struggles: subordinate social agents have to draw upon economic, political and ideological structures if they are to defeat entrenched elite groupings and refashion social relations in their favour.

This objection is not at all a decisive one. Of course, it is true that a range of social mechanisms (and non-social ones besides) are efficacious in explaining interactional processes and socio-historical outcomes. But I have already pointed out that Marx's double distinction between base-superstructure and between being and consciousness does not imply a denial of this elementary fact: economic structures and processes are never simply 'material', but are also 'social' and 'cultural', and in a certain sense 'political' too. The purpose of Marx's materialist conception of history is less to deny a key role to politics and culture in shaping the historical movement of social systems, and more to affirm that particular kinds of political and cultural mechanisms (i.e. those which are directly connected to or expressive of the structural contradictions between the forces and relations of production and social classes) are fundamental in explaining the developmental possibilities and ultimate fate of all social systems.

This is still a strong claim, a materialist theory of systemic dynamics in the sense of attributing explanatory primacy to those cultural forms which are integral aspects of the forces of production (in shaping economic development), and to those political and ideological struggles which are thrown up by the fettering of the productive forces by the relations of production and resultant class malintegration. For it is not the case that any kind of politics or culture will suffice to bring about societal development or (especially) societal transformation. Far from it. Those forms of politics and ideology which soar above the 'contradictions and struggles of real life' will be of interest only to antiquarians, and will have little substantive systemic or historical impact. But it is nonetheless clear that Marx's historical materialism does not involve a neglect of politics, culture or ideology, as is commonly asserted. Yet, since it is precisely the developmental dynamic of the forces of production, and the fettering of the productive forces by relations of production, which facilitates the political and ideological struggles which govern societal elaboration/transformation, it is quite legitimate to regard the 'economic' as the decisive factor of historical advance.

These general points allow us to obtain a balanced assessment of the following much-maligned argument of Engels:

> The economic situation is the basis, but the various elements of the superstructure – political forms of the class struggle and its results, such as constitutions established by the victorious class after a successful battle, etc., juridical forms, and especially the reflections of all these real struggles in the brains of the participants, political, legal, philosophical

> theories, religious views and their further development into systems of dogma – also exercise their influence upon the course of the historical struggles and in many cases determine their *form* in particular. There is an interaction of all these elements in which, amid all the endless host of accidents (that is, of things and events whose inner connection is so remote and so impossible to prove that we can regard it as non-existent and neglect it), the economic movement is finally bound to assert itself.[150]

The standard objection to Engels' formulation is twofold. First, that it crudely and falsely abstracts economic relations from social relations and social consciousness, suggesting a relationship of 'external causality' between structure and superstructure. *Contra* Engels, we are told, 'social being' and 'social consciousness', economy and society, are 'interpenetrated', presupposing one another so closely that it is scarcely plausible to separate them even in thought. Second, that it compounds this error by insisting that economic generative mechanisms are privileged in the sense that these alone exercise the decisive influence in determining socio-historical outcomes. In the latter case, of course, Engels is taxed by the critics for transforming historical materialism into a monistic theory of horizontal causality in social systems, according to which economic structures or 'economic conditions' are 'the ultimately determining factor in history'.

Neither of these criticisms is valid. The first is the easiest to dispose of. At the risk of repetition, if the distinction between structure and superstructure is interpreted, not as a broad distinction between 'social being' and 'social consciousness', but as a specification of the hierarchical ordering of emergent structures in social systems, it is clear that no implausible abstraction of 'consciousness' from the practices of economic production or class struggle is implied here. The second objection to Engels' above-abbreviated statement of historical materialism has more substance to it than the first. His argument here and elsewhere is clumsy in the sense that it can be interpreted as expressing the view that the economy always and everywhere determines the long-term fate of any society or social system, even if in the short- or medium term superstructural factors (law, polity, ideology, etc.) are capable of arresting or facilitating its historical dynamic.

However, notwithstanding the ambiguities of Engels' terminology here and elsewhere, it does seem more reasonable to interpret his account of the historical interface between structure and superstructure, not as 'determination in the final analysis' (as the Althusserians would have it), but as a statement of reciprocal but unequal interaction between the two.[151] Now, such an understanding of structural dynamics certainly is logically consistent with a materialist theory of history. Yet it is one which avoids economic monism without collapsing into pluralism. For, according to this view, although socio-historical outcomes are shaped 'horizontally' by a plurality of socio-cultural mechanisms, a 'structured dialectic'[152] if you like, at the same time those mechanisms derived from the structure have a long-run tendency to 'assert their own movement as necessary' *vis-à-vis* those derived from the superstructure.

But is Engels' interpretation of historical materialism as an account of the 'reciprocal but unequal interaction' between structure and superstructure theoretically defensible? An affirmative answer to this question is implicit in my defence of Marx's structural and historical sociology outlined in Chapter 4. There I argue that the 'interaction of two unequal forces' (socio-economic base and politico-ideological superstructure) which provide history with its dynamic is a function of two kinds of structural relationship. The first of these is the contradiction internal to most modes of production between forces and relations of production. This supports Engels' thesis of the 'dominance' of the 'economic movement', even against obstruction from 'conservative' elements of the superstructure, by virtue of the tendency of class relations to fetter the productive forces in a way which brings about convulsive crises and societal decline. How does this work?

Because class-based relations of production, and the superstructural forms which act to stabilise them, eventually become a barrier to crisis-free economic growth, they inevitably fall under ever increasing pressure from internal and external forces (domestic class unrest and intra-class economic and military competition from rival states) to undergo reorganisation by whatever means in the interests of unfettered economic development. Often these pressures build up until they become irresistible forces for progressive change. In this case, 'economic dominance' manifests itself 'positively', in the sense of stimulating or motivating class agents to engage in struggles to reform or overturn social relations, even if this is only top-down reform which preserves in a modified form the powers and privileges of existing elites. On other occasions, however, 'progressive' classes pioneering new forms of production and wealth creation fail to break the power of ossified property forms and their attendant superstructures, or entrenched elites fail to respond appropriately to the economic constraints (introducing counter-productive or token reforms, etc.). In this case, 'economic dominance' asserts itself 'negatively', by means of the 'common ruination of the contending classes'[153] or even 'barbarism'[154] (i.e. the internal disintegration or regression of a society, or its subordination to economically and hence militarily stronger states).

The second form of structural relationship which explains the tendency of the 'economic movement to assert itself as necessary' is that of the 'relative autonomy' and 'structural dependence' of the superstructure from and upon the economic base. This works as follows. First, since 'core' superstructural forms (such as polity, education and law) are indispensable to the vested interests of propertied elites to secure their privileged position in the relations of production, it is uncontroversial that these will tend to develop in ways which promote (or which at the very least do not contradict) the dominant economic relationship between exploiting and exploited classes. Second, since those agents who occupy positions of power and authority in superstructural relations or institutions draw their (normally privileged) life-chances from the surplus product or surplus value pumped out of the direct producers by the exploiting class, it follows also that they (in common with previous generations of superstructural role-incumbents) will undergo greater or lesser directional pressure to identify their interests and functions with those of propertied elites, meaning that over time there will be a strong tendency for superstructural emergents to be forced into line with structural emergents.[155]

Naturally, this does not mean that those superstructures closely tied to the economic base must develop in ways which guarantee the reproduction of existing class relations. Their relative autonomy is such that those elite groupings who live off the surplus in cultural and political spheres (i.e. those who command the armies, the police forces and the priesthoods) do tend to develop particular interests of their own, particularly in obtaining for themselves and the institutions they control higher prestige and material privileges than those which accrue to those operating in other branches of society. The relative autonomy of the politico-ideological superstructure from the economic base may even become a drain on the mode of surplus extraction, endangering the relations of production upon which the reproduction of social institutions and material culture is 'ultimately' dependent.[156] Again, in these circumstances, the 'structural dependence' of the superstructures on the relations of production allows the 'dominance' of the economic in a negative way. The failure of the superstructures to adequately safeguard the relations of exploitation in which they are rooted must ultimately lead either to their overthrow by subordinate classes, or the weakening or even collapse of society under pressure from economic decline and internal strife, or failing this, the military or economic subordination or destruction of society at the hands of propertied elites from foreign territories. But the prohibitive sanctions of allowing those superstructural emergents which are 'functional' to dominant property relations to 'get out of line' is for the most part sufficient to ensure that those with vested interests in their preservation prevent them from doing so or rapidly bring them to book if they do.

The existence of such relationships of structural dependence (of polity, law, major cultural institutions, etc., upon economic production and exploitation) is what justifies the Marxist view that societies are systems, or totalities, following their own logics of development, rather than a heterogeneous ensemble of 'autonomous' structures or practices, moving in no particular direction. The latter view is, of course, virtual orthodoxy among contemporary postmodernist scholars, and for many Weberians, for whom history is 'meaningless flux'. Both sets of theorists follow Nietzsche's example in reducing social reality to a 'flat space' of competing power centres, none of which are anterior or basic to the others. By doing so they avoid the error of dissolving the economic, political and ideological aspects of society into one another only at the heavy price of undermining any conception of society as a 'unity-in-difference'.

But the either-or dichotomies of monism versus pluralism are no more exhaustive of the scientific possibilities than are those of individualism versus holism, or voluntarism versus determinism. A 'principle of pluralism' cannot be inferred from the failings of monistic reductionism, any more than the failings of holism prove the case for individualism or vice-versa, but has to be justified on theoretical and empirical grounds. Yet most practitioners of 'multi-factoral' historical sociology appear oblivious to this fact. For them it is a matter of 'common-sense' that either historical dynamics are determined by socio-economic mechanisms alone or they are the indeterminate resultant of a multiplicity of distinct or 'autonomous' causal factors (economic, political, military or ideological), none of which have any greater explanatory significance than the others in shaping societal outcomes.

Conclusion

The fundamental aim of this chapter has been to show that a fully adequate social theory and sociology must be constituted as a specific application of emergentist materialism to the human and social worlds. Thus, whereas previously I have been concerned with demonstrating the efficacy of an emergentist ontology of society and attendant methodology of social analysis, in opposition to various forms of reductive social theorising, here I have sought to show that sociological emergentism is both supportive of a dialectical materialist understanding of society and history and is substantially deepened and enriched by being reconstructed as such. Failing this, it becomes vulnerable either to idealist regress (the fate of practically every major form of sociological theory) or to a depthless descriptive empiricism (as exemplified by Weberian and postmodernist theory) which is incapable of coming to terms with the fact of evolutionary directionality in societal development. Indeed, as in the case of Weberian and postmodernist approaches, the attempt to show that neither materialism nor idealism offers adequate understandings of society and social process invariably ends up collapsing into idealism in practice. So it is that postmodernists end up with 'textualism' (the reduction of social structure and social interaction to 'discursive practices'). And so it is that Weberians end up treating ideology and culture as 'freefloating' phenomena, as magically uncaused by anything external or anterior to itself (e.g. Weber's postulation of a mystical 'rationalisation process' as lying at the historical root of capitalism, and his attempt to show that religious ethics are not explainable in terms of class relations or material circumstances).

By contrast, my conclusion that neither idealism nor pluralism are defensible, either as ontology or method in the social sciences, is drawn logically from the philosophical ontology of depth realism, which as we have seen is based upon the activity and results of the empirical sciences. The stratification of nature, in particular the relations of ontological presupposition and vertical determination which lead from lower-order to higher-order structures of the material world, is plainly inconsistent with theoretical models of the social world which either treat 'culture' or 'consciousness' or 'discourse' as its primary reality or which collapse it into a depthless space of autonomous practices or structures where everything determines everything else in a kaleidoscopic fashion. Such is indicative of the fact that explanation of 'ideal elements' must always be sought in underlying structures, whether the 'situational logics' defined by emergent social relations or the non-social structures anterior or basic to these (e.g. human biological needs and interests).

Yet because the higher-order ideological and ideational structures of human-social reality are never autonomous of the social and material circumstances of their production and reproduction, but are rather shaped crucially by the life-worlds of their human authors and bearers (as determined by their positioning in social relations), this is strongly suggestive that the ultimate explanation of societal evolution and/or transformation must also be a 'materialist' one. Paradoxically, this is acknowledged by Weber, in one of his more insightful moments, where he points out that human agents will not for the most part tolerate too great a discrepancy between their cultural values or beliefs and their material interests. As we have seen, since those material social structures which frame the life-experiences and life-chances of differently situated individuals in effect exert directional pressure upon agents to reproduce and elaborate cultural structures ('ideal interests') in a manner which is broadly consistent with their vested social interests and experiences in social relations, it follows that there is a long-run tendency in any social system for the latter to 'accommodate' or 'correspond' to the former.

Naturally this does not mean that 'ideal elements' passively register 'material elements', or that the former are not indispensable to any passage of social interaction leading to systemic elaboration or reproduction. But it does mean that those 'ideal elements' which feed into structural statics or modification or even transformation are always energised by and expressive of the 'contradictions of real life', the latter of which explain why such cultural properties are efficacious in these crucial respects and determine also the systemic possibilities which result from their translation into social agency.

Thus emergentist Marxism, as social theory, can logically sustain an understanding of society as 'vertical determination' (of superstructure by structure and substructure) and of history as 'horizontal determination' (reciprocal but unequal interaction between base and superstructure in shaping socio-systemic outcomes). I will pursue these themes in Chapter 4. Before doing so, however, it is necessary to obtain an adequate understanding of the human agents (and their social interaction) who are alone responsible for society and history-making. This is the task of the next two chapters.

2 Organisms, subjects and society

The purpose of this chapter is to lay down the foundations of an understanding of human agency and social interaction compatible with realism and Marxism. This will be conducted as follows. First, I will offer an introduction and defence of Marx's theory of human nature, and account for its necessary theoretical function in historical materialism and any useable theory of society. My basic argument here is that the Marxian theory of 'species-being' allows us to grasp certain fundamental facts about social relations and social process which would otherwise be baffling, and offers an account of human nature which is in keeping with the findings of contemporary research into human origins. Second, I will seek to add more theoretical substance to the above by considering the adequacy or otherwise of 'naturalistic' and 'sociological' accounts of subjects, agency and society. This will suffice to buttress my defence of realist social theory (in the foregoing analysis) by revealing the shortcomings of endorsing an 'understratified' view of individuals (as agents and interactants) which collapses them into the 'flat place' of either social interaction or their 'pre-given' psycho-organic or subjective properties (i.e. as organisms or subjects).

Taken together, my critique of naturalistic and sociological models of the interface between individual and society is designed to reveal the theoretical utility of Marx's distinction between *species-being* and *social being*. My central claim is that following Marx's example provides the theorist with the conceptual resources to avoid the abstract polarities of 'naive naturalism' versus 'sociological imperialism'.

Marx's philosophical anthropology and the concept of human nature

Despite fashionable 'anti-humanist' and 'anti-naturalist' interpretations to the contrary, the anthropological dimension of historical materialism is spelt out in no uncertain terms in Marx's *Comments on James Mill*, *The Economic and Philosophical Manuscripts of 1844* and the *Grundrisse*. This is also quite manifest in Marx and Engels' collaborative work *The German Ideology*. The starting point of Marx and Engels' social theory is precisely their rejection of the idealist view of Hegel and his followers, that the human and natural worlds are but epiphenomena of God or 'Absolute Spirit', and that human beings are themselves a semi-divine species, a race of rational beings, set apart from the rest of organic nature by the Creator's 'ultimate purpose'. In place of idealism, Marx and Engels postulate the materialist datum that instead of being counterposed to nature, human beings should be recognised as a constituent part of nature, an aspect of nature's biological evolution, as absolutely continuous with nature, as completely dependent upon nature, and as totally immersed in nature.

As Marx himself puts it:

> The life of the species, both in man and in animals, consists physically in the fact that man (like the animals) lives on inorganic nature; and the more universal man (or the animal) is, the more universal is the sphere of inorganic nature on which he lives. ... The universality of man appears in practice precisely in the universality which makes all nature his inorganic body – both inasmuch as nature is (1) his direct means of life, (2) the material, the object, and the instrument of his life-activity. Man lives on nature ... nature is his body, with which he must remain in continuous interchange if he is not to die. That man's physical and spiritual life is linked to nature means simply that nature is linked to itself, for man is a part of nature.[1]

Indeed, it is this recognition that the material roots of human society, culture and history reside precisely in organic and inorganic nature, which doubtless informs Marx's claim in the *Manuscripts* that 'history itself is a real part of natural history – of nature developing into man'.[2] And it is, of course, this same naturalistic conception of the 'micro-foundations' of social life which underpins Marx's critique of Lassalle's argument that 'labour is the source of all wealth and culture' in his *Critique of the Gotha Programme*. Thus, for Marx,

> labour is not the source of all wealth. ... Nature is just as much the source of use-values (and it is surely of such that material wealth consists!) as labour, which itself is only the manifestation of a force of nature, human labour-power.[3]

Philosophical materialism, once translated into social theory, thus postulates the essential complicity between human beings and nature, between human history and natural history. Such an understanding dictates in turn that social theory has both a definite method and point of departure when analysing human society and history:

> The first premise of all human history is, of course, the existence of living human individuals. Thus the first fact to be established is the

> physical [i.e. biological] organisation of these individuals and their consequent relationship to the rest of nature. Of course, we cannot here go into the actual physical nature of man, or into the natural conditions in which man finds himself – geological, oro-hydrographical, climatic, and so on. The writing of history must always set out from these natural bases and their modification in the course of history through the actions of men.[4]

In other words, the scientific or materialist investigation of humanity's life-process must start from the biological constitution of human beings and from the physical structure of the material environment with and within which they are compelled to interact in the production and/or procurement of their cultural and economic needs. Only after elaborating these 'natural bases' – 'the actual physical nature of man [and] the natural conditions in which man finds himself' – can sociological and historical analysis proceed; in effect by examining the manner in which the psycho-organic and environmental foundations of human society are modified or even transformed through history by the socio-cultural mode and activity of modern *homo sapiens*.

The materialist conception that instead of standing apart from nature human beings are in fact a constituent part of nature, is only the starting point of Marx and Engels' philosophical anthropology. The fact that humanity is a part of nature, arising as a product of biological evolution, and remaining always dependent on the physical environment for its intellectual and material sustenance or livelihood, does not mean that human beings should not be clearly differentiated from the rest of nature. It should be recalled that Marxian philosophy and social theory was developed not only in opposition to Hegelian idealism, but also to the mechanical materialism of the radical enlightenment. A genuinely dialectical materialism demanded a transformation of the meaning of materialism as it was then understood by Feuerbach and the utopian socialists.

Marx and Engels were thus amongst the first to recognise that mechanical materialism inevitably ends up negating itself in a kind of elitist idealism, since in order to overcome the radical determination of human beings by the biological, environmental and socio-cultural facts of their life-process, it has to postulate the existence of 'great individuals', 'visionaries' or 'charismatic leaders' who are magically emancipated from these conditional pressures. As Marx himself puts it:

> The materialist doctrine that men are products of circumstances, and that, therefore, changed men are products of other circumstances, forgets that it is men who change circumstances and that the educator must himself be educated. Hence, this doctrine is bound to divide society into two parts, one of which is superior to society.[5]

The Marxian solution to the impasse of mechanical materialism is a dynamic one. Rather than portraying human beings as determined by a mute or static biological constitution, and as merely adapting themselves to a pre-given and essentially unchanging physical environment, Marx and Engels instead posit the role of creative human agency in modifying or even transforming the natural and social worlds. They also stress the manner in which the changed circumstances which result from this activity (and the actual process of changing these circumstances) simultaneously changes the nature of its human authors. Thus: 'Men, developing their material production and their material intercourse, alter, along with their actual world, also their thinking and the product of their thinking. It is not consciousness that determines life, but life that determines consciousness'.[6]

So, in contrast to Feuerbach and his followers, Marx and Engels stress both the essential unity between humanity and nature, and the radical difference between the two. Although for them philosophical materialism still constitutes the basis of the analysis of both nature and society, it is nonetheless the case that the peculiar status and function of the species-capacities of human matter (as a force for consciously reacting upon and modifying the social and material facts of human existence), requires a *distinct* materialist approach which transcends behaviourism and determinism, and which makes a clean break with the mechanical causality associated with the purely physical sciences.

It follows from the Marxian critique of mechanical materialism that the key to understanding human society and history lies in uncovering the defining characteristics of humanity's species-being. This is because in the absence of such an account of the psycho-organic powers and dispositions of human persons, it is impossible to explain how they are able to differentiate themselves from the rest of organic and inorganic nature and react back upon it in a redirective or transformative way. What, then, is the Marxian theory of human nature?

On the one hand, of course, Marx and Engels clearly reject the notion of an unchanging human nature (i.e. a human nature which is not the product of evolutionary history and which is not amenable to further evolutionary change under certain circumstances). To endorse such a metaphysical abstraction as this would, from their point of view, constitute a violation of the dialectical method which stresses the historical status of all of nature's elements and interconnections. One of Marx's major criticisms of Feuerbach was that the latter conceived of human nature as an eternal essence, totally abstracted from the socio-cultural mode of modern *homo sapiens*, from humanity's natural history, and from the specific social relations emergent from these bases. '[T]he essence of man … can with him [Feuerbach] be regarded *only* [my emphasis] as 'species', as an inner, mute, general characteristic which unites the many individuals only in a general way'.[7] For Marx, by contrast, the concrete or actual characteristics of human persons have to be regarded as a simultaneously socio-cultural and evolutionary psycho-organic construction:

> [B]ecause he [Feuerbach] still remains in the realm of theory and conceives of men not in their given social connection, not under their existing conditions of life, which have made them what they are, he never arrives at the actually existing, active men, but stops at the abstraction 'man'.[8]

On the other hand, however, Marx and Engels certainly did accept that human persons in widely different societies, societal contexts and historical epochs share fundamental characteristics in common. This apparent contradiction between humanity's species-nature and its socio-cultural nature dissolves once we recognise that these two aspects of the human life-process are interwoven and mutually reinforcing, with each providing necessary enabling preconditions for the historical development of the other. Norman Geras' attribution to Marx of an analytical distinction between 'human nature' and the 'nature of humanity'[9] (or between 'species-being' and 'social being') thus appears to me to rightly identify a contrast in Marx's work between the relatively permanent (albeit historically produced) characteristics and tendencies of human persons which exist in a wide variety of societies throughout history, and those provisional and contingent characteristics which individuals take on as a result of their immersion within specific kinds of socio-cultural relationships.

From this point of view, the precise nature of human beings in any concrete societal and historical context depends on the interrelationship between 'human nature' and 'the nature of humanity' – that is, on the interface between their 'species-being' and their 'social being'. It follows from this, in turn, that the task of social analysis is not to conflate these two dimensions of 'human reality' (i.e. its social and non-social components), or reduce one to the other, but to examine their interplay over time.

But what are these relatively enduring attributes or dispositions of modern *homo sapiens* which transcend specific cultures or societies? Broadly, the Marxian conception of human nature defines it in terms of a wide range of powers, capacities, qualities and tendencies which are quite unique to human beings (to the best of our current scientific knowledge). These include sociality, intelligence, self-consciousness, rationality, linguistic capacity, and redirective-constitutive labour, as well as certain universal emotional dispositions and elementary behavioural norms.[10] The Marxian conception of human nature also defines it in terms of a range of universal psycho-organic needs and interests (to be specified).[11]

Now, the 'capacities' and 'tendencies' component of human nature is theoretically significant for Marx because it furnishes historical materialism with an explanation of how human society and socio-cultural development is possible. The theoretical function of the 'needs' and 'interests' component of human nature, by contrast, is to furnish historical materialism with part of the explanation of why society and history have a dynamic.

Addressing the former, Marx stresses four species-capacities in particular. These are: intelligence, self-consciousness, sociability and labour. These he appears to regard as especially essential enabling prerequisites of humanity's socio-cultural mode of existence, of humanity's cultural history, and of the wider species-powers which human beings have acquired during the course of their social and biological development. To grasp his meaning here let us examine briefly the role of each of these 'human capacities' in historical materialism.

The fairly self-evident role in historical materialism of human 'intellect' or 'consciousness' (i.e. the powers of abstraction, reflection and intentionality) and self-consciousness (i.e. the 'I' who does the reflecting and purposive acting) as a gift of human nature (or the interface between human biology and the object-world it encounters from birth) rather than a product of social conditioning and cultural learning, has long been a source of discomfort to those Marxists and non-Marxists who would like to pigeonhole Marx and Engels as 'social determinists', 'anti-humanists' or 'anti-naturalists'. And yet it is Marx's contention that one of the more important species-capacities peculiar to human beings, which sets them apart from the animals, is precisely conscious intelligence and self-consciousness, since it is these powers which enable human beings to meet their material and other needs in a wide variety of ways and which make human society and culture possible. As Marx argues:

> The animal is one immediately with its life-activity. It does not distinguish itself from it. It *is* its life-activity. Man makes his life-activity itself the object of his will and of his consciousness. He has *conscious* life-activity. ... Conscious life-activity distinguishes man immediately from animal life-activity.[12]

Human beings are thus capable of utilising their superior mental equipment to reflect upon their conditions of existence, subjectively raising themselves above the social and material facts of their 'life-world' in order to formulate new or innovative ways of changing or even transforming these conditions, before translating reflections and abstractions into conscious intentional practical activity geared towards these ends. In other words, unlike other animals, which are condemned by their biology to simply reproducing themselves and their narrow range of specialised behaviours, human beings can transform themselves and their social and material circumstances precisely because they possess the mental power to abstract themselves from their activity and the products of their activity, and hence dream up innovative ways of modifying or improving them. It should go without saying, of course, that without this universal species-capacity for conscious and self-conscious activity, there can be no more possibility of human beings qualitatively differentiating themselves from the rest of nature than there can be of a distinctively human history.

It is important to stress, however, that Marx and Engels do not regard these human qualities of consciousness and self-consciousness as purely static or contemplative ones. Rather their contention is that these species-powers, although an essential prerequisite of human society and social history, have nonetheless been developed socially and historically. From this perspective, although human persons are biologically endowed with the capacity to engage in self-conscious reflection upon the social and material circumstances of their life-process, they develop and refine these (and other powers) by putting them to work – i.e. by translating them into concrete practices or activities in relation to the world. Thus, whereas Marx and Engels argue that human consciousness and self-consciousness is dependent for its historical development upon the cumulative progress of practical human activity in the material world, they are also clear that human consciousness and self-consciousness are on their own insufficient preconditions for the existence of a recognisably human society or history.

It follows from these arguments that abstract appeals to 'mind', 'consciousness' or 'rationality' will not alone suffice to provide the 'genetic micro-foundations' of complex socio-cultural organisation and elaboration. On the contrary, as Marx and Engels were the first to grasp, it is precisely because human beings are by nature conscious and self-conscious *producers*, i.e. labouring animals, that society and humanity have a history as opposed to an endless cycle of mere adaptation to external circumstances. Thus:

> Men can be distinguished from animals by consciousness, by religion or by anything else you like. They themselves begin to distinguish themselves from animals as soon as they begin to produce their means of subsistence … Men have history because they must produce their life, and because they must produce it … in a particular way.[13]

It is this conception of the interrelationship between human practical activity – i.e. labour – and human consciousness which allows us to make sense of Marx's famous assertion that '*labour* is the essence of man … it is just in his work upon the objective world … that man proves himself to be a *species-being* … through his production nature appears as *his* work and *his* reality'.[14] There is no question here of Marx reducing human nature to 'labour' or 'production', as is often suggested, for human beings can only be producers (as opposed to mere adaptors) given the species-dispositions of abstraction, reflection and intentionality listed above, which themselves are emergent from the organic structure of the human brain. (That Marx held this view is explicit in his own claim that the redirective labour of human beings 'is *conditioned by their physical organisation; their consciousness is determined in just the same way*'.)[15]

Rather than deny the reality of species-dispositions other than labour, Marx's point is instead that labour constitutes both a practical demonstration of the existence and importance of these wider capacities – i.e. the sphere of activity where they are manifest – and the vehicle by means of which these capacities are tested and developed in practice. Thus, precisely by engaging in redirective and constitutive labour upon the physical world in the realisation and expansion of their subsistence, human beings expand their control and practical knowledge of nature, and simultaneously refine and enhance their own natural powers and attributes of sociality, intelligence, self-consciousness and rationality.

Of crucial importance in understanding these above aspects of human nature, and their relationship to Marxian sociology, is the final dimension of species-being I referred to earlier – namely human beings as essentially social or cooperative animals. The importance of this element of human nature, for Marx and Engels, is that it allows them to account for the fact of humanity's perpetual immersion in socio-cultural relations without resorting to some or other convoluted version of the 'ruse of reason'. This in turn enables them to expose the totally fallacious logic which dwells behind liberal social theory's efforts to abstract individuals, and their properties and characteristics, from the historically developed social relations of which they are a constituent part.

Much of the power of Marx's critique of political economy stems from the fact that he scrupulously uncovers the social and historical prerequisites of the primitive theoretical categories of private property and the atomised individual, which lie at the heart of liberal social and political thought. Thus he notes how the social relations of commodity production generate the impression that 'in this society of free competition, the individual appears detached from the natural bonds etc. which in earlier historical periods make him the accessory of a definite and limited human conglomerate'.[16] So, in contrast to the claims of the methodological individualists of his own day, Marx argues that it is simply because human beings are sociable by nature which explains why they are to be found in society in the first place:

> The human being is in the most literal sense a *zoon politikon* [an animal which lives in communities], not merely a gregarious animal, but an animal which can individuate itself only in the midst of society. Production by an isolated individual outside society ... is as much of an absurdity as is the development of language without human beings living together and talking to each other.[17]

From this point of view, the fact that human beings are social animals by nature renders the task of counterposing an anthropology of human beings to a sociology of human relations an utterly pointless endeavour. The sociable or cooperative mode of humanity's species-life ensures that an anthropology of human beings is closely related to a sociology of society. And so to counterpose human nature to social relations (or anthropology to sociology) is as foolish as to abstract individuals from society and to treat them as being in possession of a privatised rationality and individuated subjectivity which is divorced from the social characteristics of the human species.

Marx's theory of human nature as a structure of tendencies and powers: a defence

The above concludes by exposition of Marx's account of the 'capacities' and 'tendencies' peculiar to human organisms. Whatever one makes of its veracity or otherwise, what cannot be doubted is its internal coherence. But how useful and plausible is the Marxian account? Considerably so, I would be inclined to argue. The following arguments are intended to provide a useful contribution to establishing that this is indeed the case.

Materialism versus idealism

One important strength of Marx's thesis that humanity's natural psycho-organic powers of sociality, intelligence, self-consciousness, rationality and language are historically developed and enhanced (and in a certain sense historically produced) through the interplay between nature and productive labour, is that it enables us to break decisively with the elitist and idealist notions of human nature and human personhood associated with most hitherto existing western philosophy. The problem with these is that they tend to treat human persons as definable wholly in terms of 'consciousness, 'mind', 'self-consciousness' or 'self-identity' conceived apart from their practical activity as 'abstractly mental labour'.

This point is well made by Alex Callinicos:

> The proposition that men and women are first and foremost *producers* radically challenged basic assumptions about society that had been accepted by almost all earlier thinkers. Aristotle had defined man as a rational animal. This definition separates the power to think and reason from all other activities, and especially from the daily drudgery of manual work to which most people in history have been condemned. ... Aristotle was the product of a slave society. The ruling class of the ancient world despised manual labour as an activity fit only for their slaves. (The Roman legal definition of a slave was *instrumentum vocale* – a tool that talks.) Aristotle's image of the good man is that of a slave-owner who, free from the need to work for his living, is able to pursue the higher things of the mind. The same separation of mental and material labour, itself a reflection of the class societies in which they lived, was made by all the great bourgeois philosophers, from Descartes to

> Hegel. All treated the life of the mind as the only important thing about human beings, and all assumed that someone else would do the work to provide them with the sordid material goods – food, clothing, lodging – that they needed in order to pursue the truth.[18]

The substance of Marx's objection to those views of human beings which reduce them to their mental powers of 'consciousness' or 'rationality' can be summarised as follows. First, to define human beings as rational animals alone is to abstract 'consciousness' from its biological and socio-historical prerequisites. Second, and more importantly, this preoccupation with the spiritual life of the species (and human individuals), which completely ignores the ways in which human beings are combined in socio-cultural relationships, hides from view the social and material preconditions (i.e. class relations) which enable certain individuals to specialise as producers of ideas (as thinkers, theorists, theologians, philosophers, etc.). Finally, such concepts of human nature mystify the most fundamental source of progress in human knowledge. For this is seen falsely as stemming in its entirety from the 'abstractly mental labour' of ideologues. For Marx, by contrast, knowledge arises from

(i) the practical interchange between human beings and nature (especially via the labour-process) in the production and expansion of their needs, and
(ii) the practical struggles of the downtrodden to comprehend and alter for the better the circumstances of their lives.

Sociality and its emergent properties

Unlike cultural determinists of a functionalist, structuralist or 'postmodern' persuasion, an endorsement of Marx's account of human nature allows the theorist to explain why people are to be found in societies in the first place. We can, in short, follow Marx's example in accepting that human beings are by nature intensely sociable or collaborative creatures, genetically predisposed to form and live within collectivities or communities, due to their psychological and physical need for identity and fellowship with those of their own kind. Such a position is hardly controversial amongst a growing number of contemporary anthropologists and evolutionary biologists, for whom the biological evolution of modern *homo sapiens* has involved the natural selection of genes which greatly encourage sociable and cooperative behaviours and interactions.[19]

Relatively untouched by the intellectual fads of postmodernism and post-structuralism, and protected from the abstract individualism of orthodox liberal social theory by the nature of the empirical archaeological and anthropological data, many would endorse the following account of the evolutionary origins of genetic human sociality provided by Nancy Makepiece Tanner:

> Selection in favour of sociability would intensely favour the more intelligent young who could effectively execute the new behaviour. ... Reorganisation (of the brain) could have happened quite rapidly: young who did not make it and died before reproductive age did not pass on their genes. Selection would have favoured young who were curious, playful and cued in to the behaviour of other group members, imitating tool making skills and environmental know-how, learning to recognise and interact with a wide and diverse social network.[20]

By way of contrast with Marx's approach, a useful illustration of the conceptual weakness which overcomes social analysis where it neglects the sociality of human nature is to be found in John Rawls' famous theory of 'justice' and 'community'.[21] As is well enough known, Rawls bases his principle of distributive justice on certain strong assumptions about the nature of human beings (although paradoxically he describes these as 'weak assumptions'). These are that humans are 'distinct individuals' prior to forming 'relationships and engag[ing] ... in co-operative arrangements with others',[22] and that their social interactions entail 'mutual disinterest', which (in the circumstances of 'moderate scarcity') necessitate the need to construct principles of justice to regulate conflict. From this perspective, 'a sense of community describes a possible aim of antecedently individuated selves, not an ingredient or constituent of their identity'.[23] The function of justice is accordingly to supply an objective mechanism to reconcile the conflicts and competitive self-interest of mutually disinterested and asocial selves.

But Rawls' failure to acknowledge that human beings are predisposed by their genetic makeup towards sociality perhaps informs his complete lack of purchase on the self-evident fact that 'people conceive their identity – the subject and not just the object of their feelings and aspirations – as defined to some extent by the community of which they are a part'.[24] Certainly Rawls cannot accept that human persons are constituted as the persons they are partly by their socio-historical situation.[25] Yet it is, of course, the reality of the communal allegiances in which individuals subjectively invest themselves, as these are shaped by cultural tradition and informed by the sociality of human nature, which demonstrate the poverty of treating human persons as purely individuated selves.

These normative and emotional commitments of persons to their communities are often of such intensity that 'communal identities' are often incorporated into their very sense of self. This community need not necessarily be identified with a total society or nation-state (although for many individuals it undoubtedly is); it may in fact be identified with a particular 'micro' environment of human interaction (e.g. family or neighbourhood) or in terms of membership of a particular social class or ethnic group. Indeed, much of the enduring appeal and strength of nationalist and ethnic identities in the modern world, ruthlessly exploited for their own vested interests by imperialists and racists alike, is most likely the product of the inherent human need of persons to define themselves in relation to some kind of human community (imaginary or real, alienated or otherwise) of which they believe themselves to be members.[26]

Social labour and language

Endorsing Marx's entirely reasonable belief in the innateness of conscious human sociality and labour (i.e. social labour) also provides us with the conceptual resources to explain how another of humanity's species-powers – the biological capacity to acquire and use language – becomes translated into the actuality of language acquisition and use. For it is by engaging in ongoing social interaction, particularly that which involves practical activity in relation to the world, that human infants learn and develop their linguistic skills. And it is by immersing themselves in the daily constitutive practices of social life (i.e. food procurement, shelter building, tool manufacture, etc.) that anthropologists best obtain a reliable grasp upon the linguistic norms and cultural traditions of 'alien' societies.[27]

By logical extension, in a historical and evolutionary sense, it is nothing other than the collaborative or social mode of human nature (particularly where it is mediated by cooperative labour) which allows the translation of the elementary forms of human consciousness and rationality into verbal or written modes of communication, which then feed back into the evolution of human sociality, facilitating in turn the further historical development of rationality and consciousness. Thus Marx is right to argue that '[l]anguage is as old as consciousness, language is practical, real consciousness that exists for other men as well, and only therefore does it exist for me; language, like consciousness, only arises from the need, the necessity of intercourse with other men'.[28]

This latter argument concerning the socio-historical basis of language is often treated with the utmost scorn by naive naturalists. But it is not in the least bit controversial. It is, of course, no accident that the only animal (and other) species to acquire some form of complex 'language' are those biologically oriented towards a *social* mode of *economic* existence. Those species which engage in some or other form of social cooperation in procuring (and/or distributing) their means of subsistence precisely require some form of communication to coordinate their social and economic activities. Social labour is thus uniquely adaptive from the point of view of natural selection in the direction of language acquisition and use. Glynn Isaac makes the argument as follows:

> It is clear that the adaptive value of food-gathering and division of labour would be greatly enhanced by improvements in communications; specifically, the passage of information other than that relating to the emotions, becomes highly adaptive. This has proven to be the case in other zoological phyla that have made the acquisition of food a collective responsibility, as is shown, for instance, by the so-called language of the bees and other social insects.[29]

But it is important to be clear that this emphasis on the socio-economic basis of language-acquisition in general throughout organic nature should not blind us to the novelty of human language. The difference between human language and the primitive modes of communication found in some animal and other species is that the former is an emergent property of conscious beings, and as such expresses abstract concepts removed from immediate reality, whereas the latter is the property of unreflective creatures, and as such constitutes rudimentary patterns of sound (or chemical signals and/or bodily movements) which are utilised unconsciously to coordinate immediate and instinctual behaviours.

Nonetheless, irrespective of these crucial differences between human consciousness and language and the modes of 'thinking' and communication associated with other species, three general points can be made with certainty. First, the forms of consciousness of all gregarious species are necessarily social in character, irrespective of whether these 'mentalities' constitute the 'herd consciousness' of unreflective creatures or the 'reflexive consciousness' of human beings. Second, there can be no language worthy of the name outside social relationships.[30] Finally, complex forms of verbal communication can only arise in biological species whose sociality has a practical application in a cooperative mode of economic activity.

Thus, unlike post-structuralist and postmodernist approaches which fetishise human 'language', seeing it as the key to explaining society and culture (hence separating human beings, society and history from material reality), the materialist conception of human beings (as inherently social producers) animates an account of human agency and social interaction which allows contemporary anthropology to actually comprehend the development of human language. The paleaoanthropologist Richard Leakey explains:

> The question of why language evolved was once easily answered. It was believed that the organisation required of a band of people involved in co-operative hunting demanded an efficient mode of communication, that is, speech. But in fact hunters rarely talk when they are in search of prey, and the hunting dogs of Africa conduct highly complex and co-ordinated hunts without the benefit of language as we know it. This hypothesis for the origin must therefore be seen as far too simplistic. ... Our ancestors moved from being opportunistic omnivores to operating a

> food-sharing economy based on meat and plant foods. This eventually led to the establishment of a hunting-and-gathering economy. … The emergent hominid way of life involved co-operation in food-gathering, systematic and reliable sharing of food, social life focusing on a series of temporary home bases and probably a division of labour. Language within *this* context is clearly much more beneficial than it would otherwise be for mundane tasks, such as passing on instructions for making stone tools or planning a hunting expedition. Certainly, language would facilitate these activities, but they do not *demand* the spoken word in the same way that a co-operative economy and complex social life do.[31]

Social labour and socio-cultural evolution

Despite the ritualistic abuse heaped upon it by those who accuse Marx and Engels of 'economic reductionism' or 'productive force determinism', another great strength of the Marxist conception of human beings as essentially conscious producers is that it establishes the conceptual foundations of an entirely plausible and (to my mind) uncontentious materialist theory of agency (and hence socio-cultural development or 'progress'). Given these aforesaid species-powers and dispositions (of sociality, intelligence, self-consciousness, rationality and labour), Marx's argument is simply that human beings, being 'somewhat rational' social producers, will tend to act in ways which develop their modes of social labour (provided social and material constraints are not prohibitive). This they will do in order to reduce their vulnerability to the capricious forces of nature and to meet and expand their needs in more efficient, less arduous, less time-consuming and more innovative ways. Yet in doing so, human beings will inevitably develop their knowledge, along with these above species-capacities and traits, since the development of the tools and techniques of social labour, and the growth in the productive forces this allows, simultaneously enables the accumulation of a deeper and broader base of practical know-how in relation to nature, which each successive generation of persons can reflect and react upon in seeking to further develop its needs.

So, from this point of view, the cumulative growth in the product and technology of social labour – which necessarily accompanies improvements in the productivity and economic output of the human labour-process – correspondingly generates cumulative advances in human knowledge of practical constitutive tasks *vis-à-vis* the material environment. This in turn enables a simultaneous and ongoing historical refinement of the human powers of abstraction, reflection, rational thought and linguistic ability. At the same time, however, in developing their productive forces, human beings also allow themselves the capacity to construct and sustain increasingly sophisticated and differentiated socio-cultural relations (e.g. systems of material culture and distinct political and other institutions). This is because an expanding economic output creates the possibility of a greater societal investment of human and material resources in social functions other than those directly involved in the production or procurement of the means of subsistence.

Note how well this materialist conception of human nature, and the labour theory of culture which stems from it, fits hand-in-glove with the latest research hypotheses of palaeoanthropology, archaeology and neurobiology into humanity's socio-cultural origins and development:

> Modern *homo sapiens* have a number of distinct advantages over their nearest relatives today: a somewhat larger brain size in proportion to body weight, a hand structure which makes the operation and manipulation of tools vastly easier than even for a chimpanzee, vocal cords which, unlike those of the apes, permits the clear articulation of sounds, and the capacity to live in social groups. It is undoubtedly the social character of human relationships which has enabled them to exploit their other, perhaps marginal, evolutionary advantages. From this and the use of tools comes the key characteristic of human beings living in society: the change in their relationship to the natural world as they attempt to control and manipulate it. From this and the activity of goods production to satisfy wants, which flows from it, comes the steady transformation of human social relationships which has characterised the history of the past few thousand years.[32]

Marx's theory of human nature as a structure of needs and interests: a defence

Enough has now been said in defence of Marx's account of those species-capacities or causal powers which define human nature. But if the species-powers of intelligence, self-consciousness, sociality and labour have a quite definite analytical function in historical materialism (in providing a 'genetic' explanation of why human persons are predisposed towards living in societies or communities, and of how complex socio-cultural relations and 'history' are possible), then what explanatory role do human needs and interests perform?

An extremely important one, I would contend. As suggested earlier, apart from providing historical materialism with its 'fundamental premises' –

> [m]en must be in a position to live in order … to make history. … But life involves before everything else eating and drinking, housing, clothing and various other things. … The first historical act is thus the production of the means to satisfy these needs, the production of material life itself …[33]

– the concept of human needs and interests also furnishes Marxian theory with an elementary 'micro' explanation of the ongoing process of *social conflict and class struggle* which provide socio-cultural elaboration/transformation with its historical dynamic. The simple fact that human beings have basic material needs (i.e. for sufficient food, clothing, shelter, hygiene, sexual relations, leisure,[34] voluntary or 'free' social intercourse,[35] fellowship and identity with their own kind,[36] 'breadth and variety of activity',[37] 'fresh air and sunlight',[38] health and safety at the workplace,[39] etc., to ensure their psychological and physical 'well-being'), and thereby possess interests in ensuring that these needs are met, supplies them with urgent imperatives to modify or even overthrow those hierarchical or unegalitarian (i.e. class-divided) social relations (and attendant vested social interests) which retard or deny all of them.

As should be clear from the above, such needs and interests are not confined to or defined by the mere satisfaction of the minimum standards required to ensure human survival. The social and productive mode of humanity's species-being ensures that what counts as satisfying human 'well-being' is always conditioned by the level of development of the productive forces: the more advanced are the productive forces of a society, the greater is the abundance of material resources which might be distributed amongst its members, and the higher or more generous the cultural definition of basic human needs contained therein. Nor are such historically generated human needs and interests mere artificial socio-cultural wants or desires. If social relations are capable of sustaining a level of economic output and productivity which is capable of improving the 'life-chances' and cultural and political opportunities of the entire societal community, it is perfectly acceptable to regard the continuing retardation or frustration of these by vested social interests as a denial of *real* needs and interests.

In view of this, where social relations permit the possibility of higher generalised human life-chances, greater political representation or enfranchisement in the running of society, and improved access to culture, education and leisure, humans will quite rightly regard their psycho-organic well-being as being compromised (and will therefore be discontented and angry) if this potential is not realised or at least striven for by those in positions of power or authority. Furthermore, where a majority of humans discover a mismatch between the capacity and success of society in improving their life-chances, they will sooner or later become embroiled in convulsive social struggles, and sometimes organised into collective agents, geared towards modifying or overturning those social relations and vested interests implicated in the denial of their elementary needs and interests.

Equally importantly, insofar as class-divided societies always entail *exploitation* (i.e. the forcible appropriation of surplus product by an unproductive elite from the direct producers), and insofar as exploitation always involves the denial of material and cultural resources and adequate political representation to a majority of a society's members which might otherwise have been employed to improve their well-being, we are also compelled to endorse Marx's view that asymmetrical or hierarchical social relations are contrary to objective human needs and interests. Of course, Marx is not denying that class-divided societies and capitalism in particular are 'progressive' in a certain sense compared to those societies which went before (i.e. in the sense of allowing the development of the productive forces). But nonetheless, his ethical critique of class society and capitalism is undoubtedly informed by his Promethean humanism, according to which social forms are assessed according to their capacity to allow the 'free development of all'. Certainly, Marx is entirely justified in his belief that objective human needs and interests, far from being definable in narrowly 'economistic' terms, should instead be defined more broadly in terms of the degree of general economic, political and cultural 'freedom' or 'welfare' which is realisable by a specific societal community, given the level of development of its material productive forces.[40]

Furthermore, as properties of an intelligent, sociable and essentially cooperative species, human needs and interests are always defined by persons in accordance with normative-ethical principles of 'distributive justice' and 'fairness' of a relatively egalitarian character (again within the constraints imposed by the level of economic development of society). The plain fact is that human beings, irrespective of historical and socio-cultural context, have tended to articulate normative principles of justice and fairness in terms of the obligation of society to maintain its members at socially acceptable standards, in terms of the immorality of 'free-riding', and in terms of the ethical undesirability of permitting the existence of grossly unegalitarian social relations.[41] This is itself demonstrative of the manner in which human sociability and rationality combined provide a certain stimulus to the universal production of certain normative definitions of human needs and interests, which are not reducible to the specific social relations which individuals inhabit, and which are a powerful motivational source of their social agency aimed at societal reform or transformation.

A final plea

Despite the obvious centrality of the above account of human nature or species-being to Marx and Engels' own version of historical materialism (including their theory of human agency and social structure) there are those of a 'structuralist' persuasion who continue to deny its role in the Marxian theoretical system. For some (unfathomable) reason, the concept of human nature is deemed by many to be a 'metaphysical' or 'mystical' category, a product of Marx's immature romantic anti-capitalism, which can have no legitimate function in his mature scientific and historically informed works. But one only has to consider how incoherent, say, Marx's theory of alienated labour (the centrepiece of his critique of political economy) would be in the absence of an explicit or implicit conception of human nature as something other or more than a socio-cultural product, to realise how untenable such an interpretation must be.

Only by grasping that Marx conceives of human beings as both a socio-cultural product (as well as producer of society and culture) and a psycho-organic species-being, can one come to grips with many of the arguments contained especially in his *The Economic and Philosophical Manuscripts of 1844*. The whole point of Marx's discussion here, is that alienated labour denotes the estrangement of human persons both from their own historically developed socio-cultural needs, and from certain of their biologically-given dispositions as a species. According to Marx, not only does capitalism (and political economy) estrange the individual from his or her social relations, it also encourages a kind of fetishism which serves to subordinate society to the individual, treating social relations, the very manifestation of human sociability, as the mere outcome of anterior individuated selves and privatised utility-maximisation strategies. Now if Marx was not of this opinion, if humanity was not regarded by him as an irreducibly social species, possessing an objective need for fellowship and community, and yet alienated from its sociability (as well as from many of its wider natural needs and powers listed earlier) by commodity production and exploitative class relations, what would be the point of his claim that capitalist society 'alienates species-life *and* individual life [my emphasis] ... turning the latter, as an abstraction, into the purpose of the former, also in its abstract and alienated form ... [thereby] incorporating private property into the very essence of man'?[42]

The point of making this argument is not primarily academic. Its fundamental purpose is not to offer yet another account of 'what Marx really said' or 'what Marx really meant to say but didn't get round to'. Rather, my argument here is that reference to human capacities, needs and interests, and to human subjects as the bearer of these capacities, needs and interests (of the kind endorsed by historical materialism), is ethically, politically and analytically indispensable to any useable social theory.

Consider the alternative. Sociology and philosophy claim to appropriate a human world characterised by a multitude of social pathologies. Mass poverty, unemployment, social inequality, truncated civil and political rights, the ever-present threat of war and nuclear destruction, and so on and so forth – these are but a few of the more pressing 'problems' of our epoch, and ones which many of the most distinguished and resourceful practitioners of contemporary social theory apparently believe they can grasp only by 'erasing the face of mankind' from social theory and society alike, and treating the human subject as a fully social construct. But this beggars the problem. One can speak intelligibly of social 'pathologies' (and indeed of 'dehumanisation', 'human rights' which are denied, 'exploitation', 'alienation', 'disenchantment' or 'anomie') only if one takes as given the existence of human needs, interests and potentialities (as derivative from human nature) which are being frustrated, and if one assumes likewise the existence of a human being who possesses enough of a 'self' to appreciate that his or her needs and capacities are not being fulfilled or fully developed by society. Without an anchorage in common humanity, there can be no objective yardstick by which one might assess the degree to which social conditions are pathological or functional, alienating or fulfilling. And without a non-social component of personal identity, there cannot be a human subject who is capable of sensing that their human needs and capacities are being retarded or affirmed by society.

Naturalistic conceptions of individuals and society

Enough has now been said in elaboration of Marx's theory of human nature. But what can be said of alternative accounts of the relationship between human nature and social order? There are two major forms of naturalism in modern social theory – sociobiology and utilitarianism – which claim to have resolved this problem. Both of these 'schools' of liberal social thought are equally committed to micro-reduction in method and upwards conflation in theory, although they differ over which level of 'human reality' (organisms or subjects) should be attributed explanatory primacy in accounting for social relations or culture.

Sociobiology For sociobiologists the 'atomistic' explanatory programme is at its most radical. All of the salient features of social behaviour are explainable wholly in terms of the general biological characteristics of human nature, and the specific genetic variations ('natural inequalities') which exist between individuals. And all important human social practices or institutions must be understood by 'discovering' the functional benefits they perform in enhancing the 'reproductive fitness' of the human genotype and the specific genes or 'complexes' of genes responsible for their emergence.

Utilitarianism More generally, however, it is recommended by naturalists that social explanation proceed with resort either to an 'economic model' of human agency and social interaction (as is argued by marginalist economics and by most versions of rational choice and social exchange theory) or to a broader 'hermeneutic model' of social behaviour which complements *homo economicus* with additional normative and affectual characteristics (as is argued by more sophisticated rational choice theorists). For the former, social action (and hence society) is grasped in terms of a narrow economist rationalism: interactants are regarded simply as 'utility-optimisers', as self-interested atoms, acting socially on the basis of the most instrumental means-ends calculations (of a cost-benefit type) of how best to meet their personal wants or desires. For the latter, by contrast, individuated 'utility-maximisation' is often watered down to 'utility-satisfaction'.[43] And although rational conduct of this kind is still regarded as the most salient feature of society, a certain space is allowed to account for all those baffling social and human properties which cannot so easily be 'read-off' from the self-interested pursuits, or egoistic psychological makeup, of 'rational man'.[44]

The naturalistic conception of individuals and society: sociobiology

Sociobiological explanations of subjects are synonymous with sociobiological explanations of human society and history. There is no gap between the different levels of analysis. As the 'founding father' of the discipline, E. O. Wilson, puts it: 'sociobiology [is] the systematic study of the biological basis of all social behaviour. ... There is no *a priori* reason why any proportion of human social behaviour must be excluded from the domain of sociobiological analysis'.[45]

Yet there is a large amount of fudge and vacillation amongst sociobiologists on the question of the meaning of their central assertion that all human social behaviour should be explained biologically. Sometimes the argument seems to be simply that 'genes hold culture on a leash',[46] i.e. that the possible *range* of human behaviours is biologically determined. But this is merely a truism which does not in the least reduce to the claim that the *specific character* of human motivation and social organisation 'is itself a direct consequence of gene action'.[47] Normally, of course, the sociobiological manifesto is firmly committed to the thesis of direct genetic control, or determination, of human social behaviours and institutions by biological human nature.

This is why Wilson, for instance, contends that 'sociology and the other social sciences ... are the last branches of biology waiting to be included in the Modern Synthesis'.[48] And this is why Richard Dawkins, to offer another example, makes the claim that human beings 'are survival machines – robot vehicles programmed to preserve the selfish molecules known as genes'.[49] From this perspective, social interaction and relationships are the unconscious tool, or expression, of the human genotype and the competitive Darwinian selective mechanisms of its atomised constituents. Sociobiology is thus firmly committed to the denial of irreducible emergent properties of human neurobiology (e.g. personal psychology and self-consciousness) and of social interaction (structure and social systems). In principle, every one of the human sciences are but 'branches of biology'.

Sociobiology's conception of human nature and social interaction: a critique

In all important respects, sociobiology's picture of human nature and of individual subjects is identical to that of social Darwinism and Hobbesian behaviourism:

> Roughly, humans are seen as [instinctually] self-aggrandising, selfish animals whose social organisation, even in its co-operative aspects, is a consequence of natural selection for traits that maximise reproductive fitness. In particular, humans are characterised by territoriality, tribalism, indoctrinability, blind faith, xenophobia, and a variety of manifestations of aggression. Unselfish behaviour is really a form of selfishness in which the individual is motivated by an expectation of reciprocal reward. Self-righteousness, gratitude and sympathy are examples of [reciprocal altruism], while aggressively moral behaviour is a way of keeping cheaters in line.[50]

But, quite apart from its arbitrariness, this formulation suffers from a number of grave conceptual defects. First, the philosophical legitimation of sociobiology's understanding of human beings is dependent on a highly suspect interpretation of scanty prehistorical and historical data. Raymond Dart's influential *The Predatory Transition from Ape to Man* gave the above concept of human nature the scientific credibility it had lost during the fall from grace of the Darwinian 'racism of empire' after World War Two.[51] Dart's thesis involved two key elements:

(i) the notion endorsed by many anthropologists of the day (and subsequently popularised by the author and playwright Robert Ardrey)[52] that modern humanity was directly descended from a ferocious carnivorous hominid (*australopithecus africanus*) which hunted into extinction its altogether more peaceable relative (*australopithecus robustus*); and
(ii) the argument that the high incidence of damage inflicted upon fossils of *africanus* and baboons (discovered at Makapansgat in South Africa), and the large volume of *particular* bone fragments of hominid and other species buried alongside these remains (e.g. hominid leg-bones and upper arm-bones and baboon hindquarters) evidenced our ancestor's genocidal and cannibalistic violence towards each other and predatory and carnivorous aggression towards other species.

Dart's radical conclusion that '[t]he loathsome cruelty of mankind to man … from the earliest Egyptian and Sumerian records to the most recent atrocities of the Second World War … forms one of his inescapable, characteristic and differentiative features … explicable only in terms of his cannibalistic origins'[53] was seized on enthusiastically by contemporaneous psychologists and biologists (most notably Konrad Lorenz).[54] More recently, the same theme has been taken up by sociobiologists, for whom contemporary 'single origins' theories of some archaeologists show that modern humans began with a single African female ancestor whose offspring 'replac[ed] ancient indigenous humans around the world … in an abrupt and violent manner'.[55]

Yet Dart subsequently admitted that he had misunderstood the significance of fossil-damage at Makapansgat (which was caused largely by natural erosion not by hominid violence). And his own views on human origins have been overtaken by more recent developments in palaeontology and archaeology. *Africanus* was not, after all, a savage carnivore predisposed towards gratuitous violence. And *homo habilis*, a food-sharing tool-maker, not *africanus*, was a direct ancestor of modern *homo sapiens*.[56]

Despite this, however, the enthusiasm of sociobiologists for indulging in *post hoc* constructions of human nature which precisely regurgitate Dart's own original (and subsequently retracted) conclusions, remains resolutely undiminished. Likewise, the 'single origins' school's almost unanimous rejection of the idea that modern humans displaced other archaic humans by violence or territorial conflict, has equally and predictably failed to dent sociobiology's faith in the primordial existence of their Spencerian-Hobbesian xenophobe. (The consensus view of the 'single origins' school is now that 'during the few thousand years of possible co-existence of neanderthals and modern *homo sapiens* extensive gene flow could have occurred between the two groups', with the latter displacing the former simply due to greater success in procuring an existence from the environment).[57]

Second, aside from the non-existent evidence from science in support of sociobiology's theory of human nature, there is the plain truth that it has been substantially undermined by an enormous volume of anthropological research, over the past thirty years in particular, into the societies of the earliest modern human beings and of their more recent archaic ancestors.[58] Whereas nineteenth-century (and early twentieth-century) anthropology was content to dismiss 'rude' societies as forms of 'barbarism' or 'savagery', lacking in culture and genuine social organisation (doubtless influenced by Thomas Hobbes' vivid portrait of human life in a state of nature: 'No arts; no letters; no society; and which is worst of all, continual fear and danger of violent death; and the life of man, solitary, poor, nasty, brutish, and short'),[59] modern anthropologists should be congratulated for demonstrating that the earliest human societies (scavenger-forager and hunter-gatherer bands) were intensely social enterprises. Such societies have been shown to entail little differentiation between the 'public' and 'private' spheres, comprised of rich and diverse traditions of symbolic culture, and enjoying what Marshall Sahlins describes as 'relative affluence … in which all the people's wants are easily satisfied'.[60]

Particularly important, for our purposes, is the knowledge furnished by the new anthropology that the original hunting and gathering societies (which characterised human socio-cultural existence and development for more than two million years during the formative period of modern *homo sapiens*) were a very great distance from being peopled by the acquisitive, individualistic, competitive, aggressive, territorial and xenophobic human beings beloved of liberal social theory. Quite the reverse in fact was true. For contrary to the expectations of today's sociobiologists, not only did hunter-gatherer peoples stubbornly refuse to construct those social institutions and cultural practices which 'Hobbesian man' dictates they should (private property, the state, the market, stratification by class or gender, inter-tribal violence and aggressive economic competition, etc.), but they also engaged in egalitarian food-sharing and collaborative (i.e. participatory) democratic decision-making as a matter of course.[61]

Leacock, Friedl and Lee summarise the available historical and comparative data as follows:

> Individual decision-makings are possible for men and women with respect to their daily routines. ... Men and women are free to decide how they will spend each day: whether to go hunting or gathering, and with whom. ... There is no differential access to resources through private land ownership and no specialisation of labour beyond that of sex. ... The basic principle of egalitarian band societies [is] that people ma[ke] decisions about the activities of which they are responsible. ... Food is never consumed alone by a family: it is always shared out among members of a living group or band. ... Each member of the camp receives an equitable share. ... This principle of generalised reciprocity has been reported of hunter-gatherers in every continent and every kind of environment. ... Sharing deeply pervades the behaviour and values of ... foragers, within the family and between families, and it is extended to the boundaries of the social universe. Just as the principle of profit and rationality is central to the capitalist ethic, so is sharing central to the conduct of social life in foraging societies.[62]

And Richard Lee reports similar conclusions in his own research into the !Kung of the Kalahari (one of the few surviving hunter-gatherer societies):

> The !Kung are a fiercely egalitarian people, and they have evolved a series of important cultural practices to maintain this equality, first by cutting down to size the arrogant and boastful, and second by helping those down on their luck to get back in the game. ... Men are encouraged to hunt as best they can, but the correct demeanour for the successful hunter is modesty and understatement. ... Whatever their skills !Kung leaders have no formal authority. They can only persuade, but never enforce their will on others. ... None is arrogant, overbearing, boastful or aloof. In !Kung terms, these traits absolutely disqualify a person as a leader. ... Another trait emphatically not found among traditional camp leaders is a desire for wealth or acquisitiveness. ... Disputes between groups over food are not unknown among the !Kung, but they are rare.[63]

Now, sociobiologists can only deal with the uncomfortable facts of the ethnographic record by resorting to their customary sleight-of-hand. E. O.

Wilson, for instance, explains away the absence of economic competition, class and gender inequality, warfare and imperialism in 'primitive communism' by simply asserting that '[i]t is to be expected that some isolated cultures will escape the[se] processes for generations at a time, in effect reverting to what ethnographers refer to as a pacific state'.[64] Therefore, in order to insulate his *a priori* concept of human nature and attendant social behaviour from empirical refutation, Wilson is compelled to ignore the totality of human development, prehistory and history up until the past 8,000 years whilst continuing to endorse a view of human origins for which not a shred of scientific evidence exists ('the most distinctive human qualities', we are told, emerged through 'intertribal warfare', 'genocide' and 'genosorption' during the 'autocatalytic phase'[65] of evolution).

Yet, despite Wilson, given the fact that

> [h]unting and gathering was a permanent and stable feature of our biological evolution through *homo erectus* to early *homo sapiens* and finally to modern man … [and] given the importance of hunting and gathering through the many thousands of generations of our forebears,

it does seem altogether more reasonable to suppose 'that this way of life is an indelible part of what makes us human'.[66] In other words, if a human nature exists, it is far more plausible to believe that 'it was moulded by natural selection during the 2.5 million year long epoch of hunting and gathering between the first appearance of *homo habilis* and the first planting of crops by 8th millennium BC *homo sapiens*'.[67] But this means that, insofar as it exists, human nature is far more likely to be the bearer of sociable, communal, altruistic, cooperative (and probably egalitarian)[68] behavioural traits and predispositions, rather than those Darwinian and Hobbesian attributes which are reckoned by sociobiologists to acclimatise human beings to life in hierarchically and competitively structured societies.

The anthropologist Richard Lee is thus quite right to insist:

> It is the long experience of egalitarian sharing that has moulded our past. Despite our seeming adaptation to life in hierarchical societies, and despite the rather dismal track record of human rights in many parts of the world, there are signs that humankind retains a deep-rooted sense of egalitarianism, a deep rooted commitment to the norm of reciprocity, a deep rooted … sense of community. … [F]or all its economic and military power and its near monopoly of the ideological apparatus, the capitalist state has not succeeded in eradicating innumerable pockets of communalism.[69]

And likewise the prehistorian Bernard Campbell is equally correct to point out:

> Anthropology teaches us clearly that Man lived at one with nature until, with the beginnings of agriculture, he began to tamper with the eco-system: an expansion of his population followed. It was not until the development of the temple towns (around 5000 BC) that we find evidence of inflicted death and warfare. This is too recent an event to have had any influence on the evolution of human nature. ... Man is not programmed to kill and make war. ... his ability to do so is learned from his elders and peers when his society demands it.[70]

Thus, *contra* the claims of sociobiology, since the mode of environmental adaptation of modern *homo sapiens* involves social and cultural learning *par excellence*, and since this mode of adaptation has been generated by the natural selection of genes which have encouraged intelligence, sociability, group cooperation and egalitarian food-sharing to an unprecedented degree, it seems entirely plausible to suppose that there can be no genetic or biological imperatives towards aggression, violence, hierarchy or individualistic 'self-aggrandisement' *intrinsic* to human nature. Precisely because the socio-cultural mode of subsistence of human beings is utterly dependent upon evolutionary adaptability in the direction of mental dexterity, sociality, cooperation and egalitarianism, it is clear enough that humans no more require genes which facilitate individualism, competitiveness, aggression or domination than they require those which generate camouflage, fur, sharp teeth or claws, physical size and strength, or speed of foot.[71]

Or to put it another way: the fact that human genes can be transmitted quite satisfactorily across the generations, without any of these above physiological or genetic traits (given humanity's cultural and technological mode of existence), must offer little encouragement to any belief in the evolutionary persistence of such innate dispositions in modern *homo sapiens*. Further, an acknowledgement of the reality that a recognisably human social existence has to depend upon a high level of brain power, rationality, and collective collaboration or cooperation between individuals, precisely demonstrates that the most adaptable human genes (from the point of view of 'reproductive fitness') must be those which reinforce or enhance these traits at the expense of those which do not.

Yet exponents of biological reductionism rarely take the time to consider the extent to which empirical data of the above kind into human origins and prehistory is compatible with their abstract 'model of man'. On the contrary, the 'instinctual nature' of humankind is often not derived simply from comparative research into human conduct and social interaction. Instead it is often informed as much by drawing crude comparisons between humans and other animals, particularly related primates, often by drawing upon data culled from researches into the behaviour of chimpanzees and gorillas.

At one extreme, naive naturalists exploit the well known fact that modern ape species probably have ancestors in common with human beings (human beings and chimpanzees share 97.5 per cent of the same genes)[72] to speculatively infer the biological nature of the latter from the former. Indeed, even a sociobiologist such as Edward Wilson, who would reject any such conflationist strategy (on the grounds that it abstracts away from the unique characteristics of humans and the variable properties of all primates), is still happy to view humans and non-human primates as sharing 'a class of behaviours that are uniform', including and especially 'aggressive dominance systems ... with males dominant over females',[73] a conclusion he would derive from anthropological researches into the social behaviours of both human and ape communities.

Hardly surprisingly, then (given the prior commitments of naive naturalists), human beings are not reckoned to do very well out of this comparison with their closest relatives. Indeed, nor do chimpanzees and gorillas do very well out of their comparison with human beings, since all are reckoned to share 'conservative' genetically determined behaviours in common.[74] Together with anecdotal evidence from the human cultural record, and research into other animal species, such selective data from primatological research and research into many other animal and insect species, is reckoned by many sociobiologists to demonstrate that Marxism and sociology generally are unscientific because they tend to blame the 'social environment' (rather than the enduring facts of human biology and hence psychology) for the pathologies of the modern world. Since ape 'communities' (in common with all animal and insect societies) are naturally aggressive, competitive and hierarchical, it is hardly surprising that human societies are organised in a similar fashion, so the argument runs. All are governed by the same laws of biological optimisation, after all. But this means that 'the key error of Marxism as a theory of history is its tendency to conceive of human nature as relatively unstructured and largely or wholly the product of external socio-economic forces'.[75]

But these arguments will not do at all. I will pay no attention to Wilson and Lumsden's above erroneous interpretation of Marx's account of 'species-being' (which should be evident from my discussion in the first section of this chapter). Leaving this aside, three major difficulties with any conceptual strategy which attempts to illuminate human nature with resort to studies of other animals are worthy of note. First, and most obviously, it is important to point out the peculiar crudity of any comparison of the purely biological nature of humans and the higher primates. For although it is undoubtedly the case that human beings and chimpanzees have near-identical genes, it is also certain that the internal organisation of these genes in each species is radically different.

Since the 2.5 per cent genetic variation between humans and chimps, together with these profound differences in their genetic configuration, is responsible for (or enabling of) such immense variations in degrees of sociality, intelligence, self-consciousness and cultural learning between the species (not to mention a whole range of emergent properties possessed by the former but not the latter), it is far from clear why it should be considered reasonable or useful to draw conclusions about human nature and interaction directly from the study of ape biology and/or behaviour. Although I would not wish to dissent from the view that studying the biology and behaviour of non-human primates can yield useful insights about human origins, evolution, capacities and needs (the latter of which might exert a certain diffused pressure or guidance upon human social behaviour), it is clear that exponents of biological reductionism have radically overstepped the mark here. After all, it should go without saying that, far from illuminating the 'nature' of human beings, the micro-reductionist strategy of sociobiology abstracts from the human 'life-world' precisely those properties of cooperation, sociality, mind, self and rationality which define it as such!

Second, it follows from this argument that the real 'romantic fallacy' is to be found not in Marx's insistence that social relations and interaction are efficacious in conditioning the concrete 'natures' of human beings in specific historical settings, but rather 'in any "naked ape" claim that we can read off from ape behaviour some inbuilt genetic impulse of human behaviour', as Chris Harman puts it.[76] As Harman rightly goes on to say, such a claim

> ignores a most important feature of the human genetic makeup which separates us from our closest cousins. They are genetically programmed in narrow ways that provide them with the behaviour appropriate to a limited range of environments, while we are characterised by an immense flexibility in our behaviour that enables us, virtually alone in the animal world, to thrive on any part of the globe. This is a fundamental difference between us and the existing apes. So gorillas are not to be found outside tropical rain forests, chimps outside wooded regions in sub-Saharan Africa, gibbons outside the tree tops of south east Asia, orang-utans outside a few islands in Indonesia. By contrast, humans have been able to live across a vast swathe of Africa, Europe and Asia for at least half a million years. Our genetic 'speciality' is precisely that we are not specialised, not constrained by any limited range of 'instinctive' behaviour.[77]

Finally, those studies into ape behaviour from which countless naive naturalists have undoubtedly derived their inspiration (at least in part) for their views on human nature, have in recent years been revealed as 'over-simple' by more contemporary research in primatology and related fields:

> Until the 1960s nearly all studies of apes were carried out in zoos, like Solly Zuckerman's famous 1930s account of life in the chimpanzee enclosure at London Zoo. They fitted the apes into a wider model of behaviour based on baboon studies (although baboons are monkeys and have quite substantial genetic differences with all the apes). They were seen as almost completely vegetarian, with little learning capacity and

> nothing that could, by any stretch of the imagination, be called culture. Above all, they were seen as innately aggressive, with the males involved in continual, vicious sexual competition for females and kept in line by a single dominant male. [But] in the last 30 years studies of chimps, pygmy chimps and gorillas in the wild have challenged any such model, suggesting that drawing conclusions about ape behaviour from life in zoo cages is about as valid as drawing conclusions about human behaviour from case studies of long term inmates in Dartmoor.[78]

Indeed, the main conclusions which have been drawn from these recent studies into ape behaviour 'in the wild' have proven extremely damaging to the arguments of sociobiologists. Harman summarises these as follows:

> (i) Chimps and pygmy chimps are much more sociable than used to be thought. Aggressive confrontations are much less frequent than friendly interactions. Most aggressive confrontations are settled without violence. (ii) Males are not involved in continual bitter competition to dominate females. ... Females initiate many sexual contacts and their co-operation is essential if males are to have special relationships with them. (iii) The role of 'dominance' among chimps and gorillas has been overstated in the past. There is no single hierarchy for all activities among chimps, and among gorillas 'dominance' often seems much closer to what we would call leadership than to domination. (iv) There is much more learned and socially transmitted behaviour than used to be thought, and much more use of primitive tools. Chimps use stones to break nuts, sticks to collect termites from holes, and leaves as sponges to pick up liquids for drinking. (v) Chimps are not completely vegetarian. They hunt small animals (for instance, small monkeys) when the opportunity arises and so get about 10% of their diet from non-vegetarian sources. And hunting is a *social* activity: some chimps will chase the monkeys, others will lie in wait, ambush and kill them. (vi) Apes do not behave as competing individuals when it comes to consuming food. If one chimp finds a source of good food ... it lets others know. And although common chimpanzees consume vegetarian foodstuffs individually (except for the mother who provides food for her young offspring), they share meat with each other, while pygmy chimps share some vegetarian food as well. (vii) Elementary forms of communication play a significant role among apes. Gestures are used not merely to attract attention but also to indicate certain intentions – as when a female pygmy chimp tells a male how she wants sex. A range of sounds are used for different purposes, for signalling danger or a plentiful source of food. (viii) The social behaviour of apes varies from band to band within each species, showing that it depends not merely on instinctive, genetically programmed factors, but also on the natural terrain they live off and the learned techniques they have for coping with this.[79]

At the risk of oversimplification, then, contemporary primatological research has revealed not only that the egalitarian and sociable tendencies of ape behaviour are more significant and enduring than its 'anti-social' tendencies, but that a significant portion of ape behaviour is clearly beyond the ken of the purely biological and ecological sciences. As is the case for modern *homo sapiens*, the mode of biological adaptation to the environment of the higher non-human primates involves genetic selection in the direction of sociality, group learning (though not symbolic culture), tool-use (though not tool-manufacture), and rudimentary food-sharing. The only difference between human beings and (especially) gorillas and chimpanzees, in these crucial respects, is that the process of biological evolution has been pushed much further in this direction for the former than for the latter. Unlike chimps and gorillas, for instance, human beings are social and cultural animals *par excellence*, and this is why the tendency towards food-sharing behaviour found in their hunter-gatherer communities was (and is) far more developed than it is in the forager-scavenger bands of the modern apes.

This being the case, I recommend the following course of action. Let us for once (but only once!) take a leaf out of the book shared by Morris, Ardrey, Lorenz, Tiger and Fox and numerous sociobiologists. That is to say, let us acknowledge that the absence of inherent anti-social tendencies towards hierarchy, domination, aggression, individualism, territorialism and gratuitous violence (allegedly manifest in the behaviour of humanity's primate cousins) is a fairly reasonable guide to their absence in the psycho-organic makeup and 'natural' behavioural dispositions of modern human beings. After all, why should we be seen as possessing such 'innate traits' or 'instinctual social behaviours' if little evidence of their existence can be found in our nearest biological relatives?

The fourth and (for our purposes) final difficulty with sociobiology's portrait of human nature and social interaction, concerns its elementary confusion of those human behavioural traits which emerge through the interplay between organism and environment, and those which can truly be said to be relatively permanent characteristics of human nature irrespective of variations in social and natural circumstances. A useful example of this confusion of the interactional and biological properties of human beings is, of course, to be found in sociobiology's treatment of territorialism and warfare in human history. The argument here is that these social phenomena are simply a 'special case' of the eternal laws of biological adaptability which animate the entirety of organic nature. As is the case for all biological organisms, human beings are, we are told, 'survival machines', predetermined by their biological makeup to enhance the reproductive success of their genes: imperialism and inter-state warfare are but socio-cultural manifestations of the genetic imperatives of biological human nature.

But, again despite biologism, modern environmental biology and physical anthropology have both made it plain enough that aggressive or violent behaviour in all higher animal species (and not just in human beings and their nearest relatives) cannot be seen merely as innate properties of the organism (pre-programmed by genetic imperatives), but arise as much (if not more) from the behavioural exigencies forced upon the organism by the environmental circumstances in which it finds itself and (as in social species) by the particular character of its relations with those of its own kind. Indeed, far from most animals being genetically predisposed towards violence and aggression, it seems that they are instinctually predisposed towards *avoiding* violent encounters where these might endanger life or limb or involve them in conflict with the members of other species which are perceived as unthreatening or lacking in hostile intent. It is only where environmental and social circumstances involve severe resource-stress or over-population that intra-species (and certain forms of inter-species) violence and aggression become commonplace.

This point is well made by Richard Leakey:

> Conflicts over mates, food and territory are commonplace in the natural world, but animals have an elaborate style of combat when settling a dispute with another member of the species, and, for the most part, they avoid inflicting serious damage on each other. One of the important factors about animal conflict is that it is more likely to happen under some types of circumstances than others. Factors such as availability of resources and territorial crowding have an important effect on the level of violence running through groups of animals.[80]

But one cannot sensibly address the sorts of issues raised by the foregoing within the conceptual frame of sociobiology's understanding of human nature and social order. The *a priori* designation of human beings as self-aggrandising, territorial, individualistic, competitive and aggressive rules out-of-court any serious (i.e. non-tautological) consideration of the role of social cooperation in human life and society, and this despite the impossibility of even imagining how, for instance, capitalist society could continue to function without a continuous daily input of self-sacrificing, altruistic and collaborative acts of social cooperation by millions of individuals (as evidenced by the chaos that engulfs the capitalist labour-process or public services when workers withdraw goodwill and 'work-to-rule'). A serious treatment of these matters would require a far more positive appraisal of the nature of human nature and behaviour than biologism is prepared to concede, and a recognition of how so many of the allegedly innate characteristics and traits of human personality, allegedly manifest in social interaction and structure, arise from the interaction of persons with the particular social and material environments they inhabit.

It is precisely because many sociobiologists have an intuitive grasp that this is the case which explains their equivocation and vacillation on this point. It is, after all, patently absurd to insist that human biology is transmitted to society and yet to deny the reciprocal causal impact of society on the individual characteristics and social activity of human beings. Yet to admit a place for the societal and material environments of interaction in any causal account of human motivation and behaviour is to call into question the adequacy of every one of sociobiology's concrete explanations of socio-cultural phenomena, all of which are gifted a biological *raison d'être*.

In other words, to concede the reality of innate human sociability, reciprocism, altruism, egalitarianism and communalism, entails an acceptance of the historico-evolutionary construction of these emergent properties of human biology during the process of humanity's unique social and economic modes of interaction with physical nature ('cooperative man', not 'Darwinian man', has adaptive survival-value). Moreover, to concede the irreducibility of the social environment, and its independent causal powers in shaping human individuals and their social interaction, entails an acceptance of the possibility that a change in socio-cultural organisation might bring about profound alterations in the characteristics, motivations and behaviours of people, and thereby bring about equally profound changes in their social action and interaction.

To accept the implications of these sorts of arguments, which accord well with historical evidence, is complete anathema to our sociobiologists, who are reluctant to court the idea that much of what they hold to be intrinsic in human nature is really the consequence of the immersion of individuals in specific kinds of structured social relations. Such conclusions would suggest that the majority of social and human pathologies which afflict the modern world – e.g. class exploitation, race and gender oppression, poverty, inequality, imperialism, etc. – could be eradicated with a transformation of social structure *without* any corresponding psychic damage to human nature. More seditiously still, such conclusions would appear to lend support to the idea that human nature (forged as it was in the epoch of egalitarian-communal hunting and gathering) would actually benefit psychically from the eradication of hierarchical, unequal and competitive modes of social organisation which precisely negate or alienate humanity's sociability.

It is, of course, impossible to say to what extent a return to egalitarian and communal ways of living would generate a psychological and material improvement in the lives of the majority of contemporary humankind. But it is likely to be quite substantial. To the best of our knowledge, for example, hunter-gatherer societies did not (and do not) generate the strains which lead individuals to suffer nervous breakdowns or become susceptible to psychotic illness. Nor is there any evidence that they suffer(ed) either from systematic gender conflict[81] or from any kind of 'crime problem' as we would understand it. Moreover, despite having only a fraction of the *per capita* economic income generated by modern class societies, pre-class communities have normally managed to support a standard of living (measured in terms of nutritional intake per head) quite adequate to the subsistence needs of their members (in sharp contrast to the unhappy fate of the labouring poor in much of the 'Third World' today under capitalism).[82]

I conclude that it is simply not the case that 'sociobiology can make valid points without overreaching itself',[83] as one sophisticated opponent of reductionism has recently asserted. A commitment to the factual existence and explanatory salience of human nature (and for that matter of natural selection as the motive force behind human evolution) need not and should not entail any kind of flirtation with sociobiology. The fundamental problem of biologism is not only its incapacity to account for the emergent properties of human biology and human agency (i.e. personal psychology and subjectivity, social interaction and socio-cultural organisation) but its failure to develop a satisfactory theory of human nature and of organic evolution in general. Thus sociobiology fails as a theory of human subjects because it fails as a theory of human organisms (and indeed of organisms generally). It is for this reason that many of the most effective critiques of biologism have come as much from practising biologists as from sociologists and anthropologists. After all, it should go without saying that an approach which does not stand a chance of coming to grips with the biological nature of animals which do not possess those 'inconvenient' properties of rationality, language and culture, is ill equipped to comprehend the nature of animals which do.

The naturalistic conception of individuals and society: utilitarianism

If biologism represents the logical consequences of 'upwards conflationism' when it is pushed to its unpalatable limits, then utilitarianism represents one step (but only one step!) backwards from the abyss. Micro-reductionism still reigns, however, for whereas biologism recommends the dissolution of structure, culture and interaction into the human genotype (and hence the collapse of the social sciences in micro-biology), utilitarianism recommends that social analysis address itself simply to the individual subject, his or her desires or wants, and the finite resources which constrain this subject's rational options for action.

In other words, unlike sociobiology (which ultimately abolishes human *subjects* as causal agents by treating significant social action and interaction as a mere by-product of the unconscious drive of the human organism to enhance or safeguard the 'reproductive fitness' of its genes), the utilitarian theory of action rehabilitates the sovereign individual as author of his or her agency, portraying it as motivated by *subjective* preferences and as structured in 'logical' ways by the rationality of the human mind (which, given the reality of 'natural scarcity', ensures that individuals generally pursue competitive instrumental self-interest above the collective good). Human agents are thus portrayed by utilitarianism as atomised individuals, self-interested 'utility-optimisers' (or in lesser versions of the approach, 'utility-satisficers'), acting socially on the basis of the most instrumentally rational means-ends cost-benefit calculations of how to best realise their personal desires, selecting which utilities will best meet primary wants, and calculating the most rational instrumental means of 'maximising' or 'satisfying' these wants. These are the core assumptions which run through the various forms of modern utilitarianism (e.g. marginalism, rational choice theory and social exchange theory).

The utilitarian conception of individuals and society: a critique

In his *Making History* (pp. 118–19) Alex Callinicos has made the point that the fundamental problem with 'utilitarian man', stemming from the theory of utility's conflation of 'all the manifold relationships of people ... [as] definite manifestations of definite qualities of individuals ... in the *one* relation of usefulness',[84] is that he is incapable of engaging in what Charles Taylor describes as 'strong evaluation' of desires and wants. 'Utilitarian man' is merely a 'simple weigher' of his options.[85] That is to say, he contents himself wholly with measuring the utility of his desires and wants (against the yardstick of individuated self-interest) without any consideration of whether these are moral or immoral, refined or unrefined, socially beneficial or pernicious, 'profound [or] superficial, noble [or] base ... fragmented or integrated, alienated or free, saintly or merely human'.[86]

By contrast, the 'strong evaluator', which Taylor recommends to us as typical of human subjects and their social conduct, judges the desirability of her wants not simply on the basis of personal utility but in the light of broader substantive (i.e. ethical and social) considerations which she appropriates from society and internalises as her own. Instead of human agents being 'reflective in a minimal sense' (i.e. reflective in the sense that they 'evaluate ... courses of action, and sometimes ... act ... out of that evaluation as against the impress of immediate desire', as is the case for 'utilitarian man'), real human persons order and act upon their desires and motivations not 'only in virtue of the attraction of the consummations but also in virtue of the kind of life and kind of subject'[87] that they wish or imagine themselves to be.

Thus human persons as 'strong evaluators' do not regard the 'ends' or 'goals' of social interaction as 'random' or 'given', as matters of subjective quantification of individual utility, but rather assess these critically in accordance with normative and moral judgements as to what is or what ought to be the case in society at large, and what is or is not appropriate behaviour for them in the light of the subjective identities they possess. Why else, for example, do revolutionary socialists sacrifice the optimisation of their private utility by disqualifying themselves from pursuing certain forms of well paid and prestigious occupations in the role-ensemble of capitalist society, or by devoting time and energy to the thankless task of flogging socialist newspapers on street corners when they could be putting their feet up in front of the telly or going to a football match? Yet if subjects are indeed 'strong evaluators' instead of 'simple weighers', and there is little good reason to doubt it, then surely we have the right to expect our utilitarians to recognise this fact and practise a little 'strong evaluation' of their own when examining the social world.

Aside from the fact that this 'evaluative realism' entails treating 'human agents' ... moral judgements as factual assertions capable of being true and false like all such assertions and rejecting the moral non-cognitivism ... that is so deeply embedded in modern Western culture',[88] it is also clear enough that it presupposes a conception of human nature and of individuated subjectivity which cannot be reconciled with the utilitarian theory of action. The very existence of Parsons' 'normative man' (and indeed of Weber's 'non-rational' modes of social action) attest not only to the irreducibility and causal efficacy of the socio-cultural levels of the human world, but also to the existence of a human person who possesses the capacity and inclination (indeed the imperative) to become a normative or moral subject and interactant.

These above considerations bring to light both the inadequacies of utilitarianism's treatment of the normative-ethical dimensions of human subjectivity as reducible to individual self-interest, and the impoverished nature of its concept of formal rationality. These problems are closely related. As Amartya Sen points out, the failure to recognise the existence and salience of human subjects as irreducibly moral beings (whose morality is in part, I would contend, conditioned by the sociability, communalism and egalitarianism of human nature) leads to the neglect of 'trust', 'commitment', 'sympathy', 'altruism' and 'reciprocity' as aspects of their affectual and normative endowment, and as powerful sources of motivation informing their social interaction.[89] The result is precisely the abject (though seldom acknowledged) failure of contemporary rational choice theory to resolve the so-called 'free-rider' problem and the associated 'prisoner's dilemma'.

The free rider problem

Consider, first of all, the question of 'free-riding'. According to utilitarianism, since human persons are primarily self-interested utility-optimisers, there is absolutely no good (i.e. formally rational) incentive for them to 'join or support organisations that provide benefits they will gain even if they do not join the organisation. Why, for example, should a person join a trade union (at the cost of time or money) if they will receive any negotiated wage increases in any case?'[90]

But perhaps the fact that people do join trade unions (and engage in numerous other kinds of collective agency) suffices to call into question the adequacy of 'utilitarian man' and his instrumentally rational action as a general feature of human social relationships – even within modern capitalist societies. After all, although it is undoubtedly the case that a fully adequate explanation of collective agency oriented towards 'public goods' is impossible without reference to the independent causal impact of socio-cultural organisation in conditioning the social interests and social powers of individuals, it is nonetheless important to stress that such sociological accounts of agency rely upon a conception of human subjects that is quite at odds with that offered by utilitarianism. It is, in fact, far more reasonable and sensible to suggest that the manifest reality of widespread reciprocity, altruism, trust, sympathy and commitment in human motivation and social interaction, particularly in the context of capitalist social relations which systematically generate countervailing pressures towards self-interest and competitive individualism, is precisely illustrative not of a 'hidden agenda' of privatised 'utility-optimisation' but of certain anti-utilitarian facts of human nature and subjectivity.

The prisoner's dilemma

Turning now to the question of the 'prisoner's dilemma'. Given that it is asserted by utilitarianism that individuals are moved primarily by instrumental rationality, it is difficult to see how rational choice theorists can explain why, for instance, political prisoners as often as not choose not to confess their 'guilt', renounce their 'crimes' or betray their comrades, despite the fact that a failure on their part to follow the 'instrumentally rational but collectively sub-optimal choice' is likely to result in their 'least preferred solution (i.e. the maximum gaol sentence)'.[91]

Treatment of persons as Sen's 'rational fools', trapped by their narrow self-interest into 'grassing-up' their friends and colleagues under pressure, or into abstaining from organising collectively in pursuit of 'public goods', not only runs counter to many of the most important facts of human society, but can be explained plausibly only by assuming that they are the kind of beings predisposed towards the aforesaid non-utilitarian motivational emotions and behavioural norms. Thus political prisoners often do not betray their confederates, despite torture and the threat of imprisonment or death, because they trust others not to betray them, or because they cannot bear the thought of putting others (especially 'significant others') through the same experience they are going through themselves, or because their commitment to their comrades (or a particular cause or organisation) is sufficient to override considerations of personal utility.

Such motivational states are not 'irrational' or 'non-rational', as utilitarianism seems to suggest. For these have not only enhanced the environmental adaptability of the human genotype, but also provide individuals with good reasons for supposing that collective agency in support of public goals and/or resistance to the pressures of the prisoner's dilemma is not always self-defeating, even in terms of personal utility.[92] Sen points out that persons are actually more rational than is allowed for by utilitarianism, since they are capable of assessing 'the modifications of the game' of rational choice by non-utilitarian normative and affectual motivations and commitments, and of refusing to regard the pursuit of self-interest as always uniquely rational.[93] This in itself is a fairly clear demonstration of the irredeemable crudity of treating instrumental rationality as the benchmark of rationality, and of reducing human behaviour to the imperatives of 'utilitarian man'.

Some rational choice and social exchange theorists are, however, prepared to admit the existence of 'limiting conditions' on the applicability of their instrumentally rational models of social action. This is precisely illustrative of the inability of utilitarianism to come to grips with the diversity of human motivation and the complexity of socio-cultural relations. Typically, such 'limiting conditions' are introduced by contemporary utilitarians to dismiss as species of 'non-rational' or 'irrational' activity those vast tracts of human behaviour and relationships which contradict the universality of self-interested utility-satisfaction.

Mark Abrahamson explains:

> These limiting conditions generally include those 'valuables that are not for sale'. Examples include love, approval, praise and admiration. What they share in common is that they cannot be purchased or given in a calculated manner. Unless they are perceived as genuine statements of true feelings, expressions of love, praise and the like are worthless to the recipient. The reciprocal debts that accumulate in instrumental relationships may simply not work the same way when people are bound together in intimate relationships. For example, after helping a co-worker in an instrumental relationship, most people feel that the other is indebted to them. Reciprocity is expected at an appropriate time regardless of the sincerity with which the help was offered. By contrast, in an intimate relationship, a different calculus may be in operation. People's willingness to make sacrifices without expecting reciprocity is greatly increased. Further, actions which might – in other situations – be regarded as entailing sacrifices may in an intimate relationship be regarded as pleasurable contributions to a relationship. In sum, reward and cost perspectives have serious limitations when applied to relationships between lovers, family members or close friends. The limited applicability arises because expressions of love, admiration, or the like are not governed by the same norms of reciprocity. On the one hand, they cannot usually be purchased. On the other hand, they cannot ordinarily be simulated; that is, offered cynically, independent of genuine feelings.[94]

But given the existence of these 'limiting conditions', one is entitled to inquire of utilitarians just how much of human agency and relationships is rightly beyond the ken of their explanatory models. After all, if a majority of social phenomena can be legitimately constructed as a 'limiting condition' on the generality of instrumental conduct in society, it is difficult to grasp the sense or 'utility' of regarding the utilitarian theory of action as the key to splitting the 'sociological atom'. Yet deny the general applicability of the utilitarian theory of action we must, and for two basic reasons. First, it is a matter of historical fact that those hunter-gatherer communities which have characterised the overwhelming majority of human existence and socio-cultural development knew precisely nothing of cost-benefit transactions. Second, even under the sway of those 'instrumental' relationships and institutions of contemporary capitalist society, it is clear enough that non-utilitarian motivations and interactions not only have a far from marginal presence, but are absolutely indispensable to the functioning and reproduction of these institutions or relations.[95]

A recognition of these aforesaid capacities and dispositions of trust, sympathy, solidarity, loyalty and altruism as elements of human nature rather than as a gift of social experience and cultural learning, also better allows us to do what liberal philosophers and social theorists have been struggling to do for generations: provide the normative principles of 'reciprocal altruism', 'distributive justice' and 'fairness' with a plausible naturalistic foundation. As Ian Craib rightly notes: '[t]he question of norms has always haunted liberal political theory, and it haunts rational choice theory'.[96] Precisely because liberalism (and utilitarianism) accepts as its starting point a metaphysical individualism whereby individuals are regarded as inherently selfish and as prior to the social relations into which they enter, to 'barter, to truck, to exchange one thing for another', the very existence of normative or ethical belief-systems in society which ostensibly recommend social behaviours governed by anything other than the pursuit of self-interested or instrumental goals, has always posed something of a difficulty for those who would follow in the footsteps of the classical utilitarians and founders of liberal social thought.

Predicated upon these preconceptions, the utilitarian argument that instrumental rationality is the benchmark of human rationality, and that social action is genuinely rational only insofar as it is consistent with purely instrumental considerations of individual utility, has forced contemporary rational choice and social exchange theorists to regard non-utilitarian norms and values as something of an oddity, as mysterious and rather suspicious entities, as essentially non-rational or irrational components of human motivation or behaviour. This is why Jon Elster, for instance, argues that 'social norms provide an important kind of motivation for action that is irreducible to rationality ... the operation of norms is to a large extent blind, compulsive, mechanical or even unconscious'.[97] And this is why, more generally, modern utilitarians draw crude analytical distinctions between 'normative' and 'rational' motivations underlying social interaction, with the former always being seen as 'having a character that cannot be explained in ... rational terms', as operating through 'shame and guilt', and as 'result[ing] from psychological propensities about which we know little'.[98]

The inadequacies of this utilitarian account of social norms (which in fact explicitly disqualifies itself from explaining them!) are fairly obvious and need not detain us long. It will suffice for our purposes to note how this most radical of individualist programmes designed precisely to 'bring men back in'[99] to social analysis, paradoxically ends up implicitly endorsing a fairly strong form of determinism which is the equal of anything to be found in the Parsonian and Durkheimian traditions. Given that utilitarianism is committed to the notion that the ends of social interaction are often explainable in terms of non-rational or irrational commitments, and since therefore persons cannot be said to have good reasons for endorsing these commitments, rational choice theorists are forced to appeal to the 'compulsive' power of norms and values in structuring social interaction.

But isn't this precisely the Parsonian schema to which George Homans counterposed his social psychology? Instead of selecting from the cultural system those norms or values which appear to fit the reality of their life-process (given their location in social relations), and instead of being able to assess critically the veracity of norms and values against a yardstick of human 'well-being', ethnographic experience or empirical evidence (as is suggested by 'evaluative realism'), individuals are strung between the twin determinations of their instrumentally rational imperative to seek out remorselessly the most efficient means to satisfy their random ends and the irresistible tidal pull of the random (normative and ethical) goals which inform their social interaction.

In contrast to such accounts, to stress yet again (at the risk of labouring the point!) the eminently plausible idea that human beings have been endowed by natural selection with species-dispositions towards sociality, communalism and altruism (and as I have contended towards egalitarianism also), the problematic nature of anti-utilitarian norms and values disappears. Once one rejects the *a priori* notion of individualists that human persons are essentially asocial animals, who enter into co-operative relations simply in order to maximise their personal welfare and interests, one is no longer confronted with the liberal dilemma of how to guarantee the co-existence of individual and society without the latter *necessarily* curtailing the freedom and liberty of the former.

From this perspective, the universal existence throughout human history and society of normative principles of 'fairness', 'distributive justice' and 'reciprocal altruism' (and those interesting common themes I have pointed out earlier which run through the diversity of socio-cultural forms these have taken) evidence not the irrationality and randomness of the normative (and affectual) ends of social interaction. On the contrary, they evidence the manner in which the non-utilitarian modes of human subjectivity encourage persons to seek out ethical standards or concepts which make sense of (and which legitimise or critique) the actual socio-cultural relations in which they always find themselves. But this means that one no longer has to follow the example of utilitarians in seeking out (invariably implausible) 'instrumental' explanations of why individuals appear impelled to produce these normative concepts (e.g. James Coleman's contention that 'fair exchange' – the principle of distributive justice – can be explained in terms of the logic of immediate contractual exchange; or Peter Blau's argument that reciprocity arises from the rational need of individuals to correct imbalances in exchange-relationships).[100] Instead it is enough to observe that these are precisely the kind of normative emergents one would expect from an intensely social and cooperative species blessed with the causal powers of self, intelligence and rational thought.

Sociological conceptions of individuals and society

The crucial thing which all non-realist forms of social theory have in common is a treatment of self-consciousness and self-identity as socially dependent, and of human nature as definable in terms of its 'plasticity' or 'openness'. There are, however, crucial differences between holists and elisionists on the question of how the social self should be conceptualised, which translate into different accounts of the explanatory function of the subject and of human agency in social analysis.

For holists, on the one hand, the 'sociological model' of the individual-society connection underwrites a treatment of agents and their social activity as animated by macroscopic 'laws' of structure or culture, operative via 'top-down' processes of socialisation or ideological conditioning, which transform 'indeterminate organisms' into human subjects and social interactants capable of functioning as agents of societal reproduction. This view is often referred to as 'the over-socialised conception of people', since it portrays individuals and their doings as passive 'puppets' or 'supports' of the social system.

For elisionists, on the other hand, the 'sociological model' of the individual-society connection facilitates a treatment of agents and their social interaction as explainable in terms of the socio-cultural practices which allegedly constitute in one and the same process both society and the subject. Normally, though not always (post-structuralism being the notable exception), this view supports a radically less deterministic portrait of the subject than is to be found in holism, and hence provides far greater scope for agency to intervene against society than is allowed for by either functionalism or structuralism. For although self is regarded here as entirely dependent upon social interaction to arise and develop (i.e. into personal identity), it nonetheless allows those who possess it the capacity to reflexively monitor their activity, and 'do otherwise' when confronted with any situation.

Anthony Giddens' summary of his own position on the relationship between self and society might just as easily have been written by any of the elisionists discussed in this chapter:

> No culture could exist without society. But, equally, no society could exist without culture. Without culture we would not be 'human' at all, in the sense in which we usually understand that term. We would have

> no language in which to express ourselves, and our ability to think or reason would be severely limited. ... The fact that from birth to death we are involved in interaction with others certainly conditions our personalities, the values we hold, and the behaviour in which we engage. Yet socialisation is also at the very origin of our individuality and freedom. In the course of socialisation each of us develops a sense of self-identity, and the capacity for independent thought or action. Socialisation is the process whereby the helpless infant gradually becomes a self-aware, knowledgeable person, skilled in the ways of the culture into which she or he is born.[101]

In the analysis that follows I will focus entirely upon elisionist conceptions of the tripartite relationship between human nature, self and society. I make no apology for my corresponding disregard of holist theorisations of the interconnections between these same strata of reality, for I take it that structural determinism is no longer acceptable in sociology (even if sociological imperialism evidently still is for many people). Indeed, it is because 'sociological imperialism' remains very much in vogue in elisionist accounts of the organism-self-society connection, and because elisionist theorising is very much in vogue in contemporary sociology, that I will devote the bulk of my analysis to addressing their views on this question. To these ends, having elaborated briefly the characteristic views of each major version of elisionist social theory on the human being and the individual subject and their connection to social relations (i.e. symbolic interactionism, post-structuralism and structuration theory), I will consider the adequacy of each of their specific views on these matters, though not necessarily in the order presented above.

Individuals and society in sociological elisionism: a brief outline

Symbolic interactionism

Interactionists conceive of social reality as fluid, and as negotiable as 'talk' or 'conversation' (since it is nothing but an aggregation of symbolically mediated exchange-relations between individuals). Now, what is true of society generally, from the interactionist perspective, is also true of the human organism and the individual subject. Four observations are in order here. First, whilst rejecting the functionalist and structuralist portrait of the unsocialised human being as *tabula rasa*, interactionists do nonetheless tend to reduce human nature to a handful of (unspecified) organic drives, and to the nebulous concept of 'flexibility' or 'plasticity'. Second, self-identity (like the character of society as a whole) is portrayed by interactionists as 'negotiated or 'constructed' in the course of interaction, and its content is regarded here as the product of the meanings or expectations which are applied to individuals by other individuals during their mutual interactions (e.g. Cooley's 'looking glass self').[102]

From this perspective, the personal attributes of individuals change in accordance with the institutional contexts they enter into, or the mechanisms of 'societal reaction' or 'labelling' to which they are subject.[103] This means that the most enduring aspects of human subjectivity or personality are those which are continually validated by others, especially by 'significant others':

> In the symbolic interaction perspective, identities are viewed as socially constructed and situational. This view ... is in marked contrast to conventional psychological theories of personality which view personal traits as rather permanently established traits that 'reside' within the individual. ... The self is, in other words, a situational product of interaction. However, it is not exclusively situational in that some qualities are regularly validated by others. This leads individuals to rather permanently regard themselves as short or tall, pretty or ugly, smart or dumb, and to present themselves to others in a congruent manner. All others are obviously not equally important in this regard. Those persons whose reactions are especially important in shaping self-concepts are referred to as 'significant others'. Typical examples include parents, especially for young children, and close friends. ... From this perspective, one's self-concept could entail any qualities that were generally responded to by others.[104]

Third, the very existence of human self-consciousness is treated by interactionists as dependent upon language acquisition and use (Mead's 'internal conversation' between the 'I' and the 'me') and the immersion of individuals in particular kinds of social activity (children's play and games) during the process of their 'primary' socialisation.[105] By 'taking on the role' or 'acting out the part' of 'significant others' (especially primary carers), young children gradually develop reflexive self-awareness, learning to imagine themselves as objects from the perspective of other subjects.

Finally, the transition of self-consciousness into a fully fledged self-identity is seen by interactionists as emergent from specific social practices. By immersing themselves in cooperative games and institutional roles, older children and adults internalise the attitudes, perspectives and obligations of the 'generalised Other' (i.e. of the total society or specific social group of which they are members) during their 'secondary' socialisation, translating these into a social conscience which becomes part of their subjective endowment.[106]

Thus, in summary, for interactionists '[t]he individual possesses a self only in relation to the selves of the other members of his social group; and the structure of his self expresses or reflects a general behaviour pattern of this social group to which he belongs'.[107] Persons are defined here as social selves, and social selves are normally identified with the institutional roles ('careers') that individuals appropriate from society and internalise as a constituent element of their personal identity.

Post-structuralism and postmodernism

Post-structuralism and postmodernism offer a similar basic portrait of social reality (in certain key respects) to those developed by symbolic interactionists. After all, these approaches share in common an emphasis on the centrality of language in constituting society (whether this is seen in terms of 'symbolic communication' or 'discursive practices') and on the essentially unstable, fragmentary and heterogeneous character of social relations (these being arbitrary cultural impositions on a fundamentally chaotic reality). Now it seems to me that exactly the same kind of argument is also true of subjects and organisms. This is because for post-structuralists, as for interactionists, the treatment of society as analogous to 'talk' or 'discourse' is designed to convey the image of subjects and of human nature as cultural constructs and as relatively plastic and negotiable.

Yet this fundamental point of contact between these approaches also marks the crucial theoretical difference between them on the question of the individual-society connection. For unlike interactionists, who seek to gift individuals certain enduring properties of subjectivity or person-hood (by dint of the 'validations' of 'significant others' and their immersion within the collective expectations or sentiments of the social group or 'generalised Other' to which they belong), exponents of post-structuralism and postmodernism wish to radicalise the 'situational self' of their predecessors and contemporaries, pushing it to its logical terminus, in effect denying personal identity any fixity or stability whatsoever.

Thus, for post-structuralists and postmodernists, the emphasis on the plural and fragmented nature of the world is designed to reveal the residual autonomy of the self as an illusion spun from the cloth of the ubiquitous 'metaphysics of presence' (i.e. the idea that the subject has immediate access to external reality and the contents of his or her own consciousness). Accordingly, post-structuralists utilise the 'linguistic analogy' in a significantly different way than do interactionists. Here it is employed to paint a portrait of self as constituted by an endless shifting play of 'signification and differentiation', which knows no 'territoriality' or stable coordinates of organisation. Therefore, from this perspective, in much the same way that a language can function only because words differ from each other, the meaning of subjects is given not by their own discrete properties, causal powers or 'inner essence', but by their 'otherness' *vis-à-vis* the constituent elements of the 'assemblages' or 'multiplicities' of which they are a part.

This basic orientation of post-structuralist sociology and social theory is well summarised by Roger Gottlieb:

> Just as there is no final theory, or given reality, so the 'subject' – a unified, knowable, discrete self residing at the heart of each person's identity – is also a fiction. This notion is another fantasy of Western thought. Personal identity is as variable, shifting and plastic as any text. As there can be no final reading of the world, or of a book, so there can be no final reading of a person. We simply interpret endlessly between the limits of birth and death. There is no 'inner truth' to persons, books or the world. All of these, in fact, are 'textual'. Human beings and language, knowledge and interpretation, cannot finally be distinguished.[108]

Structuration theory

As is well known, Giddens' structuration theory is primarily designed to provide a solution to the antinomies of 'subjectivist' or 'activist' and 'objectivist' or 'structuralist' sociological perspectives, by means of his 'duality of structure' thesis. Nonetheless its author has also sought to develop a theory of consciousness and self which 'radicalises' G. H. Mead's social psychology by combining certain of its insights with others derived from the work of Freud and Jean Piaget. Giddens summarises his approach as follows:

> There are major differences between the perspectives of Freud, Mead and Piaget; yet it is possible to suggest a picture of [self] development which draws on them all. All three authors accept that, in the early months of infancy, a baby has no distinct understanding of the nature of objects and persons in its environment or of its own separate identity. Throughout the first two years or so of life, before the mastery of developed linguistic skills, most of the child's learning is unconscious because she or he has as yet no awareness of self. Freud was probably right to claim that ways of coping with anxiety established during this early period – related, in particular, to interaction with mother and father – remains important in later personality development. It is likely that children learn to become self-aware beings through the process suggested by Mead – the differentiating of an 'I' and a 'me'. Children who have acquired a sense of self retain egocentric modes of thinking, however, as Piaget indicated. The development of the child's autonomy probably involves greater emotional difficulties than either Mead or Piaget seemed to realise – this is where Freud's ideas are particularly relevant. Being able to cope with early anxieties may well influence how far a child is later able to move successfully through the stages of cognition distinguished by Piaget.[109]

Starting from a position which rejects *tout court* the concept of a naturalistic self (on the grounds that 'a transcendental philosophy of the ego terminates in an irremediable solipsism'),[110] and which denies the possibility of non-social interaction with the object-world entering into the articulation of self and self-identity (on the grounds that this is mediated by emotions 'which are themselves constituted by social routines'),[111] Giddens claims that the emergence of self-consciousness and self-identity is a process made possible by the 'unconscious sociality' of the new-born ('the sense of ontological security ... organised cognitively through basic trust')[112] and instantiated by language-use contextualised within routinised social practices:

> The mutuality with early caretakers which basic trust presumes is a substantially unconscious sociality which precedes an 'I' and a 'me', and is a prior basis of any differentiation between the two. ... [A]cquired routines, and forms of mastery associated with them, in the early life of the human being, are much more than just modes of adjusting to a pre-given world of persons and objects. They are constitutive of an emotional acceptance of the reality of the 'external world' without which a secure human existence is impossible. Such acceptance is at the same time the origin of self-identity through learning what is not-me.[113]

Human nature and the social self in post-structuralism: a critique

Since post-structuralist and postmodernist approaches have offered the most radical version of the 'de-centring' of the self concept and 'theoretical anti-humanism', a consideration of their characteristic views on these questions seems as good a place as any to commence my critique. However, before considering to what extent logical argumentation and empirico-historical data supports post-structuralist attempts to render the self the product of a welter of sub-individual drives and trans-individual processes, it is worth taking the time to elaborate the great strength of anti-humanist and anti-naturalist treatments of the individual.

I refer, of course, to the devastating critique furnished by authors such as Foucault and Derrida of the Cartesian concept of the self. The errors of this orthodox 'philosophy of the subject' have been exposed here as consisting of subjectivism, rationalism, empiricism and atomism. Post-structuralists are quite right to argue that the self cannot be seen as purely individuated or 'self-defining', as independent from culture, as 'essentially unconnected to other people', as existing 'distinct from the body' (i.e. as a unity of consciousness), as 'only peripherally burdened with emotions', and as 'individually capable of universally valid knowledge'.[114]

Post-structuralists are equally correct to argue that Durkheimian and Freudian insights into the nature of human consciousness have successfully destabilised the sovereign individual of liberal social theory from two directions simultaneously. Thus, from this perspective, since individual motivations are shaped by a welter of unconscious drives and discursive practices, it follows that subjects can be neither the authors of their own thinking nor the foundation of all meaning, knowledge or culture. The case for post-structuralism's 'de-centring' of the self, in the sense described above, appears to me to be overwhelming.

If the important insight of post-structuralist treatments of the self is that subjectivity isn't simply an independent property of individual consciousness, it is nonetheless one which has to be recovered from a morass of error. Where post-structuralism goes wrong is in its insistence that 'de-centred' subjects entails no unitary subjects whatsoever. After all, one can readily accept that individuals are constituted as social actors through ongoing processes of socialisation and enculturation, that they possess dimensions of mind irreducible to consciousness and self-consciousness, and that personal identity is constructed through the mediation of autobiographical experiences which contain an indispensable social element; yet one can still insist that individuals possess nonetheless properties of subjectivity irreducible to unconscious psychological mechanisms and cultural practices of discursive signification.

For one thing, the fact that the human mind does possess dimensions or 'levels' below conscious self-awareness (as Freud rightly insists) does not automatically mean that it should not be conceived of as a relatively structured whole of some description, that is, as part of a unitary psycho-organic system operating relatively autonomously in relation to the environment. And, for another thing, one can legitimately argue that the human mind is 'de-centred' in the sense that it operates through processes which are partly unconscious or semi-conscious, and which are consequently 'unauthored' by intentional subjects, yet still legitimately make the observation that human beings possess also conscious elements of mind which do initiate reflective monitoring of action and intentional agency, and which do 'author' most of their socially significant behaviour. Indeed, since most social behaviour of individuals is immediately and plausibly accountable in terms of intentional explanation (rather than in terms of unconscious psychological 'instincts' or 'drives'), it does seem rather over-ambitious (to say the least) for post-structuralists to enlist Freudian psychology as an ally in their attempt to dispense with the human subject altogether.

A useful illustration of the profound logical and theoretical problems which befall post-structuralism's attempts to efface human nature and the individual subject from social analysis is to be gleaned from Foucault's work, particularly from his *A History of Sexuality*, *Discipline and Punish*, and *The Order of Things*. A major explanatory concept of Foucault's work is 'power/knowledge', which denotes relations of domination coded into signifying practices, whose function is to impose determinate structure and content on human thinking, self-identity and activity. In Foucault's words: 'The individual is not a pre-given entity which is seized on by the exercise of power. The individual, with his identity and characteristics, is the product of a relation of power, exercised over bodies, multiplicities, movements, desires and forces'.[115]

Now, at the same time as Foucault stresses the omnipotence of power, and its role in allowing the very existence of individuals as selves and social actors, it is also clear that he wishes to portray power as an unstable, fluid and essentially conflictual relationship. 'Power is war, a war continued by other means',[116] yet the very existence or presence of power always generates resistance from those subject to it.[117] Nonetheless, Foucault is quite clear that resistance does not stand a chance of usurping or overturning power, on the grounds that resistance is never itself external to the exercise of power.[118] After all, power for Foucault is the means by which 'human beings are made into subjects',[119] and this power is constituted by and within discursive practices which are inescapable because all-pervasive. This means that power can only be challenged by a counter-power which in so doing becomes itself power, a new mode of domination over bodies, collectivities and things.

But, as Callinicos and numerous other commentators have observed, the major and obvious problem associated with Foucault's concept of individuals as 'docile bodies' (i.e. as entirely animated by power relations) is that it denies him the intellectual resources to 'ground' his corresponding contention (central to his *genealogies* or *archaeologies* of modernity) that power always encounters resistance. If power is everywhere and inescapable, if individuals are but a 'prime effect' of power, it follows that the capacity of persons to resist power becomes unfathomable. To repeat an earlier point in a different context: as mere 'docile bodies', individuals cannot possibly imagine socio-cultural relations other than the ones they inhabit, they cannot possibly possess needs or wants or interests which they recognise as their own or which they regard as frustrated by society or rival social groups, and neither can they possess either good reasons or impelling motives for struggling against existing 'apparatuses' of 'power/knowledge'.

It was, of course, his awareness of this dilemma which led Foucault to postulate (initially) the 'body and its pleasures' (human nature?) and (latterly) the 'technologies of the self' (the individual subject?) as the locus of resistance to relations of 'power/knowledge'. Foucault now introduces into his social theory concepts of (presumably associal or pre-social) 'needs' and 'desires' apparently repressed by 'civilisation'. And now he portrays subjects as formed independently of power relations or discursive practices: '[p]ower is exercised only over free subjects, and only insofar as they are free'.[120] In Foucault's mature writings the freedom of individuals from the 'techniques of domination' is understood in terms of an 'aesthetic of existence'. This is comprised of social practices of a 'reflective' and 'voluntary' nature, by which individuals self-regulate their conduct and actively modify or even transform themselves, making of themselves subjects embodying political allegiances and even artistic values.[121] So, from this latter perspective, far from the social self being the 'effect' of power, it is rather a process of self-construction engaged in by 'free' individuals, which itself gives form to individual autonomy.

Where all of this leaves Foucault's earlier denial of an explanatory role for human nature, and his disavowal of the idea of an antecedently existing self at the centre of each individual's personal identity, is far from clear. On a theoretical level, of course, Foucault never saw fit to reconcile the contradiction between 'docile bodies' and 'free subjects'. The anti-humanism and anti-naturalism of his earlier writings was never formally repudiated in his middle or later work. Voluntarist idealism replaced cultural determinism, but without any explanation of how the latter related to the former or to the 'philosophy of difference'. Where before individuals were portrayed as the passive objects of the power relations into which they were inserted, now they were magically emancipated from these relational determinations, being gifted unique powers of self-determination and needs and interests irreducible to the imprint of society.

Doubtless part of the reason explaining Foucault's paralysis and equivocation on the question of the relationship between 'docile bodies' and 'free subjects', was his belated recognition that a formal break with the concepts and concerns of his earlier work would precisely capsize his post-structuralism (i.e. by bringing into disrepute the idea that reality – social, physical and psychical – is simply a structureless collection of fragments, with each particle lacking enduring characteristics of its own, and deriving instead its identity from the random and chaotic contacts it has with other particles within the 'network' of which they are all a part). For to furnish a theoretical account of *how* individuals can function as 'free subjects', interpreting the needs of the 'body and its pleasures' as a locus of resistance to power relations, would have required an explicit re-approachment with the 'essentialist' assumptions of humanism and naturalism and the despised 'philosophy of the subject'.

Whatever Foucault's own views on the formal status of the human being and the individual subject in his later years, however, what cannot be doubted is that his enterprise depends for its overall coherence upon a recognition of the explanatory salience of both these dimensions of human reality. Why is this? First, Foucault's concept of the 'body and its pleasures' must refer (albeit in a rather restrictive utilitarian way) to *organismic* needs and interests specific to human nature if it is to stand as any kind of solution to the problem of struggle and resistance. For it must be assumed that the psycho-organic needs and interests of human nature exert a strong conditional influence upon the subjectivities and conscious preferences of individuals, allowing them to articulate these as their own, if it is to be allowed that the 'body and its pleasures' stand as a fundamental locus of opposition to specific discursive practices or 'techniques of domination'.

Second, Foucault's concept of the 'technologies of the self' (i.e. practices of self-constitution and self-government), which he appears to regard as definitional of 'free subjects', can be set in motion only given the presumption that individuals enter into these practices in secure possession of certain 'determinate' or 'structured' properties of subjectivity. This is because individuals can be deemed capable of self-government and self-construction only if it is accepted that they are

(i) voluntaristic, purposive, innovative and intentional beings *by nature*, and
(ii) in possession of sufficient continuity of reflexive self-consciousness – *prior* to their immersion or involvement in the 'technologies of the self' – to assume responsibility for their own conduct and 'give form to themselves'.

All of this being the case, I conclude that the unresolved tensions of Foucault's project stand as a salutary testament to the formidable logical and substantive problems which beset any sustained attempt to eradicate 'the face of mankind' and the non-social self from social analysis.

Human nature and the social self in symbolic interactionism and structuration theory: a critique

The 'sociological conception of agency', as this is presented by interactionists and by Giddens, is to an important extent an elaboration and development of themes and assumptions which are to be found in the work of G. H. Mead and Erving Goffman (although, as I have already suggested, Giddens does 'supplement' Mead's insights with his own concept of 'innate sociality' and with others derived from Piaget and Freud). Despite variations in emphasis, philosophical vocabulary, and the detail of their respective arguments, what each of these theorists have in common is the core assumption 'that selves have social origins and are expressed in social contexts'[122] and that human nature and consciousness be regarded as indeterminate or unformed until form and content is forced upon it by the immersion of individuals within processes of social interaction or socio-cultural practices. To this one might be tempted to retort: so what else is new? After all, stated baldly in the above terms, this portrait of individuals does seem remarkably similar to the one painted by post-structuralists and postmodernists.

There are, however, two important differences between the ideas of interactionists and structurationists on the one hand, and those of post-structuralists and postmodernists on the other, which are worthy of note. First, the account of the formation of the social self in the former is far more systematic or 'theorised' than in the latter. Since Mead, Berger, Giddens and company regard the self as a *concrete* product of interaction, rather than as emergent from some nebulous or ill defined process of discursive 'signification and differentiation', they are constrained to offer *sociological analysis* in place of the abstract impressionism of the 'philosophy of difference'. This means that rather more attention is given here to the developmental stages through which self-awareness and self-identity emerges, and to the specific kinds of social activity and forms of socialisation upon which the self is allegedly dependent.

Second, as I have suggested beforehand, theorists rooted in the traditions of interactionism and structuration theory do not endorse the post-structuralist view that endorsing the social self is tantamount to displacing the subject altogether as a 'centre' capable of initiating or even 'authoring' thought and action. From this perspective, though the self is indeed socially and culturally dependent, this does not mean that the subject is reducible to his or her social relations, since interaction and socialisation furnish the individual with certain capacities – notably the ability to reflexively monitor behaviour and respond innovatively to any situation – which enable him or her to avoid being constituted as a mere 'effect' of discourse, culture or 'relationships' of whatever sort.

The respective treatments of the human being and the individual subject furnished by exponents of interactionism and structuration theory may be questioned on a number of counts. I will begin this task by examining Mead's account of the social origins of self-consciousness and self-identity, since his views on this issue are generally endorsed by interactionists, by phenomenologists such as Berger and Luckmann, and (albeit in a modified form) by Giddens as well. After this I will examine the unhappy fate of the 'social self' in symbolic interactionism, arguing that the radical 'social situationalism' of interactionists disqualifies them from explaining how individuals 'negotiate' their self-identities or find the 'internal resources' to resist societal pressures which encourage self-redefinition.

Finally, I will examine Giddens' 'radicalisation' of Mead's social psychology, especially his attempt to overcome the radical plasticity of the 'situational subject' (by postulating self-identity as the product of the individual's reflections on his or her social biography) and his appeal to the 'basic trust' inherent in human beings (as this is instantiated in 'acquired social routines' derived therefrom) to explain the possibility of self-awareness. Here I will argue that the former does not overcome the 'problem of resistance' or motive-formation which has undermined post-structuralism and interactionism, and that the latter is an illegitimate use of anthropology designed to undercut the possibility of a non-social basis of self and of naturalistic sources of personal identity.

Mind, self and society in G. H. Mead's social behaviourism: a critique

To recap: Mead and his co-thinkers identify self-awareness with the 'internal conversation' between two aspects of 'mind', that is, between the 'I' and the 'me'. Self-awareness emerges only when the individual has learned to recognise himself or herself as a 'me' as well as an 'I'. This is a capacity which is dependent upon language acquisition and use, and the participation of individuals in specific forms of social activity and cultural learning. As

Mark Abrahamson summarises Mead's approach: 'the essence of self-consciousness, the "me" in Mead's theory, is a recognition of oneself as seen by others, which emerges through child's play, playing the part of the other'.[123]

But the fundamental problem with Mead's social psychology is that it must presuppose that which it is designed to explain. Why is this? First, the process of children's play, and the capacity of infants to regard themselves as objects for others which it entails, is itself dependent on the fact that children are able to hold 'internal conversations' between themselves and others they are personifying in their play. This in turn seems to suggest that they are already aware of the distinction between 'I-not me', and of the difference between subjects and objects in their social environment, prior to engaging in play. In other words, the *fact* of child's play (e.g. Jack's capacity to imagine himself as 'Fireman Sam' rescuing Jack from the flames) appears inexplicable unless one takes it as given that children take into their play precisely those qualities of subjectivity which motivate and enable them to see themselves as an object in the eyes of other subjects.

Second, *contra* Mead, the 'internal conversations' which are constitutive of children's play do not seem to be dependent upon the prior initiation of infants into language use (although these are doubtless enhanced enormously by linguistic competence). In fact pre-linguistic children appear to play the role of others *vis-à-vis* themselves by imitating the actions, gestures, movements and vocal expressions of 'significant others', and by 'conversing' with themselves and others using imaginary words strung together without coherent order or pattern. In summary, then, the self cannot emerge from children's play if it is required to explain children's play; and language-acquisition and use cannot be indispensable to the 'me' aspect of the self if pre-linguistic children are capable of objectifying themselves in their play.

No doubt defenders of the 'sociological model of agency' might respond to the first part of my argument by claiming it involves a misunderstanding of Mead's theory of mind. It could be argued, for instance, that Mead regarded the ability of children to imagine themselves as objects for themselves (i.e. as a 'me') and their ability to 'play the role of the other', as *distinct* capacities, with the former emerging from the latter. On this view, the 'me' which is constitutive of self-consciousness is not presupposed by the fact of child's play, because it is the *process* of 'taking the part of the other' which teaches the child to imagine himself or herself as an object for others. But there are three difficulties with this kind of viewpoint which invalidate it as a solution to the problem highlighted above.

First, this interpretation has a rather insecure basis in Mead's own work. In fact Mead does not always distinguish clearly between these capacities or processes (i.e. between 'taking the role of the other' and self-objectification). And, as often as not, he seems to argue that either the developmental sequence be placed the other way round (with 'taking the view of the other' emerging from self-objectification), or that self be treated as *involving* self-objectification (rather than as constituting its outcome):

> Mind, or thought, involves the subjective structuring of a situation to permit purposive behaviour; namely, to call forth desired reactions. For such purposive behaviour to occur, the person must be able to take the view of the other, which requires self-consciousness. Self, or self-consciousness, entails a capacity to regard oneself as an object. The emergence of a self, or conception of 'me', results from a reflective interpretation of others' reactions.[124]

Second, Mead's account of the emergence of self-awareness appears to be ambiguous and confused in a more fundamental way. For having apparently argued that self-consciousness is synonymous with the capacity of the individual to regard himself or herself as an object for another person (which itself involves or depends upon 'taking the view of the other'), Mead goes on to contradict his own thesis, suggesting (in the same passage quoted above) that the act of taking an external view on oneself *requires* self-consciousness.

Finally, whatever Mead's real view on the genesis of self, what cannot be doubted is that none of the above interpretations or modifications of his approach counteract my original objection. Thus it is debatable, to say the least, whether it is possible for a child to 'take the role of the other', and hence embark upon 'internal conversations' between herself and other roles she is playing, without simultaneously imagining herself as an object for other persons. That is to say, it is difficult to imagine how, for instance, Jack can play the role of the fireman rescuing Jack from the flames (or of Jack being rescued by the fireman) unless it is assumed that he already possesses enough of a self to imagine himself as an object for another (i.e. as an object for the fireman). This being the case, it does seem likely that self-awareness pre-dates both child's play and the acquisition by human beings of linguistic competence. In view of this, the only interesting question which remains is whether a fully social account of self-consciousness can be given which places its genesis prior to language acquisition and children's play. Possibly it can. But it is nonetheless instructive that no such account has been forthcoming from the camp of interactionism.

A second major problem with the Meadian theory of mind lies in its treatment of the 'me' (and not the 'I') as synonymous with or definitional of self-consciousness. The reason why interactionists identify the former with self-awareness is that doing so makes it altogether easier for them to justify their *a priori* belief that the subject is socially and linguistically dependent. The 'I' is, accordingly, identified with a synthesis of social experience and organic drives, comprising socialised and unsocialised aspects, whereas the 'me' is identified with the possibility of purposive or planned behaviour, and with reason and reflection, and is reckoned to be dependent upon the individual being able to take an external stance on himself or herself. But there is once again much ambiguity and confusion on this point in Mead's work. For having apparently made reflexive thought and meaningful, planned goal-oriented action dependent upon the dialogical articulation by the individual of a 'me' ('[s]ociety ... is the series of "games" out of which the child's experience of diversity leads to a conception of a generalised Other and the capacity to ... think and plan in a deliberate, conscious manner'),[125] Mead elsewhere indicates that it is the 'I' which thinks and acts, and which is the source of individual originality, creativity and spontaneity.

So it is that two commentators sympathetic to Mead's project can attribute to him an account of self-formation which portrays the 'I' as very much more than a unity of psycho-organic drives and product of socialisation:

> the 'me' ... is merely the sum total of definitions of oneself given by society and above all oneself seen through the ideas of significant others. ... The 'I' on the other hand is the moving centre of all of these descriptions which are derived from others. It is the source of impulse, energy and reflection. The individual is never wholly fixed by the labels, projects and obligations which society gives. Corresponding to society's 'conversation of gestures' there is an internal conversation which uses the given language of the 'me' but may create wholly new meanings.[126]

An explanation of Mead's dilemma is to be found in his unsuccessful attempt to reconcile a fully social explanation of the subject with an emphasis on individuals as 'sovereign artificers' or authors of their own thinking and activity. The trouble with this laudable attempt of Mead's to defend the uniqueness of the individual from the encroachments of the 'social self', is that its identification of 'mind' with self-consciousness, and of self-consciousness with the 'me' aspect of personal identity, has effectively denied its author the theoretical resources to explain *how* the 'I' can be held to own the positive qualities or powers he would attribute to it. This results in a curious gap in Mead's argument. For aside from informing his readers that the 'I' is partly socialised and partly unsocialised, and that it is the source of originality, creativity and individuality, Mead does not tell us anything much about this dimension of the self at all. We do not even find out whether it is the socialised or unsocialised aspects of the 'I' which carry the greater explanatory weight in shaping the capacity of the individual for innovative thought and action. Theoretically disarmed in this way, Mead does not (and cannot) offer any grounds to justify the independence of the 'I' from the 'me'. Instead he is forced to resort to merely asserting the positive attributes of the 'I', establishing their existence by a kind of verbal *fiat*.

It is doubtless this ambiguity in Mead's work concerning the status of the elusive 'I' which has allowed subsequent practitioners of 'high' symbolic interactionism and social constructionism (and more recently of structuration theory) to downplay its significance, and effectively treat it as dependent upon the 'me' aspect of the self (as they understand it). So it is that Giddens, for example, can now claim Mead's 'I' for sociological imperialism ('intersubjectivity does not derive from subjectivity, but the other way round').[127]

A common feature of interactionism and structuration theory is thus their mutual conflation of self-consciousness, personal identity and social identity. This involves three conceptual moves. First, self-awareness is regarded as fully developed only where the individual has either acquired the outlook and attitudes of the 'generalised Other' (subject to a lengthy period of socialisation and cultural learning), or where the 'unconscious sociality' or 'basic trust' inherent in the individual is translated, via the medium of socialisation and cultural learning, into an 'emotional acceptance of the reality of the 'external world'.[128] Second, self-identity or personal identity is not always distinguished clearly from self-awareness, which is an inevitable consequence of the latter being seen as emergent from the individual's integration into the institutional roles, cultural expectations or social practices of their society or social group.

Finally, self-identity is treated as interchangeable with social identity, just as the individual as subject is treated as synonymous with the individual as role-incumbent or as social practitioner. This is because, first, an individual's self-definition is said to be dependent upon his or her constitution as a social actor, and second, the social consciousness and behaviour of the individual is regarded as having its locus in processes of enculturation and routinised conduct within institutions. Indeed, symbolic interactionism's apparent view that self-identity (and hence social identity) is synonymous with self-image or the 'presentation of self in everyday life'[129] appears to be a logical extension of the above manoeuvres, since different role-expectations require the actor to 'perform' different 'parts', and don and doff different 'personae' appropriate to the various institutional settings they occupy.

Human nature and the social self in symbolic interactionism: a critique

The fact that this account of the individual is profoundly unsatisfactory is perhaps obvious to everyone other than the naivest students of sociology. This is perhaps most obvious in the work of interactionists, which I will discuss first. Aside from the dubious moral consequences of endorsing the idea that the unsocialised 'I' possesses few 'determinate' or 'recognisable' human qualities (it is instructive that sociologists often refer to unsocialised infants as 'feral' children), perhaps the most fundamental difficulties with the interactionist approach are those of a logical character. I refer here to the fact that it is uncompelling to regard the self that is presented to others in everyday life as equivalent to the self which actually does the self-presenting. I refer also to the fact that the self cannot be equivalent to the personal and social identities of an individual, and nor can it be defined as 'a repertoire of behaviour appropriate to a different set of contingencies',[130] for the simple reason that it is required *a priori* to assemble or construct these identities and to decide which behaviours are appropriate to which circumstances.

Another way of making these arguments is to observe that there has to be more to the subject than 'frontstage' and 'backstage' performances, or indeed a fully articulated self-image or self-identity, since an antecedently existing self has to be postulated in order to explain why the individual initiates these 'presentations' of self-identity, or how the individual is capable of appropriating a personal identity from society. After all, even Erving Goffman's portrait of individuals as social performers, as image peddlers, has to take it as given that individuals possess certain enduring properties of subjectivity – namely that they are capable of 'negotiating' or 'constructing' their identities and are 'by nature' relentless, cunning schemers with an insatiable appetite for social approval. I contend that specifying these capacities must make reference to a determinate human nature and to the non-social dimensions of self.

Not only is interactionism's conflation of self, self-identity and social identity logically suspect, it is also lacking in empirical credentials. Doubtless there are many characteristics of individuals which are susceptible to self-redefinition due to the impact of processes of labelling or societal reaction. But, again, aside from the fact that the act of self-negotiation and self-renegotiation presupposes a factual and analytical distinction between self-consciousness and personal identity, it is equally certain that individuals are often highly resistant to attempts by 'society' or social group to destabilise or transform their self-perceptions.

To deny this, which interactionists in all consistency must do, is paradoxically to deny the existence of self-construction or self-negotiation, to which practitioners of this perspective are formally committed. Yet this capacity of individuals is certainly real enough, as is evidenced by the fact that they do somehow discover the inner resources to continually resist or negate the cultural 'definitions' or 'expectations' or 'attitudes' which 'significant others' or the 'generalised Other' would impose on them. This is why, for instance, the inmates of Goffman's 'total institutions' do not always or everywhere submit to practices of 'de-personalisation', designed to strip them of their individuality or destroy their identities.[131] And this is why, to offer another example, no amount of 'public labelling' or 'societal reaction' to the effect that communism is a pipedream or that capitalism 'works' will convince committed socialists to alter their beliefs to the contrary.

Nor will it do for interactionists to contend that the capacity of individuals to resist or negate the definitions or attitudes of the 'generalised Other' is derived entirely from the counter-influence exerted upon personal identity by the attitudes of 'significant others' (i.e. the validations of parents or close friends). For although it is uncontroversial that the self-images of individuals are profoundly influenced by how they interpret the views of 'significant others' towards them, it is also uncontentious that individuals seek to resist or negate the pressures which 'significant others' would foist on them as readily as those which are derived from the wider society. Why else do children seek to usurp the authority and frustrate the expectations of their parents and teachers? Why else do individuals sometimes reject the cultural and political values and lifestyle of the broader agential collectivities into which they are born and within which they have been reared? Like Foucauldian post-structuralism, interactionism's 'over-social' view of individuals founders on the problem of resistance.

One way in which interactionists attempt to come to grips with those elements of 'personality' which are apparently resistant to 're-negotiation' is by claiming that these properties of persons, inasmuch as they are derived from the 'generalised Other', are unlikely to encounter much in the way of situational disconfirmations. Another strategy of interactionists is to argue that the influence of 'significant others' and the 'generalised Other' counteract one another, with each furnishing resources which allow the individual to partially resist or negate the other. But neither of these 'solutions' render the 'social self' of interactionism sufficiently robust to account for the enduring properties of individual personality.

The first solution does not work because the 'generalised Other' has already been deemed by interactionists to be an endlessly fluid or structureless entity, subject to ongoing renegotiation or redefinition by social actors, and so cannot provide the individual with the stable objective 'frame' or 'context', which would allow this individual to ingest the common attitudes constitutive of a relatively enduring self-identity capable of transcending any specific institutional setting. This solution also fails because if the 'generalised Other' is an endlessly malleable 'structure', and cannot therefore constitute a stable source of self-identity, it follows that the primary basis of an individual's more lasting personal characteristics must be the validations and expectations of 'significant others'. Yet I have already furnished examples which indicate that individuals do resist or negate the expectations and definitions of 'significant others'.

The second solution is equally unsuccessful, since it is unclear why influences derived from 'significant others' should be gifted the strength to counteract those derived from the 'generalised Other' (or vice-versa), meaning that the decision to prioritise one over the other when accounting for the ability of the individual to resist social pressures is entirely arbitrary. This solution also fails because it is not at all difficult to propose cases where individuals have maintained a consistent and enduring personal identity, despite pressures to 'renegotiate' from 'significant others' and the 'generalised Other', or where individuals have found the capacities and motives to resist the pressures of one without utilising the resources or legitimations furnished by the other.

Whatever one makes of the above efforts of interactionists to explain the relative stability of self-identity, there can be little doubt that their tendency to elide human organisms, persons and social actors has sponsored a portrait of individuals (for purposes of analysis and explanation) as nothing other than role-incumbents, engaging in 'performances', and assuming those identities which are validated or reinforced by those they interact with. This in turn has allowed interactionists to compact or elide self-identity and social identity, where the latter is understood as the role-identities or 'masks' which individuals don and doff in appropriate institutional contexts.

One obvious flaw of this kind of approach is that such views of personal identity as 'play acting' or 'putting on a performance' lead to dubious notions such as the 'sick role' or the 'deviant career', which one finds scattered throughout the sociological literature. It often seems that individuals can no longer be anything so mundane as genuinely ill (in a physical or psychological sense), or as pressurised into illness or crime by structural or cultural constraints (e.g. poverty, unemployment, the values of consumerism or acquisitive individualism, etc.), despite the obvious plausibility of accepting the possibility of this. Nor can individuals be motivated in their thoughts and deeds by a sense of their *human* needs or interests, existing outside the social roles and institutional settings they occupy, and internalised as a constituent part of their self-identity, despite the fact that many people (most obviously full-time 'human rights' campaigners, for example) precisely select their institutional roles on the basis of a keen understanding of the interests they share in common with others as members of the same species.

The second obvious difficulty with this approach is that its compacting of self-identity and social identity (and hence of self and self-presentation) has effectively undermined the common-sense idea that it is possible and desirable to distinguish between what individuals claim to be and what they really are. For if subjects are simply their 'performances', the roles they 'act out', the images they 'present' to others and themselves, and if these are mostly situational constructs and subject to novel transformations, there can be no sense in distinguishing between image and substance when assessing who 'we' are or what 'we' believe. Yet it does not seem unreasonable to draw precisely this distinction. After all, only a fool would be so naive as to suggest that, for instance, a person who expresses racist ideas inside but not outside the workplace is one thing in the former and another in the latter. On the contrary, the personal identity of racists is identical in every situation they encounter, even if their presentation of self is tailored to meet the demands of the moment.

Human nature and the social self in structuration theory: a critique

Doubtless it is these inadequacies of the 'situational self' and 'overplastic' human being of symbolic interactionism which has encouraged Anthony Giddens to attempt their 'transcendence' (along with all hitherto existing sociological concepts) within the territory of his structuration theory. I have suggested that a fundamental difficulty with any concept of the self as the product of social meanings or definitions, internalised by individuals during their situational encounters with other individuals, is that it is ill equipped to explain either the relative permanence or stability of self-identity, or how or why individuals resist or even negate attempts by 'society' or 'social group' to mould or reshape their personal identities in ways not sanctioned by them. Giddens' contribution is to indicate a possible solution to these problems of interactionism without abandoning a fully sociological concept of the individual or of consciousness.

To these ends he puts forward two arguments. First, Giddens disposes of the pre-social self and the naturalistic dimensions of human experience, on the grounds that the organismic urges of the body are socially specified and the objects of nature impinge on individuals only through cultural mediation.[132] Second, Giddens contends that '[s]elf-identity is not a distinct trait, or even a collection of traits possessed by an individual ... [but] is the self as reflexively understood by the person in terms of her or his biography'.[133] This reputedly allows him to circumnavigate the problem of explaining the uniqueness of the individual, and of the possibility of a relatively enduring self-identity which is capable of motivating resistance to situational remodelling, since the social biography of each individual is 'unique to each ... as a constellation ... but uniquely social in composition',[134] whereas an accumulation of social experiences across the human life-cycle functions as a bulwark against pressures to renegotiate self-identity in any specific institutional setting which an individual might enter or encounter.

Giddens' claim that human consciousness, self-consciousness and self-identity are constituted entirely within and by social practices, and that therefore 'all existential problems are answered in a social context',[135] depends for its adequacy on his ability to make out a case for two separate but related arguments. These are, first, that 'the self-subsistent natural world ... impinges on us through social mediation alone' and, second, that 'possession of an "I" differentiated from all that which is "not-me" is socially and only socially conferred'.[136] Yet nowhere does Giddens offer a systematic theoretical justification of either of these positions, both of which are merely asserted on the basis of a rejection of Descartes' atomistic subjects and of the 'pre-given self' of conventional psychological theory.

This lamentable failure to defend his 'own corner', so to speak, is only the beginning of Giddens' difficulties. A more fundamental problem with his concept of the 'social self' (and of his reduction of consciousness to social consciousness) is that it is embroiled in the same kind of logical bind which has ensnared all sociological accounts of the subject. I refer here to my argument that a blanket rejection of the 'naturalistic self' simply cannot explain how individuals are capable of organising their experiences in a way which allows them to undergo processes of socialisation and enculturation (each has to recognise that social expectations apply to the same person – i.e.

to 'myself' and not someone else – over time), or how individuals are able to construct their own identities (by recognising or identifying themselves in their own activities or experiences).[137] I refer also to the fact that an explanatory concept of the pre-social self is required to explain why individuals are motivated to utilise properties, derived from their socialisation and enculturation, to construct for themselves enduring personal identities (since this refers us to the needs and emotions of a unitary psycho-organic system translated into consciousness and expressed, to some degree at least, in meaningful intentional agency).

These logical and conceptual difficulties are complemented by others more specific to Giddens' enterprise. As Margaret Archer rightly points out, Giddens' claim that 'self-consciousness has no primacy over awareness of others', or that 'trust in others is at the origins of the experience of the stable external world',[138] is hopelessly confused. The basic problem here is that the earliest human experience of and interaction with other human beings, from the 'perspective' of the new-born, is not with subjects or persons but with objects. As far as babies are concerned there is (initially) no difference between 'society' and 'nature', between subjects and objects, between the organic and the inorganic, or between the animate and the inanimate, since all are experienced sensually by the unsocialised infant (as sources of organismic frustration or reward, comfort or discomfort) as aspects of an undifferentiated world of things. But this means that '[t]rust in others cannot be the source of experiencing the stable external world, since at the start of life other people can only be experienced as part and parcel of that external world'.[139]

Giddens' claim to the contrary not only entails an 'illegitimate imputation of adult concepts (distinguishing people from animals and objects) to a baby who has no ability yet to make such distinctions',[140] but also undermines his explanation of the genesis of self-consciousness in terms of 'ontological security' or 'basic trust' instantiated in 'acquired social routines'. For if an individual is to be deemed capable of feeling either 'secure' or 'insecure', or 'trusting' or 'untrusting', in the context of his or her social relations, what has to be postulated *a priori* is a 'self which [knows] itself to be continuous over time and space', and which can 'either become secure … or [is] enough of a self to feel itself endangered in these crucial respects'.[141] In other words, since '[i]n its security or insecurity … the "I" necessarily ha[s] to be there as prior to either'[142] (given that individuals have to be granted the capacity to interpret their biographical experiences and emotions as their 'own', as belonging to the same person over space and time, if they are to regard themselves as secure or otherwise), it has to be admitted that Giddens' attempt to derive subjectivity from intersubjectivity simply does not work.

If it is accepted that self-consciousness cannot have social origins, it does seem entirely reasonable to suppose that its genesis is a function of the dialectical interface between the human organism and the object-world, in the broadest possible sense (if one is not to endorse the 'pre-given self'). But this means that Giddens is plainly mistaken in his belief that human beings cannot have socially unmediated relations with objects or with nature. Giddens' argument is that human thought and consciousness is necessarily expressed in language, meaning that the objects of physical nature and the psycho-organic 'drives' of human biology are always socially mediated and culturally specified. Yet we have seen already that the earliest interaction of the human being with persons and things (which takes place prior to socialisation or enculturation) is not refracted through language or society, since the baby-organism in possession of no cultural concepts, and unaware of the social relations into which it has been inserted, encounters an undifferentiated object-world only through its sensory equipment and organismic urges, meaning that its earliest biographical experiences are moulded primarily by biological mediation with physical reality.

Giddens does have two lines of defence still open to him, however, which might rescue his 'social self' from these above difficulties. The first of these is his 'anthropological turn' of appealing to 'unconscious sociality', 'basic trust' or 'ontological security' (as pre-social 'givens' of human nature) to explain how individuals differentiate between subjects and objects. Giddens' argument here is twofold. First, he contends that the unsocialised human being is the bearer of a 'mute sociality', which allows individuals to unconsciously feel trust or confidence in their primary carers, but not in mere things. In his words, '[t]he mutuality with early caretakers which basic trust presumes is a substantially unconscious sociality which precedes an "I" and a "me", and is a prior basis of any differentiation between the two'.[143] Second, he contends that this inherited capacity of individuals to differentiate between subjects and objects is translated (via the medium of socialisation and language-acquisition within routinised social practices) into a growing awareness of the 'I/not-me' distinction characteristic of self-consciousness (a process which entails the cultural specification of the latter, as individuals utilise their social biographical experiences to appropriate their hitherto unconscious sociality as conscious self-identity).

These conceptual manoeuvres provide a basis to Giddens' argument that 'the self-subsistent natural world only impinges upon us through social mediation', and that 'the distinction between "I/not-me" impinges on us through social mediation alone'.[144] This is because the concept of 'unconscious sociality' functions here as a kind analytical bridgehead connecting pre-social individuals with their social biography in a way which bypasses the need to refer to the interface between organism and nature when accounting for the genesis of self. From this point of view, although the concept of 'innate sociality' explains the *possibility* of self-consciousness (by allowing unsocialised individuals to distinguish unconsciously between subjects and objects), it is nonetheless the immersion of individuals within social and linguistic practices during their ongoing social biographies which explains the *genesis* of self, and the *content* of self-identity. The problem of explaining how 'trust in others' can be 'at the origins of the experience of the stable external world', or how self-consciousness can have 'no primacy over awareness of others' (given that the pre-social human being confronts initially only a world of things through organismic and sensory mediation), is thus resolved by Giddens by 'imputing ... to the inborn unconscious ... that which practical consciousness cannot deliver through undifferentiated object/person interactions where *social* routines are indistinguishable from routine occurrences'.[145]

But this argument won't do at all. The basic problem with Giddens' appeal to 'unconscious sociality' to undermine the possibility of a naturalistic concept of self and consciousness is that it is radically undertheorised. Giddens offers no arguments from evolutionary biology (i.e. in terms of natural genetic selection in response to environmental pressures) which might justify or explain its reputed existence or salience as a 'given' of human nature. On the contrary, Giddens simply asserts the reality of 'unconscious sociality', establishing its existence by means of 'theoretical fiat' or verbal imputation.

In fact good selection arguments can be offered which support a notion of 'innate sociality' peculiar to human beings and the higher primates. As we have seen, such arguments have been forthcoming in recent times, from a number of scientists working in the fields of palaeoanthropology, zoology, primatology and evolutionary neurobiology, to explain the facts of hominid evolution and human prehistory. And, interest declared, I have utilised certain of their insights to provide a naturalistic underpinning to the theory of agency outlined in the present chapter. But Giddens does not draw on any of these researches, possibly because doing so would commit him to a stronger concept of human nature than he is prepared to admit. It is this omission which lends support to my claim that his concept of 'unconscious sociality' is simply a *post hoc* untheorised improvisation, designed to insulate the social self from disconfirming arguments.

In any case, even if Giddens is right to argue that human beings possess an 'innate sociality' (and I do agree with him on this point), it is difficult to see how this 'innate sociality' translates directly into 'ontological security ... in relation to a world of persons and objects organised cognitively through basic trust',[146] as he suggests is the case. If the concept of 'human nature' is to play an explanatory function in social theory, it surely must do so by specifying a range of capacities, needs, interests and dispositions specific to human beings (subject to empirical and comparative research), rather than by imputing a uniform psycho-emotional makeup to human beings which underwrites a preference for stability or routine in social life.

From this understanding of human nature we can reasonably infer a number of propositions. For one thing, as I have pointed out earlier, a concept of human capacities and interests is necessary to specify how and why human beings 'make history'. Further, I have argued that a concept of human nature along these lines can be used to sustain a naturalistic concept of 'justice'. But a specification of human nature in these terms cannot possibly yield a human organism in secure possession of the ability to distinguish at birth between persons and things, or to experience 'trust' in the security or routines of the external world. Indeed, I would imagine that compelling arguments in terms of genetic selection or biological evolution can be made which rule out the possibility of 'unconscious sociality' being translatable into 'basic trust' or 'ontological security ... in relation to society and nature'. After all, blind trust in the external world is hardly conducive to ensuring the 'reproductive fitness' of the human organism in an environment of potential hazards.

My contention is that if the concept of 'innate sociality' is not to overreach itself, it must refer to the fact that human beings are genetically wired in a way which equips them for cultural learning and economic cooperation, meaning that individuals possess a psychological need for fellowship, community and trust and the biological capacities (adept hand and vocal organs and enhanced brain power) to sustain complicated cooperative arrangements. The concept of 'unconscious sociality' cannot, conversely, be used to impute 'basic trust' to the new-born as a 'psychological given', since this transforms a mute capacity, or even psychic need or disposition, of human sociality (to trust in others) into an actually existing mental state of pre-social individuals, sponsoring the peculiar idea that our subjectivities are directly programmed by our organic drives.

One difficulty with Giddens' endorsement of this view is that it creates a tension at the heart of his philosophy of the subject. This is because Giddens' rejection of the role of socially unmediated experiences in forging self-identity does not square with his appeal to the 'unconscious sociality' of human nature in determining the subjective orientation of unsocialised individuals towards 'ontological security' in their dealings with people and things. A second difficulty with Giddens' appeal to the role of 'unconscious sociality' in servicing 'basic trust', is that this argument appears lacking in empirical credentials and frankly implausible to boot. How can it be ascertained whether the new-born child feels secure or otherwise in its dealings with external reality? How can it be established that the new-born child 'trusts' others to always act in ways which always satisfy its needs or demands? Because neither of these things can be established or inferred from the evidence, there is simply no point in endorsing them. Yet this is precisely Giddens' preferred strategy in attempting to make out a case for the 'social self'.

In fact it does seem more reasonable to suppose, *contra* Giddens, that 'trust' in the security of the world is not an anthropological 'given', but is rather 'a secondary and subsequent development, contingently dependent upon objective routines turning out to be really and reliably routine – and thus contingent upon ... the outside world being so, rather than being a predicate for meeting stable external reality'.[147] After all, even if we accept (for the sake of argument) that babies enter the world with a 'sense of ontological security … organised cognitively through basic trust', experience is likely to teach them otherwise rather quickly, not least because the world is not so 'routinised' or 'reliable' that their urges are always satisfied, or even responded to on demand. But this means that Giddens' appeal to 'basic trust' cannot function to dispose of the logical and substantive difficulties of his own attempt to derive subjectivity from intersubjectivity. The pre-social self and the naturalistic sources of self-identity cannot be transcended with resort to 'conventionalist stratagems' of any kind.

If Giddens has to concede that the unsocialised or pre-social human being does indeed have socially *un*mediated relations with nature, which are instrumental in the genesis of self, it nonetheless remains open to him to argue that the subsequent initiation of individuals into culture and language ensures that all hitherto experiences of human beings are socially mediated, and are mediated by nothing else but society. This is, in fact, Giddens' second line of defence of his 'social self', albeit one he develops without abandoning his blanket rejection of the naturalistic sources of self-awareness (which logic indicates he must). This kind of response is not in the least bit compelling, however. For if it has to be admitted that physiological interaction with non-social reality is instrumental in allowing the human organism to constitute itself as a self, then there are no good reasons why these same non-social relations should be denied input into forming the content of self-identity, irrespective of the fact that the latter can be specified or articulated only by drawing upon cultural and linguistic resources.

Another way of making this point is to observe that our sensory or organismic interactions with nature do not simply cease once we have been constituted as socialised individuals, and nor do they magically desist from shaping the kinds of people we are or can be, or the kinds of perceptions or attitudes we are inclined to hold.

> After all it seems impossible to construe being bitten by a dog as a socially mediated experience (and of no avail to say this depends upon a society which keeps domestic pets for the same goes of near-drowning incidents), yet this event may be responsible for the person later selecting those social practices to which they *will* expose themselves.[148]

But this means that 'interactions with the natural world, physiologically mediated and reflexively understood, can *shape* our social biographies, and not vice-versa as Giddens suggests is always the case'.[149] And what is true of the relationship between individual and nature is true also of the relationship between culture and nature. Thus socially and culturally mediated our non-social relations with physical nature undoubtedly are, but equally our social relations and cultural concepts are mediated by our organismic needs and interests, and by our collaborative relations with the physical environment in our efforts to harness it to our human and social interests.

A final major problem with Giddens' disqualification from human experience of 'all socially unmediated interactions', and 'restriction of reflexivity to that which can be socially mediated' via the medium of language, is that it effectively denies human beings 'any form of private life'[150] or personal psychology. The implications of endorsing this kind of view are drawn out by John Shotter, who approvingly cites Giddens to the effect that

> motives, intentions, sentiments are not inner things represented in outer behaviour, but are in the mediatory activity (joint action) going on between individuals. ... As such, one might say, motives etc. exist less 'in' us than in the institutions between us. ... To be appropriate to its circumstances, an action need not be guided by an 'inner' representation of the 'outer' circumstances at all ... an action can be informed not so much by factors present in the source from which it issues, as by the context *into* which it is directed.[151]

This view is not exactly sociological determinism, but it is sociological imperialism. What prevents Giddens' philosophy of the subject being the former, on the one hand, is its defensible emphasis on self-negotiation and upon self-identity as the product of an individual's reflexive monitoring of their social biographical experiences. This explains how individuals 'can do otherwise' in Giddens' theory, allowing him to break with Parsons' and Althusser's 'oversocialised conception of man'. What makes Giddens' account of agency a species of the latter, on the other hand, is its characteristic view that individual motives (inasmuch as these are translated into conscious wants or beliefs) 'exist ... in the institutions between us', meaning that all meaningful and intentional human activity has a necessary external locus in society or culture.

This is, of course, yet another statement of structuration theory's denial of the naturalistic self, and of the possibility of socially unmediated interactions between human beings and physical nature. Thus, from this perspective, although individuals are not the passive recipients of the 'central value system' or the 'dominant ideology' (since they are free to select from society and culture that which they identify with or endorse), they nonetheless can specify their ideas, desires, beliefs, etc. only by drawing upon society and culture, meaning that all intentional action is socially and culturally dependent.

But to deny individuals their 'inner selves' or 'private passions' is scarcely plausible, and for three basic reasons. First, it does not seem unreasonable to contend that many of the 'routinised practices' engaged in by individuals (such as walking, jogging, swimming, gardening, sunbathing, bird-watching, etc.) are motivated by reasons or desires which have no necessary social referent or specification (in the sense of depending upon material resources or cultural norms generated by society). But this means that an explanation of why individuals pursue these and other activities (social or otherwise) has to be found in the personality differences which exist between them. Second, far from all of the rules which guide intentional individual agency being appropriated from society, or depending upon linguistic mediation (as Giddens insists is always the case), it does seem plausible to postulate the existence of 'private rules', which are forged by individuals during the process of their organismic or sensory interaction with the physical world, and which therefore refer us to personal proclivities emergent from the interface between the human being and nature.

Giddens would reject the possibility of 'private rules', on the grounds that rational thought is necessarily expressed in language, and language is necessarily social or 'public' in character. This argument is toothless, however, entailing as it does elementary errors of categorisation. For although it is true enough that 'private rules' of conduct can only be articulated via the mediation of language, hence ruling out the possibility of 'private language', it does not follow from this that the subjective dispositions or preferences of individuals which have motivated the construction of these rules have their locus or origin in social rather than personal experience.

These arguments are well made by Margaret Archer:

> If we reintroduce physiological interaction with nature, then there seems nothing objectionable about the notion of asocial rules being forged in this process. Instead, repeated experiences of falling through thin ice, with physically unpleasant circumstances, could lead to the personal 'formulation' of a rule about prior testing. Obedience to the rule is umpired by natural reality, which, being incapable of abrogating its own laws, leads to cracked ice and re-dunking, thus physically reinforcing the advisability of rule-keeping. However, just as the defence of personal psychology [does] not turn upon defending the traditional terminology of traits and attributes, neither does the defence of private life ultimately rest upon the possibility of private language. It is perfectly possible to grant the universal use of public language for the *expression* of private experience, without accepting that the feelings, urges or beliefs which people express in it are social rather than personal.[152]

Finally, Giddens' view that all human reasons and intentions are supplied by the social context in which individuals find themselves fails because it disqualifies him from explaining why individuals in specific institutional or cultural settings reject or oppose certain or all of the attitudes, values, rules, role-obligations or interests characteristic of their society or social group or both. This in turn renders it entirely mysterious why, for instance, members of the bourgeoisie occasionally 'go over' to the workers,[153] or why more generally 'individual decisions about appropriate action collide with institutional definitions, as they often do'.[154] For although individuals possess here the agential capacities to resist in thought and deed institutional definitions or specifications of their desires and beliefs, they do not possess the inner motives or inner passions which might encourage them to do so.

Doubtless Giddens would respond to this argument by claiming that individuals never negate the social environment in which their beliefs and desires are specified, but instead exchange one set of socio-cultural attitudes or sentiments for another, rather like you or I might swap one pair of shoes for another. Certainly it is uncontentious that individuals do often (or even normally) draw upon cultural resources to resist cultural expectations or attitudes drawn from other cultural resources (as, for instance, Tony Benn has drawn upon the ideas of socialism to negate the values associated with his bourgeois background and upbringing).

But this does not overcome my objection, since Giddens still requires some account of the self which allows individuals to don and doff motives or intentions, and he is still faced with the difficulty of explaining why certain individuals reject or resist those 'situational influences' which are 'closer to home' so to speak (i.e. which fit better with the social interests and cultural milieu of the 'collectivities' to which they belong) in favour of those whose impact or effect is less direct or pressing. I contend that explaining why individuals resist those cultural influences, which their social positioning and enculturation should have stripped them of external motives for so doing, demonstrates the need for social theory to endorse the existence of a stratum of personal psychology or personality, irreducible to the imprint of society, and 'forged in the space *between* biology and society'[155] and nature. After all, as Archer rightly points out, 'the fact that [society] can be refused (the hermit), reviled (the prophet), re-visioned (the idealist) or rejected (the recidivist) are forms of repudiation too varied to be explained by reaction formation'[156] to socio-cultural stimuli.

The foregoing arguments establish, against Giddens, that personal identity and social identity are not the same thing. Since neither the genesis nor the content of self-identity is entirely explainable in terms of 'social practices' or the social biographies of individuals, it follows that social theory must endorse a stratified model of the human agent, which distinguishes between the self as social actor (with attendant identities or self-presentations) and the self as the 'bearer' of an underlying and relatively stable 'personality' or 'personal psychology'. By collapsing individuals into their social biographies, Giddens destroys this distinction between human subjects and social selves, and by doing so renders his analysis of agency vulnerable to the kind of reductionism which has undermined interactionism. So it is that Giddens, in common with Goffman, more often than not treats individuals simply as 'performers', as image-peddlers, acting out 'parts', slavishly following 'routines', striving to 'keep face' or 'maintain tact' in their dealings with others.[157] The end result of all of this is a rather impoverished concept of the individual and an ambiguous conception of 'agency', as has been noted by a number of commentators.

Nigel Thrift, for example, rightly points out that, despite Giddens' avowed intention to restore knowledgeability to the subject, his treatment of individuals as practitioners, engaging in routinised rule-governed institutional action, sponsors an 'anonymous agent' who is 'devoid of spontaneity and creativity'.[158] In a similar vein, Margareta Bertilsson makes out the telling indictment that Giddens' conflation of persons and actors undermines his commitment to the subject, since in practice his concept of 'agency' refers not to subjects but to the 'dominant set of practices' which comprise a society.[159] Ian Craib, to offer a further example, is justifiably critical of Giddens' incorporation of certain of Goffman's insights into his structuration theory, making the insightful observation that this has led to an unwarranted overemphasis in Giddens' work on 'how people go on' in place of an understanding of 'what goes on' and why.[160]

Craib also argues, again rightly, that Giddens' analytical treatment of subjects as synonymous with actors has led to his portrayal of 'an emotionally impoverished world in which terms like morality and trust lose most of their strength and a comparatively empty notion of tact takes over'.[161] The culprit here, of course, is Giddens' identification of the concepts of 'trust' and 'morality' with social procedures of 'self-presentation', rather than with enduring normative and emotional emergents of humanity's psychological makeup (i.e. love, commitment, loyalty, fairness, justice, etc.).[162] That such a dissolution of subjects into their 'social practices' underwrites a superficial analysis of 'personality' or 'personal psychology' is, of course, thrown into sharp exposure by Giddens' grossly reductive attempt to explain away mental illness as resulting from a breakdown of the rules of tact and composure governing social interaction.[163]

Conclusion

To conclude this chapter I would like to make explicit two fundamental arguments which have been the centrepiece of my defence of Marx's philosophical anthropology and my critique of the 'naturalistic' and 'sociological' models of the organism-subject-society connection. These constitute the 'fundamental premises' of any workable theory of human agency and social interaction.

First, my exposure of the inadequacies of both biologism's and utilitarianism's portrait of human nature and individual subjectivity, and of contemporary sociology's dissolution or conflation of both at the level of processes of 'interaction or 'enculturation', entails not the abandonment of the concepts of 'species-being' and the 'naturalistic self' but rather their reformulation in a far more rigorous form, open to scientific procedures of empirical validation and disconfirmation. *Contra* naive anti-naturalism, a strong explanatory account of human nature, and of the non-social subject, has an indispensable analytical function in social theory, in providing 'micro-foundations' for the theory of social structure and human agency, and (as should be clear from some of my arguments in the preceding sections) in furnishing the social analyst with clear ethical and political orientations (i.e. a naturalistic principle of justice). What, then, can we say with any certainty about the nature of human nature and the subject?

(i) Human nature can be defined only with resort to meticulous historical and comparative research into human origins, prehistory and socio-cultural evolution. Only by following this procedure is it possible to demonstrate empirically which powers and properties of human beings are explainable in terms of species-being, and which are explainable in terms of social structure or agential or institutional context. To reiterate my earlier argument, I would recommend that the theorist utilise Norman Geras' attribution to Marx of an analytical and factual distinction between 'human nature' and the 'nature of humanity', with the former referring to those needs, capacities or dispositions of human beings which have an enduring and relatively permanent historical existence (as revealed by the anthropological record), and the latter referring to those ephemeral cultural characteristics which humans acquire as a result of their immersion in historically specific social relations, and within specific institutional and agential contexts within social relations (as revealed by historical and comparative sociological research).

From this historical and comparative perspective, Marx's own account of human nature appears strikingly vindicated. Humanity's species-being is clearly revealed as being predisposed towards labour, rationality, sociability, communalism, altruism, certain emotional and even normative dispositions which are explainable in terms of sociality, and quite plausibly towards egalitarianism as well. Certainly, human nature cannot be seen as uniquely adapted to life in competitive hierarchical societies, as would be claimed by most methodological individualists. For it seems indisputable that human beings were forged biologically by natural selection to cope with and sustain socio-cultural relations organised along intensely communal lines, and even in unequal class-divided societies it is apparent that cooperative and egalitarian principles of social behaviour are rather more important to the daily life and routine reproduction of social relations than those said to characterise 'Darwinian-Hobbesian man' or for that matter 'utilitarian man'. Indeed, it is a matter of historical fact that the overwhelming majority of human existence has been based on a hunting and gathering mode of economic subsistence, which depended upon an unprecedented degree of social cooperation and egalitarian food-sharing, and in which behavioural and attitudinal norms sustaining individualism, utilitarianism, territorialism, economic competition, hierarchy, territorialism and inequality did not even enjoy a marginal presence.

(ii) Human nature, as again is clearly revealed by anthropology, is definable in terms of both its behavioural and psychological plasticity, and the flexibility of its adaptability to the physical environment. That is to say, human nature may be characterised in terms of its unique capacity to enable a highly diverse range of personality-types, motivations, mentalities and modes of socio-cultural praxis, and its power to emancipate human beings from dependence upon a narrow range of material environments or circumstances. As far as the latter is concerned, humans thus possess what Marx once described as a 'universal nature'. For a lack of narrow biological specialisation allows modern *homo sapiens* to prosper in a wide range of natural habitats.

(iii) Human nature is characterised by its equally unique capacity to allow its bearers to exercise personal judgement and individual choice within the constraints and enablements pre-structured by society and nature. That is to say, human nature provides the biological capacity (indeed imperative) for individuals to interpret their interaction with the object-world in terms of the 'I/not-me' distinction constitutive of self, and as such allows human organisms to construct themselves as subjects or persons (i.e. self-aware beings who are relatively autonomous of their social and material environments). As 'strong evaluators' (rather than 'simple weighers'), human persons are irreducibly moral beings, who exercise their judgement and make their choices on a qualitative as well as a quantitative basis (though the substance of their moral and ethical beliefs is conditioned rather more directly and profoundly by their social being than by their species-being).

Talk of 'socio-cultural determination' or 'biological drives' or 'natural necessity' will not therefore suffice in any causal account of human agency or social interaction. For human nature is precisely that which allows subjects or self-conscious agents to reflexively monitor and appraise the external conditioning influences which impact upon them, select in accordance with normative considerations which behavioural responses they deem appropriate to the social and material facts of their life-process, and then act innovatively, purposively and voluntarily in the light of these considerations and choices.

(iv) Human nature cannot be defined in terms of instinctual endowment, given the negligible role this plays in human motivation and behaviour. This is because the uniquely human mode of environmental adaptation is centred upon cultural learning *par excellence*, and has thus entailed the gradual eradication from human (or more accurately pre-human) biology those genes which sustain or enhance instinctual behavioural responses to environmental stimuli.

All too often, naive naturalists (sociobiologists are particularly guilty of this) repeat the 'common-sense' error of laypersons of confusing biological instincts (genetically pre-programmed elaborate behaviour patterns – e.g. the mating rituals of many non-human species) with biological reflexes (unconscious bodily responses – e.g. blinking, suckling, crying, smiling, reaching out an arm to break a fall, recoiling sharply from a source of pain, etc.) when accounting for human social behaviour. Yet even the so-called human 'sex instinct', beloved of pop psychology, is perhaps better understood simply as an elementary human biological need rather than an elaborate predetermined pattern of behaviour. Competent or healthy human adults are not, of course, driven by sexual compulsions they cannot control or understand, and nor are they impelled to engage in specific patterns of sexual ritual (as is proven by the enormous cultural variation in courtship traditions and in the sex act itself). More generally, the biological helplessness of the human child at birth (and its corresponding dependence on society and culture to survive and develop satisfactorily) is itself precisely demonstrative of humanity's lack of instinctual endowment. To a very large extent, then, cultural learning and evolution has replaced biological instinct and evolution in modern *homo sapiens*, a fact evidenced by the virtually non-existent genetic and physical differences 'between the [cave]men of the Aurignacian and Magdalenian cultures ... on the one hand, and present day men on the other'.[164]

(v) Most importantly, perhaps, to refer to human nature and subjectivity is to specify an ensemble of species powers, capacities, dispositions and psycho-organic needs and interests, which logically must be held to exist in order to account for the existence of human society and culture. This is a transcendental argument. Thus it is, for example, quite valid to endorse Marx's attribution of the properties and powers of intelligence, self-consciousness, sociality, rationality, intentionality, purposiveness, creativity, linguistic capacity and labour to human nature and/or the 'naturalistic self' (amongst other things), for such qualities must be possessed by human organisms or persons if they are to be the kind of beings capable of sustaining and elaborating complex socio-cultural relations. Conversely, it is quite invalid to attribute any of the characteristics of biologism's or utilitarianism's abstract 'model of man' to human nature (and its emergents of mind and self), because aside from the fact that most of these dispositions are absent from the larger part of the ethnographic biography of human society, it is also the case that not one of them is functional to humanity's socio-cultural mode of environmental adaptation.

> The concept of human nature (and the naturalistic subject emergent from it) thus should not (and cannot) be used to explain the ethnographic specifics of human societies, the form of socio-cultural relations, the character and history of political and economic institutions, or even the constitution of human 'mentalities' or 'spiritualities' to be found in different socio-historical settings. All of this can be explained only by examining the historical interface between structure, culture, interaction and environment in the life of actual empirical societies. What the concept of human nature can do, however, is provide a means of explaining the handful of constants which can be found in most societies past and present,[165] offer the beginnings of a purchase on the diversity of the anthropological record, and supply an important element of the explanation of social conflict and change (i.e. in terms of suppression of basic human needs and interests which encourages resistance and struggle against the vested social interests and social relations which sustain them). Furthermore, the concept of human nature is useful inasmuch as it enables the analyst to furnish social theory with an ethical and political yardstick for measuring the degree to which empirical societies are respectively constraining or enabling of real human needs or interests ('evaluative realism' and the concept of human 'well-being').

So much for the psycho-organic and subjective 'microfoundations' of social theory and social life. But what can be said about the socio-cultural relations, agential collectivities and institutional roles which constitute the subject-matter of sociology? The second key argument I would like to draw from the preceding is that endorsing the explanatory function of human nature and the naturalistic self in social analysis is not at all tantamount to perpetrating the 'naturalistic fallacy' of collapsing society and culture into human biology, human nature or human subjects. In contrast to the 'upwards conflationist' approaches, my contention is that a fully adequate analysis of society has to study the causal interface between the 'macro' (structural and cultural), 'meso' (interactional and agential) and 'micro' (biological and subjective) levels of social systems. None is more fundamental than the others (in the sense of explaining society), for all embody their own emergent properties, and all generate their own causal powers and independent effects.

Thus, at the same time as humanity's species-being and attendant powers and capacities are transmitted 'upstream' into social interaction and socio-cultural relations (supplying the power which energises the social system, constraining and enabling socio-cultural production and reproduction, and providing a certain impetus towards the universal articulation of particular kinds of cultural norms or principles), structural-cultural and agential conditioning influences are transmitted 'downstream' to human persons (investing in them specific social interests and capacities, shaping unconsciously much of their psychological and spiritual makeup, and furnishing them with the cultural resources to construct personal and social identities for themselves). At the 'micro' level, the result of this complex dialectical interaction between these distinct layers of human and social reality is precisely the individual as the bearer or embodiment of a complex articulation of psycho-organic and socio-cultural properties. That is to say, human persons are simultaneously constituted as the concrete bearers of the specific social relations, agential collectivities and institutional roles of which they are a part (social being), of the capacities, powers, needs and interests inherent in them as members of a particular biological species (species-being), and of the process which welds these human and social elements together in the life of the individual (personal biography mediated by social and non-social experience).

It is the simple fact that the socio-cultural and agential properties of social systems are presupposed in the goals or ends which animate social interaction, and are often drawn upon by persons in order to realise their wants or desires, which counts as the decisive rebuttal of naturalistic conceptions of agency or interaction. Theories of human nature (and individuated subjectivity) will not therefore alone suffice in social analysis, because the 'nature of humanity' of a particular historical epoch is always moulded by the interface between species-being and social being in the life-process of human individuals.

3 Subjects, actors and agents

In the foregoing chapter, I have sought to lay down the foundations or 'basic premises' of a theory of social interaction consistent with social realism and critical materialism. My basic argument there is that sociology requires a strong explanatory concept of both human nature and the non-social self, if it is to avoid an amoral and apolitical indifference to human problems and social struggles, and if it is to obtain an explanatory purchase on society and history. Now my contention is that upon these 'micro-foundations' of society arises an 'interaction order', which is conditioned simultaneously by those anterior structural relations which constrain and enable the social conduct and consciousness of interactants, and by those natural properties and powers pertaining to individuals (as subjects and organisms) which enable them to function as agents of social order and/or social change. The purpose of this chapter is to conceptualise the constitution of this 'interaction order', and to understand its relationship to the structural properties of social systems and the psycho-organic and subjective capacities of individuals.

To these ends, the subject-matter of the forthcoming analysis will be organised as follows. First, I will introduce and explicate the concept of 'social interaction' or 'social action'. Then I will relate the 'interaction order' to the structural properties of society by furnishing an 'interest-explanation' of human agency, my argument being that interests (human and social) function as the bridgehead which connects interaction to structure. Next, I will outline a realist 'stratified model' of individuals as 'actors', 'agents' and 'persons' (and as the bearers of personal and social identities), and demonstrate its efficacy by means of a critical examination of the unhappy consequences of social action theory's treatment of individuals simply as role-incumbents or social practitioners. Finally, I will relate the above 'stratified model' of interaction to the subjective levels of social reality by theorising those properties of persons (mind, self and personal identity) which allow them to become actors or agents and self-construct social identities.

These tasks achieved, my completion of a useable and fully adequate Marxist account of social agency will have to wait upon the analysis contained in Chapter 4. It will be recalled that Chapter 1 contains an exposition of the explanatory primacy of social labour in bringing about the evolutionary elaboration/transformation of the human species, as part of my defence of anthropological materialism in the human sciences. In Chapter 4 I will radicalise the realist conception of social agency into one rooted in sociological materialism, by arguing the case for the explanatory primacy of social labour in bringing about subsequent socio-cultural elaboration, and for the explanatory primacy of class agency in bringing about societal transformation or reproduction.

The concept and nature of social interaction

What is social interaction? The obvious answer (and one which has considerable intuitive appeal) is that social interaction is simply the self-conscious, meaningful and intentional 'doings' or activities of human individuals insofar as these enter them into mutual relationships or interpersonal encounters. Social interaction can thus be understood as a particular form of human agency (i.e. as human agency which entails the active involvement of individuals in mutual interactional relationships), and it can be distinguished from mere behaviour by its reflexive and redirective character. Social interaction can be further differentiated between collective action and individual action, with the former referring to those practices or pursuits which involve the coordination of individual activity towards the attainment of common goals (i.e. collaborative action), and the latter referring to those types of human activity which, although socio-culturally conditioned and often dependent upon socio-cultural resources, do not do so (e.g. reading a book, listening to a CD, engaging in petty theft or sabotage at the workplace, committing suicide, etc.).

Social interaction is, in short, the obverse of social structure. Whereas the concept of social structure refers us to the patterned and enduring socio-cultural relationships which predate and postdate human action and interaction, and which exercise a conditioning influence upon both, the concept of social interaction refers us to the daily flux or flow of human activity which takes place within these anterior structural and cultural contexts, and which (often unintentionally) brings about their reproduction or modification over time.

Social interaction also typically involves different types of social action. Max Weber's attempt to conceptualise these is still the most interesting and exhaustive on offer.[1] As is well known, Weber's 'ideal typical' typology distinguishes analytically between

(i) *traditional* action (social conduct which is performed on the basis of inherited custom or habit or routine);
(ii) *affectual* action (social conduct motivated by emotional dispositions or commitments);

(iii) *rational goal-oriented* action (social conduct which involves assessing rationally the utility of a project or goal, and the most appropriate, i.e. optimal or instrumentally efficient means of achieving it); and

(iv) *value-oriented rational* action (social conduct which is oriented consistently towards the attainment of a valued end-state or ultimate goal, which subordinates all other considerations to this overriding purpose, and which does not involve a rigorous consideration of the most 'optimal' means or utility-costs of achieving it).

There are, of course, a number of profound difficulties with this formulation. In the first place, there is Weber's misconceived attempt to distinguish analytically between different modes of society, on the basis of the allegedly 'typical' modes of social action to be found within them, and his failure to contextualise adequately rational action within concrete socio-cultural relations. Both of these problems stem largely from Weber's dalliance with neo-Kantian idealism (i.e. his effort to categorise societal types in terms of the value-orientations which motivate social action) and from his reduction of all interactional, agential and structural properties of society to the beliefs and values of atomised individuals.

Second, and following on from this latter consideration, there is also a peculiar crudity to Weber's analytical distinctions between the different forms of 'non-rational' action. Aside from the problem of attributing the correct motive to a particular social act (is it affectual, traditional, value-rational or instrumentally rational?), the typology appears to be undermined by the difficulty inherent in drawing unambiguous analytical distinctions between the various forms of non-rational action (for example, an individual might have affectual attachments to a goal which is valued above all others, or might value the goal because of the impact of ingrained tradition).

Finally, and most crucially, Weber's attempt to distinguish between rational goal-oriented action (in his view the only genuinely rational action-orientation) and all the other forms of non-rational social action appears irredeemably crass, hamstrung by a crude utilitarian conception of rationality. Motivated by his ideological (or value-rational!) commitment to establish the uniquely rational character of capitalism, and the necessarily irrational nature of all conceivable alternatives, Weber's model fails to demonstrate that instrumentally rational action (i.e. social action that involves purely formal means-ends calculations necessarily indifferent to ethical or valuational judgements concerning the substantive content of the ends or goals being pursued) can be separated from rational *value*-oriented action (i.e. social action which embodies substantive evaluative commitments concerning the desirability of ends).

Thus, despite Weber, far from the institutions and social relations of capitalist society (the market, a monetary system, the business enterprise, private property, the wage-form, etc.) being comprehensible simply in terms of formal rationality, owing their salience to their technical efficiency in relating means to ends, these phenomena always involve substantive ethical and valuational judgements concerning the desirability of the kinds of objectives being pursued. (For example, a belief in the uniquely rational character of capitalist institutions is rooted in the substantive evaluation that it is especially rational to subordinate a consideration of the social content of ends to the dictates of means-ends calculability. More generally, instrumental rationality appears to be rooted in the substantive belief that 'the ends justify the means'.)[2]

The above critique might seem to lend credence to the arguments of those who believe that any attempt to build a useable *general* typology of social action is ill conceived. This is neither my intention nor my belief. There is one basic strength which can be attributed to Weber's theory of action, and one which provides one of the cornerstones of a reformulated model of interaction. This is his insistence that social action is precisely comprehensible, and hence capable of being scientifically interpreted and analysed, due to its basic behavioural and attitudinal rationality. In other words, the rational kernel of Weber's theory of action is his endorsement of what contemporary analytical philosophers would describe as 'the orthodox conception of agents'.[3] From this point of view, beliefs and values are rational if they are internally coherent or non-contradictory, and social action is rational if it is consistent with beliefs or values. The researcher attributes meaning to the social actions of individuals by assuming that persons act relatively consistently in the light of their beliefs, desires or goals. The identification of the values, objectives and expectations of the interactants in turn provides the key to understanding their activity.

Now, this 'orthodox conception of agents', which rightly takes as given the universal existence of human behavioural and attitudinal rationality, must assume also the existence of a universal human nature. As Macdonald and Petit observe, a fundamental precondition of the possibility of understanding the language and culture of an 'alien' society is the existence of what might be termed a 'principle of charity', rooted in an underlying 'principle of humanity'.[4] Broadly, for cross-cultural communication and 'radical translation' to be possible, '[i]t is essential ... that we agree in a large number of judgements', which itself is dependent upon the fact that the 'common behaviour of mankind' acts as 'the system of reference by means of which we interpret an unknown language'.[5]

The point is well made by David Wiggins:

> Presented with the human form we entertain immediately a multitude of however tentative expectations. We interpret the speech and conduct of the remotest human strangers in the light of the maxim that we should interpret them in such a way as to ascribe beliefs, needs and concerns to them that will diminish to the minimum the need to postulate 'inexplicable' disagreements between us and them. We entertain the idea, unless we are irremediably conceited or colonialist in mentality,

> that there may be something we ourselves can learn from strangers about the true, the good and the rational. ... In the absence of a belief in such a thing as human nature, I do not think that there is any idea of inexplicable error or disagreement that is available to us.[6]

In short, then, common human behaviour presupposes a common human nature and a common objective structure of physical nature, within which human persons are compelled to act and interact. Without these twin reference points of material reality and human nature, there appears no plausible way of explaining how cross-cultural communication or linguistic acquisition is possible. Thus a workable reformulation of Weber's account of social action must be rooted in 'the orthodox conception of agents' (i.e. the assumption that human beings are 'somewhat rational' in thought and deed), which in turn must be rooted in the enduring facts of human nature.

Yet a fundamental problem with Weber's model of interaction is its failure to make this above conception of rational action (i.e. action that is relatively consistent with beliefs and goals) definitional of formal rationality. For this criteria of rationality does not entail substantive considerations. The second fundamental problem of Weber's typology is, as we have seen, the crude distinctions it draws between different forms of 'non-rational' action and between 'rational' and 'non-rational' action. Nonetheless, these weaknesses do not rule out of court a defensible account of social action. Once we recognise that a concept of formal rationality involving no substantive judgements commits us to a species of rationality possessed by all competent human individuals in every human society (rather than the instrumental rationality unique to capitalism), we provide ourselves with the beginnings of an adequate understanding of human action and social interaction. Formally rational action is simply social action which is consistent with the goals, desires and beliefs of the interactant, and because it is an elementary form of action to be found equally in all societies, it is an utterly pointless endeavour to attempt to distinguish between different societal types on the basis of the allegedly 'rational' or 'non-rational' value-patterns which animate them.

Moreover, once we ally this insight with Weber's own recognition that the 'ideal-types' of action should be seen as analytical rather than empirical distinctions, it then becomes possible to grasp that concrete actions will often entail a diverse range of motivations or orientations, none of which will necessarily compromise their formal rationality. In other words, there is not always a clear distinction to be made between rational and other modes of social action: emotional, traditional and ethical orientations towards action may often be rooted in rational commitments. A useable typology of human action and interaction should distinguish between rational and non-rational action only on the basis of a rigorous assessment of the consistency with which individuals act in accordance with their beliefs and desires, within the fetters and enablements pre-structured by the socio-cultural relations they inhabit. More importantly, however, a theory of action should make its primary concern the identification and explication of the different modes of 'somewhat rational' social action (emotional, traditional, value-rational) which energise society, as these are conditioned by the agential, cultural, structural and systemic dimensions of social reality.

The function of interests and norms in social theory

In my introduction to this chapter I suggested that interest-explanation offers a solution to the problem of relating interaction and structure. But what form should this take? The most influential versions of 'interest-explanation' in the social sciences – especially those associated with contemporary rational choice and social exchange theory – have tended to identify interests with individuated wants or desires. According to Jon Elster[7] and James Coleman,[8] for example, the analytical foundations of social interaction and social order are human agents and the resources they seek to control or monopolise. Human individuals are seen as rational agents who possess subjective desires and wants which organise and motivate their interactions with others. These wants and desires constitute their interests, and individual and collective action is rational inasmuch as it is 'future-oriented and instrumentally efficient behaviour consistent with interests'. For both authors, allegiance to methodological individualism thus dictates that interests be seen 'as a taken-for-granted, natural, pre-constituted state of affairs',[9] rooted in the random self-interested ends of individuals. How plausible is this view?

Now although I would not wish to deny that one can speak meaningfully of human interests – i.e. as the ends or objectives of social interaction which can logically be inferred from the existence of elementary human needs which require fulfilling – it seems entirely questionable to me that one should treat these as the random subjective desires or wants of individuals. Moreover, although it is perfectly valid to presume that individuals are 'somewhat rational', and act socially in order to realise their individual preferences, it would be quite mistaken to predicate a theory of social interaction (and of the relationship between structure and interaction) on this basis. Why is this?

First, there are quite formidable theoretical difficulties associated with interest-explanation couched in terms of subjective preference. This has been thrown into sharp relief by both sides of the Marxist-liberal debate in political science. According to 'orthodox' political theory, 'the point of the concept of interests is to relate an agent's wants to the objective environment on which his or her opportunities for realising those wants depend'.[10] As Giddens puts it: 'interests are logically connected to wants'.[11] As Alex Callinicos has pointed out, for pluralists, social interaction (insofar as it is significant in bringing about societal change or statics) is to be explained in terms of interests which are definable as the 'expressed preferences' of individuals (the 'subjective conception of interests').[12] For Marxists, by contrast, social interaction is to be explained in terms of interests defined as those 'counter-factual wants' which individuals would hold if they were in full possession of the knowledge or information to make an informed decision as to what these should be (the 'objective conception of interests', as Callinicos describes it).[13]

The advantage of the latter over the former definition of interests is that it allows the theorist some purchase on the fact that 'an agent may not always be aware of his or her interests'.[14] For example, I may be unable to articulate my real interests due to the 'mobilisation of bias' in the political sphere or the impact of artificially induced wants in the economic sphere.[15]

Yet, although revealing the 'subjectivist' inadequacies of pluralist interest-explanations, it is clear enough that Marxist treatments of interests as 'counterfactual wants' have fundamental weaknesses of their own. In the first place, such accounts do not overcome the spectre of the 'randomness of ends' which has undermined pluralism. For if it is still individual wants which animate social agency, it is hard to see how these can be conceived objectively.

In the second place, given that individuals act on their actual preferences rather than on their 'counterfactual wants', and given that interests are identified with the latter, it is uncertain how this approach differs from pluralism as a causal explanation of social interaction, or how it can justify 'interest-explanations' in the social sciences at all. It seems to me that conceptions of interests in terms of subjective wants must either naively ignore the fact that interests cannot always be clearly articulated by oppressed or powerless groups, or sever the link between expressed wants and interests (and between social agency and human and social interests).[16]

Third, the satisfaction of subjective judgements of utility, i.e. of the wants and desires of individuals, may not always enhance the 'life-chances' or 'well-being' of human beings. I may desire to indulge in unprotected sexual intercourse, eat contaminated beefburgers, drink enormous quantities of alcohol, or inhale narcotic substances. Yet by doing so I am risking premature death or permanent disability. The concept of human interests thus presupposes an objective standard of human needs which may not always correspond to subjective individual wants. Human beings have an objective interest in obtaining or satisfying those elementary psycho-organic needs (i.e. food, shelter, clothing, cultural and leisure opportunities, sexual relations, full participation in and integration into their social relations, etc.) which satisfy or enhance their well-being. But they have no interest whatsoever in pursuing those wants which do not.

Fourth, although it is uncontentious that individuals are motivated to a large extent by their subjective desires and wants, it is equally certain that these normally are anchored in the objective biological and psychological needs of humanity's species-being. Human persons might desire and want all kinds of things, but since many of their desires are supplementary or secondary to their real needs, these are likely to be recognised by individuals as such, and will not normally be a primary motivational source of their social agency. In other words, the 'preference set' of human persons will always comprise 'first-order' and 'second-order' desires, 'primary' and 'secondary' wants, with the former corresponding broadly to their objective needs as members of the human species, and providing them with particularly impelling reasons for acting socially in their defence or pursuit.

It follows from this that the kinds of social agency which are significant, from the point of view of societal elaboration and transformation, tend to be motivated not by individuals pursuing their privatised wants, but by collectivities of individuals pursuing common goals which are defined in terms of general human needs and interests. That is to say, individuals do not normally bind themselves together into collective or corporate agents, committed to the pursuit of societal change or statics, in order to satisfy mere privatised utility-maximisation, but rather do so in order to bring about the reproduction, reform or overthrow of social relations which affirm or deny their basic human needs, and which are conducive or contrary to their fundamental human interests. For example, although members of the working class in modern capitalism no doubt would express a subjective preference for foreign instead of domestic holidays, or brand new rather than second-hand motor cars, it is highly doubtful that such concerns are uppermost in their minds when they join trade unions or offer their support to political organisations. On the contrary, the reason why workers tend to align themselves with corporate agents of this kind has rather more to do with defending their livelihood and life-chances than any drive towards the gratuitous pursuit of mere random preferences.[17]

The same is true even of members of the bourgeoisie, who form themselves into corporate agents, not for anything so trivial as the desire for a few more consumer goods or a little extra spending power, but rather to defend the very apparatus of profit-making by which they obtain their income and by which (as they see it) society obtains its wealth and prosperity.[18] Interests defined in terms of privatised wants or desires are, then, too inconsequential and arbitrary a source of human motivation to sustain an account of social agency which can explain the formation of corporate agents oriented towards macro-elaboration or reproduction, or the life-and-death social struggles which bring about societal change. Psychologistic and individualistic conceptions of human interests cannot provide secure micro-foundations for the theory of agency or interaction.

Finally, and most importantly, to reduce social interaction to the pursuit of human interests is, in any case, to completely ignore the impact of structured social relations in over-determining the objective agential interests of individuals. A naturalistic conception of 'interests' will not alone suffice, since it is the location of individuals in agential collectivities, structured in turn by prevailing social relations, which furnishes them with definite social interests which are not at all reducible to their elementary psycho-organic needs and interests as members of a particular biological species.

All human beings have the same biological needs for food, drink, clothing, shelter and sexual relations at the requisite quality and quantity to maintain human well-being. All human beings have, moreover, roughly similar psychological needs – including the need for identity, fellowship, community, egalitarian living, and a measure of control or empowerment (i.e. freedom) in the daily running of their lives. Indeed, insofar as human persons possess these psycho-organic needs, they possess also objective human interests in realising or satisfying them, and it is undoubtedly the case that such interests, when acted upon, have been the motivational source of much of the 'struggles from below' which have provided human history and socio-cultural development with its dynamic. Despite this, however, it remains the case that social struggles motivated by the denial of basic human needs can exist only in the context of hierarchical social relations which systematically generate significant asymmetries or inequalities in material resources and human life-chances (i.e. in class-divided societies). For it is only in the context of social relations, which negate or repress the objective species-needs of human beings, that it becomes meaningful to speak of human interests being the source of social struggles aimed at recovering or protecting them.

Furthermore, the mediation of human needs and interests through hierarchical social relations ensures that these often take on emergent properties and become associated with specific social powers ('structural capacities').[19] For example, although employers and wage-workers in modern capitalist society share human needs and interests in common of the kind specified above, the inter-agential relations which pertain between them, over-determined by the total social structure of which they are a part, ensure that these take on a specific socio-cultural and historical coloration. The effective monopoly possession by the bourgeoisie of the means of economic production and subsistence, and its subdivision into mutually competing economic units, ensure that the human needs and interests of its members translate into social interests defined by the competitive accumulation of capital, the appropriation of surplus value from labour, and hence the suppression of general living standards below the cultural average. At the same time, it is the specific causal powers or 'structural capacities' which members of the bourgeoisie derive from their monopoly control or possession of production and exchange (i.e. the power to exploit, hire and fire, to withdraw investment, to relocate capital, etc.) which normally enable them to safeguard these common agential interests against other social groupings.

By contrast, the separation of the proletariat from the means of production and subsistence, and the consequential need of its members to alienate their labour-power as a commodity, translate into social interests rooted in resistance to exploitation, the pursuit of higher wages, increased health and safety at the workplace, and a reduction in the working week. At the same time, since the proletariat of modern capitalism is a majority class which produces value (and hence surplus value) at the point of production, it follows from this that its members are the owners of causal powers (i.e. the power to strike, to work-to-rule, to picket, etc.) which can paralyse the profit system in the pursuit of these (above) social interests.[20]

Here, neither category of 'social interest' (capitalist or proletarian), nor the structural capacities which correspond to each of them, can be collapsed into the undifferentiated category of 'human nature'. For although anchored in human needs, these social interests can only emerge given the specific structural and agential configuration of capitalist society. The failure of rational choice theory to recognise the existence of irreducible social interests and social powers, forged in the interplay between the structural and agential dimensions of social systems, thus leads to an embarrassing exclusion 'from theoretical examination all processes related to the social construction, reproduction and transformation of such interests', and of 'how they relate to other major features of societies (such as institutions, structures, roles etc.) ... and ... to specific historical and socio-cultural contexts'.[21]

The need for social analysis to embrace a stratified conception of 'interests' is thus clear and unambiguous. From this perspective, the concept of interests refers to naturalistic interests (i.e. human interests, definable in terms of the goals, objectives or end-states which have to be acted upon and brought into being if human persons are to satisfy their objective species needs); and social interests (i.e. the specific social practices or strategies – 'modes of articulation' and the 'structural capacities' they bring into play – by which individuals may realise or enhance their human needs, as over-determined by their immersion in particular kinds of social relations, and by their agential location within these social relations). To return to my earlier example, the differential location of capitalists and workers in the relations of production ensure that each can satisfy or guarantee their well-being or life-chances, only by pursuing different (and mutually antagonistic) social 'modes of realisation' of their needs, which involve in turn the exercise of their specific structural powers.

One advantage of this account over 'orthodox' interest-explanations of social agency is that it overcomes the 'randomness of ends' associated with subjectivist definitions of interests, without breaking the link between wants and interests (human interests pertain to 'primary' or 'first-order' wants which correspond to human needs deducible from human nature) and without denying interests a causal role in explaining social agency (human and social interests, anchored in objective human needs, not random subjective 'preferences', are the major source of social agency aimed at societal reform or reproduction). Thus interests can still be conceptualised as the motor which powers social agency (furnishing persons with impelling reasons to act collectively in defence of their life-chances) and as the linchpin connecting interaction to structure (structures furnish individuals with agential interests which motivate their collective struggles to change or reproduce social systems).

A second great strength of the realist account is that the analytical distinction it draws between needs and wants, and its identification of the former but not the latter with interests, allows the theorist to account for the distance between the subjective 'preference set' of individuals and their objective needs, without making the disastrous error of assuming that ideology or power can ever be so absolute that it can function to prevent persons from recognising or acting upon the more fundamental of their human and social interests. To repeat an earlier point, since interests relate to both elementary human needs and the social mechanisms by which they can be satisfied in a given structural and agential context, it follows that the 'preference set' of individuals will generally comprise those wants which correspond with their real interests as well as those which do not. Thus, although unequal power-relations and the impact of dominant ideology does indeed prevent the members of subordinate groups from fully articulating or recognising those desires which, if put into practice, would improve their welfare, and does furthermore induce artificial wants which do not enhance and often damage their life-chances, these can no more prevent the oppressed or exploited recognising the reality of their own alienation than they can eradicate their capacity to resist it in pursuit of at least some of their basic material needs and interests.

The relationship between interests and norms in social theory

Not only does rational choice theory's 'naturalistic model' of agency furnish a grossly reductive and inadequate account of interests (treating these as reducible to subjective wants), but it also sponsors a somewhat cavalier treatment of the relationship between social norms and human and social interests. For Coleman, for instance, norms are derived from interests which, being taken for granted, are assumed to be 'norm-free' prior to their social construction (which occurs, we are told, because rational individuals need to regulate self-interest).[22] For Elster, by contrast, 'motivation in terms of interests, and motivation in terms of norms relate in a zero-sum manner … the more actors follow their self-interest the less they follow social norms and vice-versa'.[23]

The falsity of rational choice theory's reduction of social interests to human (and individual) interests is relatively easy to substantiate (and has already in large measure been substantiated in the foregoing). It is enough to add to what has already been said, that this thesis has been disproved beyond reasonable doubt by the radical differences in the way the various exploiting and exploited classes which have characterised socio-cultural life over the past 10,000 years or so have articulated their material interests.[24]

Coleman's and Elster's treatment of the relationship between norms and interests, hamstrung as it is by the crude distinction between the 'social' and the 'natural' (and in Elster's case between the 'irrational' and the 'rational') does not fare any better. First, it is utterly fallacious to regard human and social interests as 'norm-free'. The very process of recognising and articulating interests is a normative one. The normative articulation of social interests refers us to the simple fact that human beings are endowed by their natural powers of intelligence, self-consciousness and rationality to recognise the reality of their psycho-organic needs and to act in accordance with them. The normative articulation of social interests refers us to the structured historical socio-cultural and agential contexts through which human interests are mediated and thereby 'mutate' into emergent phenomena.

Second, it is also quite wrong to regard norms as unconnected to interests (however these are conceived), for it is obviously the case that the location of individuals in specific structural relations and agential collectivities grants them definite and empirically specifiable material interests, which in turn exert conditioning influences on the kinds of norms and beliefs they are likely to endorse. Elster's own example of a Sicilian vendetta, whereby the agent has to choose between acting in accordance with the social norm of vengeance (as an honour-saving device) or acting in accordance with the instrumentally rational and self-interested strategy of letting bygones be bygones (in order to avoid the risk of being killed), does not support the factual distinction he would like to make between interests and norms.[25] Not only are both these strategies (instrumental self-interest versus honour-saving vengeance) rooted in normative-valuational orientations, but neither is comprehensible without reference to social interests.

Thus, given the institutional context of Mafia rivalries, it is undoubtedly the case that following both the above courses of action would be 'rational' from the point of view of underworld business interests. Mafia vendettas, far from being motivated primarily by romantic considerations, are pursued to eradicate or discourage economic competition from rival criminal organisations. Unleashing the vendetta might indeed risk the lives of the gangsters who embark upon it. But at the same time a failure to follow it through might also endanger the goals and interests of their organisation by giving the 'green light' to rivals who would interpret this as a sign of weakness. Therefore, far from norms being unrelated to interests, as Elster would have it, often these can be explained only in terms of interests. Given the fact that interests relate both to elementary human needs, and to the social practices which individuals have to follow in order to defend or improve their life-chances (as over-determined by their place in stratified social relations), it would be peculiar indeed if these did not play a major role in normative production and articulation.

Of course, one response to the argument that interests always involve norms is to assert that rational self-interest knows no cultural boundaries. This is the preferred strategy of Elster, who counters the claim that 'rationality is simply a Western norm ... with the ... proposition that rationality in its more general features is universal'.[26] In his words, 'there can be no society where people as a rule knowingly refuse to choose the best means to realise their goals'.[27]

Unfortunately for Elster, however, this kind of manoeuvre will not do at all. In the first place, the above defence of the primacy of allegedly pre-social 'interests' over socially constructed 'norms' is ill equipped to deal with the fact that norms are not shaped unilaterally by socio-cultural relations. In fact these are simultaneously conditioned by human needs and interests of a relatively enduring kind. Although the conditional influence of species-being on the articulation of 'thought material' normally adds up to little more than a 'framework' of constraints and enablements within which cultural production takes place, there are instances where it plays a more positive causal role in shaping the content of certain norms (as is evidenced by the socio-cultural universality of egalitarian norms of 'fairness' and 'distributive justice'). [28]

Second, aside from Elster's formulation being empirically false (most historical societal types have not been characterised by instrumental rationality or economic individualism),[29] it is also hopelessly confused (e.g. note the unreflective collapse of 'rationality' into 'instrumental rationality' or 'self-interest'). Although Elster is quite right to point out that formal rationality has a universal historical significance and salience in human society, he is utterly mistaken to equate this with individuated utility-optimisation – a mode of rationality that has only come into its own since the emergence of petty capitalist and capitalist social relations over the past 450 years or so.[30]

Thus a failure on Elster's part to articulate a stratified or differentiated concept of rationality, which is capable of grasping the analytical distinction between *formal* rationality (the logical consistency with which individuals order their beliefs and act in accordance with beliefs and desires) and *substantive* rationality (the specific cultural forms which rational thought and action takes in different kinds of society 'and in different institutional contexts within a society'),[31] allows him to flatten the historical diversity and complexity of humanity's socio-cultural 'life-worlds'. And this in turn encourages his sanctioning of arid, contextless generalisations which if not false are merely truistic (e.g. 'like the platitude that in all societies, as a rule, people choose the best means to realise their goals').[32]

Persons, agents and actors: a realist model of interaction

The preceding discussion introduces the concept of 'social interaction' or 'social action', and seeks to make out a case for grasping the interface between interaction and structure in terms of interests (human and social).

The analysis so far can be summarised as follows. First, social interaction is defined here as those intentional and self-conscious goal-oriented 'doings' of people which involve the coordination of individual activities, the immersion of individuals in mutual interpersonal encounters, or the location of individuals in socio-cultural relations which either provide them with reasons for acting or furnish them with the resources to do so. Second, human agency and social interaction is conceived as being 'somewhat rational' in formal terms (both attitudinally and behaviourally).

Finally, my contention is that it is precisely this 'formal rationality' of human nature which makes it reasonable to suppose that interactants generally seek to act socially in accordance with their interests. Thus, although socially structured power or ideology (or both) is often sufficient to partially deflect individuals in subordinate positions from either comprehending the relationship between their human and social interests (i.e. by mystifying which social interests or 'modes of articulation' are appropriate to defending or enhancing their life-chances), or acting entirely consistently in accordance with either, these are rarely sufficient to prevent them from recognising that they do indeed possess fundamental human needs ('primary wants'), or from attempting to act upon these wherever circumstances permit.

But, whatever the merits of the above formulations, it is doubtful whether these add up to a fully adequate account of social interaction (or of the relationship between interaction and structure). This is because this understanding of the 'interaction order' is a relatively undifferentiated one, which consequently compacts or flattens the rich complexity of social action, and the specific modes of social practice which comprise it, into a homogeneous standard or model. A fully adequate account of interaction has to recognise that the different forms of individual and collective action which animate society must be distinguished analytically from one another, not only on the basis of the typical kinds of subjective motivation or orientation which underpin them, but in terms of the objective structural, institutional and agential 'collectivities' within which social interaction is contextualised.

This is because it is these latter 'frames' of action which determine the range of social practices which are permissible within their respective boundaries, and the nature of the social powers or 'structural capacities' exercised by human agents by dint of their membership of them. Furthermore, I have made the point (in Chapter 2) that a fully adequate understanding of society also has to theorise the properties/powers and needs/interests inherent in human beings by dint of their membership of a particular biological species (i.e. articulate and defend a 'strong' explanatory account of human nature). For whereas the former explains *how* it is human beings can engage in goal-oriented activity, the latter provides a large measure of the explanation of *why* they actually do so (i.e. why human agents seek to translate their species-powers into intentional social activity aimed at the reproduction, modification or transformation of the social relations they inhabit).

In place of an undifferentiated category of 'social interaction', in short, is required a *stratified* typology, of both the distinct social properties which social action takes on as a result of its anchorage within different societal contexts, and of the distinct species-attributes and imperatives of human beings that generate the power which animates social action (and hence the entire social system). Whereas 'social interaction' or 'social action' is best grasped as a kind of 'umbrella' concept covering the manifold types of goal-directed individual and collective activity operative in society, a realist reconstruction of this concept enables the theorist to investigate the interplay between the emergent properties of human persons and their social interaction in shaping socio-cultural processes and outcomes.

To these ends, I would endorse Margaret Archer's injunction to stratify the category of 'people' into a tripartite distinction between 'Subjects', 'Social Agents' and 'Institutional Actors', with the latter concepts referring, respectively, to individuals either as members of agential collectivities (e.g. nation-states, ethnic groups or social classes) or as bearers of institutional roles.[33] Thus, from this perspective, constructing a satisfactory account of individuals and their social interaction entails drawing an analytical distinction between 'species-being' (the psycho-organic tendencies, attributes, needs and interests of human beings), 'agential action' or 'social agency' (the individual and collective activities of human persons insofar as these are conditioned responses to the objective distribution of 'life-chances' structured by their membership of agential collectivities and by inter-agential relations), and 'institutional action' or 'role-action' (the individuated and collaborative activities of people as conditioned by the institutional roles they appropriate from society and personify in subjectively specific ways).

Further analytical distinctions can (and should) be made within this typology. First, 'species-being' can be stratified into its constituent elements (thereby allowing the theorist to distinguish between primary and secondary characteristics of human nature, and the relative importance of each in accounting for social process). Second, 'social agency' or 'agential action' can be internally differentiated between individual agency (i.e. individuals' personal responses or reactions to their material and cultural 'conditions of life', as conditioned by the agential collectivity of which they are a member), and collective agency (i.e. the group responses of persons – articulate or inarticulate, organised or unorganised – to their agential circumstances). Finally, 'agential action' can also be internally differentiated between what Margaret Archer has described as *primary agency* (i.e. those relatively uncoordinated and unorganised responses or reactions – atomistic or collective, articulate or inarticulate – by individuals to their agential and inter-agential situations in society)[34] and *corporate agency* or *organisational agency* (i.e. the institutional forms of coordinated or collaborative action by the members of a collectivity which is either self-consciously oriented towards the attainment of public or strategic goals – e.g. political struggles, military conflicts, diplomatic transactions, commercial explorations',[35] etc. – or towards the pursuit of societal reform or even transformation).

Organisational agents might thus include 'vested interest groups, promotive interest groups, social movements and defensive associations'.[36] Equally, in rare cases, they might also constitute political organisations geared towards the pursuit of a revolutionary transformation of an existing social system and its replacement by an entirely different one – the 'unprecedented form of agency' as Perry Anderson describes it.[37] Typically, organisational agency is a mode of social action which is self-consciously oriented towards the defence or pursuit of agential interests, as these are 'overdetermined' by the structured relations between agential collectivities.

Now, although the aforementioned distinction between 'institutional action' and 'agential action' (or between the 'Role-Actor' and the 'Social Agent') is indispensable in theorising the dynamics of social interaction, and how this feeds into institutional change or statics in the role-ensemble of society (more on this later), it is nonetheless important to stress that it is the latter which enjoys explanatory primacy in bringing about macro (i.e. structural) change or stasis in social systems. This is because the structural relations between agential collectivities, by shaping asymmetrically the distribution of finite material resources available to each, and by defining the objective social interests which the members of a collectivity have in common *vis-à-vis* the members of another, provide social agents with a powerful impetus towards (or compelling reasons for) engaging in collective action aimed at the defence, reform or overturning of existing social relations. Social agency is, then, a privileged mode of social action, because it relates individuals most directly or intimately to the systemic features of the societies they inhabit. By contrast, there is of course no corresponding dynamic underlying role-action within the institutional framework of society which could conceivably be held responsible for generating the same societal effects. This is because inasmuch as individuals are the bearers of social roles, they are 'bound in' by the normative requirements which go with them, and there are fairly stringent limits to the degree to which they can reinterpret their social roles and yet remain incumbents of them.

It is precisely the causal primacy of the nexus between human nature and social agency in accounting for how and why structural and cultural change or stability takes place, which justifies my focus, in the analysis that follows, upon these particular aspects of the 'people' which animate social systems. The basic tripartite model for approaching the explanation of societal change or its absence must therefore be rooted in the dialectical interplay between 'species-being' and 'social agency' (the latter as conditioned by overall structural social relations), with 'institutional action' emerging from 'agential action', and both institutional action and social agency having their anchorage or 'micro-foundations' in the species properties and dispositions inherent in self-conscious human beings.

Since time and space do not allow a full treatment or defence of the analytical distinctions I have drawn in the concept of interaction, I will devote the remainder of this section to justifying just two of them – namely those between corporate and primary agency, and between social agency and role-action.[38] First I will examine the interface between corporate agency and primary agency in generating *structural-cultural* and *agential* elaboration or statics in social systems. Then I will examine the interface between social agency and role-action in generating *institutional* elaboration or statics within the role-ensemble of society. These tasks completed, the fourth and final section of this chapter will be devoted to accounting for those properties of persons (mind, self-consciousness and personal identity) which allow them to become agents and actors and self-construct social identities.

Corporate agency and primary agency

What is the relationship between corporate agency and primary agency? As the organised and self-conscious political expression of agential interests it is, of course, easy to regard corporate agency as a uniquely privileged mode of social interaction, insofar as bringing about structural-cultural change or stable reproduction is concerned. This is because 'only those who are aware of what they want, can articulate it to themselves and others, and have organised in order to get it, can engage in concerted action to re-shape the structural or cultural feature in question'.[39]

By contrast, primary agency, as a mode of social agency which lacks collective organisation and worked-out political objectives or strategies, and which in the normal course of events generates aggregate societal effects unknowingly and unintentionally, simply by being a part of the social environment (as individuals 'react and respond to their context as part and parcel of living in it'),[40] can just as easily be portrayed as simply a 'passive' enablement of societal change or statics. From this point of view, the best way of interpreting the distinction between organisational and primary agency, is to regard the former as alone acting positively in bringing about structural or cultural morphogenesis or stasis, whereas the latter functions instead to furnish the 'raw material' (i.e. social interests and structural powers) which motivate and enable individuals sharing a common location in social relations to form organisational agents geared towards furthering or defending their life-chances.

One obvious strength of this account is that it is capable of specifying the differential circumstances which have to obtain if structural-cultural and agential change or stability are to occur in a society. Such an account begins with corporate agents engaging in self-conscious social action, and interacting strategically with primary agents in pursuit of their agential interests in a given structural and cultural environment. In acting strategically on their interests, corporate agents generate (intentionally or unintentionally) molecular changes in the social environment they share with primary agents, pressurising the latter to respond to their changing conditions of life in different ways, either by formulating their own corporate agents or by reacting in a relatively unorganised and sometimes spontaneous (atomistic or associational) manner.

This 'unleashes a stream of ... environmental pressures and problems which affect the attainment of the [former's] promotive interests',[41] forcing them to modify their own strategic agency, as they seek to continue the pursuit of their interests in a context reshaped by the corporate and primary responses of the latter. At the 'macro' (i.e. systemic) level this process will result 'in either morphostasis or morphogenesis depending on the outcome of interaction'.[42] At the same time, however, 'since social interaction is the sole mechanism governing stability or change, what goes on during it also determines the morphostasis or morphogenesis of [a]gency itself'. This is because 'in its attempt to sustain or transform the social system, [agency] is inexorably drawn into sustaining or transforming the categories of [c]orporate and [p]rimary [a]gents themselves'.[43]

In social systems characterised by a conjunction of cultural hegemony (i.e. a dominant culture shared in common by the various elite groupings which constitute its socially dominant class) and structural monolithism ('the superimposition of elites and a heavy concentration of resources which together [constrain the] crystallisation of opposition'),[44] as was notably the case in many of the ancient and medieval Asiatic societies which comprised the 'tributary mode of production', the processes that might lead to structural-cultural and agential elaboration are more often and more likely to be short-circuited by countervailing pressures towards stable reproduction. (I will not say that agential pressures towards change in these societies were extinguished altogether, since 'morphostatic' social systems, as opposed to 'morphostatic' situations within societies, exist only in the imagination.)

One important reason for this state of affairs is that primary agents, in these societal circumstances, encounter both powerful ideological constraints on their ability to articulate cultural dissent (i.e. a hegemonic dominant culture embodying few manifest exploitable internal contradictions), and equally powerful material and institutional constraints on their ability to articulate and mobilise their agential powers or 'structural capacities' in an effective manner. In the tributary mode of production, for instance, this took the form of a powerful centralised state apparatus which possessed the organisational capacities – military and political – to prevent the direct producers translating their fermenting unrest into corporate agency oriented towards societal reform or revolution.[45]

A second reason for this state of affairs is that the ruling classes which dominate relatively stagnant societies are as much constrained by 'the absence of ideational or organisational alternatives'[46] as they are enabled by the manner in which cultural hegemony and structural monolithism dovetail in curtailing effective organised opposition to their rule. In these circumstances, structural and cultural domination tend to complement one another in ensuring that system reproduction predominates over system elaboration, since elites 'have no immediate alternative but to live together' and 'every interest in continuing to do so'.[47]

If stable system reproduction may often arise from what Archer describes as 'the superimposition of structure and culture',[48] which operates to hold back the emergence of corporate agents from the ranks of the propertyless and disenfranchised, it follows that system elaboration or transformation is best facilitated by social relations which pre-empt or break down the material and ideological hegemony of powerful social groups which erode the incapacity of primary agents to fully articulate and promote their interests. Such a state of affairs has not been untypical of most historical societies (it is societal stagnancy, not change, which is a special case and requires particular explanation), because it is only in exceptional cases that the overall configuration of a social system allows unopposed domination by a unified class or elite.

Normally, of course, social systems provide a greater or lesser scope for 'the progressive expansion of corporate agents, of those who are numbered among them, and a divergence of the interests represented by them, thus resulting in substantial conflict between them'.[49] This in turn generates the potential for social change. For unless there are especially stringent structural and cultural constraints operative within hierarchical social relations, which function to discourage primary agents from articulating their interests and organising collectively in their defence or promotion, there is no compelling reason to suppose they will not do so.

The drama of morphogenesis/morphostasis thus involves the following process. Corporate agents, the organisational capacities of dominant elites or classes, act purposively in defence or pursuit of their agential interests, thereby shaping the social environment which primary agents inhabit, forcing the latter to respond to their changing (and usually worsening) social and material circumstances. This reaction of primary agents to the strategic pressures placed on them by corporate agents will either take the form of passive aggregate responses to environmental stimuli (in which case system dynamics will at best offer them stagnant and at worst declining life-chances), or it will take the form of organised resistance (in which case system elaboration at least offers them the promise, contingent upon a successful struggle against their oppressors, of improved life-chances and a greater degree of societal enfranchisement generally).

Which of these scenarios is most likely to develop in any specific interactional context is contingent not only upon the structural and cultural configuration of the social system in question, and the structural powers and material resources which primary agents possess or can mobilise, but also upon their general state of consciousness (anger or apathy, demoralisation or willingness to fight, greater or lesser political awareness of agential interests, etc.) on the eve of a major crisis. On the one hand, where the responses of primary agents to the strategic pressures exerted upon them by corporate agents are merely passive aggregate ones, or where these assume organised forms which are quickly curtailed or extinguished by dominant elites (due often to the economic and political immaturity of subordinate groups), the overall result is agential elaboration by and structural reform on behalf of the propertied and powerful alone, as dominant groups adjust their strategies and goals, in accordance with the ever-changing problems and pressures posed by the mere environmental presence and reactions of the propertyless or otherwise oppressed to their social situation. Hence the 'morphostasis' of structure and agency.

On the other hand, where the responses of primary agents to the effects of corporate agency take the form of organised collaborative resistance to the powerful and propertied, which can no longer simply be crushed (given the maturing political and economic strength of the former), the result is the growth of the category of corporate agents, the decline of that of primary agents amongst the previously unorganised (as the former become absorbed or transformed into the latter), and the initiation of 'bottom-up' processes of reform or transformation in the interests of the disenfranchised or propertyless where social struggles are successful. Hence the 'morphogenesis' of structure and agency respectively.

The morphogenesis of structure and agency: the example of British social policy

I will illustrate this rather abstract picture of the dynamics of societal and agential elaboration with the concrete example of the evolution of British social and welfare policy between 1750 and present times. It is (or should be) common knowledge that during the early phase of industrialisation (1750–1860), prior to working-class suffrage in the latter nineteenth century, the state power was transparently and unequivocally a 'committee for managing the common affairs of the bourgeoisie' and landed gentry. This state of affairs was reflected in the pattern of social policy during this period.

Some of the most significant innovations in social policy introduced by the state here included the formation of a police force independent of the military (created to control 'riotous assembly' and safeguard the property of the wealthy in the growing urban centres),[50] the construction of a large-scale system of penal institutions (to incarcerate the mass of urban paupers, beggars and petty thieves generated by the expulsion of the peasantry from the land and the violent fluctuations in the labour market),[51] and the strengthening (or introduction) of vicious legal sanctions designed to counteract 'property crime' (hangings, floggings, mutilations, deportations, etc.).[52]

Other crucial policy initiatives were the following. First, the revamped Masters and Servants Act – originally introduced in 1721 – which granted employers draconian contractual powers over their workers. Second, the Combination Acts of 1799 and 1800, which criminalised working-class political and economic organisation and agitation. Third, the New Poor Law of 1834, which was designed to terrorise workers into accepting bare subsistence wages and the most inhuman of working conditions under threat of the workhouse. Fourth, the Enclosure Acts, which arbitrarily redefined common property as private property, and which lent state backing to the efforts of landlords and capitalist farmers to turf the peasantry off the land. Finally, laws against vagrancy and trespass, and the periodic banning of trade union organisation and the right to demonstrate (during periods of heightened class tension and social unrest).[53]

My account of the 'morphogenesis' of the 'interventionist' British state thus commences with structural and agential 'morphostasis'. In this scenario, the grossly asymmetrical balance of power between the propertied and the propertyless (i.e. the abstraction of the newly forming proletariat from any formal or informal representation in the institutional structures of economy and polity) enabled the corporate agents of the former to pursue their interests largely unhampered by the latter. Agential elaboration during this period, in so far as it was causally efficacious in stimulating social policy initiatives, was enacted exclusively by the propertied, in response to the problems posed by the presence and reactions of (initially) primary agents to a social world not of their own making, involving the introduction of new organisational capacities (legal and institutional) designed to allow the continued pursuit of their interests in a social environment modified by social interaction. By contrast, organised agential responses by the propertyless during the later part of this period (e.g. the Luddite revolt of 1811–13, the Chartist movement of 1837–48, and the formation of the earliest trade unions in the 1820s), rooted as they were in an undeveloped minority working class, tended to be short-lived, and were destroyed by military repression before they had a chance to establish and elaborate themselves and generate a strategic impact upon state policy-making.[54]

The initial faltering efforts of primary agents to self-organise in resistance to exploitation were, in short, shipwrecked by a combination of the organised power of a confident ruling class and their own political and economic immaturity. Because of this, agential elaboration by the working class was no more advanced at the close of this period than it was at the beginning. The 'nightwatchman state', concerned only with establishing the political and economic preconditions of untrammelled capitalism, hence reigned supreme. And even those few social policy initiatives (e.g. the Factory Acts of 1825, 1833, 1844 and 1847) which appeared to benefit labour (by reducing the number of work-hours children had to submit to employers) were stimulated not so much by working-class pressure, but by concerns amongst sections of the bourgeoisie and the state elite that overworked children were subject to 'moral degradation' (and were thus in need of ethical education if they were not to become a threat to 'legitimate' society), hampered the future stability or flexibility of the labour market, and generated the potential for unrest amongst their elders (whose wages were being undercut). In any case, of course, pressure from other sections of the business lobby ensured that the factory legislation of this period had either a negligible impact on the reality of child exploitation (the new laws were not rigorously enforced and sanctions were not readily applied to transgressors), or worsened the living standards of the proletariat as a whole (working-class parents were not paid higher wages to reimburse them for the loss of their children's income).[55]

In the subsequent period of British history (1860–1939) the domination exercised by the propertied classes over the state was to become substantially modified (though not, of course, eradicated or even seriously undermined).[56] The pattern of structural and societal reform still remained for the most part 'top-down', controlled mostly by the corporate agents of the state and capital, and was motivated as much by external rather than internal agential pressures. But at the same time the gradual consolidation by the working class of their own corporate capacities (i.e. trade union organisation and latterly party political organisation), which were developed in response to the huge strategic pressures placed on them by the corporate agents of the propertied during the previous period, did ensure that subsequent social and welfare reform became somewhat 'watered down' (a little less stick and a little more carrot).

The limited and inadequate social reforms from the mid-nineteenth- to the early twentieth century were motivated primarily by three major agential concerns. First, political fear by the elite of an increasingly mobilised and organised working class and its potential to press for radical reforms or even 'socialist reconstruction' (even where it was not yet doing so). Second, its corresponding awareness that a measure of reform (especially in health, social security and education) was necessary to maintain the competitiveness of British capital *vis-à-vis* international rivals. Third, its attempts to prevent the 'moral contamination of the 'respectable' working class by the 'feckless residuum' of casualised workers who were reputedly prone to 'malingering' and riotous assembly.

The corporate agents of the working class thus had to be conceded a certain measure of progressive legislation to contain their grievances (or potential demands) within the bounds of the existing social order, and to negate the appeal of socialism. At the same time, the utmost repression had to be exercised to liquidate the threat of the 'residuum' by means of slum clearance, the sterilisation or deportation of 'undesirables', and the disqualification of its members from any welfare protection. Furthermore, the cumulative experiences of military weakness (as exposed by the Crimean and Boer wars) combined with relative economic decline (as revealed by the speed at which Germany, the USA, Japan and France were catching up and in some cases overtaking Britain in terms of labour productivity and volume of output) ensured that measures would have to be taken to improve the health, education and hence motivation of the working class if the long-term survival of the Empire was to be safeguarded.[57]

That such agential concerns were to the forefront of social policy during this period is evidenced by the very nature of the welfare legislation provided. The public health legislation of the 1870s, for instance, was not the product of working-class or union agitation, but was introduced by the state to stabilise the labour market and safeguard the health of the rich (in the wake of a number of large-scale cholera outbreaks – originating in the urban slums – which for the bourgeoisie had the unfortunate 'side effect' of wiping out skilled workers and members of their own class as well as the unskilled, unemployed, and 'undeserving poor').[58] Moreover, a concern with improving the efficiency of Britain's economy and armed forces was, for example, the dominant motivation informing the introduction of the 1906 Education Act (which sought to give local authorities the – discretionary, of course! – power to finance the provision of school meals for working-class children).[59]

More generally, of course, state provision had to be held within the most stringent fiscal limits (to limit the tax burden on capital) and was specifically designed not to compromise in the slightest the stable reproduction of the low-wage economy.[60] At all costs, the workers and their families had to be discouraged from indulging in the delights of unproductive 'sponging' (or punished by means of welfare disenfranchisement or stigmatisation for a life of unproductive or 'dissolute' conduct). Social services and welfare relief had therefore to co-exist with the workhouse system and be as sparse and punitive as possible. Indeed, even where market considerations had no direct relevance to social policy – as was true, for example, of the provision of old-age pensions in 1908 – the cold hand of liberal financial orthodoxy ensured that the provision offered was paltry to say the least. So it was that Lloyd-George's 'new deal' for the elderly added up to a mere five shillings a week for individuals and 7*s.* 6*d.* for couples (which was insufficient to lift its incumbents out of absolute poverty) and was restricted to people over seventy years of age (during a period where average life expectancy for workers was considerably less than this).[61]

Furthermore, the social hierarchies and politico-ethical values of the propertied had to be manifest in social policy and welfare reform, lest the workers perceive they were receiving 'something for nothing' and come to expect 'user-friendly' socialistic-type reforms from a benevolent state in the future. National Insurance, for instance (in its original incarnation in the 1911 Act), aside from being funded largely from the wages of the working class (the 'one in five rule'), was to be held to the bare physical minimum to ensure subsistence, and was to discriminate on the basis of 'deserving' and 'undeserving' poor.[62]

The same liberal moralism and social authoritarianism was also evident in the workings of the Old Age Pensions legislation of 1908, which sought to exclude from coverage those infirm workers who were unable to 'prove' that they had been habitually employed in a 'respectable' trade.[63] And, in a similar vein (to offer another example), education provision which was first proposed during the 1830s (the heyday of Chartism) to counter the perceived 'seditious' influence of the informal schooling provided within the working-class community, was later introduced (in the 1870 Act) and subsequently strengthened (in the 1891 and 1902 Acts) with the quite explicit purpose of 'gentling the masses' – i.e. preaching a respect for property, nation and empire – and introducing working-class children to the bare minimum of literacy and numeracy necessary for their future roles in the labour market.[64]

The major reason why the workers' movement was prepared to go along with welfare reforms which were at best perfunctory (and at worst punitive) is explainable rather more in terms of ideological than material weaknesses. For the trade union bureaucracy now possessed the political and organisational resources to campaign energetically for genuinely progressive welfare reform in the interests of the propertyless, and this was especially the case following the concession of the working-class franchise and the formation of the Labour Representative Council in 1900 (excepting of course the period from 1894–1907 in the aftermath of Taff Vale). The pro-liberal political stance of the labour movement, forged as much by poor education, intellectual poverty and a lack of knowledge of socialist theory as it was by sound argument (though also by a large measure of political opportunism), ensured that its political and industrial leaders could imagine no alternative to the orthodox deflationary economic programme practised by bourgeois governments prior to the 1930s. Consequently, a system of universal state benefits or pro-labour intervention in the workings of the market to counteract the boom/slump cycle was for them a utopian hope. Indeed, this was a belief which lamentably became enshrined in the 'do-nothing' social policies of the first Labour administrations of 1924 and 1929–31, whose most disgraceful failing was their refusal to combat growing unemployment and to alleviate the poverty caused by unemployment.[65]

Nonetheless, despite the ideational poverty of the union leadership (and latterly of the Labour Party's parliamentary elite), the very existence of these reforms, and of others which *were* campaigned for by the unions (most notably the introduction of old-age pensions in 1908), would quite possibly not have emerged at all, were it not for the pressures exerted on the state and capital by the developing industrial and political organisational agencies of the working class. It is, in this respect, an interesting historical fact to note that the working-class franchise (introduced in the 1867 and 1884 Acts) was only conceded by the state *following* the introduction of many of these early tentative moves towards a welfare state worthy of the name, and following the defeat of the revolutionary Chartist movement of 1837–48 (which itself gave the subsequent development of the trade union movement in the 1850s, 1860s and 1870s a huge impetus).[66]

A more complex pattern of social policy has been evident in the early post-war years (1945–74). Initially, the dynamics of societal elaboration were no longer expressed simply in terms of 'top-down' reform (exploiting the ideological weakness of oppositional corporate agents) but expressed for the first time also powerful and ideologically coherent 'bottom-up' pressures for change. The construction of the Beveridgean welfare state between 1945 and 1951 reflected the convergence of two powerful social blocs: state monopoly capital and organised labour. Capital required a comprehensive welfare state not only in order to placate a working class radicalised by the experience of thirty years of war and depression and of promises of 'a home fit for heroes', but in order to equip the workers with the higher level of cultural and technological know-how required for successful competition in the post-colonial world (mere literacy and numeracy would no longer suffice). The labour movement, by contrast, wanted progressive welfare legislation and quality public services for the simple purpose of improving the quality of life of its members, and it emerged from the war with the organisational resources (industrial and political) to campaign effectively for them.[67]

This temporary and uneasy alliance between rival corporate agents representing opposed social classes was made possible by the economic logic of 'state monopoly capitalism' and the ideological forms it gave rise to. The effective discrediting of supply-side monetarist economics by the Great Depression allowed the dominance of a new intellectual orthodoxy – Keynesian demand management and deficit budgeting – which held that governments could guarantee economic growth and stability by boosting domestic demand through full employment, government borrowing and public expenditure.[68] Not only did this new Keynesian orthodoxy render welfarism less ideologically unpalatable to those vested interest groups organised in defence of capital, hence weakening their resistance to the demands of the TUC and Labour Party, but it also gifted the labour movement the ideological capacities it had previously lacked to argue convincingly for radical reform in all areas of social life (the neo-classical argument that inequality, poverty, deflation and the minimal state were indispensable to economic success could now be trumped).

The end result of this social interaction between rival corporate agents was hence the relatively benign 'Butskellism', which dominated the thinking of Labour and Conservative governments alike throughout the post-war boom.[69] The greater ideological and organisational power of the labour movement (which in the context of full employment could only gather strength, and with it the confidence to fight for yet wider political, social and economic reforms), in harness with the greater capacity of capital and the state to surrender reforms (in the context of the boom), allowed the construction of a social environment (the 'permissive' society as today's reactionaries describe it) in which manifold new corporate agents (oriented on a wide and broad base of issues, including race, gender, environment, etc.) could emerge and flourish. Here corporate agency and primary agency now found itself immersed in a social environment positively bloated with promotive interest groups, in which the unorganised sections of the populace were declining (the morphogenesis of agency), and in which laissez-faire capitalism developed into organised or corporate welfare capitalism (the morphogenesis of structure).

It is a commonplace that the subsequent period of state welfare reform and social policy (1974 to the present day) has seen the initiatives and trends of the previous period thrown into sharp reverse. Why has this been the case? As we have seen, the so-called 'Butskellism' (welfare state capitalism), which generated a social environment in which the organisation of primary agents (into unions, political parties, pressure groups, single-issue campaigns, etc.) gathered pace, was rooted in and dependent upon a particular combination of economic, class and ideological circumstances, which was itself the outcome of the previous hundred years or so of social interaction. The balance of class forces brought about by a strong, articulate and mobilised labour movement, in harness with the changing economic needs of capital and the changed economic logic of corporate capitalism (which together allowed an ideological convergence of sorts between capital and labour on the issue of welfare and social reform), created in the conditions of the long post-war boom a temporary and unstable truce between the rival corporate blocs.

As long as this truce remained in place, the state elite could take on the coloration of a corporate actor which stood above the opposing class interests of civil society (or more generally between oppressors and oppressed). The trouble was, of course, that the state submitted voluntarily to the political demands of organised labour (and other corporate agents rooted in the oppressed) only inasmuch as these could be reconciled with the interests of the propertied, and this in turn was dependent on the post-war economic boom continuing indefinitely. Once the limits of capitalist expansion were reached at the close of the 1960s, and the system crashed into a new period of chronic crises and generalised stagnancy from the 1970s onwards, the compromise became unworkable, and the class aspect of the state was thrown into sharp relief. Hence the sharp 'rightwards turn' in social policy since the mid-1970s. The state and corporate capital now acted together to 'roll back' welfare spending and the gains of the labour movement and other promotive interest groups.[70]

A new 'morphostatic' situation gradually emerged in social policy, as oppositional groups generally found themselves unable to influence government thinking, as the trade union movement declined in membership, confidence, militancy and organisational capacity, and as the major party political opposition (the Labour Party) meekly adapted itself to the agential interests of big business and its allies in the state machine. (In the latter case, of course, the capitulation of 'New Labour' to big business has been carried through by cravenly exploiting the demoralisation of the workers' movement to justify a stampede to the right which renders its politics indistinguishable from those of the unabashedly pro-bourgeois parties.)[71]

Again the question needs to be asked: how was it that one of the most organised and powerful labour movements in the western world (the product of patient advance over a century or more) became demoralised and defeated by the strategic corporate actions of the state and capital within the space of a mere ten years? Once more the answer is to be found in the ideological vacuity of Labourism, which fed into a weakness of leadership when the crisis of the 1970s finally broke. As argued earlier, the changing 'needs' and logic of capital in the immediate post-war context of 'state capitalism', as expressed intellectually in neo-Keynesian economic theory, provided the leadership of the labour movement with the ideological resources to justify the gradualist and reformist stance it had adopted unwaveringly since its origins. Previously when capitalism had lurched into crisis, as in the 1930s, the TUC's and Labour Party's uncritical acceptance of supply-side economics (the so-called 'Treasury View') ensured the political and industrial paralysis of its organisational powers. Just at the point where the workers required strong leadership and firm action to combat mass sackings, the erosion of workplace rights, wage cuts and public spending cutbacks, the corporate agents of labour were unable to offer it, bound as they were to the idea that crises could only be combated by a policy of retrenchment, deflation and wage controls.[72]

With the renewed onset of the pre-war boom/slump pattern and generalised economic stagnation in the period after the mid-1970s, and the resultant effective discrediting of Keynesianism as a viable alternative to monetarism, the same intellectual paralysis inevitably resurfaced. As before, the leadership of the labour movement found itself politically disarmed by its inability to justify reforms in a context where it was no longer respectable to believe that one could 'spend one's way out of a crisis'. A failure to articulate a genuinely socialist ideational and political opposition to capitalism (which would have demonstrated that a fight for socialist relations of production was the only solution to the crisis) ensured that no concerted or unified opposition to attacks on welfare, public spending, full employment, employee rights and conditions, and trade union organisation was ever mounted.[73]

My account of the morphogenesis of structure and agency in relation to welfare reform and social policy thus concludes unhappily with stagnation or 'morphostasis', as progressive social elaboration runs into the limits imposed by bourgeois social relations in the epoch of long-term capitalist decline.[74] The future for welfare and progressive social legislation looks bleak indeed, as the government continually seeks to implement never-ending rounds of cuts in health, education and social security (as a proportion of GDP and as measured in terms of a failure to provide annually a level of resources which would prevent a cumulative decline in the quality of provision), as the official political opposition devote their policy not to improving the situation of the working class, minorities and the poor but to reassuring business that 'the economy is safe in our hands', and as the trade union bureaucracy 'sits on its hands' and insists that the workers must 'wait for Labour' (or now wait for Labour to be returned for a second term!).

Such political opportunism and ideological vacuity must always be the norm where the crisis of capitalism is so deep and so intractable that reformism can no longer justify itself by delivering reforms. At the time of writing, society stands at the crossroads of the organic crisis where further progressive agential and structural morphogenesis cannot be contained within the boundaries of the existing social system, and can only be released by the revolutionary replacement of capitalism with a classless socialist society. Yet, given the political stance of corporate labour ('reformism without reforms'),[75] the morphostatic scenario seems likely to persist until such time as the propertyless, under-privileged and oppressed break with the reformist politics of the trade union bureaucracy and replace the Labour Party with new corporate agents capable of better representing their interests.

Morphogenesis and structural transformation: the dynamics of social revolutions

I contend that the foregoing conceptualisation of the dynamics of societal morphogenesis/stasis works reasonably well as an account of the dynamics of structural-cultural and agential elaboration within the bounds of a given social system. This is because here corporate agents do indeed appear to be the sole 'positive' causes of social change or stasis. But I now want to argue that it has limitations as an account of those 'bottom-up' revolutionary social struggles which seek to overturn social systems in the interests of the propertyless. This is because primary agents are, in hierarchical societies entering into organic crisis, more often than not the major source of the social struggles which shake them to their foundations, spontaneously exploding into radical unrest or protest, often outflanking those corporate agents (in terms of militancy) which reputedly represent their interests, and acquiring elementary organisational forms in the very act or process of entering into struggle.

This was notably the case, for instance, in the 1905 revolution in Russia. Here the (largely) non-unionised working class responded to the privations of Russia's disastrous war against Japan (in the context of political repression and economic backwardness) by spontaneously erupting into a wave of strikes in St Petersburg. This gave rise on their part to the organisation of a mass demonstration (ending in the Bloody Sunday massacre) and, in response to this repression, a general strike, the establishment of the St Petersburg soviet, mutiny in the navy, even an uprising in Moscow, and all of this (bar the Moscow insurrection) without much prompting by the opposition parties (which were taken aback by events).[76] The same basic pattern has been repeated in other revolutionary and semi-revolutionary situations – for instance, in the Portuguese revolution of 1974, and in the events of May 1968 in France.[77]

One important reason for this capacity of primary agents to set in motion sudden and dramatic processes of (prospective) societal change is that, despite their lack of organisation and a worked-out political strategy for pursuing their interests, they often embody a keen political awareness of their own agential interests, and with this a high degree of anger and resentment at the manner of which society and its vested interests operate to deny or frustrate these. In these situations it often requires only the introduction of a particularly insensitive government policy, the outbreak of a political scandal or crisis, a major military defeat, or a dramatic change in the fortunes of the economy, to ignite the 'touchpaper' of mass unrest or protest amongst those who have hitherto appeared to act entirely passively, apathetically and atomistically in response to structural and agential pressures. At the same time, however, processes of radical primary agency, precisely because they are initiated by people who lack fully articulated political goals or strategies, and who furthermore lack tactical experience of agential struggles and organisational know-how to conduct these successfully, do require corporate agents oriented to their interests if they are to stand a realistic chance of fully formulating and achieving their objectives. For when confronted by the organised power of the state and capital, the propertyless simply cannot afford the luxury of an 'on the spot' or 'trial and error' learning process in the heat of the struggle between them.

The failure of the 1905 revolution in Russia, and of more recent revolutionary socialist opportunities in China (1925–7), Germany (1919–23), Chile (1972–3) and Iran (1979–80), are chilling reminders of the unhappy consequences which can befall the working-class movement where it lacks organisational capacities and experienced (and non-opportunistic) political leadership.[78] Conversely, the equally unhappy fate of, for instance, the British Labour Party and trade union movement in recent years (the 'great moving rightwards show')[79] is a salient testament to the political degeneration and paralysis which can engulf corporate agents where the primary agents they are anchored in and purport to represent lack the confidence (in this case due to the experience of class betrayal and defeat) to pressurise their representatives to campaign energetically in defence of their real (i.e. objectively structured) interests.[80]

It was, of course, an awareness of the complexity of the interplay between corporate and primary agency in bringing about system change or stasis which led the greatest of proletarian revolutionists, i.e. Lenin, to rethink his own elitist formulae of *What Is To Be Done?*.[81] His subsequent realisation (in response to the events of the 1905 revolution) that the working class could *spontaneously* acquire a revolutionary socialist outlook and some of the organisational capacities to act upon it (instilled in them to some degree by the exigencies of collaborative labour and factory discipline) encouraged him to postulate a more dialectical relationship between class and party (or between primary agency and corporate agency), whereby both would perform a positive causal role in ushering in a socialist society.

On this view, instead of initiating a socialist uprising, the function of the revolutionary party was to offer organisational know-how and advice on tactics and strategy to the working class, prior to and during their entry into the fray, to demonstrate in practice (by gaining the trust of the workers) its right to assume a leading role in any revolutionary situation, and to act as the 'memory' of the working class movement (i.e. distil the lessons – theoretical and practical – of its previous defeats) and thereby ensure that the revolutionary workers would not repeat the errors of previous struggles. At the same time, however, the function of the revolutionary party was also to learn from the experiences and insights of workers in struggle, to strive to involve the most able and militant workers in party activity, and to utilise their spontaneity, militancy, creativity and enthusiasm in order to blow away the bureaucratic sclerosis instilled by party routine and procedure (which often ensured that the Bolsheviks were more to the rearguard rather than to the vanguard of potentially revolutionary situations).[82]

The invaluable lesson to be learned from generations of activists wrestling with the problems of socialist organisation and its relationship to working-class struggle is simply that both primary and corporate agency can equally be a positive force for societal change. Indeed, certain kinds of societal change – namely the revolutionary transformation or overturning of a social system – are quite impossible unless primary and organisational agents both play a positive causal role in social struggles. For these can only succeed given mass participation by the organised and hitherto unorganised alike. It is only where corporate agents attempt to substitute themselves for primary agents during social upheavals, or where primary agents are forced to embark upon radical struggles in the absence of corporate agents oriented on their interests, that movements aimed at revolutionary structural and cultural remodelling tend to fail.[83] It should go without saying, of course, that social movements 'from below' powered by both organisational and primary agents are those which stand the better chance of ushering in structural or cultural reform within a given social system.

The key difficulty with the realist conception of social agency is, therefore, that it drives too deep a wedge between corporate and primary agents, making it something of a mystery how the latter can spontaneously transform themselves into the former, and in doing so often outflank and outdo established organisations formally based on their interests. In other words, if primary agents are to be conceived simply as 'objects to whom things happen', as collectivities of individuals who 'neither articulate projects nor mobilise for their attainment', or who 'cannot be strategically involved in the modelling or remodelling of structure or culture',[84] it becomes impossible to explain how many of the fiercest class struggles in history could have occurred at all. After all, such class struggles often take place in social contexts where 'morphostatic' situations prevail (i.e. where vested interest groups have extinguished or curtailed the emergence of corporate agents pertaining to the disenfranchised),[85] and furthermore are often responsible for creating the corporate or organisational forms which enable subordinate groups to win for themselves an effective say in future strategic decision-making.[86]

The purpose of making this argument is not to suggest that the realist understanding of primary agency is simply wrong or misplaced. Rather it is to suggest that it is over-simple, capable of grasping certain ways of being a primary agent but not of others. To bridge the chasm between primary agency and corporate agency, it is necessary to define the latter simply in terms of the organisational capacities which primary agents self-construct in response to the strategic pressures exerted upon them by vested interest groups, without making any assumptions as to whether or not the former are actually capable of strategic collective action or collaborative political mobilisation in defence of their interests. This is, I suggest, an empirical question, contingent upon an analysis of the society and social situation in question. From this viewpoint, instead of being necessarily passive or apathetic, primary agents will or will not be so depending on the level of political radicalism, militancy and self-awareness of their agential interests which they may or may not have achieved.

To speak of primary agency, then, is to address not only the unorganised responses of the under-privileged and propertyless to their social situation, but also their general state of consciousness, and that of their most 'advanced' sections at any particular time. Though both appropriate organisational forms and radical political consciousness are indispensable components of any revolutionary transformation of social relations, they cannot be conflated into a single analytical category (i.e. of 'corporate agency'). This is because corporate agents tend to be thrown up by the social struggles of primary agents (which indicates the former are capable of articulating projects and engaging in collaborative strategic action)[87] and have often operated deliberately to repress (i.e. 'constitutionalise') the militancy and struggles of those primary agents they represent, hampering the prospects of radical structural change in their interests.[88] The 'unprecedented form of agency' (socialist revolution) thus requires not simply mass participation by primary agents (who in the process of acting and struggling in defence of their interests assume organisational capacities) but also the intervention of a particular form of corporate agent (i.e. a revolutionary Marxist party independent of reformist organisations and yet anchored in the workplace and community of the propertyless) if it is to succeed.[89]

Social agency and institutional action

The necessity of drawing an analytical distinction between the social agent and the role-actor, and of conceiving of the latter as emergent from the former, can be demonstrated easily enough by revealing the shortcomings of so-called 'social action' perspectives, of the kind to be found in most versions of the 'sociological conception of agency'. For symbolic interactionists, functionalists and social constructionists alike, human beings are generally regarded as synonymous with social selves, and social selves are regarded as synonymous with social actors whose interests are definable in terms of the social roles (especially the normative 'rules' which are applicable to roles) which they appropriate from society as their own and impersonate or personify in specific ways.[90] From this perspective, in other words, social interaction is explainable in terms of the normative rules which are said to govern or 'pre-script' the institutional roles which individuals select from society and 'act out' in a particularistic style.

The problems with social action theory as it is conceived above may be usefully summarised as follows. First, quite apart from 'putting out of business' the human person emergent from the interface between the psycho-organic makeup of humanity's 'species-being' and the experiential life-process of the individual, the failure of its practitioners to distinguish between the agential and institutional dimensions of the 'interaction order' leads to an inability to theorise the dynamics of collective action, and to a refusal to admit that different role-positions in society might allow their incumbents to function either as 'macro-actors' or 'micro-actors' in everyday interaction (hence undermining their view of social order as resulting from an aggregation of micro-transactions between 'laypersons'). Second, social action theory's 'under-stratified' view of social interaction (as composed solely of the institutionalised doings of rule-following role-incumbents) encourages a 'de-centring' of the processes which generate social malintegration and macroscopic change in social systems, and thereby often helps sustain an unwarranted consensus model of society.

Third, this collapse of agential action or membership into role-action ensures that action theorists cannot furnish an adequate explanation of the genesis of rules and roles (i.e. of why social groups construct and reproduce the institutional roles and rules they do). Finally, nor can its practitioners' grasp of individuals as role-incumbents account for how social interaction might modify or even transform the role-ensemble of a society (i.e. introduce to it new roles and attendant rules of social conduct or transform or abolish old ones), or of why individuals are motivated to select the institutional roles they do from society. I will elaborate on each of these arguments in turn.

John Scott has made the observation that social action theory offers 'only a partial view of collective agency'. As he puts it, for action theorists, '[t]he formation of small groups, business enterprises and political enterprises is recognised, but not explained, and they are seen as having only a shadowy existence as part of the "framework" of social life'.[91] The reason for this 'absence' in social action theory is twofold. Most obviously, of course, it is explainable in terms of its practitioners' 'populist predilection' for revealing the roots of social order in the activities or transactions of micro-actors, conceived simply as 'lay persons' or 'ordinary members of society'.[92]

Since this kind of approach sees its task as adducing the 'interaction order' from a non-hierarchical aggregation of micro-transactions between 'lay actors' or 'ordinary members of society', it is clear enough that it is ill equipped to offer a theory of collective action (this requiring explanation in terms of common interests shared by members of social groupings occupying the same basic 'situation' or 'circumstances' in society). After all, having reduced society to an aggregation or repetition of micro-transactions, social action theory can provide no coherent account of contradictory social interests, which may motivate collaborative projects of societal replication or transformation, and nor can it grasp the specific social powers (i.e. 'structural capacities') which members of different collectivities may draw upon during their mutual interaction, and which shape the trajectory of their interaction.

This 'relational individualism',[93] in which contemporary social action theorists trade, furthermore seems to undermine the warranty of stratifying the 'interaction order' on the basis of the differing degrees of power which actors can mobilise in pursuit of their interests in the course of their daily institutional doings. Social action theorists do often recognise that the role-ensemble of society is populated by macro-actors as well as micro-actors (e.g. Berger and Luckmann's observation that some actors wield 'bigger sticks' than others),[94] but they logically cannot theorise why this is the case, since at the very least this requires an explanation of how or why the daily 'renegotiation' of social reality by micro-actors always yields a recurrent 'institutional pattern' whereby particular individuals remain in control of resources denied to others which allow their decisions to 'stretch widely in space and time'.[95]

As Mouzelis rightly points out, the basic assumption underlying micro-sociology (that all social phenomena 'are made up of aggregations and repetitions of many … micro-events')[96] ensures that its practitioners cannot grasp 'role-play' as energised by hierarchical transactions in which those decisions taken at the top of institutions subsume those taken by subordinates at lower levels.

> For instance, meso encounters between junior managers of some particular organisation may be hierarchically connected with encounters of employees lower down in the organisational hierarchy, as well as with the macro transactions of senior managers. … The latter interactions (which do not necessarily entail many actors but rather powerful ones) are certainly no mere aggregates of those played lower down in the organisational hierarchy … since decisions taken at the top tend to become the value premises that those in subordinate positions have to consider when they take their own, more limited decisions.[97]

In fact, the hierarchical ordering of institutional encounters in society can be explained only by referring the role-array to inter-agential relationships governing the reproduction of asymmetrical distributions of economic, political and cultural goods, which confront interactants as emergent structures. For unless the 'interaction order' is treated as comprised of social agents and role-actors, it is unclear how the analyst can avoid regurgitating 'functionalist' explanations of stratification which portray the ranking of institutional roles as corresponding to 'common values' and determined by their respective contributions to the 'needs' of society.

The second reason for social action theory's relative neglect of collective agency (and social agents) is no less difficult to comprehend. Where 'interaction' or 'praxis' in the here and now is held to be constitutive of all things social and cultural, it is inevitable that the agential dimension of society must be confined to a nebulous or peripheral role in social analysis. This is because the category of 'social agency' refers us to 'collectivities' of individuals sharing interests, social capacities and life-chances in common (by dint of the positioning of these groupings *vis-à-vis* various distributions of resources and the relationships of domination and subordination which pertain between them) which are causally efficacious in shaping people's attitudes and conduct, irrespective of their activity or interests as rule-governed role-incumbents or social practitioners. Now, it is obvious that social agency can bring about macroscopic structural change in a way beyond the reach of role-actors, not least because actors are forced to operate within the constraints of their institutional roles or 'praxes', whereas agents may operate collectively on the basis of broader social and human interests which are not 'hemmed in' by narrow sectional obligations or rules.

It is, of course, for this reason that it is possible to talk of 'social movements', which are precisely concerned with modifying or transforming overall social structures, not with tinkering with particular institutional rule-role sets. Thus, where actors and agents are conflated, or where the latter is collapsed into the former, this inevitably gives rise to an inherently partial view of interaction and a relatively static picture of social life, since reference to institutions and role-play neglects important sources of conflict or social malintegration (e.g. stratification by class, gender or ethnicity, the struggles of the oppressed against the oppressor, etc.) and directs attention instead towards the functions of social organisations and institutional roles. Lacking an account of inter-agential incompatibilities or antagonistic interests, as these are predetermined by pre-structured asymmetries of resources, social action theorists consequently often find themselves drawn into the impasse of opting for a consensus model of society and attendant demonisation of social disorder.

For example, this subsumption of social agency under institutional role-action explains why Berger and Kellner's famous analysis of the institution of marriage abstracts from it those realities of gender inequality and oppression which ensure that it cannot be portrayed simply as a 'partnership' in which the participants 'construct not only present reality but ... past reality as well, fabricating a common memory ... project[ing] the future in accordance with this maritally defined identity'.[98] More frequently, however, this under-stratified view of the 'interaction order' encourages action theorists to account for conflict by making their appeal to 'institutional imperfectations' generated by the plurality of functions which constitute societal organisation (e.g. as is recommended by Berger and Luckmann in their more 'radical' moments).[99] Yet this strategy is indefensible, not least because it is unclear why a mere differentiation of societal functions should necessarily generate either institutional strains or discord between different roles, particularly since the 'interaction order' is said to be 'negotiated' collectively by a community of lay actors. Why, for instance, should the institutional roles of doctor and lawyer generate antagonistic values, interests or 'sub-universes' of meaning?

Contra the theoretical logic of social action theory, it is possible to grasp institutional strains within the role-array of society only by relating these to agential collectivities and agential relations as these are 'bounded' within the constraints and enablements of an emergent social structure. For example, cut-throat rivalries between business firms in the marketplace, and social conflict between managers and workers within the business enterprise, do not stem from the 'institutional segmentation' of functions in the socio-technical division of labour. On the contrary, these forms of social malintegration issue from the fact that the business enterprise is inserted within social relations of commodity production which pressurise each unit of capital to 'out-compete' its rivals under pain of foreclosure, and from the fact that workers and capitalists have opposed interests by virtue of the fact they constitute propertyless and propertied social groupings, with the income of the latter derived from the economic exploitation of the former. In this case, institutional strains in the economic structure of society (e.g. the boom/slump cycle) stem from structural contradictions of the capitalist mode of production mediated by antagonistic intra-class and inter-class relationships and conflicts. Again, only by distinguishing the 'role-actor' from the 'social agent' is it possible to obtain an explanatory purchase on the facts of this matter.

The incapacity of social action theory to account for the origins, or indeed possibility, of the normative rules and institutional roles which characterise a society, can be illustrated by studying the genesis of particular institutional forms. Consider, for instance, the example of trade unions. Given that social agency is regarded by action theorists as interchangeable with social action, and given that social action is regarded as 'rule-governed' or 'rule-following' role-action (by definition within an institutional set-up), it has to be admitted that it is entirely mysterious how trade unions could ever have come into existence. After all, it seems indisputable that rules governing the institutional doings of trade unions cannot explain the social interactions which brought these into being, since such rules can emerge only from the fact of trade union organisation itself. In other words, as emergent properties of the formation of trade union organisation, 'rules applicable to them would only actually be involved after they had been formed'.[100]

This argument has a more general application. Consider the example of the origins and subsequent development of the British welfare state outlined earlier. What were the normative 'rules' which governed or underwrote its emergence? Certainly, the emergence of the welfare state was constrained and enabled by pre-existent legal and cultural norms (as were trade unions). But these 'rules' were secondary to the fundamental objectives of welfare reform (stabilising the social order, 'gentling' the masses, improving the efficiency and exploitability of labour, etc.). Furthermore, such rules of 'doing welfare' were in any case developed *ex-post* by the trial-and-error practical exigencies of developing a welfare system and social policy worthy of the name. Once again, as in the case of trade unions, explanations of social interaction in terms of rule-governed role-action cannot here account for *how* the 'rules' of 'doing welfare' were ever articulated (these were after all the products of social interaction!) or *why* social groups were ever motivated to formulate these 'rules' in the first place.

Explanations of social interaction solely in terms of role-action, in short, appear to be tautological, presupposing that which they are supposed to explain. This crucial failing of role-theory reveals yet again the need to root social actors in an anterior interactional context (i.e. the agential collectivities into which they are born) if social causes are to be found for new institutional forms. For it is the agential location of individuals in hierarchical social relations which furnishes them with social interests (as determined by the differential life-chances and respective degrees of autonomy and control in society which pertain to the members of the collectivity of which they belong) in articulating or defending certain forms of institutional arrangements. And it is these same agential interests which supply individuals with the motives or reasons to act collaboratively in so doing (I will return to this argument shortly).

If the concept of 'agential interests' (and hence social agency) will suffice to supply the hinge which links institutional structure and social interaction, then there appears no good reason why it should not be regarded also as the mechanism which explains institutional elaboration (or its absence) in the role-ensemble of a society. By contrast, social action theory has, of course, never been able to explain how or why institutional change occurs in a social system. This is because once social interaction is treated as animated by interests which are determined by the social roles (and attendant normative expectations) which individuals internalise as part of their self-identity, it becomes well nigh impossible to ground role-change in coherent human motives or reasons (rooted in turn in objective interests).

In other words, once the interests of human agents are defined in terms of the roles they adopt from society, and once these roles are regarded as 'pre-scripted' by normative rules or conventions, it becomes hard to imagine how individuals muster the 'internal' (personal) and 'external' (social) resources to act collectively in the modification, or even transformation, of either the roles they inhabit or the role-ensemble of society as a whole. Social interaction becomes trapped in what Archer describes as 'normative conventionalism',[101] whereby individuals have choice as to how they impersonate or personify roles, freedom within the constraints of roles, but no choice or freedom as to whether they follow or endorse the normative obligations associated with roles. The result is, again, a curiously static picture of social life, which rides roughshod over the historical fact of ongoing institutional elaboration in the role-ensemble of capitalist society, in which 'role-clash' is posited as the only source of structural and institutional change, but cannot be justified theoretically (given the collapse of the human person and personal identity into the social self and social identity respectively).

The lesson to be learned from the failings of social action theory is that, although an account of individuals as role-actors does indeed capture certain important features of the people which animate social systems, this will not suffice as a general account of social interaction. The key error of social action theory lies not in its regard of individuals as role-incumbents, tightly circumscribed by normative rules, but in its reduction of social agency and human person-hood to role-action. The fact that the characteristics which pertain to individuals as members of agential collectivities (e.g. under-privilege, poverty, powerlessness, propertyless, exploitation, oppression and their opposites) are those which 'people acquire involuntaristically and *not* as roles that they occupy through choice'[102] is what justifies the realist view that social agency and role-action are not interchangeable, and that the former is interest-governed rather than rule-governed or rule-following.

Margaret Archer makes the point as follows:

> It is defensible ... to view [the properties of agents – i.e. 'privilege' and 'under-privilege', etc.] as positions rather than roles because of the impossibility of specifying any but the fuzziest and most highly contested normative expectations associated with them. Whilst systems of social stratification, especially rigid and unidimensional ones, *may* generate roles associated with particular strata (such as Brahmin, Nobles or Literati), this is contingent to stratification rather than being a necessary and internal feature of it. The quintessential features of all stratification systems, namely 'propertylessness', 'powerlessness' and the lack of prestige (together with their opposites), are ... distributions of positions with determinate life chances rather than an array of roles with clearly defined normative expectations.[103]

After all, it is clear enough that individuals (and collectivities of individuals sharing the same relationships of domination/exploitation and subordination with other agential groups and similar life-chances) may possess interests in common without translating these into role-action. The unemployed and poor still have real interests in decent jobs and high wages (and, of course, in socialist equality) even where they do not 'play' or 'perform' the 'role' of voter, trade unionist, demonstrator, rioter or revolutionary activist.

Most important of all, however (to return to an earlier point), a treatment of individuals as role-actors, social agents and human persons ensures that the plain fact of institutional elaboration is no longer mysterious. For individuals can now be plausibly seen as possessing interests (human and social) which are external to roles and which gift them potent reasons or motives for acting collaboratively to modify or transform the roles they occupy or are subject to. 'Normative conventionalism' can thus be circumnavigated where

> Adam as Agent is allowed on the scene. For we become Agents *before* we become Actors. After the Fall, the rest of humanity enters society through the maternity ward doors and we immediately acquire the properties of Agents through belonging to particular collectivities and sharing their privileges or lack of them – as males/females; blacks/whites; foreigners/indigenous; middle class/working class. ... [T]he 'under-privileged' confront plenty of exigencies, given their poor life chances, and thus have the best of reasons for struggling towards collective organisation (unionisation, franchise and civil rights movements, feminism), just as privileged Corporate Agents find good reason in protection of their vested interests to try to contain or repress the former. In the struggle between them ... the extant role array undergoes considerable transformation. New positions get defined under the prompting of promotive interest groups, though they will bear the marks of compromise and concession in the course of interaction against opposition. Equally the defence of vested interests may prompt role changes precisely in order to defend interests themselves (Kings will accept any form of constitutionalism in order to remain King – but a Constitutional Monarch is a very different role embedded in a much modified role-set). In short, the re-grouping of Social Agents provides the motor which generates new role-rule sets as some of its unintended consequences, thus providing an account of their development in terms of non-rule governed action, which is not open to Social Actors as encumbents of roles hedged by normative conventions. ... Another way of putting it is that Agency makes more room for the Actor, who is not condemned to a static array of available positions.[104]

By way of illustration of this argument, let us reconsider my earlier example of the evolution of the British welfare state and social policy (in this case between 1945 and 1951). As we have seen, the interactions between the rival corporate agents of capital and labour (and between the corporate agents of the propertied and the primary agents of the propertyless) led to the rapid post-war construction of a system of universal social and welfare provision. The impact of these agential interactions (the regrouping or remodelling aspect of social agency) on the role-ensemble of British society was profound. Whole new institutional sectors were formed (involving modified rule-role relations). Others were rapidly expanded in response to the demands of organised capitalism and greater societal enfranchisement, including those associated with teaching, the medical profession and social work, as well as more 'mundane' occupations concerned with ancillary and clerical functions. Can it seriously be doubted that the dynamic of social agency provided here the stimulus for institutional remodelling, in the absence of which it would not have taken place?

More generally, of course, unless one regards the social roles which comprise the institutional structure of society as over-determined by dynamic processes of agential regrouping, it is difficult to explain the higher or lower levels of income, autonomy, 'elasticity' and prestige which correspond to different occupational roles (other than by resorting to functionalist-type accounts of 'societal needs'). How else, other than in terms of agential dynamics, for instance, can the modification (by means of state intervention) of the formerly arbitrary and draconian powers of the capitalist entrepreneur over his workers be explained? How else, other than in terms of the differential agential origins and history of vocational groups, do we account for the differing fortunes (in terms of income, job security and working conditions) of the legal and medical professions on the one hand and the teaching and social work professions on the other? Without an anchorage in anterior agential interaction, such social phenomena are placed beyond the ken of sociological explanation.

A final major strength of drawing an analytical and temporal distinction between social agency and role-action (both of which are nonetheless social aspects of the individual's life-process), and between interest-related and role-governed social interaction, is that it allows the theorist to furnish a major part of the explanation of why persons select the roles they do from society without departing company from interest-explanation. Again, social action theory is unable to do this, because having identified reasons with interests and interests with roles (and the normative rules connected to them), it has to assume that 'the initial choice [made by individuals] of a [role] position is contractarian, a contract which it is non-rational to enter in prospect but which can be rational in retrospect or rationally corrected' (because individuals cannot have a reason to adopt a role and attendant social identity if they possess 'no prior interests upon which reasons can work').[105] In sharp contrast to this kind of approach, the realist stratification of the 'interaction order' into its differentiative dimensions allows the analyst to account for why persons select their social roles from within a (greater or lesser) range of institutional options, in terms of the social interests they inherit at birth by simply being a member of a particular agential collectivity.

From this perspective, the agential contexts into which individuals are inserted (class, ethnicity, gender, etc.) will determine the differential 'opportunity costs' (constraints and enablements – material and cultural) attached to pursuing different kinds of social position (or positions) within the institutional sector of society, and hence provide persons with rational motives for restricting their initial role-choices (and those corrected by experience) to that part of the role-ensemble which appears to be within reasonable reach. Urban working-class blacks, for example, are not likely to 'achieve' the role of barrister or high court judge, given the reality of discrimination by class and ethnicity and economic and cultural subordination, and so are unlikely to regard the pursuit of such roles as a sensible 'career' option.

On this basis, and from this starting point, a complete or fully satisfactory account of why individuals select the specific social roles they do, from within those areas of the role-ensemble which are accessible to them, can be constructed by analysing those additional social, personal, biographical and psychological factors which might 'bring the residual contractual element [of role-selection] into the area of sensible choice'.[106] Committed socialists and black nationalists, for instance, are not likely to apply to join the police force, given the facts of their personal identity, irrespective of whether such a 'career-move' is within reasonable reach. Such an option is available only to those in possession of what Theodor Adorno once described as the 'authoritarian personality'.

Self, personal identity and social identity: a stratified model of people

The foregoing argument indicates the need to anchor the role-actor not only in the social agent but also in the human person. In practice this means that a distinction has to be drawn between personal identity and social identity. A distinction should also be drawn between the human being and the human person, between human nature and the human subject, or between mind (or consciousness) and self, with the latter being conceived as emergent from the interface between organism and environment (because it is from human self-consciousness or self-awareness that both personal and social identity are emergent). Again, the necessity of distinguishing analytically and factually between mind, self, personal identity and social identity is best demonstrated by reminding ourselves of the conceptual weaknesses which have befallen those social action perspectives (especially those associated with 'high' symbolic interactionism and social constructionism) which have been most explicit in collapsing the first three strata into the last. What are the relevant arguments here?

I have suggested that 'over-social' views of the individual fail for four basic reasons. First, the existence of self-consciousness cannot be seen as dependent on social interaction (e.g. G. H. Mead's children's play and dialogic speech-acts), because an antecedently existing self has to be postulated to explain the possibility of cultural learning and the ability of infants to acquire linguistic concepts and to self-objectify in their play. Second, the self cannot be seen as synonymous with the properties of personal and social identity, since a precondition of individuals engaging in the 'presentation of self in everyday life', or initiating 'frontstage and backstage performances' of self, is the *a priori* existence of a self which is precisely capable of 'self-negotiation', 'self-monitoring' and 'self-presentation'. Finally, personal identity cannot be treated as synonymous with social identity, least of all with self-presentation (i.e. the self as a reflected identity forged by 'labelling' or 'societal reaction'). For it is a matter of empirical fact that individuals do somehow summon the 'internal resources' to resist the definitions or expectations of society or social group, whilst it seems uncontentious that a distinction has to be made between the self which is 'self-presented' and the self which does the 'self-presenting'.

The only solution to the antinomies of symbolic interactionism's and social constructionism's theory of 'mind, self and interaction' is to make out a case for five basic claims. The first argument I would like to make is that mind or consciousness is a natural capacity of humanity's species-being (dependent upon the psycho-organic organisation of human beings and generated historically through processes of natural selection) whose contents are not exclusively social or cultural. My second argument is that self-consciousness has a naturalistic foundation, since it is emergent from the interchange between organism and environment. In practice this means that self or subject should be identified with Mead's 'I' (not his 'me'), and hence freed from dependence on society, culture and language.

My third argument is that Mead's conception of the 'me' (the individual's capacity to see him- or herself as an object for another person, and later the social group to which they belong), far from being constitutive of the 'I/not-me' distinction, should be regarded instead as a socio-cultural and linguistic articulation, refinement or development of the self. From this point of view, the 'I and the 'me' (or the 'I/not-me' dialectic of the self) stands for the individual's sense of unitary subjectivity, i.e. his or her sense of bodily and spiritual continuity in and relative autonomy from the world, whereas the Meadian conception of the 'me' represents the translation and transformation of self-awareness into personal identity.

The fourth argument I would like to make is that personal identity is emergent from the interface between self-conscious subjects and their social and material environment, comprises social and non-social dimensions, and is the source of the capacity of human persons to resist those socio-cultural definitions or expectations (i.e. processes of 'societal reaction' or 'labelling') which the 'generalised Other' or 'significant others' would impose on them during ongoing social interaction. My final argument is that the 'looking-glass self', the self as a matter of situational definition, the self that is identified with the roles which the individual internalises as his or her own and with the 'masks' which they don and doff in different institutional contexts, refers us not to personal identity but to social identity.

The function of the distinction between personal and social identity is not therefore to differentiate between the naturalistic and social sources of the self, but to give theoretical content to the common-sense (and intuitively correct) notion that the self-identity of individuals comprises relatively stable and enduring properties as well as more ephemeral or situational ones. Such a distinction is necessary, furthermore, not simply in order to explain the distance between self-identity and self-presentation, between substance and image, but also in order to explain the self-evident fact that self-identity simply cannot be arbitrarily redefined or reconstructed every time an individual comes within hailing distance of the 'attitudes' or 'reactions' of those who inhabit the various institutional contexts that they inhabit.

The naturalistic foundations of human consciousness

The necessity of the analyst to grasp human consciousness naturalistically (i.e. as a property of the organism and as requiring no social referent or locus) may be demonstrated by briefly reminding ourselves of the basic philosophical difficulties which have undermined sociological accounts of mind (which see consciousness as an abstract potential of the brain, but necessarily dependent on culture to emerge). Two key difficulties spring to mind here which are worthy of note.

First, it appears contentious that 'society' or 'culture' or 'language' be held as necessary enablements of a 'recognisably' or 'distinctively' human consciousness. This is because accepting this position places human beings below the level of many animal species, whose members do apparently possess sufficient consciousness (and continuity of consciousness) to make enduring elementary distinctions in the object-world during the experiential flow of their life-cycle, and who do utilise their interactional experiences with physical nature in a way which allows them to engage in elementary learning processes. More concretely, this position paradoxically places human beings below their nearest primate relatives (chimpanzees, pygmy chimps, gorillas and orang-utans), since these are all animal species whose members appear capable of a degree of forward planning in their dealings with each other and with the 'significant objects' (e.g. foodstuffs, natural enemies, etc.) which populate their environment.

Thus, if it is true that '[t]here are no pre-existing ideas … and nothing is distinct before the appearance of language'[107] (i.e. if there is really no 'rational' or coherent cognitive process prior to enculturation), it is certain that 'animals would be unable to hunt, cats would not find their way home, chimps would not engage in primitive tool-use, and infants would not acquire language'.[108] Although it is undoubtedly the case that the pre-social capacity of the human mind to make 'logico-rational' distinctions in the object-world and to plot or initiate intentional conduct is not at all synonymous with cultural and linguistic 'constructions' of reality, it is equally certain that the former must be prior to and enabling of the latter. All too often, it seems, sociological imperialists 'confuse the capacities of the (human) mind with its (social) contents'.[109] The naturalistic components of consciousness emergent from human neurobiology cannot so easily be disposed of.

Second, nor is it true that processes of dialogic communication or signification transform human consciousness into a fully cultural consciousness (by intervening between individual thought and external reality), thereby excluding other mediating influences (i.e. non-discursive social relations and non-social experiences) from impacting upon individual thought and activity. If this were indeed the case there would be no possibility of cultural or linguistic change or reform, since neither social nor natural reality could function here to stimulate or motivate redefinitions of given situations or objects, by contradicting or challenging established symbolic representations or constructions of these.

If the simple fact that pre-linguistic children can be socialised into culture shows that the causal powers of intentionality, abstraction and reasoning power, possessed by all competent human infants, simply cannot be a gift of culture (however great a role cultural factors have played in the evolution of the human brain or in enhancing the intellectual powers of concretely situated individuals), then, equally, the plain fact that (for instance) 'politically correct' controversies over appropriate language-use can ever arise evidences that the cultural contents of individual thought (as these are expressed in linguistic signifiers) are conditioned to a large extent by non-discursive experiences of non-cultural 'objects'.

After all, if the contents of human consciousness are drawn exclusively from the 'inherited store' of signifiers or symbols contained in a culture, and if these symbols or signifiers impose order or meaning on social and physical reality, it is difficult to imagine not so much how, but why, individuals are moved or impelled to reinvent or redefine the meanings of their material situations and social relations. To explain cultural and linguistic change, in other words, it is necessary to refer to changes or developments outside culture or language.

For example, until recently, established linguistic practice in academia and literature entailed the generic use of 'man', 'mankind' and 'he' when referring to all things human. Since the late 1970s, however, this has changed very rapidly, with '(s)he' or 'he/she' or 'she/he' being substituted for 'he', 'people' for 'men', and 'humankind' or 'humanity' for 'mankind'. As John Molyneux rightly observes, this development

> was possible because this particular linguistic reform was a product of a real movement and a real change in the consciousness of millions of women and men which in turn arose from real changes in material

conditions and social relations (the influx of women into paid employment, higher education and the professions, the pill, abortion rights).[110]

But if non-discursive or extra-cultural 'social objects' are causally efficacious in shaping human consciousness (as for instance the social situation of propertylessness conditions the thinking of the propertyless poor), what is the warranty of denying that non-social relations with the material objects and processes of physical nature can do the same?

The fact that the contents of mind are not exclusively social or mediated culturally is not difficult to demonstrate. For example, it is (or should be) uncontroversial to believe that exposure to, say, the English winter climate will normally ensure that individuals respond by wrapping up warmly and/or turning on their heating appliances. One would expect the opposite behaviour during the warm summer months. Here non-social interaction with physical reality (the impact of the weather on the human body) furnishes individuals with pressing interests and hence good reasons to respond in the appropriate or rational ways (to avoid overheating or overcooling). It is of no avail to appeal to the 'socialisation' or 'cultural tradition' to explain the facts of this matter. For if cultural 'rules' do exist which govern these kinds of behaviour, these can be explained only in terms of physiological signification and bodily interaction with nature. In any case, socialisation or cultural learning is dispensable in these situations (even if it remains useful or desirable). Lest parents neglect to inform their young offspring of the lamentable consequences of inappropriate clothing in specific weather conditions, physical reality will itself teach them the lesson in due course! Clearly non-social relations with the natural world do have an important input into the contents of human consciousness and into certain forms of social behaviour.

What applies to the relationship between individuals and nature applies equally to the interface between culture and nature. One would, for instance, have to be blind not to notice the profound impact of the physical environment upon, say, the cultural traditions and economic relations of the aboriginals of the Australian outback. Nor will it suffice to undermine the above observation by arguing that 'primitive' societies are 'closer to nature' than modern ones, or that the latter have emancipated their cultural structures and social relations from any kind of 'determination' (however loose) by physical circumstances. Socio-cultural practices and structures are always anchored in human biology, itself a power of nature, of nature acting upon nature, whereas the greater 'autonomy' of industrial societies from the natural world is itself a function of a closer approximation here of cultural knowledge to material reality – that is, of a closer relationship between culture and nature.[111]

Not only are sociological accounts of consciousness entirely unsuccessful, but they are also entirely superfluous. In recent years developments in neurobiology and AI (Artificial Intelligence – the study of computers) have allowed philosophers to develop anti-reductive materialist theories of consciousness which have managed to avoid the twin pitfalls of mechanical determinism and idealist irrationalism (or the unstable combination of the two in Cartesian dualism). The most interesting and ingenious of these attempts to overcome 'the mind/body problem' has undoubtedly been provided by the American philosopher of mind Daniel C. Dennett.[112] A brief exposition and defence of his arguments should therefore suffice to make the case for endorsing a naturalistic account of consciousness.

Dennett's work has been concerned with developing two complementary theoretical approaches to the study of mind. The first of these is his 'synchronic model' of consciousness, which seeks to reconcile his view of mind 'as a natural phenomena whose activities are continuous with those of the physical world' with his corresponding view that 'human beings are 'intentional systems' whose behaviour cannot be explained without ascribing to them beliefs, desires and other mental states'.[113] The second is his 'diachronic model' of consciousness, which seeks to anchor the historical origins of mind in purposeless mechanical biological evolution (defined by him as an 'algorithmic process'), from which consciousness has arisen from unconscious then semi-conscious organic matter in a sequence of developmental stages.

Dennett's 'synchronic model' of mind is designed to illuminate the irreducibility of 'mental states' to 'physical states' without making appeal to Descartes' mysterious 'mind stuff' (a disembodied essence lurking somewhere in the brain which is the author of self and intentionality). The centrepiece of his argument is that just as a digital computer is best understood as an assemblage of hierarchically ordered sub-systems, each of which is less 'smart' than the total system of which it is a part, and each of which undertakes progressively more complex functions than those from which it is composed,[114] so it is that the human mind functions in the same basic way.[115] In other words, like the computer, the human mind is for Dennett a composite structure of 'homunculi', in which the 'highest level design breaks down … into a committee or army of intelligent homunculi with purposes, information and strategies', and in which each of the 'intelligent homunculus' is organised 'into smaller … less clever homunculi'.[116]

Dennett summarises this argument as follows:

> In an organism with genuine intentionality – such as yourself – there are, right now, many parts, and some of these parts exhibit a sort of semi-intentionality, or mere *as if* intentionality, or pseudo-intentionality – call it what you like – and your genuine, full-fledged intentionality is in fact the product (with no further miracle ingredients) of the activities of all the semi-minded and mindless bits that make you up. … That is what a mind is – not a miracle machine, but a huge semi-designed, self-redesigning amalgam of smaller machines, each with its own design history, each playing its own role in the 'economy of the soul'.[117]

As Callinicos rightly says, the point of Dennett's argument is to provide an explanation of how 'all the complexity and richness of human mental life ... can somehow emerge from brute, mindless matter' which has assumed a particular level and complexity of organisation. 'The analogy of the computer, composed of progressively less intelligent sub-systems, shows that there is no sharp dividing line between mind and matter but a series of continuous gradations which blur this distinction'.[118] 'Mind' or 'consciousness' emerges, from this point of view, where the inherently and radically decentred hardware of the brain and central nervous system (each part of which has its own separate 'design history') becomes combined for a unified function, thus 'giving their union vastly enhanced powers',[119] a process dependent upon the long historical interface between organism, environment and (latterly) culture during the formative years of modern *homo sapiens*.

It follows from these arguments that 'mind' is not the gift of some kind of cosmic super-subject (the 'soul' residing behind the physical circuits of the machine-organism). Nor is it the product of any specific area or 'special centre' of the brain (as is argued by a school of thought Dennett describes as 'Cartesian materialism').[120] And nor is it the 'simple effect' of the physical structure of the brain and nervous system as a whole. On the contrary, mind constitutes the 'virtual capture' of the brain's 'parallel multi-track processes of interpretation and elaboration of sensory inputs' by a 'higher level design' (the 'Joycean machine' as Dennett calls it).[121] This 'higher level design' *subsumes* the lower-order strata and processes from which it has emerged. This means that conscious thought does not reduce to 'brain states' because mind is precisely that which *organises* a flux of 'simultaneously active channels of operation' and accompanying 'varieties of perception ... or mental activity' into a serialised 'stream of consciousness'.[122]

The purpose of Dennett's 'diachronic model' of mind is simply to account for the historical basis of the 'stream of consciousness' emergent from mindless organic matter. As Callinicos points out, whereas in *Brainstorms* and *Consciousness Explained* Dennett 'uses AI to help offer a static analysis of how human brains as they exist *now*, as organs of a certain living species, perform certain complex mental functions',[123] in his *Darwin's Dangerous Idea* he has constructed an evolutionary history of mind which traces 'the gradual accretion, over billions of years, of the sort of Design – of functionality and purposiveness – that can support an intentional interpretation of the activities of organisms (the "doings" of "agents")'.[124] As Dennett himself argues, given certain 'basic premises' specified by Darwin's theory of evolution (most notably 'resource stress', 'the struggle for existence', random genetic variability within populations of organisms, 'the strong principle of inheritance', and the concept of 'differential reproductive fitness' of specific genetic structures),[125] it is reasonable to postulate consciousness as the end product of a particular 'algorithmic' sequence of natural selection. From this point of view, 'mind appears historically through a succession of steps along a continuum, in which intentionality gradually appears in forms which (relative to the final step) appear crude and stupid'.[126]

I will not dwell here on the reasons this mode of adaptation was set in motion: suffice to say that such genetic traits were selected because they enhanced the behavioural flexibility of human beings and their hominid forebears, allowing them to escape dependence on a narrow range of habitats. For current purposes it is enough to make the point that Dennett has articulated a formidable challenge to theological notions of teleology in nature and idealist appeals to 'skyhooks' or 'mind-first' principles[127] (which descend to earth from on high to account for the strata which support 'mind' or 'spirit') without lapsing into the crudities of 'central state materialism'. As he puts it: '[g]ive me ... regularity – the mere purposeless, mindless, pointless regularity of physics – and I will show you a process that eventually will yield products that exhibit not just regularity but purposive design'.[128]

Consciousness, self and self-identity

Of course, many contemporary sociologists would endorse my claim that human intelligence and reasoning power be gifted a biological foundation and naturalistic genesis, on the grounds that the living human body is pre-social, and that human consciousness is emergent from the physical structure of the human brain as this has undergone evolutionary elaboration in interaction with nature and culture. However, much controversy continues to surround my corresponding belief that human self-consciousness or self-awareness (i.e. the 'locus' or 'centre' around which personal identity and social identity is constructed) should equally be gifted a naturalistic foundation. Indeed, whereas philosophers are divided on the question of the genesis of the human subject and his or her relationship to social process and social relations, sociologists have (as we have seen) tended to be dismissive of any notion of the pre-social and extra-social self. Their preference is instead to regard human self-consciousness as either the product of anterior socio-cultural structures, or as forged in the process of daily social interaction, ongoing social 'practices', or the free play of 'discourse' or 'language games'.

Contra sociological imperialism, however, a concept of self, relatively independent of socio-cultural determinants or conditioning pressures, is absolutely indispensable if the theorist is to even begin the job of explaining society and social change. The first step towards demonstrating that this is indeed the case involves specifying the dependence of social relations on properties of self-consciousness and personal identity.

Margaret Archer explains:

> Justification of the above ... consists in specifying what properties define a human person and demonstrating that these same properties are necessary conditions of social life itself. Such a defining feature has

> appeared to many to be the continuity of consciousness. The idea that a person is something which is aware of its persistence and progress through time is thus to advance the continuity of consciousness as part of what we mean by personal identity. This continuous sense of self is ... the indispensable contribution which our humanity makes to our social life. For unless there are persons who know themselves to be continuous over time, who work as self-persisting recorders, then nothing would prompt the attempt to survive in society, and likewise nothing would secure the survival of society. Survival itself would not be on the agenda. Though it is otiose, perhaps it makes matters more graphic to stress that activities which take place over time, like reflecting or acting themselves, as well as prudence and deferred gratification, strategic intervention, planning or hoping all depend upon a continuous sense of self. This being the case, then those collective and individual actions of actors and agents who do things like acknowledging their vested interests, weighing these interests against one another and weighing them against their values, would not enter the picture. The same goes for becoming members of social movements and for personifying roles in particularistic ways. In all these cases, unless there is self-awareness that it is the *same* self who has interests upon which constraints and enablements impinge *and* that how they react today will affect what interests they have tomorrow, then questions about the meaning and explanation of social action never arise.[129]

Thus, in order to explain how persons appropriate role-expectations and responsibilities from the institutional sector of society, act in the light of social interests and cultural values, and construct for themselves personal and social identities, it is necessary for them to have a sense of self (logically anterior to their social interaction) which recognises that these are consistently applicable to them irrespective of time or place. In other words, the individual has to be attributed sufficient powers of self-reflection to define their experiences and projects as belonging to or as initiated by the same person over time, if they are to be deemed capable of meeting their social obligations and taking responsibility for their social activity. Without this continuous sense of self, social obligations and expectations could never impinge upon individuals, because they would not be the kind of beings capable of recognising them as such.

For example, unless the incumbent of an institutional role is self-aware of his or her continuity as a distinct individual over time, there is nothing which can ensure that he or she will be capable of recognising that the rules and obligations attached to a role are as much applicable to their activities in the future as they are in the present, or have been in the past. Furthermore, unless one takes as given the existence of a continuous sense of self, irreducible to social interaction, it becomes difficult to see how, for example, role-clash in the institutional sector of society is even possible. For

> [u]nless a person has a sufficiently continuous sense of self to recognise that both roles are theirs and that performing the two will mean confronting their incompatibility sooner or later, then there is neither a personal dilemma nor any social impetus to avoid the impasse (by resigning, reinterpreting etc.).[130]

The purpose of the above argument is to suggest that human self-consciousness or self-awareness is not only *irreducible* to social relations or social process but is also *basic* or *primitive* to social life generally. It is, of course, this latter assertion which is normally treated with the greatest scepticism by those who would endorse some or other version of the 'over-social' or 'over-socialised' view of individuals. Many sociologists would perhaps attest to the view that a continuous sense of self-identity is indeed a necessary condition of role-action and agential action, and that a useful distinction between personal identity and social identity can be drawn, and yet insist that this sense of self is nonetheless a gift of society and culture (i.e. the product of primary socialisation or the earliest social interactions of the human infant). From this point of view, although symbolic culture and complex social organisation presuppose human beings in possession of a sense of self, a defence of the social roots of self-awareness can nonetheless still be made by claiming that primary socialisation functions to transform 'indeterminate organisms' into selves who *subsequently* play their part in reproducing society or culture.

Such socio-cultural reductionism fails, however, and for four basic reasons. First, it is obvious enough that a necessary precondition of human socialisation and cultural learning getting started at all is the existence of a particular kind of animal organism (the living human body as the repository of certain natural causal powers and tendencies) which is already capable of making elementary classifications or 'rudimentary distinctions in the flux of experience',[131] including the primary distinction between itself and the environment it inhabits. Yet, as we have seen,

> to accord authority to the social over human thought ultimately depends upon establishing that society is essential to the possibility of human thought at all. Yet ... society can enjoy no such primacy, for human beings are born into a undifferentiated world such that the primary task has to be the differentiation of objects, meaning that the distinguishing of social objects cannot be a predicate but only a derivative of a general human capacity to make distinctions – including ... the crucial one between 'myself' and the rest of the world.[132]

Equally importantly, before a human being can acquire cultural and linguistic concepts of self from the society they inhabit, they must first be capable of grasping social concepts and possess enough of a *sense* of self to regard these as applicable or relevant to their own life-process. Without this *a priori* sense of self there can be no secure basis or impelling motivation for the cultural articulation of concepts of the self, nor for individuals to appropriate specific social definitions of the self as their own. For if the latter is to be internalised by people, it has to be assumed that humans are the kind of beings who possess the need (indeed radical imperative) to articulate their sense of continuity of unitary subjectivity, and of the distinction between themselves and the world they inhabit. Indeed, if this point is conceded, if it has to be admitted that human beings are indeed the repositories of these powers or abilities, and are capable of authoring these kinds of initiatives, then why not regard them as being the bearers or authors of others? As Ian Craib rightly observes: 'The subject refuses to lie down'.[133]

Second, in logical extension of Margaret Archer's argument that it is necessary to posit a continuous sense of self to account for the possibility of role and agential action, it should count as the decisive rebuttal of purely sociological conceptions of subjectivity to point out that one can explain the capacity of pre-linguistic human infants (who as yet have not been constituted as social selves) to internalise the cultural rules, linguistic norms and appropriate conduct of their native society only by accepting that they possess enough of a self (i.e. self-awareness of their own continuity in the world) to regard these rules or expectations as being consistently and continually applicable to themselves over time. Unless one assumes *a priori* that self-consciousness is anterior or prior to social consciousness, that personal identity is more primitive than social identity (and that the latter are emergent from the former), it becomes almost impossible to explain how socialisation and cultural learning can ever get off the ground. Thus to explain how, for instance, G. H. Mead's social actors or Giddens' social practitioners are capable of internalising the collective expectations and norms of the 'generalised Other', which precisely allow them to participate in those habitualised or routinised practices which reproduce society, it has to be assumed that they do actually possess beforehand sufficient properties of subjectivity or self-reflection to recognise themselves in the obligations and expectations of the Other.

Failing this,

> the implication for society is that nothing gets done, for without selves which sense that responsibilities are their own, and which also own expectations, then the latter will have all the force of the complaint that 'something ought to be done about it'. Thus the strongest forms of socialisation theory ... ultimately cannot work with completely indeterminate material: it has to be determinate in this one way at least, that of acknowledging itself to be the same being over time.[134]

Thus Marx's own insistence on a naturalistic conception of human self-consciousness can be verified transcendentally, that is, by positing what state of affairs must logically exist in the world (in this case a pre-social self) if human society and culture is to be possible at all.

Third, in recent years research into the mental capacities of many species of non-human primates has radically strengthened the case for rejecting a sociological explanation of human self-consciousness. This is because such studies have uncovered evidence of self-awareness amongst certain species of great apes and Old World monkeys which in no plausible sense can be accounted for in terms of symbolic enculturation, socialisation or language-use within ongoing social relationships (unless one is to count 'vocalisation' as 'verbalisation' or elementary tool-use, social imitation and economic cooperation as 'culture'). For example, incidents of 'tactical deception' amongst baboons, chimpanzees and gorillas are now extremely well documented in the relevant literature ('including ... concealment, distraction, the creation of misleading indications of intent, and manipulation of innocent bystanders'),[135] and these are strongly suggestive of the existence in these species of a sense of self.

As Richard Leakey and Roger Lewin rightly point out:

> The significance of deception goes well beyond its just being another social tool. The agent of deception must have an idea of what response its actions will provoke in the target. The agent must be able to put itself in the mind of the agent. In other words, in order to practice deception, an individual must have a clearly developed sense of self.[136]

Equally significantly, complementary researches into the taught linguistic skills of certain apes in captivity (and particularly into the manner of which these apes use human language to express their feelings and desires) also appears to be strongly indicative of the existence in these species of a sense of self-awareness which *predates* their immersion or integration into symbolic culture. In the words of primatologist Patricia Marks Greenfield,

> we have demonstrated that a pygmy chimpanzee – a species virtually unstudied before from the point of view of language – has not only learned, but also invented, grammatical rules that may well be as complex as those used by human two-year-old children.[137]

But given that purposive language use in human infants is comprehensible only given the presumption that they have already acquired a sense of self (because mastery of linguistic concepts and elementary grammar is dependent upon individuals being able to distinguish themselves from the object-world and recognise the applicability of linguistic signs and rules to themselves over time), it does not seem unreasonable to impute equivalent 'subjective givens' to the higher non-human primates. Indeed, the capacity of chimps and (to a lesser degree) gorillas to learn and use human sign language is particularly demonstrative of the existence here of a pre-social self in a slightly different sense. This is because these linguistic abilities may be acquired (by means of human instruction) by animals whose own sociality is insufficiently developed or refined to account for them sociologically, as is proven by the fact that that symbolic language use does not arise 'spontaneously' or 'naturally' in any primate species other than *homo sapiens*.

Thus when, for instance, the captive chimp Washoe signs 'come love hug sorry sorry',[138] in response to disapproval by her keepers or teachers at some or other item of her behaviour, she is demonstrating that she is capable of putting herself in the head of the Other and recognising certain of her emotions and behaviours as her own and assuming responsibility for them ('I' have upset 'you'; by doing so 'I' have upset 'myself'; 'I' must make amends to 'you'). Equally when, for example, another captive chimp (Kanzi) responds in the appropriate way to complex instructions (such as 'go to the bathroom' or 'pick up the ball and give it to Rose'),[139] what we are witnessing here is behaviour which is dependent upon the possession by its progenitor of a sense of self. For this is conduct which can be enacted by Kanzi only given his own awareness of his own distinctiveness from the world, his own continuity in time and space, and his knowledge that the expectations of others apply consistently to himself and not to others ('you' want 'me' to go to the bathroom; 'I' will go to the bathroom).

Yet these elementary cognitive elements of self – which explain how Washoe and Kanzi can use grammar as competently as two-year-old humans – pertain to a species whose 'natural sociality' does not equip its members for life in complex symbolically mediated relations, and whose sense of self cannot therefore be attributed in any plausible way to socio-cultural causes or antecedent conditions. I contend that if closely related non-human primates possess an elementary sense of self which is primitive or basic to their integration into their natural communities, it is reasonable to suppose that the same holds true of human beings.

Third, it seems clear enough that the human body is itself crucial to our identification as persons, and this of course is anterior to any specific society or culture which human beings inhabit. The human body is, in other words, a pre-social source of self-identity. Bodily continuity in the life of an individual is precisely required 'in order to connect experiences together as part of one consciousness'.[140] This is because the biological or physiological unity of the human body, and the fact of its relative autonomy from the rest of organic and inorganic nature, enables and indeed impels persons to define themselves as unitary subjects (despite the express orders of a certain school of continental philosophy whose practitioners nonetheless do generally acknowledge 'themselves' as authors of their 'own' publications).

More precisely, given that human beings possess species-capacities of intelligence, abstraction and reasoning power, it is a necessary function of their possession of physical bodies which persist over space and time (and which constitute their consciousness) that they interpret or sense themselves as relatively self-subsistent and unified selves confronting an external or independent object-world. The genesis of self-consciousness and self-identity cannot then be attributed to 'social facts' (however these might be conceived). For it is a prerequisite of our enmattered or embodied constitution, and of the mental powers which this bodily constitution defines, which allows (and perhaps compels) us to imagine our experiences, consciousness and the contents of our consciousness as our own property, as belonging or pertaining to us and not to others.

The living human body is a crucial source of this pre-social reflexive self-awareness in a slightly different sense. As the bearer of a range of species powers and capacities (i.e. consciousness, intelligence, rationality, cultural and linguistic learning, etc.), and as the possessor of certain psycho-organic needs, it would be naive indeed to imagine that these biologically given capacities and needs do not have an important input into what individuals become as persons. It is, after all, uncontentious that the motivational source of humanity's earliest interactions with nature and society is precisely needs-satisfaction (i.e. the baby's demands for nourishment, comfort or warmth). Moreover, the mechanism by which humanity's natural powers are articulated and elaborated is precisely this process of needs-satisfaction, which in being set in motion allows individuals to appropriate the properties of the species as their 'own', that is, as a constituent element of their personal identity.

This argument does not, of course, add up to the contention that self-identity is reducible to human biology, or to the specific genetic makeup of individuals, as would be claimed by sociobiologists. Whilst differences in individual 'psychology' are causally influenced by the unique genetic organisation of living bodies, and whilst these genetically influenced variations in the psychic nature of individuals often feed in to their definition of themselves as people, it would be quite wrong to regard these as making a fundamental contribution to personal identity. For whereas genetic differences might at best be a cause of variations in temperament or emotional endowment between individuals, render them more or less competent at particular social skills, or predispose them towards or against certain sensory experiences (which might in turn impact upon the manner of their self-definitions), these are nonetheless likely to be a less significant source of personal identity than the experience and activity of persons in the material world during their life-cycle.

Nonetheless, the fact that personal identity is forged primarily through interaction with external reality should not allow us to lose sight of the fact that 'human beings must have a particular physical constitution' to be capable of constructing and sustaining enduring personal identities. 'Even in those cases where the biological may be socially mediated in almost every instance or respect, such as child-care, this does not mean that the mediated is not biological nor that the physical becomes epiphenomenal'.[141] After all, it is a peculiar kind of conceptual blindness which encourages sociologists to insist one-sidedly on the social mediation of personal identity without recognising that this property of persons is equally and simultaneously mediated by human biology and physical nature.

My argument thus far establishes the need of social theory to endorse the existence of a pre-social human self-awareness in order to explain how society and culture (and personal identity and social identity) can be possible at all. The fourth and final failing of 'over-socialised' and 'over-social' accounts of the individual, however, is their refusal to endorse the causal power and explanatory salience of what Margaret Archer describes as 'those human relations which cannot be construed as social relations',[142] yet which shape the personal and social identity of individuals – that is, the extra-social components of self-consciousness.

Of course, to accept that human beings may have 'non-social relations with non-social reality, which as part of [their] consciousness is also part of what [they] are as persons'[143] is complete anathema to those analysts who would insist that all human experience must be socially mediated (i.e. through culture and language) and that the social mediation of human experience must ensure that an unbridgeable chasm exist between culture and nature. But 'the things which the self senses ... are not exclusively social (nor are they only mediated to us through society)'.[144] And it is these 'things' (the undifferentiated object-world which the human baby organism initially encounters, and the structure of material nature within which persons are necessarily immersed throughout their lives) which play an important role in conditioning the personal and social identities individuals acquire during their life-cycle.

Again, this argument is well made by Margaret Archer:

> [The extra-social self] ... is a necessity which arises out of our embodiedness. We are born into a world which comes to us as one made up of undifferentiated objects, including people, out of which we gradually have to *learn* to discriminate the social from the non-social. In other words, the object/people distinction is an acquired one and we acquire it in that order. Not only ... is this predicated upon our human capacity for learning such distinctions, but crucially upon our surviving long enough to do so! As animals, our bodily needs for food, drink and warmth require an immediate relation with things that are really nutritious, thirst quenching and warming. Survival depends upon these being regularly experienced and therefore these experiences cannot wait upon their social definition (instead the basis for signification is physiological) nor upon the recognition that they are socially mediated. ... In the beginning, the provenance of these necessities is irrelevant, i.e. *whether* or not they do in fact depend upon social provision, or divine providence for that matter. Direct interaction with the otherness of nature is necessarily prior to being able to distinguish social others: for survival, the sequence cannot be the other way round.[145]

But, as Archer rightly goes on to argue,

> if we do from our beginnings ... have non-social experiences of non-social reality ... then why should we not continue to do so for the rest of our lives? Hunger, thirst and discomfort may be our first prompts to extra-social exchanges with nature, but there is also Marx's important insight that we are committed to *continuous practical activity in a material world*, where subsistence is dependent upon the working relationship between us and things, which cannot be reduced to the relations 'between the ideas of men'. In this sense, cumulative experiences of our environment will foster propensities, capacities, aversions which sift the social practices we later seek or shun, and thus the social identity which we then assume because of something we already are as persons.[146]

Now, to admit that human beings can and must have non-social experiences of non-social reality throughout their lives, and that these experiences shape their social identities by defining them as persons, is to do no more or less than concede that material reality (as well as society) places constraints and enablements on our activities and thinking, and hence on the manner in which we think about ourselves. We have already seen that it is entirely reasonable to suppose that non-social exchanges with non-social reality are efficacious in shaping the consciousness and activity of individuals. How then can it be denied that these 'natural relations' have an important input into the constitution of an individual's self-identity and social identity?

After all, physical damage or neglect of the human body (which is not at all culturally specific) may often retard the development of a 'stable' or 'balanced' personal identity, or indeed damage one that has already been constructed, as is evidenced, for example, by the psychological insecurity and intense unhappiness which often afflicts people who have undergone childhood abuse or trauma. Equally, persistent and pleasurable experiences of physical reality (e.g. plenty of space, stimulating environmental 'things' to experience and manipulate, clean air, sunlight, exercise and access to the material goods which ensure physical and mental health or well-being, particularly when enjoyed in childhood) will certainly contribute to the articulation of a robust self-image in later life. And, more generally, those interactions with non-social reality which individuals find rewarding or punitive, pleasurable or otherwise, will, as we have seen, contribute to how they imagine themselves as people, which will in turn constrain and enable the kinds of social roles and social identities they appropriate from society and personify in particularistic ways. For example, an individual who is susceptible to sea sickness is not likely to seek out employment as a deckhand.

I conclude that it is reasonable to accept that the 'I/not-me' distinction (the individual's self-awareness of his or her own continuity in and relative independence from the world) does not arise specifically from *social* interaction and is not mediated by society and culture alone. But how, then, can self-consciousness be explained? The only sensible answer to this question is this: a sense of self must be emergent from and mediated by non-social interaction with physical or material reality.

As Archer rightly points out, it does seem uncontentious that self-consciousness arises because the psycho-organic urges or drives of the human infant force it into engaging in bodily exchanges with the object-world ('the reality of the external world initially being established through bodily testing of the food and drink coming to it from "outside" which generates an "inner" satisfaction only available from "outsider" sources'), being 'forged between the [individual's] experiencing of [his or her] own organismic needs and inner inability to satisfy them'.[147] On this view, baby organisms learn to distinguish themselves from the material environment (which is initially experienced as an undifferentiated object-world), and later human infants learn to recognise themselves as objects, by confronting the manner in which the physical environment operates relatively independently of their own behaviours, providing constraints and enablements on the exercise of their desires from 'outside', supplying the external means to satisfy those elementary bodily needs (e.g. food, drink, warmth, comfort, etc.) which cannot be realised with resort to their internal resources. In simpler words, non-social (i.e. bodily) interaction with non-social reality enables and impels new-born and developing infants to interpret their experiences in terms of the 'I-not me' distinction, since it is these interactions which force the human organism to confront the fact that the world is not a mere extension of ego or will.

Self-objectification from the view of other subjects

The obvious advantage of the above naturalistic account of self-consciousness, over treatments of human persons as social selves, is that it allows the theorist some kind of purchase on how human infants are able to commence along the path of self-objectification in the eyes of other persons. Since human infants obtain an elementary sense of self by means of non-social exchanges with non-social reality, they therefore enter into processes of socialisation and cultural learning with precisely those qualities of subjectivity which are required to explain their capacity to 'take the role of the other' and later self-construct personal and social identities. Broadly, unsocialised and pre-linguistic human beings are from birth inserted in socio-cultural relations, being forced at once, as they seek to satisfy their desires, to interact with objects and persons, learning gradually to differentiate between them, not through immersion in or exposure to any specific social practice or cultural activity (i.e. Mead's children's play and games), but through the different kinds of interaction which are necessarily involved when relating to subjects and objects respectively.

In other words, subjects become distinguished from objects because in practice it is impossible for children to relate to them in the same way. Objects do not, of course, 'act' at all, do not possess human emotions, operate (insofar as they function at all) in relatively routine and predictable ways, and are either passively manipulable or passively impervious to the child's will. Subjects, by contrast, do 'act', do resemble the child physically and emotionally, do not function passively or entirely routinely, and are neither entirely manipulable nor entirely indifferent to the child's wants. In sharper contrast still to objects, subjects exercise will and power over children, offer them warmth, comfort and nourishment, and strive to interact or communicate with them.

Infants consequently learn through practice and experience that certain 'objects' (i.e. persons) differ from mere 'things'. They sense that certain objects resemble themselves, possess qualities which are mysterious and awesome and yet not dissimilar to their own, act autonomously of themselves and things, and possess feelings and will as they do themselves. It is, of course, a short step from here, and one as much contingent upon biological maturation as socialisation, for young children to subjectively identify themselves with those persons who are a part of the everyday landscape of their lives, imaginatively placing themselves in the role of these 'significant others' during their play, before later acquiring the more impersonal roles of the 'generalised Other' as they immerse themselves in cooperative games and complex role-play.

Unlike 'over-social' views of persons, in short, the great strength of this realist account of the subject is that it is capable of making a meaningful distinction between the primary (non-social) and secondary (social) components of self-consciousness. Self-consciousness has naturalistic roots in human biology (those species-powers of intelligence, abstraction and reasoning power inherent in the conscious brain which allow, indeed impel, individuals to interpret their bodily intercourse with the object-world in terms of the 'I/not-me' differentiation) and non-social interaction with material reality (the process by which the conscious brain is forced to confront the externality of the world beyond its own embodied self). This elementary pre-social and extra-social (but not pre-given) self, forged in the interface between the psycho-organic powers and needs of the living body and the object-world, constitutes the 'core' or 'centre' of individual personality, the subject who thinks, self-monitors, self-negotiates and initiates innovative and spontaneous action.

At the same time, however, the self as a matter of social definition, the self as socially and linguistically dependent, is no mere fantasy of the endlessly inventive sociological imagination, but is rather a subsequent stage in the cultural and linguistic articulation of the self, emerging as individuals translate their sense of unitary subjectivity into social concepts of personhood, self-identity and social identity. Thus Mead's 'me' (the self as an object for the 'community') is indeed as much dependent on language-use and social interaction as it is upon the prior existence and subsequent development of the causal powers of human nature inherent in the living body. For it is uncontentious that 'taking the view of the other' requires a context (i.e. society) which enables a distinction between subjects and objects to be drawn. And it is equally certain that the conceptual appropriation and articulation of self-identity must always be expressed in linguistic symbols derived from society, and is conditioned by social experience. Equally, however, Mead's 'me' would be a complete non-starter if human beings did not possess properties of self-consciousness both prior and supplementary to their construction as social selves.

Personal identity and social identity

The social construction of the capacities which Mead identifies with the 'me' is also an early stage in the individual's self-construction of a personal identity. The subsequent articulation by individuals of an enduring personal identity (elaborated during the process of their experiential life-cycle) is thus an emergent property of an enhanced and developed self-awareness which is characteristic of self-objectification from the point of view of other subjects and the 'societal community' or 'generalised Other'. But of what is personal identity constituted?

As indicated earlier, personal identity has social and non-social components. This is one way it may be distinguished from social identity, which as the name implies is entirely social in content (although it may be negatively influenced by non-social experience). The non-social or naturalistic sources of personal identity include those psycho-organic needs and capacities of humanity's 'species-being' which self-conscious individuals learn to recognise as their own property, and also all those personal aversions and preferences, emotional dispositions, and physical and mental capacities of individuals, co-conditioned by their specific genetic makeup and bodily interaction with material reality, which they regard as crucial to their self-perception or self-definition.

The social sources of personal identity, on the other hand, include those processes of primary and secondary socialisation by which individuals acquire social skills with which they identify, and the cultural and linguistic concepts by which they express and develop these skills, and along with these their self-identities. The social sources of personal identity refer us also, once again, to those personal capacities, emotional dispositions, sensory likes and dislikes, etc., which individuals regard as definitional of 'who they are' (insofar as these are conditioned by social experience and socialisation), and to those cultural and political values which individuals often internalise as their own and actively seek to personify in thought and deed.

If personal identity is comprised simply of that which individuals recognise and endorse as definitional of the kind of subjects they are, of what does social identity consist? Social identity is best understood as a kind of 'special case' of personal identity, a kind of 'optional extra' which individuals may or may not acquire, given the kind of life they lead as members of society. More specifically, social identity refers us both to those aspects of self-identity which are invested in the social roles which individuals appropriate from society and self-consciously internalise as their own property,[148] and to the self as presented by the individual in a particular interactional or institutional context (under pressure from socio-cultural expectations or obligations).

Consequently, although all persons possess a personal identity, forged by biographical experience and the allegiances, propensities and capacities this sponsors, not everyone possesses a social identity. For only those persons who 'feel at home' in the social roles they have chosen (or have had foisted upon them) can invest themselves subjectively in them, whereas those who regard the 'attitudes' of the Other as plain wrong or worse may not always be prepared to don and doff the masks expected of them. Unskilled factory workers, for instance, are unlikely to regard their occupational role as an important element of their self-identity, given its monotony and low status, preferring instead perhaps to subjectively invest themselves in their hobbies or leisure pursuits or political activities.[149] Equally, to offer another example, even in the inhospitable political and cultural climate of Nazi Germany, not all socialists or anti-racists donned the mask of orthodox or official opinion in their everyday dealings, irrespective of the appalling personal risks of not doing so.[150]

There are at least four good reasons why this analytical and factual distinction between personal identity and social identity needs to be drawn. The first of these is that it allows us to obtain some kind of purchase on the dynamics of 'role-clash' in the institutional sector of society. Since personal identity relates to those experiential processes by which individuals acquire self-knowledge of and assume self-responsibility for their human needs and interests, and of their personal capacities and wants, it follows that social roles which satisfy neither of these things will foster a reappraisal by individuals of their purpose in personifying them, and possibly a subjective or actual withdrawal from them (as these are compared with alternative roles or identities). The second important reason why personal and social identity ought to be differentiated, is that doing so allows us to grasp some of the reasons why individuals appropriate certain social roles and attendant social identities, but reject others. Since personal identity often relates to those social experiences (agential or cultural) by which individuals internalise ethical and political values or allegiances, it follows also that these will also impact upon the kind of roles or social identities which they actively seek or shun.

The third important reason why personal identity and social identity cannot be treated as interchangeable is that it is the former which explains the capacity of individuals to resist the latter (i.e. oppose or reject the social 'attitudes' and 'definitions' of 'significant others' and the 'generalised

Other'). Hence personal identity, insofar as it involves self-awareness of human interests, personal capacities and cultural and political allegiances, and insofar as it is defined by biographical life-experience, does gift individuals the 'internal resources' to resist those situational processes of 'societal reaction' or 'labelling' which might adversely subvert or alter their self-perceptions or self-definitions.

The final major reason why personal identity and social identity must be distinguished one from the other, is that by doing so we allow ourselves to make sense of the fact that the individual does indeed don and doff social roles (and with them social identities) without ceasing to be either a subject or the same person over time. Personal identity thus enables human beings to function as coherent, unified and purposive agents, capable of recognising, articulating and acting upon their human and social interests, and in so doing defining and redefining themselves as actors. In other words, personal identity, emergent from self-consciousness, is what enables individuals to function as agents and actors, and hence reproduce, elaborate or transform structure and interaction alike in pursuit of their interests.

Conclusion

In the previous chapter I developed a materialist theory of the naturalistic foundations of social interaction and social structure, which is informed by critical realism. Human nature and the individual subject is understood here as possessing 'determinate' and 'structured' properties irreducible to the imprint of society, which precisely explain the possibility of complex societal organisation and history-making. In this chapter I have sought to grasp the 'interaction order' which rests upon these 'micro-foundations' and its relationship to the organismic-subjective and structural levels of society.

In doing so I have sought to make out a case for three basic arguments. First, social interaction is best understood as 'somewhat rational' human conduct, involving the coordination of individual activities or those activities of individuals which are necessarily situated in socio-cultural relations (in the sense that these relations supply them with resources for acting or with reasons for so doing). Second, the 'interaction order' is comprised of distinct strata – subjects, agents and actors – with agents and actors 'emergent' from the organismic and subjective properties of individuals. Finally, 'interests' (human and structural) should be regarded as powering the interface between structure and agency.

The point of my first argument is to synthesise the best elements of the Weberian and structuralist traditions of sociological theory, and thereby to overcome the key weaknesses of each. From this perspective, social interaction is authored by rational subjects, and is precisely comprehensible and hence capable of being analysed objectively because it is 'somewhat rational'. Yet it is situated in social relations which define what is to count as rational social conduct by shaping the 'situational logics' in which individuals are embroiled, and by furnishing them with the ideational resources by means of which they make sense of these situations.

The point of my second argument is to obtain an explanatory purchase on why and how social systems are replicated, elaborated or transformed over time. Interaction is the sole 'cause' of all things social and cultural. But interaction has to be grasped as comprised jointly of agential action (i.e. conduct energised by structurally determined inter-agential relations and by attendant agential 'circumstances' and interests) and role action (i.e. conduct which is explainable in terms of the institutional roles or functions which individuals select from society), if social analysis is not to regurgitate the errors of social action theory (i.e. the neglect of collective action, the overemphasis on social integration, the inability to theorise institutional elaboration, the collapse of the interaction order into a non-hierarchical flat place of micro-transactions, etc.). From this point of view, 'normative conventionalism' (the tight circumscription of interaction by rules attached to institutional roles) can be overcome by grasping institutional reproduction and elaboration as powered by the struggles and interests of broader collectivities of individuals, who are not 'hemmed in' by narrow role commitments.

The purpose of my final argument is to show how explanations of social interaction in terms of 'interests' can be made which avoid the polarities of structural determinism and voluntarist idealism. My fundamental claim here is that interests cannot be understood in 'subjectivist' or 'psychologistic' terms, as the random 'preferences' of individuals, as is recommended by exponents of the 'orthodox conception of agents' (so much in vogue for modern rational choice theorists). On the contrary, these must be grasped 'objectively' as corresponding to the psycho-organic needs of humanity's species-being, as these are mediated by the social relations and agential collectivities into which individuals are involuntarily deposited at birth.

Put simply, individuals possess basic human needs which must be fulfilled on a daily basis if they are to survive or prosper, and possess therefore human interests in ensuring that these needs are met. At the same time, however, the location of individuals in social relations and agential collectivities determine both the degree to which their human needs are fulfilled or frustrated, and the kinds of social strategies or practices ('modes of realisation') which they must pursue if they are to safeguard or enhance their life-chances.

It is the interface between human needs and the social 'positions' individuals occupy in social relations which ensures that the former are translated into agential interests (i.e. those social modes of realisation of human interests which correspond to agential collectivities as defined by inter-agential relations). Understood thus, and translated into the categories of Marx's historical materialism, the concept of social labour connects human interests and needs to economic structure (the forces of production), whereas the concept of class interests connects class structure to class struggle (the relations of production). This allows the theorist to postulate a dynamic historical account of societal process rooted in their mutual interplay.

But why should social labour and class agency be 'privileged' in this way as the mechanism which explains the overall dynamics of social systems? The analysis contained in the next chapter will seek to answer this question.

4 Structure, power and conflict

The purpose of this chapter is twofold. First, to outline a realist account of social systems which neither reduces structural properties tautologously to some or other form of 'organised' interaction, nor reifies them by gifting them hydraulic powers of determination by virtue of which individuals function simply as agents of their functional requirements. Second, to utilise this general model of 'structure' or 'structural properties' to outline a logically coherent and conceptually defensible *materialist* understanding of society or 'social system' along the lines outlined and defended by Marx and Engels (i.e. one which avoids the twin pitfalls of reductionism and determinism, on the one hand, and voluntarism or 'spontaneism', on the other).

My point in attempting to establish the explanatory power of Marx's structural sociology (which doubtless many would find terribly old hat) is that a hierarchical model of structural constraints, enablements and impulses (such as that articulated by Marx's base-superstructure model of the social system) is the only way to avoid collapsing socio-historical analysis into two unacceptable positions. On the one hand, a 'cultural focus', which leads directly to the mind-numbing relativism of analytical philosophers (such as Winch and the contemporary theorists of post-structuralism and the sociology of knowledge), for whom the concepts and practices of a particular society cannot be understood outside the socio-historical context of their articulation, and for whom the 'symbol sphere' or 'language' appears to have consumed the whole of society. On the other hand, the 'orthodox' Weberian view, which denies directionality to societal process, and which grasps historical outcomes as the radically indeterminate products of a chaotic flux of equivalent causal 'factors' (the 'economic', the 'political', the 'military', the 'cultural', etc.).

I take it that both these views are false: the former because it is an implausible species of reductionism which leads to the wildest form of idealism (and furthermore renders sociological analysis a non-starter); the latter because it is refuted by the plain fact that it is indeed possible to speak of 'development' or 'evolution' in historical process, and because societies are relational and cannot therefore be disarticulated into autonomous elements or spheres of activity or power. This being the case, my argument is that

Marx's analytical distinction between structure and superstructure, properly understood, offers the theoretical tools to achieve two important ends. First, to avoid collapsing society into an 'undifferentiated totality' without departing from the view that society is a system (not a fluid combinatory of autonomous practices, institutions or modes of social action). Second, to grasp history as 'progress' and as 'totality', in the sense of possessing an 'inner logic' which imparts to it a 'vertical' directionality by virtue of which it can be grasped as a whole. Before embarking upon these tasks, however, it is necessary to consider the meaning of the concept of 'structure', the relationship between 'structure' and 'culture', and the manner by which structures shape social interaction and human agency.

Structure and culture in social analysis

The concept of social structure has a long pedigree in the social sciences. Explicitly or implicitly, overtly or covertly, the idea of social structure has been central to most schools of sociology and social theory, at least from the work of Marx onwards. There is, indeed, something to be said for the argument, forcefully put by Margaret Coulson and Carol Riddel, that 'the idea of social structure is *the* lead off point, and the *anchorage* idea of sociology'.[1] Certainly, this has been the case in the work of many of the classical sociologists. Marx's 'social relations', Durkheim's 'social facts' and Parsons' 'action systems', for instance, are all conceptual efforts to grapple with the patterned nature of social life, and to get to grips with the manner in which individuals confront an 'objective' social world which appears to shape their thinking and activity from 'outsider sources'.

Doubtless it is this which explains why the history of sociology has been (amongst other things) the history of consecutive conceptual efforts to grasp the nature of social structure. The compressed historical span since the Second World War has thus already seen the rise and fall of functionalism, conflict theory and various forms of structuralism, all of which were undoubtedly 'macroscopic' in orientation. Indeed, even those sociologists who have sought consciously to reduce the concept of structure to the epiphenomenon of the social action of isolated individuals, have not been able to rid themselves easily of the need to resort to 'structural' or 'institutional' analysis. Max Weber's philosophical writings are, of course, a case in point. Having theorised the conceptual and methodological poverty of 'holism' (as he saw it), which for him falsely postulated the existence of irreducibly social phenomena, Weber went on to produce a voluminous output of substantive historical sociological work which precisely analysed the causal influence of 'collectivities' or 'constellations' upon social action in various socio-historical contexts.[2]

There are a number of reasons for seeking to explain human and social life in terms of 'structure' or 'structures'. First, as indicated above, it does seem indisputable that societies possess a certain interdependence of social practices or social functions, i.e. systemic properties, which persist over time and which involve persistent regularities or patterns of social interaction, of which the interactants concerned are often unaware. As Alex Callinicos rightly observes: 'We can [refuse] to regard them [structures] as self-reproducing organisms and still refuse to apply the term "society" to any set of human relationships which showed no capacity to continue across generations'.[3]

Second, societies (or more generally social systems) always entail specific kinds of social relationships, particular kinds of 'institutional patterns', configurational regularities of social interaction of a distinct nature, which precisely enable us to distinguish meaningfully between them. To refer to structure in this sense is thus to draw attention to the manner of which specific configurations of social relations at any given point in time exert a causal influence or conditional guidance upon the consciousness and conduct of the human agents who govern them.

Third, 'to say that a society has a structure is to say there are limits to the extent to which it may vary without becoming an instance of a different kind of society'.[4] Here the concept of structure allows the theorist to discern the point at which an accumulation of quantitative changes in a society brings about its qualitative transformation.

Finally, and most importantly, the concept of structure allows us to grasp the fact that social relations and institutions have an 'autonomous' and 'external' character and significance, one which does not depend in the least upon the particular nature of the interactants who animate and reproduce them:

> When I perform my duties as a brother, a husband or a citizen and carry out the commitments I have entered into, I fulfil obligations which are defined in law and custom and which are external to myself and my actions. ... Similarly, the believer has discovered from birth, ready fashioned, the beliefs and practices of his religious life; if they existed before, it follows that they exist outside him. The system of signs that I employ to express my thoughts, the monetary system I use to pay my debts, the credit instruments I utilise in my commercial relationships, the practices I follow in my profession, etc. – all function independently of the use I make of them. Considering in turn each member of society, the following remarks could be made for each single one of them.[5]

Thus we can endorse Erik Olin Wright's injunction to define social relations as 'sets of empty spaces',[6] and thereby insist upon a meaningful distinction between social interaction (and the human agents who are responsible for it) and social structure. The social roles of 'teacher' and 'pupil', for example, pre-exist the current generation of actors whose daily doings reproduce or elaborate them (which implies their externality from current interactants and their social action) and furthermore exert a conditional influence upon the institutional practices and role-identities of their individual incumbents (which implies their autonomy from current interactants and their social action).

The above observations establish the case for seeking to understand societies in terms of the structures they possess. But what is structure? In keeping with the general view of contemporary sociologists, I would endorse the position that 'social structure refers to the enduring, orderly ... relationships between *elements of a society*'.[7] Structure is societal organisation, the relationships between 'parts' of a social system.

But what is the ontological status of structures grasped in these terms? My contention is that the concept of social structure is the obverse of the concept of social interaction. Whereas social interaction refers to the conscious and self-conscious activity of human beings, and especially the ways in which this activity or 'agency' continually reproduces or reshapes society, social structure refers to the resultants, or effects, of this activity, the manner in which the action and interaction of the dead confront the activity and thinking of the living as an inherited environment of 'institutions', 'distributions', 'artefacts', 'language habits', 'belief-systems', 'ways of living', and so on and so forth, which both frustrate and facilitate the possibilities of agency and consciousness of those here present. Socio-cultural structure is, in other words, 'the traditions of all the dead generations' (i.e. certain of the 'emergent properties' of previously materialised social conduct), which in 'framing' or 'bounding' the activity and thinking of contemporary flesh-and-blood interactants in definite and specifiable ways ensures that societies or social systems either tend to persist in a given form, or are modified or transformed on the basis of a pre-determinate range of developmental possibilities. The concept of structure thus draws our attention to the fact that 'society is more than the sum of the people in it',[8] or indeed of the totality of their interpersonal relations or interactions.

Such an ontological understanding of structure means that social analysis must take on a specific methodological orientation. Specifically, the function of structural analysis is to offer 'a guide which tells us where to look in trying to explain any social phenomenon sociologically'.[9] Since individuals and their interaction are always contextualised within an environment comprised of structures (to which it is rationally oriented), it follows that the explanation of social conduct 'should be sought first in the way that society is organised'.[10]

In other words, whatever the impact of human agency and interaction in reproducing or elaborating the structural properties of a society, it is nonetheless always with structures that any explanation of social phenomena must commence. Structures explain the social conduct which allows them to persist or which causes them to perish (given certain premises about human organisms and subjects – namely that individuals have psycho-organic needs and capacities which they self-consciously articulate as such and attempt to act upon), just as human agency explains the elaboration, replication or overturning of these same structures over time (given the same anthropological premises as specified above).

The nature of structural and cultural conditioning

In the foregoing I have suggested that structures 'explain' social interaction (even if social interaction explains structural change or statics). But how do they do so? Certainly not by operating as hydraulic *determinations* of human action and consciousness, as is suggested by structuralists and functionalists. On the contrary, as Margaret Archer has recently pointed out, structural conditioning is essentially a mediatory process, which is best grasped as an 'objective influence which conditions action patterns and supplies agents with strategic directional guidance'.[11] This it does by defining the objective situational logics in which interactants find themselves or enter into during their life-cycles. In Archer's own words: 'It is the situations to which people respond which are mediatory because they condition (without determining) different courses of action for those differently placed, by supplying different reasons to them'.[12]

There are three aspects to structural conditioning (as a mediatory process) by virtue of which 'directional guidance' is imparted to the social conduct of interactants (and hence to socio-cultural dynamics). These are: involuntary placement, vested interests, and opportunity costs.[13] First, 'involuntary placement'. To grasp the meaning and import of this concept it is necessary to remind ourselves that the social environment is *pre*-structured by material and cultural emergents prior to the doings of those here present. These emergent structures 'account for what there is (materially and culturally) to be distributed' amongst a society's members, 'the shape of such distributions',[14] and the manner of which these distributions are related to one another and to institutions in a 'structure of structures'. Such emergents also account 'for the nature of the extant role-array, the proportions of positions available at any time and the advantages/disadvantages associated with them',[15] and other societal properties besides.

In the case of societal 'distributions' of cultural and material goods, it is scarcely plausible to deny that interactants are inserted involuntarily at birth into agential collectivities, which by virtue of their asymmetrical access to resources provide their members initially with differential life-chances. But this is scarcely any less true of individuals as role-incumbents. In this case, although interactants have a certain freedom over which of these to appropriate as their own from society (within constraints imposed by the facts of their agential origins and upbringing), it nonetheless remains certain that 'such exercises of voluntarism do not free agents from involuntaristic involvement in structures and their situational conditioning'.

Thus:

> Most of us have the choice of whether to marry or not, but agential awareness of the structural powers which this would entail (legal responsibility, financial communality, canonical obligations and juridical restrictions on exit) may serve hermeneutically to prompt avoidance. Yet the alternative choice of 'partnership' may dodge those particular situational constraints attaching to the marriage project, but it is not a method of gaining immunity from all structural influences; these agents have merely 'exchanged' one potential situation for another form of situational conditioning (the law still arbitrates on custody of children, relative entitlements to common goods, eligibility for certain benefits, etc.). Similarly, opting for single or celibate status is not to opt out of situational constraints, but to be embroiled in a different set.[16]

Second, 'vested interests'. The significance of the involuntary placement of interactants within 'positions' or 'places' within social relations is that it distributes different vested interests to those differently placed. Vested interests are definable as those appropriate modes of social praxis which agents occupying a particular socially constructed situation in society can or ought to pursue, if they are to enhance or defend their life-chances or well-being (whether individually or collectively *vis-à-vis* the members of other social groupings differently situated).

For those sections of a 'societal community' whose members occupy positions by virtue of which they monopolise a disproportionate share of or access to a society's means of economic, political and cultural production and consumption, these vested interests will include pursuit of those social strategies or practices which allow them to maintain their position of power, privilege and authority relative to subordinate agential collectivities. For those members of society who are occupants of social groupings which are collectively disenfranchised relative to the advantaged (in terms of having restricted access to authoritative and allocative resources which are materially available and which would by virtue of their redistribution allow them to sustain improved life-chances or well-being), it is clear that vested interests are those structurally determined praxes which would allow agents in subordinate positions to either wrest control of those resources necessary to end their subordination (or, failing this, to at least improve their life-chances by obtaining a more equitable share of a society's resources), or to join the ranks of privileged or advantaged groupings.

This being the case, whatever the peculiarity of the vested interests which pertain to differently situated collectivities of agents in social relations, it is certain that 'one of the main antecedent effects of structures ... consists in dividing the population ... into those with vested interests in maintenance and change respectively, according to the positions in which they find themselves involuntaristically'.[17] In other words, the significance of structural conditioning here is that vested interests (in maintenance or change) are a function of the involuntary placement of interactants in different situations or positions in social relations *vis-à-vis* various distributions of material and cultural goods.

But this means that agents' vested interests (as opposed to their wants and desires) are not subjectivist phenomena. On the contrary, they are 'objective features of ... situations'[18] by virtue of the fact that emergent structures, by defining the general standards of living of differently placed collectivities of people, determine which courses of social action are best suited to improving or protecting the lot of their members. For example, collective methods of industrial struggle and union membership are, for members of the working class, more effective social means of achieving greater autonomy and higher life-chances in capitalist society than 'individualistic' modes of self-aggrandisement. This is because the proletariat's agential situation of propertylessness denies its members the economic and cultural resources to compete as equals with members of the middle class by means of individuated mobility (I will return to this argument below).

Third, 'opportunity costs'. Now, it is apparent that structural conditioning grasped in terms of 'involuntary placement' and attendant 'vested interests' is a necessary but insufficient condition for asserting that structures 'explain' the interaction which reproduces or elaborates them. After all, specifying objective vested interests does not itself provide a structural interest-explanation of social agency and societal dynamics. Agents might not recognise which courses of social action are appropriate to their social circumstances or positioning (perhaps because, being 'undetermined' by structural emergents, their interpretations of their situations are always 'open' or fallible; or perhaps because the effectivity of dominant ideology is sufficient to prevent them recognising where their vested interests lie). Equally, having recognised their vested interests, agents may choose to disregard them (perhaps because afraid of the consequences of pursuing them, or perhaps because they find their pursuit distasteful or ethically reprehensible).

Furthermore, agents may find subjective wants more compelling sources of motivation than whatever objective social interests they possess. As Archer rightly points out,

> [s]ince a vested interest is not a 'social force' nor do people's responses have anything in common with billiard balls' unreflective movements, then their influence depends for its efficacy upon them being found good by large numbers of those who share them (though not necessarily upon them being found best by all in the same position).[19]

What is needed, in short, is the specification of some kind of mechanism which would allow vested interests to be transmitted (however imperfectly) into forms of social consciousness and specific modes of social practice geared towards their pursuance or defence.

The mediatory mechanism, by means of which the vested interests attached to structural situations in society become efficacious in explaining the conduct and consciousness of interactants, is that of opportunity costs. 'Without in any way depriving agents of their fundamental interpretative freedom, nevertheless real structural influences mean that objective opportunity costs are associated with different responses to frustrating or rewarding experiences, which condition (without determining) the interpretations placed upon them'.[20] 'Opportunity costs' are attached to the various modes of social praxis or activity by which individuals may pursue their human needs and culturally constructed wants, meaning that particular action-responses to structurally determined agential circumstances are likely to induce either rewards (in terms of greater societal enfranchisement or improved life-chances) or costs (in terms of reduced autonomy or freedom of action and stagnant or declining life-chances) – or a different balance between the two – and indeed to induce these effects differentially for members of different agential groupings.

Naturally, the existence of these 'opportunity costs' attached to different modes of social praxis does not function as a hydraulic determination of human agency and consciousness. One reason for this is that human beings are 'sovereign artificers' whose powers and properties of self, intentionality and rationality allow them sufficient autonomy of action and thought to resist the most stringent of structural constraints. Furthermore, structural conditioning does not generate passive agents 'deterministically doomed' to follow their vested interests, because the existence of differential 'opportunity costs' attached to different social practices does not make it certain that agents will seek to forego penalties and facilitate rewards (or to subordinate vested interests to subjective wants or beliefs).

For example, there is no reason why particular members of powerful elites or socially dominant classes should not choose (for ethical, political or altruistic reasons) to renounce the privileges of their background and upbringing – perhaps by covertly supporting and funding workers' resistance to capitalist exploitation, or by handing over their fortunes to charity. Nor is there any reason why individuals occupying role-positions of high status and income in institutions should not decide for the same reasons to sacrifice both, in favour of the more modest pickings associated with other (perhaps more socially beneficial or intellectually demanding) institutional functions – such as resigning a company directorship to train as teacher or doctor, or to bring up a child. Nonetheless, this having been said, it remains certain that most individuals will act and think in rough accordance with their vested interests, not least because freedom of action and interpretation is precisely freedom to orient towards opportunity costs, in a way which minimises punishing constraints and facilitates rewarding experiences. Thus most will find those reasons for pursuing vested interests more compelling than those which recommend alternatives, as they evaluate the latter against the balance sheet of costs and benefits.

The mediatory influence of opportunity costs is twofold. First, they function 'through allocating different costs for the *same course of action* to those who are differently situated'.[21] This they do by placing individuals in agential groupings which have greater or lesser access to those various societal distributions of economic, political and cultural capital which facilitate individual mobility or 'success' (in terms of obtaining those scarce institutional functions which confer high income and status), thus hampering those in 'disadvantaged' positions in social relations from competing on equal terms with those from 'advantaged' backgrounds for occupancy of these same 'privileged' role-positions.

And so, although the existence of opportunity costs grasped in this way does not preclude individuals in disadvantaged or subordinate positions from achieving 'upward mobility' into the upper reaches of the institutional hierarchy, they do nonetheless function to ensure that greater costs (e.g. financial hardship during further education or training) and risks (e.g. the real possibility that these costs will be in vain due to a limited number of opportunities or discrimination) are attached to the project of individual advancement. For the disadvantaged, such costs or risks, or to put it another way, this asymmetry between costs or potential costs and the advantages or potential advantages which are likely to result from paying them, are often sufficient (in perhaps a majority of cases) to either discourage this kind of project from being initiated or to successfully derail it before it has a chance to yield results.

Second,

> differential opportunity costs not only affect the ease or difficulty of undertaking the same course of action for groups which are differently situated, they also condition which projects are entertained by them and thus serve to explain why it is that these can be systematically and diametrically opposed.

This is the case because the 'connections between the antecedent setting of life-chances, the vested interests associated with them, and the opportunity costs predisposing towards different projects can account for divergent trends amongst those variously situated'.[22] In other words, the objective positioning of individuals in social relations, which ensures they must follow specific kinds of social strategies if they are to most effectively enhance or defend their vested interests, at the same time exerts a certain pressure over them to behave in the appropriate ways (i.e. to maintain existing powers and privileges, or avoid increasingly punitive restrictions on their freedom or consumption).

It is for this reason, for example, that individualistic modes of self-advancement (social mobility up the institutional pecking order) are the preferred and normal strategy of members of the middle class to achieve or sustain their life-chances and secure autonomy at work. By contrast, for members of the working class the strategy which is normally relied on (and for many positively preferred) is that of collective mobilisations (i.e. union organisation and action) for these same purposes.

By way of further illustration of this argument, I will consider the above example – the directional guidance exerted by structures (by means of vested interests and attendant opportunity costs) to the kinds of collective social practices which are likely to be pursued by workers to improve or defend their conditions of life and work – in greater detail. Now, workers who fail to take strike action in response to the projects of employers to 'rationalise' production or 'streamline' the labour force (in favour say of a 'work-to-rule' or an appeal to 'public goodwill') are unlikely to succeed in protecting jobs or conditions of work. This is because such a strategy entails a failure on the part of the workers to effectively utilise their 'structural capacity' to halt the production of value and surplus value upon which the accumulation of capital (and hence the profitability of capitalist enterprise) depends.

By failing to take the appropriate 'collective' response, however, workers send a signal to the employers that they lack the 'stomach' for a determined confrontation, and by doing so encourage the latter to seek out yet more concessions and retreats (more 'flexible' practices justified in the name of 'globalisation', etc.). The logic of this process is therefore a downward spiral of growing working-class passivity and declining confidence, together with steadily declining life-chances and autonomy at work, until such time as an explosion of anger (or desperation) propels the workers to take more determined or resolute action which has the potential to redress the balance (and which in doing so re-educates them as to which strategies are better suited to effectively assert their vested interests against the employing class).

Thus, as my example shows, although structurally determined 'opportunity costs' attached to different modes of social praxis or action do not determine or guarantee that interactants adopt consistently the appropriate means to defend or enhance their vested interests, they do provide a purchase on the question of why they often do so (despite attempts at ideological obfuscation by opposing interests and the 'fear factor' of defeat and its consequences). Workers in Britain and elsewhere, for instance, despite the setbacks and defeats of the 1980s, still possess the 'structural power' of the mass strike to reverse the trend of labour market 'restructuring', and we can be sure that steadily increasing frustration and anger at their growing relative disadvantages in society will prompt its exercise again in the near future.

To claim that this is indeed the case is not, of course, to minimise the significance of those countervailing generative structural pressures (such as a less favourable balance of class forces from the point of view of the proletariat than existed in the 1970s, brought about by the isolation and defeat of the workers' struggles in the 1980s, the spectre of mass – though now declining – unemployment, the vacuum of political leadership and ideology on the left, etc.) which have prevented them from doing so. These structural constraints have clearly sapped the militancy and confidence of the Western working class, and continue to do so. But it nonetheless remains the case that the rising pressure of mass discontent at the base of society (faced with growing poverty, relative disadvantage, insecure temporary employment, crumbling public services, lack of adequate industrial or political representation, etc.) cannot be contained indefinitely.[23] It is this steady accumulation of costs attached to proletarian inactivity and passivity, which guarantees that convulsive confrontations between the state and capital on the one side and the workers on the other (by 'traditional' means of mass industrial struggle) are likely to break out in the none-too-distant future.

The Marxian concept of social structure

My contention is that the basic concepts of Marxian sociology furnish the analyst with the best available theoretical tools to grasp the manner of the interface between the various structural elements which comprise any social system. The task of this section and the next is to provide good arguments in defence of this strong claim. I will start by describing in the broadest terms the philosophical basis of the 'materialist conception of society'. Then I will outline the core theoretical concepts of the Marxian account of structure (i.e. 'mode of production', 'forces of production', 'social relations of production', 'structure – i.e. base – and superstructure', etc.). A critical appraisal of the more enduring and influential claims of the orthodox liberal critique of Marxian sociology (i.e. the argument that Marxism equals 'technological determinism' and 'economic reductionism') will be integrated into the discussion proper.

The philosophical and anthropological premises of historical materialism

It will be recalled that my discussion of Marxism thus far has involved the articulation of three basic points. First, the simultaneous and combined importance of anthropological and sociological premises in historical materialism, with the former underpinning the latter, providing 'naturalistic' and 'humanist' micro-foundations to Marx and Engels' theory of society and culture (Chapter 2). Second, the manner in which both these aspects of Marxian theory arise from a totalising dialectical and materialist philosophy of nature, which postulates the explanatory and historical primacy of matter over mind, of being over consciousness, and which thus regards human thought as emergent from underlying physical and biological structures, and the contents of this thinking as a 'reflection' of material reality (social and physical) rather than vice-versa (Chapter 1). Finally, the manner in which 'philosophical materialism' (grasped as a dialectical ontology of nature specifying a stratified material world of irreducible levels, extending from basic chemical and physical structures to the higher structures of biological and human reality) underwrites an account of human nature as a 'differentiated totality', whereby its distinctive physical architecture and emergent properties (of intentionality, self-consciousness, rationality and culture) are seen as evolutionary products of the historical movement of social labour, as human beings and their hominid ancestors have acted to procure a material subsistence from the physical environment (Chapter 1).

It is this stratified or differentiated concept of human nature which constitutes the foundation of Marx and Engels' understanding of interaction, structure and system. To reiterate the relevant points. For Marx and Engels, it is the core activity of social labour in the procurement or production of the basic material necessities of life (food, clothing, dwellings, etc.) which has allowed and which continues to allow humanity to enjoy a cultural existence and history. Further, this core activity of material production has also played an absolutely central role in the *self*-creation of humanity as a particular biological species with distinct capacities and needs.

From this perspective, in the same way as humanity's species-capacities of intellect, self, rationality and language arose as an evolutionary emergent from the 'basic' or 'core' human activity of social labour for subsistence (as part of the lengthy historical process during which our hominid ancestors evolved into fully modern human organisms), so humanity's subsequent socio-cultural history and development has been made possible and given a powerful stimulus by the ongoing historical interchange between productive social labour and the physical environment (and the economic structures which have arisen from this interaction between humanity and nature, and which feed into the process as a causal power or generative mechanism in their own right). This is because the dialectic between socio-economic production, its emergent properties (the ensemble of economic structures which every generation of agents find 'already made') and material nature, generates the output of economic resources which are necessary to support non-productive social activities and which thereby enable (in the sense of providing 'conditions of existence' for) the construction and increasing differentiation of non-economic social structures over time.

The mode of production as structure and action

The famous Marxian distinction between base (i.e. structure) and superstructure is sketched out above in the simplest terms. Before examining the meaning and efficacy of the structure–superstructure model, however, it is worth considering how Marx and Engels conceptualise the 'base', if only because many of the most influential critiques of historical materialism (especially the claim that Marxism is a form of technological determinism) have precisely based their authority upon its misunderstanding.

It is important to make the point that for Marx and Engels the mode of production is both 'structure' and 'action', and as such cannot be identified simply with the 'base' (as I have interpreted it as emergent structures). In other words, Marx and Engels do not clearly distinguish between the 'structural' and 'activist' aspects of the mode of production, between the mode of production as the 'core' or 'fundamental' social practice and the mode of production as a configuration of social structures which are 'basic' to other social structures in a social system. Yet it is clear that, although Marx and Engels often treat the mode of production as synonymous with the labour-*process*,[24] they also define it in a way which simultaneously acknowledges both the activity or agency of material production to transform nature and generate use-values, and the fact that in producing their means of life economic agents enter into 'definite relations', and encounter 'specific circumstances' which are independent of their will, not of their own making, and which correspond to a 'definite stage' of development of the productive forces.[25]

Marx and Engels' focus on the dual nature of the mode of production is quite legitimate, not least because the explanatory primacy of the mode of production as structure in Marxist theory is in part derived from the fundamental importance which Marx and Engels attach to the *process* of material production in sustaining human and social existence on a daily basis. Yet it is important to delineate the two meanings of 'mode of production' if we are to derive from their writings a theory of the interface between 'action and its environments'. That these distinct aspects of the mode of production are normally conflated by Marx and Engels is not surprising. They did not, after all, possess the conceptual tools (i.e. an emergentist ontology of the social world) to add theoretical substance to their own insight that 'men make history but not in circumstances of their own choosing'.[26] This being the case, I propose to do so on their behalf.

Consequently, in the analysis that follows, the mode of production as structure will be treated as an accumulation of material wealth or economic resources and technical know-how upon which agents draw in the labour-process, the institutional functions or role-positions which comprise the 'organisational properties' of the labour-process, and the pre-structured 'distributions' of means of production and/or subsistence which (where appropriate) shape the class positions and attendant vested interests of interactants, in advance of their economic or other practices, and which feed into the 'institutional properties' of the labour-process. The mode of production as activity, by contrast, will be treated simply as both the productive 'doings' of agents in reproducing their material existence and expanding their material and other needs in ongoing interchange with nature (via the medium of the labour-process), and as the exploitative 'doings' of non-producers in appropriating surplus-labour or surplus-product from the direct producers by whatever means or methods are available to them.

Forces and relations of production as emergent social structures

An important source of confusion amongst Marxists and non-Marxist interpreters of Marx centres upon the respective explanatory function of the two constituent elements of the mode of production – the forces of production and the relations of production. There are a number of possibilities here. First, there is the 'conventional' view, held by the orthodox Marxists of the Second and Third Internationals (e.g. Kautsky, Plekhanov, Stalin, etc.), and powerfully restated in more recent times by the analytical philosopher G. A. Cohen,[27] which contends that the forces of production are more fundamental than the relations of production, since these alone hold the key to societal dynamics. Productive forces *select* production relations according to their capacity to further socio-economic development or 'progress'. Second, there is the polar opposite view (whose most important contemporary allegiants include Robert Brenner and Alex Callinicos), which holds that it is the relations of production which are the most basic structure of the mode of production, on the grounds that production relations determine whether or not the productive forces develop or stagnate, and because it is in any case impossible to speak meaningfully of productive forces in abstraction from the social organisation of the economy.[28] Finally, it has become fashionable more recently still to interpret the mode of production (somewhat eccentrically) as forces and relations of production plus politics and ideology. 'Social relations of production appear in specific economic, ideological and political forms', as one leading light of the approach puts the argument.[29]

My contention is that the easiest way to grasp the concept of 'mode of production' in Marxian theory is by drawing out what for Marx distinguishes forces of production from relations of production. For only by doing so can we grasp the interrelationship between them. What constitutes the forces of production? In my view, and also I believe in Marx's view, forces of production have a material, social and ideational aspect. The 'material' and 'social' dimensions of the 'forces', on the one hand, refer us to labour-power and the institutionalised forms of cooperative social 'activity through which men and women seek to meet their needs by acting on and transforming nature', which 'implies a certain organisation of production, the possession of the appropriate tools, and so on'.[30] More specifically, the socio-economic aspect of the 'forces' entails a particular technical organisation of work by means of which labour-power is combined with means of production (raw materials, tools and technology), and a corresponding mode of social cooperation by means of which this union between labour-power and nature is accomplished, which together determine 'the methods of labour and thereby its social productivity'[31] at any given point in time.

The 'ideational' aspect of 'forces', on the other hand, refers us to the inherited store of technical (and sometimes scientific) know-how which is directly integrated into the labour process, and which also determines the manner of which labour-power and means of production (the 'objects' and 'instruments' of labour) are combined in everyday economic activity. As Marx puts it, 'general social knowledge has become a *direct force of production*'.[32] Marx also appears to identify forces of production as those modes of wealth-creation associated with rising social classes which have not as yet been constituted as the dominant relations of production in a society.[33]

Relations of production, by contrast, are specific kinds of social relations which are the dominant economic (or politico-economic) structures of the society in which they are embedded. More specifically, relations of production are, as Callinicos rightly says, those 'relations which ... concern the control of the process of production and the distribution of its products'.[34] Where these relations of production predetermine an unequal distribution of the means of production in a society, they give rise (or are equivalent) to relations of economic exploitation, i.e. class relations.

Marx makes the argument as follows:

> Wherever a part of society possesses the monopoly of the means of production, the worker, free or unfree, must add to the labour-time necessary for his own maintenance an extra quantity of labour-time in order to produce the means of subsistence for the owner of the means of production, whether this proprietor be an Athenian aristocrat, an Etruscan theocrat, a Roman citizen, a Norman baron, an American slave-owner, a Wallachian boyar, a modern landlord or a capitalist.[35]

As is well enough known, Marx's theory of class, and of the relationship of classes to relations of production, is never spelled out by him explicitly. The third volume of *Capital* breaks off at precisely the point where Marx is set to make clear his own approach to this question. Nonetheless, it would be quite wrong to suppose that Marx's theory of class cannot reliably be derived from his theoretical writings taken as a whole, especially the three volumes of *Capital*. Certainly, this is the view of G. E. M. de Ste Croix. His interpretation of Marx's approach appears to me to go right to the heart of the matter:

> *Class* (essentially a relationship) is the collective social expression of the fact of exploitation, the way in which exploitation is embodied in a social structure. By exploitation I mean the appropriation of part of the product of the labour of others. ... A class (a particular class) is a group of persons in a community identified by their position in the whole system of social production, defined above all according to their relationship (primarily in terms of the degree of ownership or control) to the conditions of production (that is to say, the means and labour of production) and to other classes. ... The individuals constituting a given class may or may not be wholly or partly conscious of their own identity and common interests as a class, and they may or may not feel antagonism towards members of other classes as such.[36]

Clearly, then, class structures are integral to relations of production which correspond to a certain stage of development of the productive forces – specifically those 'forces' which provide material 'conditions of existence' for an unproductive group to emerge in society. Class-based relations of production, by concentrating certain of the means of production in the hands of a tiny minority of non-producing 'owners', allow this privileged group the structural capacity to appropriate surplus-labour or surplus-product from a subordinate class of 'direct producers', who are forced to yield to economic exploitation in exchange for some kind of access to the means of subsistence. This asymmetrical distribution of the means of production determines not only the effective control of the means of wealth-creation by a particular exploiting class, but also the extent to which the subordinate or exploited class exercises control over its own labour-power: the lesser the degree of control exercised by the exploiting class over the means of production, the greater the degree of control exercised by the subordinate class over its own labour-power.

Relations of production, insofar as these are rooted in class exploitation, must therefore always entail a structurally determined antagonism between classes, so that 'class struggle itself becomes an intrinsic rather than a contingent consequence of the structure of class relations'.[37] Furthermore, where there exists this asymmetry of distribution of the instruments and materials of labour, i.e. where there exist relations of exploitation, there must also exist an unequal distribution of the means of subsistence, which in turn stimulates a class conflict over the distribution of the social product as well as over control of the production process.

A final set of observations. Aside from the above interpretation of relations of production, it does seem reasonable to infer from Marx's writings an additional important dimension to his treatment. Jon Elster makes the point, during his discussion of pre-capitalist societies, that a theoretically adequate conceptualisation of relations of production should include an account of the non-producing owners, i.e. of the internal configuration of the propertied class or classes. This he does on the grounds that 'the nature of the non-producing owners would presumably enter importantly into analysis of the furthering or fettering of the productive forces by the relations of production'.[38] This seems to me a defensible view of Marx's meaning. For example, whatever one thinks of Marx's own discussion of the so-called 'Asiatic mode of production' (and I do not think very much of it), it is nonetheless apparent that his designation of the Oriental civilisations as 'stagnant', as incapable of internally generated development, precisely depends upon some conception of the manner in which the nature of the 'non-producing owners' acts as a brake on economic 'progress' or evolution.

Furthermore, as Callinicos rightly observes, Marx's claim that 'capital exists and can only exist as many capitals, and its self-determination therefore appears as their reciprocal interaction with one another',[39] would be equally incoherent if we were to attempt a definition of capitalist relations of production in abstraction from the internal characteristics of the capitalist bourgeoisie as a particular social class.[40] Callinicos' point is that Marx's theory of capitalist development and crisis hinges crucially upon the role of *intra*-class economic competition in generating the dynamic of 'accumulation for the sake of accumulation, production for production's sake', and hence the periodic over-accumulation of capital.[41] As Marx puts it:

> Competition is nothing more than the way in which the many capitals force[e] the inherent determinants upon one another and upon themselves ... the influence of individual capitals on one another has the effect precisely that they must conduct themselves as *capital*.[42]

Callinicos and Elster are therefore right to argue that a fully satisfactory account of the relations of production in any society must therefore include an analysis of the internal configuration of the class which 'owns' or otherwise possesses productive property.

To summarise the preceding discussion. The mode of production in Marxian analysis can be legitimately grasped as a particular configuration of socio-economic structures – the forces and relations of production. The forces of production are the organisational properties of the socio-technical labour-process – especially the manner or form by which labour power and means of production are combined in a particular economic system in order to transform nature and generate use-values – and the 'bank' of scientific and technical knowledge which is integrated into material production, and which is developed on the basis of human interaction with nature via the medium of social labour.

The relations of production consist of 'the relationship of the direct producers to the means of production and their labour-power, the nature of any non-producing owners, and the mode of appropriation of surplus labour from the direct producers by any such owners' (i.e. the mode of class exploitation as determined by these structural elements).[43] Relations of economic exploitation entail an asymmetrical distribution of the means of production (and hence consumption). The form of exploitation (or surplus extraction) thus determines or is synonymous with 'the class structure, so that classes are defined relationally, by their objective relationship both to the means of production and labour-power and to other classes. Exploitation in turn gives rise to class struggle',[44] which powerfully shapes the dynamics of social systems.

The mode of production and structural conditioning: orthodox objections

This above understanding of the mode of production in Marxist theory enables us to dispense with three common objections to historical materialism. First, the argument sometimes encountered that Marx is unable to distinguish analytically between forces and relations of production in a way that allows him to grasp their interplay in determining the constitution and dynamics of economic and social systems. Second, the contention, most recently repackaged by Ernesto Laclau and Chantal Mouffe, that Marx's structural sociology 'reifies' or 'fetishises' the objects, instruments and products of labour, in effect treating 'the economy ... as a mechanism of society acting independently of human action'.[45] Finally, the claim that by seeing specific production relations and wider social structures as a simple 'effect' of a given stage of development of the productive forces, Marx is guilty of 'technological determinism'. I will address each aspect of the 'orthodox critique' in the order I have presented them above.

It is, of course, perfectly true that productive forces are an indissolubly human and social phenomenon. But it is also equally certain that Marx makes no attempt to deny that this is the case. There is simply no question of Marx's distinction between forces and relations of production being one between purely 'technical' and 'material' factors (i.e. technology, tools, raw materials, human skills and the economic output of social labour) on the one hand, and those social relations which determine the production and distribution of the social product, on the other.

Since, for Marx and Engels, the productive forces in their 'structural' aspect are precisely the resultants of human and social activity, and precisely entail social organisation (i.e. the socio-technical organisation of the human labour-process), it follows that the distinction between productive forces and production relations must be grasped as one between relations among social positions which enter into the production or procurement of use-values, and those relations among social positions external to the labour-process which determine the distribution of the means of production or procurement and social product (including the mode of surplus extraction). But this means a meaningful distinction between forces and relations of production can be made without abstracting the former from membership of society or from any kind of dependence upon human agency. Clearly, productive forces, as emergent properties of the historical interface between social labour and material nature, cannot be construed as detaching the developmental dynamic of the productive forces from the socio-economic practices of human beings.

This interpretation of the productive forces in Marxian sociology enables us to dispense also with the argument that historical materialism

> is not simply a theory that accords a privileged place to economic factors [but] is, more specifically, a form of technological determinism [according to which] the rise and fall of successive property regimes are explained by their tendency to promote or fetter technical change.[46]

Along with the related (though not identical) charge of 'economic determinism' or 'economic reductionism' (see next section), the claim that

Marxism equals 'technological determinism' has traditionally been the major objection of 'bourgeois' intellectuals to historical materialism since Marx first formulated his approach in the 1840s.

Indeed, this is a view which is much alive and kicking today. The following curt dismissal of Marx's historical sociology along these lines by Tony Spybey, to offer one contemporary example, is far from untypical:

> Under the terms of historical materialism, societies must pass through the epochs of ancient, feudal and capitalist, each with its respective 'relations of production': 'master and slave'; 'lord and serf'; 'capitalist and worker'. When the 'relations of production' of an epoch cease to be appropriate for its technologically advancing 'forces of production', a major contradiction is created in the social structure and revolutionary change is regarded as inevitable. For this reason, historical materialism is sometimes referred to in terms of 'technological determinism'.[47]

In order to get to grips with the orthodox interpretation of Marx's account of the relationship between the mode of production and societal process it is necessary to make a concession. For like all stereotypical views, there is *some* kind of textual basis for interpreting historical materialism as a species of technological determinism. For example, Marx does at one point argue that

> it is not only what is made but how, and by what instruments of labour, that distinguishes different economic epochs. Instruments of labour not only supply a standard of the degree of development that human labour has attained, but they also indicate the social relations within which men work.[48]

Whereas elsewhere he makes the claim that

> social relations are closely bound up with productive forces. In acquiring new productive forces men change their mode of production; and in changing their mode of production, in changing the way of making their living, they change all their social relations. The windmill gives you society with the feudal lord; the steam mill society with the industrial capitalist.[49]

But it is also the case that even these apparently extreme statements of technological determinism have an ambiguity which renders any secure interpretation of them as such of doubtful validity. Consider the first passage cited above. To claim that the economic product and level of technological development of a society furnishes a useful conceptual means of distinguishing between different 'economic epochs' does not necessarily add up to the view that this is the only acceptable way of doing so. There is no indication here that Marx is distinguishing between modes of production or modes of economic exploitation on this basis. In fact the application of his argument appears to be much narrower than this, referring instead to the structured relationship between means of production and labour-power – that is, to structural properties of the forces of production. Least of all is there any suggestion that Marx is claiming here that *social systems* are determined by the level of development of the productive forces. Rather, he seems to be arguing that the level of economic and technological know-how (i.e. the methods of social labour) 'indicates' or 'is associated with' the 'social relations within which men work'. Understood in this way, such a viewpoint seems to me to have little in common with the notion that the objects, instruments and products of labour (i.e. the means of production and subsistence) unilaterally explain the labour-process, let alone the more radical idea that productive forces select production relations.

Similar problems call into question the adequacy of a 'mechanical materialist' interpretation of the second passage cited above. It should be obvious, after all, that it is at least possible that Marx is (again) not claiming here that productive forces are the sole 'cause' of relations of production or wider social relations. After all, he does explicitly say that social relations are 'closely bound up with', not determined by, the forces of production. Aside from this, it is clear that Marx's claim that the 'windmill gives you society with the feudal lord ... the steam-mill society with the industrial capitalist' does not necessarily indicate a strict causal relationship between forces and relations of production, with the latter responding passively to developments in the former. Indeed, even when taken solely on its own terms, i.e. even when this passage is abstracted from its wider intellectual context, it appears equally plausible to interpret it as a statement of correspondence between a certain level of development of the instruments, techniques and productivity of the labour-process and the specific kinds of production relations associated with it.

Whatever one makes of passages of the above type, however, what cannot be doubted is that there are remarkably few of them to be found in the substantive works of either Marx or Engels. Any attempt, therefore, to comprehend Marx's sociology on the basis of such isolated remarks, in abstraction from the bulk of his theoretical and historical writings, is bound to degenerate very quickly into misunderstanding, even vulgarisation. In fact, contrary to what he argues in the first passage cited above, Marx does not attempt to analyse 'economic epochs' in terms of their material instruments of production and associated level of labour productivity. Instead, he distinguishes modes of production one from the other in terms of their characteristic relations of production, in particular (where appropriate) in terms of their distinct modes of class exploitation, by means of which surplus labour is extracted from the direct producers by non-producing 'owners' or 'controllers' of certain of the means or conditions of production. This is why, for example, Marx does not draw a crude distinction between 'foraging', 'pastoral', 'agrarian' and 'industrial' modes of production, instead differentiating between 'primitive communism', 'slavery', 'feudalism', 'capitalism', etc.

By way of confirmation of this argument, it is necessary only to consider a couple of examples from Marx's theoretical writings. In the third volume of *Capital*, for instance, Marx insists that the

> specific economic form in which surplus-labour is pumped out of the direct producers determines the relationship of rulers and ruled. It is always the direct relationship of the owners of the conditions of production to the direct producers ... which reveals the innermost secret, the hidden basis of the entire social structure.[50]

Elsewhere, in the first volume of *Capital*, Marx argues that

> [w]hat distinguishes the various economic formations of society – the distinction between for example a society based on slave-labour and a society based on wage-labour – is the form in which this surplus-labour is in each case extorted from the immediate producer, the worker.[51]

Such passages, and numerous others, hardly evidence a commitment on Marx's part to reducing relations of production to forces of production, especially 'forces' conceived in narrowly 'technicist' or 'materialist' terms.

But if the relationship between productive forces and production relations in historical materialism cannot plausibly be interpreted as one in which the former 'determines' the latter, of what does it consist? Does Marx wish to say that productive forces, though not the unilateral 'cause' of production relations, are nonetheless the more 'fundamental' structure of the mode of production? If so, in what sense are the 'forces' more 'basic' than the 'relations'? Does his own rejection of technological determinism commit him to the view that production relations are 'basic' (in an explanatory sense) to productive forces? Or does Marx wish to argue that the mode of production, not one or other of its constituent structures, has primacy in explaining social systems?

My own view of Marx's meaning on this question is, on first sight, a paradoxical one. On the one hand I believe that Marx does indeed regard productive forces as 'basic' to production relations. Yet on the other hand I am convinced that he is committed to a view which sees the mode of production or 'economic structure' as a totality (not either one of its constituent structures), as enjoying explanatory primacy in shaping the constitution and dynamics of societies. To see why this is the case, however, it is necessary first to dispose of the 'either/or' positions cited above.

Marx's most famous compressed statement of structural causality – i.e. the 1859 Preface to his *A Contribution to the Critique of Political Economy* – can be used to justify either the primacy of productive forces or the primacy of the relations of production in historical materialism. Chris Harman, for example, argues for the primacy of the 'forces' over the 'relations', on the grounds that for Marx 'relations of production correspond to forces of production, not the other way round'.[52] Alex Callinicos, by contrast, appears to endorse the opposite view, partly because production relations are for him (and for Marx, he believes) responsible for furthering or fettering productive forces, and partly because he seems to regard an effective debunking of technological determinism as depending upon the ascription of dependent status to the latter *vis-à-vis* the former.[53]

G. A. Cohen's defence of the primacy of productive forces over the relations of production, on the other hand, is rooted in his belief that that the 1859 Preface identifies three distinct hierarchically ordered structures in society: the forces of production, the 'economic structure' (the relations of production), and the superstructure, the first of which 'selects' the others in accordance with their functionality to economic 'progress'. In his words:

> Now the sum total of relations of production in a given society is said [by Marx] to constitute the economic structure of that society, which is also called – in relation to the superstructure – the basis, or base, or foundation. The economic structure, or base, therefore consists of relations of production only: it does not include the productive forces. It is true that to exclude the productive forces from the economic structure runs against the usual construal of Marx, but he actually said that the economic structure is constituted of relations of production. ... People mistakenly believe that the productive forces belong to the economic base because they wrongly think that the explanatory importance of the forces ensure their membership of it. But while the forces indeed possess this importance, they are not part of the economic base, since they are not economic phenomena. To stay with the spatial metaphor, they are below the economic foundation, the ground on which it rests.[54]

But what is remarkable about each of these interpretations of the mode of production as structure (or structures), and of the relationship of the mode of production to the other structures of society, is their uncertain status in Marx's own account in the 1859 Preface and elsewhere. Each of them obtains for itself a superficial plausibility by highlighting particular statements or comments of Marx on this question, whilst ignoring those which at least partially contradict the opinion which is being derived from them.

Consider, first of all, Callinicos' view that Marx's method involves 'starting from the relations of production, and treating them, not the forces of production, as the independent variable'[55] in any explanation of societal process. Although Callinicos is correct to observe that Marx does indeed tend to identify modes of production in terms of their respective relations of production and/or modes of surplus appropriation, this hardly proves his case, for what is ignored in his account is Marx's own insistence that developing productive forces collide with, or bring under pressure, existing relations of production, primarily by bringing into existence the material and social preconditions (i.e. new forms of wealth-creation which are incompatible with the vested interests of established 'ruling' classes, newly developing or rising social classes, etc.) for challenging, and indeed overthrowing, these established relations. Clearly, in Marx's view, productive forces have a dynamic all of their own, by virtue of which they 'rebel against' the existing social organisation of production and exploitation. Indeed, Marx is also quite specific in his insistence that production relations 'grow out of production itself',[56] which certainly supports the legitimacy of an interpretation of the former as 'basic' to the latter.

Consider now the legitimacy of Harman's converse view that 'forces' enjoy explanatory primacy over 'relations' in shaping both the economic structure and wider social relations of society. Harman is quite right, of course, to point out that Marx argues in the 1859 Preface that production relations 'correspond to' productive forces and productive forces 'rebel against' production relations, and not vice-versa. But this is surely sketchy evidence in support of an interpretation of historical materialism (such as Harman's) which treats the latter as exercising primacy over the former in explaining social structures and societal dynamics. 'Forces' may well be 'basic' to 'relations' in the sense that these provide them with 'conditions of existence'. But to admit this much does not mean that relations of production are any less important than productive forces in accounting for what happens in society or history by virtue of the conditional influence both exert upon superstructural forms and the consciousness and conduct of interactants.

A different set of objections apply to Cohen's arguments. These appear to me to rest upon a highly dubious distinction between 'material' and 'socio-economic' structures, i.e. upon 'a set of contrasts between nature and society',[57] which in this sense exists nowhere in Marx's writings. Indeed, such an interpretation seems to square ill with the simple fact that Marx's critique of liberal political economy was designed primarily to reveal the falsity of its fetishisation of historically specific socio-economic relations as 'formally rational' (i.e. 'technical-material') relations between individuated subjects and various objects of utility, and of its treatment of socially generated categories (private property and the abstract individual) as the naturalistic foundations of social order.[58] We are thus expected by Cohen to accept that Marx abstracts 'material relations' from 'social relations', having criticised his opponents for having done the same.

In any case, of course, Cohen's interpretation of the Preface is substantially undermined by Marx's contention that 'the mode of co-operation [i.e. the socio-technical structure of material production] is itself a "productive force" '.[59] It is, after all, difficult to see how the productive forces can be anterior to the socio-economic structure of society if the 'forces' themselves have an indissolubly 'social' character. Though Cohen is right to point out that Marx does describe the 'sum total of ... relations of production' as constituting 'the economic structure of society', it is also true that Marx argues in the same passage that '[i]n the social production of their life, men enter into definite relations ... of production, which correspond to a definite stage of development of their productive forces'.[60] Elsewhere Marx makes the claim that 'the formation of the economic community' is 'founded' upon the mode of surplus-extraction, which in turn 'reacts upon production as a determining element'.[61] Passages such as these are hardly compelling proof of Marx's abstraction of forces from relations of production, or of his treatment of the latter as alone comprising the economic 'base' of society.

The real relationship between forces and relations of production

There is, in short, precious little substantive evidence supporting a view of historical materialism as privileging in a causal sense either productive forces or relations of production, in shaping one another and the wider social structure of a society. The most that can be said is that forces and relations of production are both (for Marx) aspects of the 'economic structure' of society, which is held to be the 'base' or 'basis' or 'foundation' of all other social relations in a society. But if neither 'forces' nor 'relations' can be plausibly seen as 'causing' or exercising 'dominance over' each other and the total social structure of which they are a part, of what does their relationship consist?

My own view, arrived at in part by means of elimination of plausible alternative views, is that the interrelationship between forces and relations of production has to be grasped in terms of the distinct range of constraints, enablements and impulses which each places on the other and on societal development as a whole. The significance of the productive forces in the Marxian schema lies in their function of defining the possibilities for an investment of material and human resources in structural and cultural elaboration or differentiation in any specific society or social system. The forces of production determine what is materially possible in any historical epoch (in terms of enabling the existence and persistence of certain kinds of social and cultural structures, practices or forms of consciousness, and ruling out the existence or persistence of others). Productive forces also generate a certain impetus towards the 'selection' by interactants of the appropriate structural forms which would allow their unfettered development. It is in these senses that productive forces are 'basic' or 'foundational' to production relations. The former furnish material 'conditions of possibility' of the forms which the latter can take, and exert a certain directional pressure upon interactants (belonging to a rising class based upon new forms of wealth-creation) to act in ways appropriate to further their development.

To offer an obvious example. It is only after the productive forces have developed to a point where they permit the generation of a surplus-product, over and above the basic consumption needs of the direct producers, that it becomes possible for class-based relations of production to emerge on the historical canvas. In this situation, forces of production enable the existence of class-divided relations of production (which themselves allow a further development of material subsistence and hence a growth of the human population). Yet at the same time they preclude a return to 'primitive communism' (because the expanding populations to which agricultural production gives rise cannot be supported by foraging modes of wealth-creation, and because exploiting classes in any case use a portion of the surplus to maintain the armed forces necessary to defeat any attempt to restore these). And they preclude also an advance to socialist relations of production centred on the abolition of economic and political inequalities (because these require the development of productive forces to the extent that society can support a decent life for all, and not just for a tiny minority, i.e. up to the point where an insufficiency of goods and services to satisfy all fundamental human needs can be overcome).[62]

I have contended that such productive forces also generate a certain stimulus towards the reorganisation of production relations in a way which promotes their further development. On the one hand, the development of the productive forces in Europe, from at least the fifteenth century onwards, generated a powerful impulse to the rise of capitalist relations of production, as Marx put it, 'in the interstices of feudal society'. Thus:

> From the early 19th century onwards, on the other hand, the development of the productive forces has created an increasingly powerful impetus towards socialism. The increasing socialisation of production, the growth of the world working class, the rise of the world economy, the advances of science and technology ... all press humanity in the direction of social ownership and democratic planning.[63]

There are four basic reasons why productive forces provide this impulse towards the reorganisation of production relations. First, class-based relations of production always place fetters upon the development of material production, which throws society into crisis and thereby opens up a 'space' in which oppositional currents to the *ancien régime* can prosper (i.e. by articulating ideas which promise a solution to the problems of society and mobilising struggles against the old order). Second, and as we have already seen, the cumulative development of the productive forces of society provides 'conditions of possibility' for the construction of new production relations, which are better equipped to allow further economic development, which 'somewhat rational' agents (appropriately placed and with vested interests in so doing) are bound to grasp the potential for sooner or later. Third, 'vested interests' and attendant 'opportunity costs', in acting in ways appropriate to these vested interests, are associated with those social agents whose livelihood depends upon the advancement of new forms of wealth-creation or social ownership, which collide with the vested interests of agential collectivities centred on socially dominant modes of economic exploitation (i.e. in extinguishing or controlling the threat of new productive forces to the established social relations from which they derive their privileges), and which in so doing motivate a struggle between them, the outcome of which determines the future developmental possibilities of society.

Finally, relations of production always invest in the agents of subordinate classes not only vested interests in developing the productive forces beyond the existing economic organisation of society, but also the 'structural capacities' to do so. In other words, there are powerful and objectively determined factors working in favour of the overturning of existing relations of production by the developing forces of production these have themselves (at least in part) engendered. For example, under capitalism, the structural capacities of the working class include:

> its immense numerical superiority over the bourgeoisie; its concentration in workplaces and the cities; the dependence of the bourgeoisie on the working class for all its operations including the operation of its state; and the fact that the working class can rule society without the bourgeoisie but the bourgeoisie cannot exist without the working class, which means that the bourgeoisie has to go on defeating the working class indefinitely but the proletariat has only to defeat the bourgeoisie once (in the world historical sense).[64]

Such structural factors of the capitalist mode, generated by the relentless expansion and centralisation of production, and hence of the working class, impart a certain directional impulse towards the establishment of socialist relations of production. This is by virtue of the fact they make the eventual victory of the proletariat over the bourgeoisie not only a possibility but also a probability (though not of course an inevitability: this depending on the outcome of the struggle between classes during 'critical periods' where the balance of power between them is virtually even).[65]

The significance of the relations of production, by contrast, consists of the fact they generate a social integument which facilitates and stimulates a certain quantitative and qualitative development of economic output and labour productivity, yet which acts as a brake or barrier on this development of material production beyond a certain point. As Marx puts it: 'From forms of development of the productive forces these social relations turn into their fetters'.[66] This does not mean that the social relations of production determine whether or not there is any economic development in a society. A treatment of structural conditioning as structural hydraulics is, after all, ruled out by Marx's theory of 'species-being', which allows for a certain weak tendency of the productive forces to develop irrespective of socio-historical context, under the stimulus of rational human interests (in expanding consumption, taming environmental pressures, allowing greater leisure opportunities, etc.). This being the case, the explanatory function of production relations does not consist of the fact that they are (normally) sufficiently constraining of human agency to fix or extinguish this tendency of the productive forces to develop. To repeat the basic point: production relations exert a conditional influence upon productive forces by virtue of their capacity to further or fetter their development. They do not 'select' or 'cause' productive forces, any more than productive forces 'select' or 'cause' production relations.

Relations of production constrain and further productive forces, in the sense they shape both the tempo of economic development and the scope for economic progress and consumption which is possible in a society without endangering the reproduction requirements of its economic structure. This capacity of relations of production to do so is a function of their internal organisation. Hunter-gatherer social relations, for instance, are capable of supporting the consumption of a band consisting only of twenty or thirty persons, and they constitute a barrier to economic development beyond the narrow requirements of 'simple reproduction' (though they enable a level of consumption for all which is entirely adequate to elementary human needs). This is because foraging social relations are based upon procuring, not producing, the means of subsistence from the material environment, which by its nature provides little potential to increase labour productivity, and no stimulus whatsoever towards a division of labour beyond that of sex.

Capitalist social relations, by contrast, give rise to a dynamic of economic growth which outstrips by far the rate of economic development of any previous mode of society, and which generates the material potential to sustain an equivalence of consumption on a global scale without denying anyone a decent standard of life. Yet these relations can only do so by sustaining 'societal scarcity' in tandem with convulsive crises of 'overproduction' and 'overaccumulation' which threaten the stability of the whole system. This is because capitalist production relations are based upon two great 'separations' – of the direct producers from any access whatsoever to the means of production, and of the property-owning class into separate yet interdependent units of capital in a competitive marketplace – which pressurise the latter (under pain of bankruptcy) to continually strive to increase the rate of exploitation (i.e. productivity) of the former and to accumulate resources in expanded production, irrespective of the limits of the market to absorb the output of labour. Here, prohibitive opportunity costs, attached to practices which are not conducive to the pursuit of optimum profitability and maximum exploitation of labour in the marketplace, ensure that most members of the propertied class precisely conduct themselves as capitalists.

Production relations, where these are organised as class relations, thus fetter the productive forces by virtue of the fact they generate vested interests among the powerful and propertied in preserving an asymmetrical distribution of the means of production and consumption, upon which they must act in defence if they are to preserve or enhance their life-chances or advantages generally, respective to other class groupings. In the case of feudal and tributary society, for example, production relations typically fetter productive forces by overburdening the subsistence agrarian economy with the profligate consumption and other expenditures of an unproductive group, thereby giving rise to terrible famines and the collapse of peasant production (due to an insufficiency of use-values) during periods in which agricultural yields are lower than average. In the case of capitalist society, by contrast, production relations typically fetter productive forces, not by generating an insufficiency of use-values to meet the culturally defined expectations of rulers and ruled, but by stimulating a periodic expansion of economic investment and output (subject to the competitive pressures of 'many capitals') beyond the limits of the market, and by undermining the basis of capital accumulation, and hence profitability, by replacing workers with machines (subject to these same competitive market pressures).

In any social system, therefore, the potential of the productive forces to develop, and the nature of their development, depends crucially upon the extent to which the social relations of production and economic exploitation (i.e. class relations) retard or facilitate (or indeed distort) the rational imperative of human agents to improve the methods and productivity of social labour. The less the structure of class relations operates to fetter the capacity or inclination of interactants to pursue their human interests in developing material production, or the more the class organisation of society functions to subsume rational human needs and interests under vested interests rooted in the competitive accumulation of wealth ('production for the sake of production'), the greater is the capacity of the relations of production to facilitate or even impel a more rapid tempo of development of productive forces than would otherwise be possible.

Structure and superstructure in Marxian sociology

Before addressing the meaning of the relationship between structure and superstructure in Marxian sociology, it is necessary to consider briefly the question of what comprises the superstructure. To make clear an earlier argument: the actual or immediate contents or products of human consciousness have nothing to do with the superstructure, since these are bound up with social interaction, not with the resultants of this interaction.[67] Nor is the superstructure to be identified only with legal and political relations (plus other ideological forms which are 'functional' to the base), as is suggested by G. A. Cohen's interpretation of Marx.[68] Certainly, Marx does argue that the economic structure of society is the 'real basis upon which rises a legal and political superstructure'. But he also claims elsewhere that

> upon the different forms of property, upon the social conditions of existence, rises an entire superstructure of distinct and peculiarly formed sentiments, illusions, modes of thought and views of life. The whole class creates and forms them out of its material foundations and out of the corresponding social relations. The single individual, who receives them through tradition and upbringing, may imagine that they form the real motives and the starting point for his own activity.[69]

Clearly, Marx identifies the superstructure with social ideas generally, as well as with political and legal relations. The superstructure is, then, best grasped as an ensemble of emergent social and cultural structures which arise on the 'economic foundation'. It is, in other words, comprised of every social and ideational structure which is not part of the base. This does not necessarily mean that every cultural or social property which is to be found in the superstructure is directly explainable in terms of the economy. (An endorsement of the contrary view seems to explain Cohen's desire to resist 'overpopulating' the superstructure.) For one thing, the 'real basis' of 'social relations', which for Marx gives rise to 'modes of thought and views of life', includes human organisms, their species-capacities and needs, and the law-governed physical environment which furnishes the labour process with its raw materials.[70] Furthermore, Engels makes the point that social ideas and institutions are generated by the reciprocal interaction of superstructural spheres, not simply by the economic base as 'sole active cause'.[71] This means that non-economic social and cultural structures have economic and non-economic 'material foundations', and are shaped by horizontal generative mechanisms as well as by vertical ones.

Enough said (for the moment) about the superstructure. Let us now address the relationship between base and superstructure. Now, the structure–superstructure model should 'be seen as making a distinctive claim about the *kinds* of structures which have primacy in explaining social systems, namely that these are the forces and relations of production'.[72] But of what does this 'primacy' consist? Perhaps unsurprisingly, in view of its centrality to Marxist sociology, intense controversy has always surrounded the appropriate way of grasping the interplay between 'economy' and 'society' in historical materialism, and a number of different 'solutions' to this question have been mooted by Marxists over the years.

For the 'orthodox' Marxists of the Second International, Marx's claim that the mode of production is the 'real basis' of society was commended as an unequivocal statement of technological determinism: productive forces determine economic relations which in turn determine social relations. For the humanist New Left, by contrast, Marx's argument was treated simply as 'metaphor' or 'heuristic', the usefulness of which was often more misleading than illuminating. From this point of view, Marxism was better grasped as the 'philosophy of practice' (as Gramsci famously put it), not as a structural sociology.[73]

In response to these opposing positions, the structural Marxists attempted a compromise position which insulated Marxism from the terrible twins of voluntarist idealism and economic determinism. For them, the relationship between structure and superstructure became reformulated either as economic 'determination in the final instance', or less ambitiously as a statement of the passive, restrictive impact which the economy exercises over society.[74] Finally, in more recent years, of course, it has become fashionable to interpret the structure–superstructure model as an empirical thesis applicable only to capitalism (where economy and class are said to be dominant, unlike in pre-capitalist societies where politics and status are more important).[75]

Structure and superstructure: traditional objections

Why this diversity of opinion on the theoretical status of base and superstructure in historical materialism? An interesting explanation of why this has been the case is provided by David Lee and Howard Newby.[76] For them the logic of Marx's structure–superstructure distinction, as a particular application of the materialist method in the human sciences generally, sponsors a fatalism which is difficult to square with the 'emancipatory', 'libertarian' and 'humanist' dimensions of Marxist thought. In other words, Lee and Newby postulate an unresolved tension right at the heart of Marxism, between, on the one hand, a theory of human agency (Marxism as the 'philosophy of practice'), and on the other hand, a theory of 'structural causality' in which economic facts are 'ultimately determining'. It is this tension at the heart of Marxist discourse (between 'humanism' and 'economism', between 'voluntarism' and 'determinism') which has fuelled the ongoing dispute between those who have appropriated different aspects of his philosophical legacy (humanist Marxism versus scientific Marxism). Yet the problem is that the 'materialism' of Marx sponsors a 'depressing and dehumanising philosophy of history', whereas the 'humanism' of contemporary neo-Marxists overcomes this only at the price of presenting 'a sanitized version of Marxism which is less distinctively Marxist'.[77]

Whatever one makes of this argument, at least Lee and Newby recognise that there is room for 'ambiguity' on the manner of which Marx's social theory should be understood: 'humanist' or 'economist', 'activist' or 'structuralist', 'emancipatory' or 'determinist'. By contrast, a depressing feature of the overwhelming majority of post-war opinion in the Western academy on this question has been its inability to concede even this much. Under the baneful conditional influence of Cold War politics and ideology, the Western intelligensia has generally seen fit to endorse Max Weber's crude dismissal of Marxism as an 'antiquated doctrine … which satisfies the dogmatic need to believe that the economic "factor" is the only "real" one, the only "true" one ... which "in the last instance is everywhere decisive" '.[78]

Particularly in the aftermath of the collapse of the Eastern Bloc, and with the spectre of 'communism repentant',[79] it is doubtless this fact which explains how it is that Tony Spybey, to offer a random example, can still find a publisher in the 1990s prepared to publish his (staggeringly unoriginal) view that

> [t]he appraisal and criticism of historical materialism may be continued on the basis of [its] economistic bias. The crucial mechanisms and dynamics of change ... are located exclusively in the economic institutions of human societies. This implies a neglect of other institutions, in particular the politico-military institutions associated with the wielding of power and authority. ... The proposal that a single type of social institution can be seen as functional for change is one that must be treated with suspicion.[80]

The very best thing that can be said of the argument that either Marx or Engels endorse economic reductionism is that it is (to put it diplomatically) 'considerably overstated'. Two simple observations should suffice to make this clear. First, although there are undoubtedly a number of passages in the works of Marx and Engels (some examples of which I have already analysed) which it is possible (though not always plausible) to interpret in this light, it is nonetheless the case that the attribution of a reductionist world-view to either of them can be sustained only by isolating such passages from the wider theoretical context of their writings.

Second, aside from considerations of this kind, it is clear that Marx's most famous exposition of the structure–superstructure model, and of his distinction between 'social being' and 'social consciousness' (in the 1859 Preface), is notable chiefly for the manner in which it avoids postulating the monocausal determination of political and ideological relations by economic structures:

> In the social production of their life, men enter into definite relations that are indispensable and independent of their will, relations of production which *correspond* to a definite stage of development of their material productive forces. The sum total of these relations of production constitute the economic structure of society, the real *foundation*, on which *rises* a legal and political superstructure and to which *correspond* definite forms of social consciousness. The mode of production of material life *conditions* the social, political and intellectual life-processes in general. It is not the consciousness of men that determines their being, but, on the contrary, their social being that determines their consciousness.[81]

Since Marx is quite clear here that the relationship between economic structure and politico-ideological superstructure is not a determined one, in which the latter is a passive reflection of the former, it does seem uncharitable, to say the least, to place the blame for the vulgarisation of Marxism as economic reductionism on the Old Man's 'muddled' ideas. Taken at face value, after all, Marx's argument grasped as a whole commits us only to the notion that the social and material facts of human existence 'determine' (in an unspecified way) human consciousness, including perhaps the products of human consciousness. I have already suggested (in Chapter 1) that this is an entirely defensible thesis, and not one which necessarily entails an implausible separation of thought and action in the daily life-process of individuals. As a statement of the structural relationship between 'economy' and 'society', on the other hand, Marx's argument is far more qualified and subtle. The language here is of 'correspondence', 'rootedness' and 'conditioning', not of 'determination'. For Marx, the economic structure no more appears to 'cause' the superstructure than, say, the foundations of a block of flats determines the internal configuration and furnishings of the dwellings which reside above.

Clearly, then, whatever Marxism is, it is not simple economic determinism. But is there perhaps more substance to Lee and Newby's more interesting claim that there exists a 'tension' or 'ambiguity' between 'determinism' and 'activism', between 'materialism' and 'humanism' in Marxist thought? In fact, there is not. The latter aspect of this argument is easiest to dispose of. As we have seen, Marx's theory of 'human nature' (upon which his humanism is based) is a materialist account of the genetic foundations of conscious human agency. As such, Marx's endorsement of materialist ontology and method in the human sciences generally does not in the least contradict a 'voluntarist' account of human agency. Clearly, it is not being denied by him that 'structures' or 'societies' are made and remade by the conscious and self-conscious doings of individuals. All that is being argued is that the 'voluntarism' of social action has its material basis in humanity's species-being.

The first part of Lee and Newby's argument poses a greater challenge to Marxism than the second. Nonetheless, it does not present insuperable problems for the version of historical materialism I am seeking to articulate and defend in this chapter. I have already suggested that Marx does not (as he ought) distinguish clearly between 'action' and its 'environments'. Inasmuch as he fails to do so, his sociology is certainly 'ambiguous'. But once we put Marx 'right' on this matter (in the manner I have suggested) the 'tension' in his theory disappears. Just as the social world is populated by both structures and subjects, so it is possible to speak of 'conditions' and 'consciousness', of 'determination' and 'voluntarism' in social life. Lee and Newby, by contrast, offer no conceptual means by which this 'ambiguity' in Marxism can be resolved. Because they themselves do not distinguish between 'action' and its 'environments', perhaps they are forced into squeezing Marxism into either/or polarities: structure or action, economism or humanism, determinism versus spontaneism; or to put it another way, Marx's base–superstructure model of society versus Marx's 'philosophy of practice'.

Structure–superstructure as a thesis of vertical causation in social systems

Despite the variety of interpretation on the question of the appropriate way of grasping Marx's structure–superstructure model, it is my own belief that a thorough examination of the joint works of Marx and Engels allows of only one 'reasonable' understanding of this matter (in the sense of not being contradicted by the textual evidence). I do not believe, nor can I see how, the textual data supports a view of the relationship between structure and superstructure as mere 'metaphor', or as 'ideal type' or 'heuristic device' (and certainly not as economic reductionism). Nor do I see how the 'explanatory primacy' of the mode of production can be interpreted only in terms of the restrictive impact it has on the wider social structure of a society, or as 'determination in the final instance', as the Althusserians would have it.

Freed from these dead-ends, my own interpretation of Marx defends the primacy of socio-economic 'base' *vis-à-vis* politico-ideological 'superstructure' in terms of the following arguments. First, the 'foundational' role of the mode of production in generating 'conditions of existence' for non-economic social structures (and the practices which govern them), and in furnishing a determinate range of material constraints and enablements upon which these structures and practices are dependent and within which they are 'bounded' in empirically specifiable ways. Second, the explanatory significance of the mode of production as the central determinant of the vested interests and hence political consciousness and conduct of interactants. Finally, the explanatory significance of the mode of production in shaping the content of political and juridical relations, and especially of those cultural and ideological forms which are 'functional' to its stable reproduction, or which express the 'contradictions of real life'.

The role of economic structures in enabling and setting limits to non-economic structures and practices

The notion that the mode of production is the 'basis' or 'foundation' of all non-economic social activities and structures in society, in the sense of generating 'conditions of possibility' for their existence and development, has already been elaborated in Chapter 1. It is therefore sufficient for my current purposes to simply reiterate the relevant points in summary fashion.

The foundational status of the economic structure of society in Marx's sociology has a twofold character in this sense. On the one hand, it has a 'diachronic' dimension or aspect. This is because the mode of production in human history must have had an existence prior to non-economic practices and structures. This makes it an entirely defensible argument to claim that the former is 'basic' to the latter, the 'source' from which the latter is 'emergent' and in which it is 'rooted'. As Marx puts it: 'The first historical act is ... the production of the production of material life itself'.[82]

On the other hand, the mode of production has a 'synchronic' dimension or aspect. This is because the mode of production precludes certain superstructural forms, for example

> a feudal base is incompatible with universal suffrage and parliamentary democracy and obviously could not give rise to the philosophy of John Stuart Mill, the economics of Adam Smith, the novel as the dominant literary form or the paintings of either Rembrandt or Jackson Pollock.[83]

Yet at the same time the mode of production generates the surpluses of time and resources (human and material) which allow any society to support and further elaborate non-productive activities, and therefore non-economic emergent structures.

This aspect of Marx's latter argument is well summarised by Roger Gottlieb:

> The mode of production is a central determiner of social life because it sets the limits to and provides the resources for all other human activities. The level of technological, scientific and productive development determines how much time and energy we have for activities other than simply meeting our survival needs. The mode of production provides the resources to support non-labouring intellectuals, artists and researchers. Thus the possibilities of philosophy, art and theoretical science exist within bounds determined by how developed the productive forces are. This development not only makes certain activities possible, it rules out others, making old ways of life impossible and demanding new forms of human interaction. The more technology is developed, for instance, the less people need to trust in superstition. The more production is socialised and geographically interdependent, the less meaningful small political boundaries can be. From small dukedoms we forge nations. Out of nations we forge a united Europe.[84]

As Chris Harman rightly points out, Marx's view that socio-economic structure is 'basic' to politico-ideological superstructure, in the senses described above, is derived from his corresponding view that 'there exists a core activity at any point of history which is a precondition for everything else that happens [in society] – the activity of work on the material world in order to get food, shelter and clothing'.[85] Since social labour to procure the means of subsistence generates the resources which allow the reproduction and elaboration of forms of activity external to material production, so it is equally the case that those emergent economic structures, which flesh-and-blood agents inherit from previous generations of toilers, function to support the wider structures of society in the same fashion, and shape the potential to which these can be elaborated or developed by those here present.

As Engels famously puts it:

> Political, juridical, philosophical, religious, literary, artistic, etc., development is based on economic development. But ... [i]t is not that the economic situation is *cause, solely active*, while everything else is only passive effect. There is, rather, interaction on the basis of economic necessity.[86]

Thus it is the productive labours of the dead generations which support superstructural emergents and which prefigure the scope and form of their subsequent development by human agents: structure is 'basic' to superstructure because the activity of material production to sustain human life is 'basic' to all other socio-cultural activities. In other words, the mode of production as 'structure' and 'action' is what enables the possibility of those modes of socio-cultural practice which give rise to the development or differentiation of superstructural spheres over time.

The decisive role of economic structures in shaping the political consciousness and agency of interactants

I have suggested that Marx is committed to a view of structural conditioning whereby the socio-economic base of society explains the political thinking and agency of interactants. This thesis is obviously more controversial than the one I have attributed to Marx above. Nonetheless, it is defensible and plausible if it is understood as follows. That is, not as a thesis specifying that every aspect of political consciousness or form of activity must have an economic motive or locus. But as a statement of the primacy of those 'situational logics' governed by productive force development and class membership in determining the general 'conditions of life' and 'vested interests' of human agents, and by logical extension which of those politico-cultural values or attitudes in currency in a society are likely to form the core of their thinking, and thereby feed into collective struggles to reproduce, reform or transform an existing social system. In the following exposition I will attempt to add some substance to this argument.

As noted earlier, where social relations of production involve an uneven distribution of the means of production (and hence subsistence) they give rise to class-divided societies, whereby a non-productive group utilises its effective control over certain of the conditions of labour and wealth-creation to extort surplus labour or surplus product from a class of 'direct producers'. By stratifying the 'societal community' into vastly divergent socio-economic circumstances, with grossly asymmetrical access to material and cultural goods, class-divided relations of production distribute contradictory vested interests (plus attendant opportunity costs in acting appropriately in their defence or pursuit) to concretely situated agents. These 'conditions of life', which are bounded by the class positioning of agents in the relations of production, along with the vested interests which agents possess by virtue of their class positioning (and upon which they must act if they are to defend or improve their life-chances), together feed into the social consciousness of interactants as conditional influences, shaping the general outlook and hence politico-cultural activity of those subject to them. Indeed, they do so not as one structural generative mechanism amongst a plurality of equivalents (e.g. nationality, ethnicity, gender, etc.), but as the fundamental one, which as such explains rather more of the content of human political thinking and agency than do the others, or such is my contention.

What is the warranty for endorsing this simple though controversial argument? Marx has a decisive answer. This is simply that class relationships have a fundamental significance in shaping inequalities of access to authoritative and allocative resources, which other modes of stratification simply do not have to an equivalent degree. Class has explanatory primacy in conditioning the socio-political thinking and activity of interactants (for structural change or replication) by virtue of its key role in determining the access of interactants to the basic necessities of food, clothing and shelter, not to mention leisure, cultural and educational opportunities, together with effective means of political representation in a society.

Though it is certain that other forms of 'disadvantage' and 'inequality' (even domination) exist in society, that these are as 'real' as class divisions, and that these are by no means insignificant, they are nonetheless less important than class relations in these crucial respects, not least because class relations are relationships of exploitation, which by their very nature must involve 'domination' together with an asymmetrical distribution of the means of production and consumption. Since the interests and experience of agents are shaped crucially by their respective access to the means of material and cultural production and subsistence, it follows that the content of their political consciousness and action (and those forms of cultural identity and activity which are explainable in terms of their conditions of life) must be explained primarily in terms of class.

By way of elaboration of these (exceedingly contentious!) assertions, I will address what is perhaps the key objection to them. I refer to the popular view of sociologists that any talk of the 'primacy' of class over other modes of inequality (in the senses I have described) is an 'essentialist' error, on the grounds that class is but one form of 'stratification' or 'domination', others such as race and gender being equally or more important. What are the grounds for accepting this argument? In the extended analysis that follows I will seek to answer this question. This I will do by focusing on the examples of stratification by race and sex, for the simple reason that these are normally seen as particularly decisive counter-examples to the primacy of class as I have conceived it. What is the warranty for supposing that these determine the life-chances or conditions of life (and hence vested interests) of interactants to the same extent as stratification by class? What are the implications of stratification by race, gender and class for the articulation of human agency? I will address each of these questions in the order I have presented them above.

Employment, pay and property by sex, race and class in modern Britain: empirical indicators

Important inequalities exist between men and women, and between ethnic groupings, in terms of property ownership. It is reasonable to surmise that white males possess on average about 3.35 times more wealth than non-white males per head of the population,[87] and survey data indicate that only 40 per cent of marketable wealth in the UK economy is owned by women (according to figures for the early 1970s).[88] Major inequalities also exist between men and women, and between ethnic groupings, in terms of access to Professional or Managerial Class (PMC) positions. Contemporary research indicates that 27 per cent of white male economically active persons, but only 21 per cent of non-white male economically active persons, were employers, professionals, administrators and managers in 1988–90 (a mere 12 per cent of whom were Africans or West Indians).[89]

Survey data also show that:

(i) 32.1 per cent of male employees but only 24.7 per cent of female employees in full-time work were occupants of PMC posts in 1979;[90]
(ii) 15.8 per cent of all working males but only 10.5 per cent of all working females were employers, higher professionals or administrators in 1993; and[91]
(iii) only 3 per cent of high court judges, 5 per cent of company directors, 14 per cent of barristers and solicitors, 17 per cent of full-time university lecturers and 4 per cent of academic professors were women in 1991.[92]

To this I might add that inequalities of wealth and access to PMC positions goes hand in hand with inequalities of income between men and women, and between whites and non-whites, who are incumbents of the same or similar occupational positions in the labour market.[93]

Nonetheless, empirical indicators from other sources are strongly suggestive of the fact that such economic inequalities between women and men and between whites and non-whites are much narrower than those structured by class relationships. This is particularly evident in the case of property ownership. According to government figures for 1991, the lower 50 per cent of the population (comprised largely of manual workers, unemployed manual workers, plus their dependants) own a mere 8 per cent of national wealth. Taken as a whole, the working class (approximately 70 per cent of the population) own just 21 per cent of national wealth.[94]

One does not need to be a mathematician to work out that females (approximately half of the population) own nearly twice as much property as proletarians (approximately three quarters of the population). Nor does one need to be a statistician to grasp that the average distribution of wealth per head for non-white males is vastly greater than that for proletarian males and females. For whereas it is defensible to surmise that individual non-white males own on average less than 30 per cent of the property of individual white males, it is also uncontentious that proletarian men and women in semi-skilled and unskilled occupations own a share of property per head which is half that of non-white males (and eighteen times less than that accruing to male and female members of the 'professional-managerial' and employer classes).[95]

That class relations also play the major role in determining pay differentials in the occupational structure is also beyond serious question. This can be demonstrated by comparing the inequalities of income which exist in the labour market by race, sex and class. Empirical research has shown that in 1978 manual workers received on average roughly 47.5 per cent and unskilled manual workers just 41.5 per cent of the pay of higher professionals, managers or administrators.[96] Since subsequent years have seen the abolition of wages councils, the return of mass unemployment, the shifting of the burden of direct and indirect taxation from rich to poor, and the weakening of trade union organisation and working-class militancy, it is reasonable to suppose that these relative differentials in income between members of the PMC and the manual working class have been considerably widened.

How do these figures compare with those which reveal the extent of inequalities of pay by sex and race? The *New Earnings Survey* reveals that in 1984 women workers earned on average only 74 per cent of the hourly rate and 66 per cent of the gross weekly earnings of male workers.[97] Nicholas Abercrombie and Alan Warde report that non-manual and skilled manual workers from ethnic minorities earned only 78 per cent and 89 per cent respectively of the income of their white counterparts in 1986.[98] Again, stratification by class clearly gives rise to significantly greater inequalities in the 'market situation', and hence life-chances of interactants, than does stratification by race or sex.

The causal primacy of class membership or positioning, in shaping the access of interactants to high-status positions within the occupational structure, is perhaps less clear than it is for determining occupational income differentials and the distribution of property. Nonetheless, it is no less decisive. Data from social mobility surveys are particularly instructive here. David Glass' famous 1949 study, for instance, reveals a high degree of social closure by class: 53.4 per cent of the sons of professionals and higher administrators were themselves professionals, higher administrators, managers or executives, whereas only 0.8 per cent of the sons of unskilled manual workers, 1.3 per cent of the sons of semi-skilled manual workers, and 3.3 per cent of the sons of skilled manual workers were occupants of these same positions.[99] Subsequent research into social mobility has revealed a significant weakening of the rigidity of the occupational structure by class, but enormous inequalities of access and opportunity remain firmly in place.

According to the Oxford Mobility Study of 1972, for example, 64.8 per cent of the sons of higher professionals, high-grade administrators, managers in large industrial concerns and large proprietors were to be found in these same occupations. By contrast, only 14.9 per cent of the sons of unskilled, semi-skilled or skilled manual workers were found to be occupants of these role-positions.[100] These findings of the Oxford study have been confirmed by more recent research by Marshall *et al.* (1988).[101] According to this, 59.6 per cent of sons from PMC backgrounds (as defined by the occupational position of 'chief childhood supporter') were themselves occupants of PMC positions as adults, whereas just 20.2 per cent of sons from manual working-class backgrounds were found to be incumbents of these same positions.[102]

Though these data are not strictly analogous to or contemporary with those cited above for the distribution of the occupational structure by sex and ethnicity, they nonetheless do suggest that the class membership of interactants has far greater causal significance than their racial or sexual characteristics in determining their access to the 'new middle class' of professionals, administrators or managers and the employing class. Certainly, the relative degree of participation by individuals from working-class backgrounds in the upper reaches of the occupational hierarchy is less than for individuals who are women or who are from non-white ethnic groupings. Thus 24.7 per cent of full-time female workers were members of the PMC in 1979, whereas only 16.6 per cent and 20.4 per cent of adult males from skilled working-class backgrounds were to be found in the same category in 1972 and 1988 respectively (most of whom were certainly in full-time employment). Thus 21 per cent of non-white adult males were members of the PMC in 1988–90, whereas only 15.6 per cent of adult males from semi-skilled and unskilled working-class backgrounds were to be found in the same category in 1972, and only 20 per cent in 1988.[103]

Furthermore, the relative differentials in opportunity which exist between the sons of working-class and middle-class parents, in terms of obtaining access to the PMC, are at least twice as great as those which exist between men and women or between white and non-white ethnic groupings. Thus whereas white males are roughly 1.3 times more likely to be found in the PMC than non-white males, and whereas male employees are roughly 1.5 times more likely to be found in the PMC than female employees, male employees from PMC backgrounds are 2.95 times more likely than male employees from manual working-class backgrounds to be found within this occupational bracket.[104]

Further evidence for the primacy of class relations in determining the access of interactants to the PMC can be derived by comparing the occupational positions of men and women on the basis of their class origins. Research by Stanworth and Giddens has revealed that out of a sample of 460 company directors, only 1 per cent had manual working-class origins.[105] This compares to 5 per cent of company directorships which are held by women, according to research already cited. Unfortunately, however, a paucity of studies examining the class composition of other elite occupations (such as university lecturers, professors, barristers, solicitors, judges, etc.) means that general conclusions cannot be drawn here in relation to the 'primacy debate'. We know the extent to which women are under-represented in certain elite professions, but not the extent to which individuals from working-class families are.

Fortunately, aspects of Marshall's research can be used to illuminate this issue. Marshall's data reveal that 41.4 per cent of females, compared to 59.6 per cent of males, whose chief childhood supporter belonged to Class I (whose members are defined as higher professionals, higher-grade administrators, managers in large industrial concerns and large proprietors) were themselves to be found in these same positions or in lower Class II positions within the PMC (such as lower professionals, lower-scale administrators, managers in small businesses, etc.). Marshall's data also show that 57.2 per cent of females, compared to 59.4 per cent of males, whose chief childhood supporter was a member of Class II were also to be found in Class II or I.[106] Clearly, men from PMC backgrounds have relative advantages over women from the same backgrounds. In fact, women from Class I origins have opportunities for occupational success which are about two thirds of those enjoyed by men from the same class.

But these relative disadvantages between men and women within the PMC are minute beside those which exist between men and women from different social classes. For example, as I have already pointed out, of males whose chief childhood supporter was a skilled, semi-skilled or unskilled manual worker, a mere 20.2 per cent managed to 'make it' into the ranks of the PMC, according to Marshall's figures for 1988. For women from the same class position, the figure for 1988 was a paltry 14.5 per cent.[107] Thus, whereas women from the upper bracket of the PMC have opportunities for remaining within the PMC as a whole which are a third less than those of men from the same class situation, the opportunities for occupational mobility into the PMC by men from manual working-class backgrounds are less than half of those of women from middle-class backgrounds (for working-class women more than a quarter less than for working-class men), and little more than a third of those enjoyed by men from middle-class backgrounds. This is surely fairly decisive evidence of the primacy of class membership over sexual makeup in limiting and/or facilitating the occupational opportunities of interactants.

Education by sex, race and class in modern Britain: empirical indicators

A sober appraisal of the available empirical data on the distribution of educational opportunity and access in contemporary Britain is again unambiguously supportive of the primacy of class over gender or ethnicity in shaping the life-chances of interactants. Consider first of all the distribution of elementary and A-level qualifications by sex, race and class. Now, girls have 'outperformed' boys in terms of acquiring GCSE, CSE and O-level passes at grade C or above for more than thirty years.[108] Indeed, since the 1990s girls have begun to 'outperform' boys in terms of acquiring A-level qualifications as well.[109] There is no reason to be believe this trend will not continue, especially since it is probably explainable by differing socialisation patterns for male and female children which have proven to be extremely enduring. This being the case, it is by no means unreasonable to suppose that the current unequal distribution of elementary and further qualifications by sex in the population at large will not persist beyond the next twenty years.

Recent research has also indicated that differential educational attainment between ethnic groupings in terms of obtaining elementary and secondary qualifications is increasingly being undermined. Important inequalities still exist between whites and non-whites at these levels, but they are less significant overall than previously. Thus 17 per cent of whites and 13 per cent of non-whites (including 16 per cent of West Indians) of working age had achieved GCE O-levels in 1988–90, whereas 24 per cent of whites and 16 per cent of non-whites (including 24 per cent of West Indians) of working age had achieved A-levels or their equivalents during the same period.[110] These figures paint a more optimistic picture than others for 1981–2 which showed that 17 per cent of white- but only 6 per cent of black school leavers had achieved five or more graded O-level results, and that 13 per cent of white- but only 5 per cent of black school leavers had achieved A-level results.[111]

By contrast, the prospects for undermining proletarian disadvantage in terms of acquiring elementary and secondary qualifications remain as bleak as ever. Males and females from manual working-class backgrounds (and especially males) continue to 'underachieve' sharply, relative to middle-class males and females. These relative differentials in educational success at these levels between those from working-class and middle-class backgrounds are far greater than those which exist between those from white and non-white ethnic groupings. Non-whites find that their chances of obtaining A-levels are about two thirds of those of whites, whereas persons born into 'professional' middle-class families are nearly four times more likely to achieve A-level qualifications than those born into unskilled manual working-class families.[112] Whites find that their chances of ending up without any educational qualifications are about 16 per cent less than for non-whites, whereas persons born into unskilled manual working-class families are more than eight times more likely than those born into professional middle-class families to end up with no educational qualifications.[113]

What is true of the relationship between class and ethnicity is also true of the relationship between class and gender. The fact that the emergent structure of educational disadvantage at secondary school and college level is shaped far more significantly by class than by gender is thrown into sharp relief by the following statistics. Whereas 33 per cent of males and 40 per cent of females had no educational qualifications in 1988–90, the equivalent figure for people from unskilled manual working-class backgrounds was a staggering 60 per cent.[114] Whereas 59 per cent of males and 53 per cent of females had GCSE, CSE, O-level or A-level qualifications in 1992, for people from skilled, semi-skilled and unskilled manual working-class families the equivalent figures were only 41 per cent, 37 per cent and 29 per cent respectively.[115] Whereas 36 per cent of males and 17 per cent of females aged 16–59 had A-level qualifications or their equivalents in 1992, only 4 per cent of individuals from unskilled manual backgrounds, 6 per cent of individuals from semi-skilled backgrounds, and 8 per cent of individuals from skilled manual backgrounds, had managed to do the same by 1990–1.[116]

The further up the education system one travels, the tighter becomes the correspondence between educational disadvantage and class background, and the weaker (in relative terms) its association with gender or ethnicity. Figures show that roughly 46 per cent of the intake of universities are women, and that that a significantly larger percentage of all non-white school leavers than white school leavers are now to be found entering higher education establishments (though this is partly explainable in terms of higher unemployment rates for non-whites than for whites).[117] Research data also indicate that 11 per cent of men but only 6 per cent of women (aged 16–69), and that 8 per cent of whites compared to 9 per cent of non-whites (aged 16–59), have degrees.[118] In terms of access to and success in higher education, then, it is reasonable to conclude that whites no longer have (statistically significant) relative advantages over non-whites, and that the relative advantages which men have over women are marginal. By contrast, men continue to hold significant advantages over women in terms of obtaining degrees and postgraduate qualifications (though with the growing equalisation of the numbers of men and women entering university, this inequality is likely to be further eroded over the next few years).

The relationship between class membership and access to and success in higher education is altogether less ambiguous than this. The reader will be unsurprised to learn that persons from manual working-class backgrounds are far less likely than either women or non-whites to go to college or university, or to achieve degree qualifications. This can be established definitively by the following measures.

First, by comparing the relative inequalities of access to higher education which exist between whites and non-whites, and between men and women, with those which exist between people from different class backgrounds.

From this perspective, whereas stratification by ethnicity no longer appears to translate into (statistically significant) inequality of access to higher education institutions, and whereas stratification by gender ensures that only 46 per cent of the intake of universities are women, stratification by class ensures that only 1.1 per cent of the intake of universities are from families whose head of household is an unskilled manual worker (according to figures for 1984).[119]

Second, by comparing the relative inequalities of access to university for women and men from different class backgrounds. From this perspective, whereas 40 per cent of men and 24 per cent of women aged 25–29 not in further education, who had attended a university or polytechnic as their last educational establishment, had fathers in professional or managerial occupations, only 1 per cent of women and 3 per cent of men (who fell into these categories) had fathers in unskilled manual employment.[120]

Third, by comparing the relative inequalities of access to higher education for whites and non-whites from different classes. From this perspective, whereas 37 per cent of whites compared to 56 per cent of non-whites aged 16–19 went into higher education in 1988–90, only 47 per cent of non-whites from unskilled or semi-skilled manual working-class backgrounds, compared to 69 per cent of non-whites from professional-managerial or employer backgrounds, did the same.[121]

Finally, by comparing the relative inequalities of achievement in higher education (in terms of acquiring degree qualifications) which exist between men and women and between whites and non-whites, with those which exist between people from different class backgrounds. From this perspective, whereas 9 per cent of non-whites compared to 8 per cent of whites aged 16–59 had acquired degrees or their equivalents in 1988–90, and whereas 7 per cent of women compared to 12 per cent of men aged 16–59 had done likewise by 1992,[122] only 3 per cent of persons aged 25–59 from unskilled manual working-class families, compared to 32 per cent of persons of the same age category from professional middle-class backgrounds, had achieved as much by 1990–1.[123]

Furthermore, whereas 56 per cent of men and 47 per cent of women aged 25–59 born into professional middle-class families had attended a higher education institution by 1990–1, only 20 per cent of men and 11 per cent of women from skilled manual backgrounds, and 10 per cent of men and 6 per cent of women from unskilled manual backgrounds (of the same age bracket), had done likewise.[124] This means that persons from unskilled manual working-class backgrounds are more than three times less likely than persons from professional middle-class backgrounds to enter higher education, and thirteen times less likely than persons from PMC backgrounds to secure a degree or equivalent qualification. By contrast, there are no (statistically) significant disadvantages at these levels between whites and blacks, whereas the chances of middle-class women going into higher education are roughly 85 per cent of those of middle-class men, and those of women securing a degree or equivalent more than half of those enjoyed by men.

The primacy of class relations in shaping the political consciousness and social agency of interactants

My argument establishes that class relations have primacy over other structures of inequality by virtue of the fact they have by far the greater efficacy in shaping the situational logics of interactants. What are the implications of my account in terms of the shaping of political consciousness and agency and the articulation of social interests? I have made the claim that the 'fateful power' of class relations in defining the life-chances of interactants ensures that class interests are 'basic' to their political thinking and activity. What is the meaning of this proposition? For the most part it means that agents will recognise that class interests are fundamental to whatever other interests or identities they possess, and will tend to act upon these in preference to others, where they have the confidence to do so (unless prevented or discouraged). It is for this reason that 'the history of all hitherto existing society is the history of class struggle'.[125] But clearly, this is not always the case for everyone, since mechanisms of class subordination are reinforced by other oppressions, and the uniqueness of individual experience does not always provide an accurate guide to which of these are basic.

This being the case, I contend also that even where agents do perceive that their life-chances are shaped primarily by structures other than class, and even where they imagine that interests and identities other than class are of greater significance in shaping the content of their political actions, this is in fact a false consciousness, itself explainable in terms of class positioning, which can be revealed as such by examining the social content of the ideologies and agency of those who espouse such views. For example, despite the fact that many urban working-class non-whites doubtless regard institutionalised racism or perhaps racist attitudes as the fundamental cause of their social disadvantages, if it can be shown that the grievances they articulate are primarily class issues, and if it can be shown that the forms of resistance which they engage in response to inequality and deprivation are modes of class agency, it follows that my thesis of the primacy of class relations in shaping the political thinking and activity of interactants is defensible. This, I suggest, can be demonstrated satisfactorily.[126]

Yet I am not committed to arguing that for each and every interactant class relations are primary in the ways I have described above. It is important to grasp that the purpose of my argument is to postulate the primacy of class in shaping the life-chances and agency of *collectivities*, not of *individuals*. For particular individuals, structures of inequality other than class will indeed be more significant in determining their life-chances, even if this is not the case for most. Who would doubt, for instance, that this is sometimes true of the victims of sexual violence or of racially motivated assaults and police 'fit-ups'? Such experiences might well lead those who have been subject to them to conclude that racial or sexual domination are the fundamental forms of subordination in society. However, it remains the case that such experiences are untypical in the sense that most blacks and (especially) most women have not endured them. The disadvantaged life-chances and economic exploitation associated with the class situation of the propertyless, on the other hand, is the inescapable experience of all proletarians, whether men or women, black or white.

It is also important to be clear that my argument is not a statement of the correspondence of class interests and class consciousness. To say that class interests are basic to the social agency and political consciousness of interactants does not mean that interactants always and everywhere accurately represent either their immediate or their long-term class interests.[127] It is enough to say that agents will more often than not regard class as the central determinant of their situation in society, and will think and act politically, whether appropriately or otherwise, in the light of this awareness (though they will for the most part be subject to systematic 'directional guidance' to draw upon 'traditions' of industrial struggle and political action which are at least appropriate to their immediate class interests). Nor is my argument a statement of structural determinism. Agents will normally tend to base their agency upon their (immediate) class interests, or upon a rough approximation of these, because a long-term failure to do so will incur punishingly prohibitive opportunity costs in the form of declining life-chances, which, being 'somewhat rational', most will be reluctant to pay.

This close connection between class membership and the political consciousness and social agency of interactants exists as much for bourgeois women and non-whites than for their proletarian counterparts. Yet the interplay between them is often more immediately or directly discernible in the case of the latter. This is for the simple reason that workers suffering at the sharp end of inequality, poverty, poor housing, substandard education and lack of autonomy at work (where they can get work) simply cannot afford the luxury of 'constructing' their social experiences in a way which relegates class issues and grievances to a subordinate or secondary status. Class issues and interests will be immediately relevant to or present in their thinking and agency, even where these are not recognised as such, or are confused with interests other than class. Working-class blacks and women, for instance, will articulate vested interests (e.g. for employment, a minimum wage, union rights, decent housing, properly funded welfare services, subsidised childcare facilities, an end to paramilitary policing, etc.) which are unambiguously explicable in terms of class positioning, notwithstanding whatever beliefs they might have to the contrary.

Indeed, they will tend to regard these as 'more real' (i.e. less abstract) than those 'purer' ethnic or gender interests championed by patriarchy theorists and black nationalists (such as 'wages for housework', the overturning of 'traditional' sex roles, equality of participation in the occupational sphere, even withdrawal from 'colonial' or 'patriarchal' society, on the assumption that 'whites' and 'men' possess objective interests in the subordination or oppression of blacks and women by virtue of the material and other benefits which they purportedly derive from it). This is for the simple reason that a politics of gender and ethnicity conceived apart from and in opposition to class interests is alien to the real experience of proletarian women and non-whites, by virtue of the fact it stands in contradiction to fundamental aspects of their 'social being'. Little wonder that social movements oriented on patriarchy theory and black nationalism (which seek to organise women and blacks irrespective of class) have quickly found themselves fractured and undermined by class antagonisms. Little wonder that the contemporary politics of race and sex (as these are conceived by feminism and black nationalism) have been unable to secure activist organisational roots within the working class, and can no longer even enlist mass passive or inactive support from working-class women or blacks.[128]

This is not to say that authentic gender and ethnic interests and identities are not integral aspects of the 'social being' of women and blacks. Certainly, issues such as racially motivated police harassment, racist attacks, domestic violence, inequalities of opportunity and pay in the labour market, abortion rights, and so on, are (or can be reasonably interpreted as) important sources of antagonism in society between men and women or between black and white. Nonetheless, it is reasonable to suggest that for a majority of women and blacks, such antagonisms are not seen as being rooted in irreconcilable differences of interest between themselves and men and/or whites, nor as more fundamental forms of advantage and disadvantage than those which are shaped by economic and class factors. Least of all are sexist and racist divisions interpreted by most women and blacks as forms of domination by which *all* men oppress and dominate women, and by which whites subordinate blacks. Nor are they likely to be understood in these terms under any circumstances. This is not simply because the 'social being' of women and ethnic minorities is too complex and contradictory to be grasped by such simple and straightforward concepts. It is also because theories of ubiquitous male and white domination offer no practical political means by which such oppressions can be successfully undermined, and as such are usually seen as rather pointless.[129]

A survey of black youth in 1980s Britain has revealed, for instance, that unemployment, low pay and state oppression are more fertile sources of discontent than racially motivated assaults or white prejudice generally.[130] Today, working-class blacks are more likely to identify particular institutions of racial-class domination (especially the state) rather than 'whites' as 'the enemy'. Recent research also indicates that most blacks in the UK (86 per cent) recognise the need for 'people of Asian/West Indian origin [to] ... join trade unions alongside white people'.[131] Other surveys have documented a steady erosion and increasing marginalisation of racist attitudes amongst whites in the UK since the 1950s,[132] together with a sharp rise in 'mixed race' relationships, including marriage.[133]

Elsewhere the point has been made that women and men generally have a need to enter into intimate relationships with one another, to marry each other, to share their lives together, and continue to do so for reasons of 'romantic love', which inevitably cuts against any simple identification of the relations between them as unambiguously and necessarily antagonistic or oppressive.[134] Since the same can hardly be said of the relations which exist between capitalists and workers, or between white racists and blacks, it is clear enough that gender and familial relations cannot be perceived simply or largely as rooted in the oppression and exploitation of women by men, as a form of serfdom or servitude[135] or suchlike, despite the fact that real societal inequalities exist between the sexes, and that particular interpersonal relations between particular men and women involve the exploitation and oppression of the latter by the former.

Such material realities simply do not square with the social analyses offered by feminism and black nationalism. Thus, whereas women and blacks will identify with aspects of the description of their subordinate status in society, as this is presented by patriarchy theorists and black nationalists (for the simple reason that they do experience sexism and racism which adversely shapes their life-chances), this awareness will rarely translate into positive endorsement of (and least of all activist support for) the formal ideas and politics of those who espouse such views. Indeed, though especially alien to the real experiences and interests of working-class women and ethnic minorities, the political ideologies of black nationalism and patriarchy theory are hardly compatible even with the life-worlds of bourgeois women and blacks (because the experience of such individuals of racism and sexism is far less acute and vicious than for their proletarian 'brothers' and 'sisters', and is often different in kind). This being the case, it is scarcely surprising that feminism and black nationalism today have neither an organisational basis nor a substantial following amongst women or non-whites of any social class.

Yet it is true that middle-class women and blacks are more inclined than their working-class counterparts to construct gender or ethnic interests and to identify which explicitly downgrade or deny class issues or interests. It is for this reason that modern feminism (oriented on patriarchy theory) and black nationalism (oriented on the ineradicability of white racism) is the exclusive preserve of PMC women and blacks respectively and is dominated by bourgeois politico-cultural values and attitudes.[136] This ideological orientation is sometimes explainable in terms of class opportunism pure and simple. Black and female members of the employing and managerial classes, for example, have vested interests in propagating the fashionable idea that gender and ethnicity are the fundamental divides in society, because this absolves them of responsibility for the exploitation of *all* proletarians (whether men or women, blacks or whites) and erects ideological barriers to the unification in struggle of a working class divided by race and gender.

More often, however, it is accountable in terms of self-deception, as this is shaped by the specificity of their class positioning and experience. In this case the emancipation of middle-class blacks and women from the brute realities of material subordination and disadvantage, by granting them the space to take their privileged class-determined life-chances 'as given', allows them to project their relatively marginal disadvantages *vis-à-vis* white and male members of the same class as the fundamental forms of inequality for all blacks and all women, and to fondly imagine they are part of a 'community' unified by sex or race. Yet, despite this, the content of their social consciousness and agency is normally better explained in terms of class positioning and attendant vested interests, irrespective of their views to the contrary. This is, of course, indicative of the fact that 'gender interests' and 'race interests' do not generally override 'class interests', even for those who wish to claim the reverse is true.[137]

The decisive role of economic structures in shaping the function and content of superstructural forms

I have contended that, for Marx, the structure of the mode of production is primary in conditioning political relations and certain forms of culture and ideology (especially those which have a 'political' or 'economic' dimension or function). How should this 'primacy thesis' be understood? As implied above, not as a thesis of the 'absolute determination' of every item of superstructure by structure. This would rehabilitate the dishonest (or ignorant) caricature of Marxism proffered by the likes of Laclau and Mouffe, for whom 'the base/superstructure model affirms that the base ... determines the superstructure, in the same way that the movements of a hand determine the movements of its shadow on a wall'.[138] Rather, Marx's argument must instead be grasped as a specification of the central role of relations of production in conditioning the core content and function of those superstructural emergents (especially legal and political structures and ideologies) which are immediately relevant to either sustaining or challenging an existing mode of production and class exploitation. That such a view is defensible, even plausible, will (I hope) be demonstrated in the analysis that follows.

The first point to make is an obvious one. Not all elements of the superstructure more or less express the vested interests of the propertied or even the 'middling' classes. This is for the simple reason that the economic structure of a society is not a monolith, but is rather 'a contradictory totality, a unity of opposites',[139] by virtue of the fact that it is comprised of a relationship of economic exploitation (and hence of political domination) between classes with respect to the means of production, which imparts to interactants (by virtue of their agential positioning) differential life-chances and vested interests (in societal replication or change). To make the point more economically: since the economic structures of class-divided societies are dialectical, so the same is true of their superstructures. This being the case, certain cultural or ideological forms, and certain institutional structures (especially forms of political organisation), are always articulations or expressions of the conditions of life and vested interests of subordinate classes, whereas others entail a contradictory synthesis of the world-views and vested interests of rival or opposed classes.

Classic examples of the former include the original teachings of Jesus Christ prior to their adaptation in a distorted form as the official religion of the Roman empire (teachings which inverted Greek and Roman views of the poor and destitute as 'base' or 'unworthy' and of the rich as 'noble' and 'upstanding', and developed the idea that private property and profit-making is immoral),[140] the socialism of Marx and Engels and those classical Marxists (Lenin, Trotsky, Luxemburg, Gramsci) who have sought to develop their intellectual and political legacy, and the revolutionary theory and practice of the Leninist form of party organisation. A classic example of the latter is, of course, the ideological and organisational emergents of the reformist 'trade union consciousness' of workers under capitalism, such as parliamentary socialism, Labourism and the bureaucratised reformist parties of western Europe, all which are rooted in an unstable (and normally unworkable) compromise between the interests of capital for higher profits and labour for higher wages and greater autonomy or self-determination at work.

That Marx did not regard the politico-ideological superstructure as performing only a conservative function (in stabilising the relations of production) is also implicit in his claim that 'consciousness must be explained from the contradictions of material life, from the existing conflict between the social productive forces and the relations of production'. There can be no doubt that, for him, the superstructure must be grasped as a 'site of struggle' in which 'legal, political, religious, aesthetic or philosophic forms' are those by which agents become conscious of the conflict between the forces and relations of production 'and fight it out'.[141]

The second point to make is that particular elements of the superstructure have a crucial 'functionality' in respect of the reproduction requirements of the 'dominant' mode of production in any society, whereas others do not. On the one hand, those 'parts' of the superstructure which do possess this functional (practical and ideological) utility to relations of production – such as 'the law, the judiciary, the police, the military, the education system',[142] political ideologies, political institutions, etc. – are immediately or directly subject to 'directional pressure' to accommodate themselves over time in terms of their content to the vested interests of those class groupings who control or otherwise possess the means of wealth-creation.

> Thus a modern capitalist economy could not co-exist with laws which were anti-capitalist in that they either looked back to feudalism by, for example, prohibiting usury (lending money and charging interest) or

> anticipated socialism by banning the employment of wage-labour or legalising the expropriation of the rich by the poor.[143]

On the other hand, those 'parts' of the superstructure which do not possess this functional importance to relations of production (such as certain forms of 'other-worldly' religious doctrines, etc.) are not subject to this intense 'directional pressure' to develop in ways which 'fit in' with or which do not contradict or otherwise obstruct the dominant economic relationships (which is not to say that many of these cultural structures are not profoundly ideological). Thus

> a capitalist economy can ... coexist with art that yearns for the feudal past (the pre-Raphaelites in Victorian England, the poetry of Ezra Pound, the fantasy novels of J. R. R. Tolkien) or makes propaganda for the socialist future (the plays of Brecht, the paintings of Leger and so on).[144]

Capitalism can also co-exist with a variety of different religious and philosophic forms. This means that certain elements of the superstructure are more or less 'determined' by (or more or less 'autonomous' of) the economic base than others. Which falls into which category cannot be settled by *a priori* schematic classifications, but only by empirical investigation. As Franz Jakubowski puts it: 'Any analysis of the extent to which ideological and material relationships interpenetrate must be made individually, according to each particular case'.[145]

Naturally, my argument does not mean that those elements of the superstructure which are embroiled in tight functional relationships with the base are passive effects of structural hydraulics. Interaction (motivated by vested interests and the punitive opportunity costs of not acting consistently in their defence or pursuit) is the mechanism by which superstructural emergents are brought into correspondence with the structural emergents of a society. But it is vested interests, as these are determined by the involuntary positioning of agents in the relations of production, which generates the impulse for the propertied to act in the appropriate ways, i.e. to utilise their structural capacities (as owners or controllers of wealth and property) to force superstructural spheres into a 'functional' relationship (of compatibility or accommodation) with the mode of production.

Yet it is important to note that functional relationships of correspondence or accommodation between structure and superstructure (or rather between structure and those elements of the superstructure which have immediate practical and ideological implications for the economic structure) are never 'harmonious' or 'integrated'. The collision of vested class interests in society, as these in turn are shaped by relations of production, ensure that these superstructural relations are always 'sites of struggle'. Nonetheless, it remains the case that, excepting periods of mass or revolutionary class struggle which call into question the existing organisation of social relations, the balance of class forces must always be such that the vested interests of the propertied are normally far better represented than those of any other agential grouping in those superstructural spheres which are especially conducive to the 'functional requirements' of the dominant economic relationships of a society.

Economy and polity

I have suggested that those elements of the superstructure which have particularly close links to the economic structure of society are political (i.e. state) and legal relations. Constraints of time and space compel me to focus on a single example – the relationship between economy and polity in class society (especially in capitalism, but also in pre-capitalist societies).

The close correspondence between economy and polity is derived, in the first place, from the fact that the state owes its historical existence to inter-class antagonisms which are rooted in a certain level of development of material production:

> The emergence of the state presupposes a relatively highly developed division of labour. On the one hand, it presupposes that human labour is already productive enough to ensure that not all physically capable individuals actually carry out directly productive labour for their own means of subsistence, but they are already in a position to be employed on social interests which do not directly coincide with their own interests as individuals. On the other hand, the emergence of the state presupposes that there is already an opposition between individual and social interests; that production and appropriation no longer occur socially, as in primitive communism, but that appropriation takes place by means of exchanges between individuals. This mode of production causes society to split into classes, which are distinguished from each other by their position in the production process; the main result of this is that conflict occurs between those classes which possess the means of production and those which do not. This is why the state becomes necessary.[146]

The historical origin of the state, in other words, is to be found in the conflict between exploiting and exploited classes:

> It is the admission that this society has got itself entangled in insoluble contradiction and is cleft into irreconcilable antagonisms which it is powerless to exorcise. But in order that these antagonisms, classes with conflicting economic interests, shall not consume themselves and society in fruitless struggle, a power apparently standing above society, has

> become necessary to moderate the conflict and keep it within the bounds of 'order'; and this power, arisen out of society but placing itself above it and increasingly alienating itself from it, is the state.

But this means that the state is 'as a rule the state of the most powerful, economically dominant class' of a society, a mode of class domination. As such, it is reconstituted anew to service the vested interests of every propertied class which rises to predominance in society, and in this way is brought into correspondence with 'every stage of the relations of production':

> The ancient state was, above all, the state of the slave-owners for holding down the slave, just as the feudal state was the organ of the nobility for holding down the peasant serfs and bondsmen, and the modern representative state is the instrument for exploiting wage-labour by capital.[147]

The mechanism by which state structures are brought into 'functional correspondence' with changes in 'property relations' is of course the social agency of a rising propertied class (such as the bourgeoisie within the 'womb' of feudal society). Yet the agency is more or less successful in the long run because of the pressure of structural constraint. Initially the state has to reconcile the interests of old and new propertied classes (e.g. the aristocracy and the merchant capitalists in 'late feudalism'), increasingly dependent as it is upon the revenue of both, and this modifies its social functions and the content of its political actions (the sponsorship of markets and trade as well as the legal protection of landed wealth and bonded labour). Later on, however, as old production relations are increasingly subverted by new (e.g. as petty capitalism supplants feudalism in the countryside), the polity – or rather the state elite – is placed under ever-greater directional pressure to identify more closely with the vested interests bound up in the latter, since more and more of its revenue and patronage depends upon the economic activities of the newly ascendant class, without access to which it could not hope to maintain its bureaucratic structures nor its political control over a given territory. (I will develop this argument shortly in greater detail in the context of a discussion of the specificity of the interplay between polity and class in capitalist society.)

These structural constraints need not be derived entirely or even solely from the domestic scene, however. The pressure can be regional or even global. Where a new mode of production has achieved predominance in one society, in one area of the globe or even internationally, other societies or regions will quickly come under pressure to follow the same course. Assuming that the new mode of production is 'progressive' (in the sense that it allows a greater tempo of economic development than the old), the punitive opportunity costs attached to clinging to unreformed political structures which are bound to archaic property relations (and attendant vested interests) are likely to include either military subordination (the external destruction of the state) or social and political decline more generally (together with the risk of overthrow of the state elite from within and its replacement with another more conducive to capitalistic interests and development).

The history of early modern Europe provides ample examples of both contingencies. In Spain, for instance, the absolutist monarchy was unable to reform itself (stuck as it was between the landowners and the great merchants), and faded from the scene as a great power, losing control of much of its empire, presiding over a lengthy period of social dissolution and economic backwardness, before disintegrating altogether. In France, by contrast, the absolutist state was eventually overthrown by a petty-bourgeois-led coalition, resulting in the creation of a republic accompanied by a period of rapid economic growth and the establishment of a new empire. Elsewhere, of course (most notably in Germany and Japan in the later part of the nineteenth century), the state elite was to the forefront in promoting successful capitalist industrialisation, motivated by the desire to partake of a slice of the economic cake to be plundered from more backward societies or regions, and to avoid being subordinated to more developed industrial powers.

But this tight correspondence between economy and polity is often disguised by the fact that the latter must simultaneously function as the guarantor of the conditions of class exploitation against the threat posed by the propertied classes of foreign territories. The state must be an instrument of domestic class domination and of intra-class competition on a wider stage (whether regional in the conditions of late feudalism, or global as under the auspices of modern capitalism). And this means that a fundamental part of the state's activities must be concerned with the mobilisation and exercise of military power.

Doubtless a failure to grasp this fact explains the belief of many neo-Weberian sociologists (and Marxists influenced by their pluralistic conception of social causality) that 'historically ... the primary function of the state has been external, in continuing struggles with other states for territory and power',[148] meaning that the logic of 'exterminism' or 'military accumulation' or 'political competition' is beyond the ken of class analysis, following as it does from a dynamic which is autonomous of the mode of production.[149] Such a conception of state relations and class relations as comprising 'two parallel systems' or discrete sources of social power, each 'driven by different imperatives',[150] probably explains the (entirely logical) view of those (such as E. P. Thompson and Anthony Giddens) who argue that combating the threat posed to humanity by the 'global military order' is a separate matter to the struggle for socialism against capitalism, and one which requires an independent movement which is capable of uniting 'all good people' across class lines.[151]

Yet there are a number of good reasons for rejecting this neo-Weberian perspective. First, international state relations since the Bolshevik revolution have undoubtedly been shaped by the 'twin concern of the dominant classes in advanced capitalist societies ... to defend the "national interest" against all other capitalist states and ... to prevent the spread of "communism" anywhere in the world'.[152] To interpret the latter as a 'classless' phenomenon is thus to miss the whole point of the Cold War. For this was a conflict between rival systems of *property relations* on a global scale, waged by military, ideological and economic means, and initiated by the USA and its allies to ensure that non-western parts of the world system remained 'open' to commerce under the auspices of 'neo-imperialism', irrespective of the social and human costs of this 'strategy' for innumerable 'Third World' peoples (chronic underdevelopment and attendant mass poverty).[153]

Second, in the period prior to the challenge posed by 'actually existing socialism' to bourgeois property relations (the so-called 'age of imperialism' between 1875 and 1914), the drive of the advanced western states to forge or expand empires or zones of influence was motivated primarily by economic motives, themselves shaped by developments in the relations of production (notably the rise of state monopoly capitalism, the expansion of production beyond the limits of domestic markets and their existing satellites, the growing propensity of the system to crisis, etc.).[154] Thus, whatever the origins of the state system, its subsequent development has bound it ever tighter to capitalist social relations and interests.

Third, the historical and empirical evidence mobilised in defence of the thesis of the autonomy of polity from economy, in both pre-capitalist and modern capitalist societies, is often flimsy to say the least. To illustrate my claim I will consider the arguments of Theda Skocpol (perhaps the leading 'state-centred' theorist) and Nigel Harris (a distinguished Marxist writer influenced by the state-centred approach).

First Skocpol's arguments. Skocpol cites a number of examples of state autonomy from modes of production and class agents.[155] Basing her account on Hugh Heclo's *Modern Social Politics in Britain and Sweden*, and focusing on unemployment insurance and pensions, Skocpol claims that 'civil service administrators in both Britain and Sweden have consistently made more important contributions to social policy development than political parties or interest groups'. State elites, not society-centred agents, have pushed for social and welfare reforms, and lobbying pressures from outside the state apparatus have been much less important. 'Socioeconomic conditions, especially crises, have stimulated only sporadic demands from parties and interest groups'.[156] I will consider her British example.

Of course, it is true that public policy-making in Britain has often been shaped by state interests and imperatives, such as stabilising the social order upon which state power rests, and has been fashioned in response to the perceived failings of previous policy rather than by direct pressure from propertied or business elites. But Skocpol nonetheless overplays her hand here. Certainly, the historical development of unemployment insurance and old-age pensions in the early part of the twentieth century can hardly be seen as a classless agenda. Pensions were a longstanding demand of the trade union movement, and unemployment insurance was introduced piecemeal in an attempt to both stabilise the capitalist order (during a period where mass unemployment was becoming seen as a breeding ground for social discontent) and to ensure that unemployed workers remained fit enough to work once prosperity was restored. Further, it is scarcely plausible to accept that these state decision-making processes have not generally been shaped indirectly by relations of production and attendant dominant class interests, even where they have not been campaigned for openly by class agents. Such indirect influences include the constraints placed on state agents by the imperatives of the economic system (domestically and globally), and by the fact that, by background and enculturation, state elites are sympathetic and attuned to the interests of propertied elites and the functional requirements of the economic order upon which class power rests, and rarely initiate or at least persist with policies which are patently harmful from a business point of view.

So, even if it were true that dominant class interests have not generally been the motive force behind the unfolding of social and welfare policy in Britain (whether organised in parties or pressure groups), this being pushed instead by state actors, it is not clear this in itself would 'prove' the autonomy of state agency from class and economic structures or processes. After all, the relative acquiescence of powerful sections of the bourgeoisie to the historical development of social policy in Britain between 1850 and the present day itself requires explanation. And, in fact, this lack of concerted class opposition to state-sponsored initiatives in social and welfare reform by the majority of the capitalist class, and the willingness of much of this economic elite to allow state elites to introduce and perpetuate such reforms, may be legitimately interpreted as evidencing a relative correspondence of interests between the state and capital on the question of the goals of social and public policy-making. In fact, as I have shown elsewhere in the current undertaking, social and welfare policy in Britain from its eighteenth-century origins simply cannot be understood without a class analysis.[157]

In any case, why choose the narrow example of social policy (and particularly just two aspects of social policy - unemployment insurance and pensions) to demonstrate the efficacy of 'state-centred' analysis? There are, after all, other examples which appear more cut-and-dried. Skocpol could have cited the well documented cases of the (often successful) opposition of the British civil service to the policies of the elected government on a whole range of economic and social issues. Yet the fact that such opposition takes place, and is often successful, is not at all suggestive of the autonomy of polity from class. This opposition is, after all, both in and against the state, not a simple collision between society and state. Moreover, it is a commonplace that such civil service obstruction of the policies of elected governments has been rather more directed against Labour administrations than Tory ones. Indeed, especially against Labour administrations which have purportedly stood for socialist reforms of the economy and a certain redistribution of wealth from the richer to the poorer sections of society, plus higher taxation levied on business to support public services (i.e. pro-working-class and anti-capitalist reforms). By contrast, where Labour governments acquiesce wholeheartedly to right wing, pro-capitalist, pro-market policy agendas, the opposition of the unelected elite state to their rule is considerably reduced. This is exactly what has occurred in Britain under New Labour.

In defence of her thesis of the autonomy of the state from class and economic relations, the main historical evidence which Skocpol cites is found in her *States and Social Revolutions*. This contains substantial empirical surveys of the classical social revolutions in France, China and Russia. For reasons of space I will focus on her treatment of the French Revolution.[158] The centrepiece of Skocpol's argument is that in this case the activities of state, as these were constrained by relative weakness and lack of independence from internal and external pressures, explains why the revolution occurred and was successful in reorganising social and state relations.[159] This, for her, is indicative of the fact that state decision-making, as this is shaped by state interests, is at least as important as social and class interests and forces in determining the trajectory of societies. What are we to make of this argument?

In fact, the historical details of Skocpol's account of the revolution are mostly uncontentious, and few Marxists would have any problem accepting these. And most would accept her argument that states are significant macro-actors in their own right, with interests and capacities apart from those of class. The problem with her analysis is the theoretical conclusions which are drawn from it. Certainly, Skocpol is right to say that a major factor explaining the overthrow of the French monarchy was its failure to develop a rational taxation system to support its political activities and territorial ambitions, this leading to an acute fiscal crisis of the state. And certainly Skocpol is right to argue that the absolutist state failed abjectly to implement those reforms which would have dealt with the problem (a new land tax levied on the privileged orders generally, plus an end to the exemptions enjoyed by the clergy and nobility in particular). Skocpol is also right to cite military weakness – as revealed in unsuccessful wars with Britain for control of colonies – as exacerbating the internal crisis of the French state.

But these failings were crucial only in the context of the general crisis of the French agrarian economy (overburdened to breaking point by a combination of low productivity, high prices and the crushing weight of state and local taxation). This engendered peasant uprisings in the countryside and food riots in the towns.[160] Moreover, the tax system was inefficient and antiquated (not to mention grossly asymmetrical) precisely because it was skewed towards serving the interests of the landowners, top merchants and bishops (themselves substantial landowners), and those recruited from their ranks who staffed the bureaucratic structures of state. It was, of course, precisely because the monarchy and top state officials were closely integrated into the existing semi-feudal structure of class relations (dependent as they were upon the patronage of the landed elites) which ensured their paralysis on the issue of self-reform in the run-up to 1789 and during the 'municipal revolution' which subsequently unfolded.[161]

All of this being the case, the theoretical difficulty of Skocpol's 'state centred' interpretation of the French Revolution is revealed by the following facts. First, a combination of socio-economic and political grievances fuelled the revolution, underpinned by the growing social and economic decline of landlordism and the growth of petty capitalism, not simply or primarily the variable of 'weak government'. Second, the international pressures placed on the French state which exacerbated the internal crisis were a function of more advanced capitalist development in England and Holland, which ensured that French absolutism was increasingly disadvantaged militarily on the world stage. Third, this revolution was a class rebellion led by a petty-bourgeois coalition against the privileged orders of state and society. Fourth, the state bureaucracy and ruling monarchy of French society was essentially an integral part of the landed aristocracy, and in fact owed its historical origins to feudal production relations, and its political predominance to the weakening of these same relations. Finally, only an analysis couched in terms of class relations and interests can explain why the French state failed to introduce reforms which might have eased the pressures leading to revolution.

But this means that a 'society-centred' understanding of the French Revolution is more illuminating than a 'state-centred' one, despite Skocpol's claim to the contrary. Paradoxically, this is conceded by Skocpol where she says that the French state was undermined by the manner of which 'agrarian relations of production and landed dominant classes impinged upon state organisations'[162] in the context of international economic and military pressures:

> The revolutionary crisis developed when the old regime states became unable to meet the challenges of evolving international situations. Monarchical authorities were subjected to new threats or to intensified competition from more economically developed powers abroad. And they were constricted and checked in their responses by the institutionalised relationships of the autocratic state organisations to the landed upper classes and the agrarian economies.[163]

Quite so. But isn't this a rather odd defence of Skocpol's thesis of the autonomy of state relations from class relations, i.e. to identify the lack of autonomy of French absolutism from propertied elites as the major cause of its demise? Yet this is basically Skocpol's explanation ('weak administration' in the face of 'evolving international situations') for each of the great social revolutions of the nineteenth and twentieth centuries.

Consider now the arguments of Nigel Harris. In his attempt to establish 'the general indifference of private capital to what I have identified as the primary function of the state' (i.e. waging war for the purpose of acquiring 'power' or 'territory'), Harris claims that '[c]apital swallowed the Second World War, the Korean War and the Vietnam War without a bleep'.[164] He also goes on to argue that much state legislation, which is purported by Marxists to be in accordance with the interests of capital, is not actively promoted by the business lobby, and as such cannot be understood in terms of a class analysis, being better grasped in terms of the political interests of the state elite to ensure the social cohesion of the territory it administers.[165] His purpose in making these arguments is to illustrate his belief that military conflicts between states generally defy any kind of explanatory reduction to underlying modes of production, class relations or class interests.

Harris cites the example of anti-immigration controls in defence of this thesis. Though he acknowledges that these might serve capitalist interests by dividing the working class between 'natives' and 'foreigners', hence making collective resistance to capitalist exploitation more difficult, he denies that this evidences the subordination of the state to capital. Thus: 'We can indeed invent reasons as to why capital favours immigration control, but are these the reasons immigration controls exist?'[166] This is because such legislation has normally been campaigned for not by big capitalists but by 'right wing conservative and openly fascist political forces'[167] who are most committed to nationalist identities and interests. The indifference of private capital to anti-immigration policies is, Harris contends, a measure of the dispensability of such measures to the functioning of the modern trans-state economic system (which depends, we are told, on the free movement of commodities, capital and labour).[168] After all, '[p]rivate capital has an interest in dividing the working class only when it is united and threatening',[169] and such unity has been conspicuously lacking most of the time.

But these arguments are plainly inadequate. Consider Harris' example of immigration controls as evidencing the 'autonomy' of state policy-making from capital and class structure in recent times. This is remarkably weak. As Callinicos rightly points out, capital does indeed have an interest in the existence and persistence of these state measures, irrespective of whether or not the working class is 'united and threatening'. After all, only by keeping the workers divided can their unified resistance to capitalist rule be forestalled. Harris is quite right to point out that big capitalist interests were not to the forefront in pressing for a tightening of anti-immigration policies in the recent past. Yet the forces which did promote them were hardly 'classless' phenomena, for these had their locus in the petty bourgeoisie, who have often been mobilised by capital as the 'bribed tool of reaction' (as Marx once famously put it).

In any case, of course, it is far from clear why the failure of big capitalists to lobby for tighter anti-immigration policies evidences an 'indifference' on their part to such a policy. If, as Harris claims, trans-state capitalism has a 'need' for the free movement of migrant labour, why has it not been the case that vociferous demands have not been forthcoming from major industrialists, financiers or shareholders for the relaxation of immigration controls? (On the contrary, state policy-making has moved firmly in the opposite direction in recent years in the advanced western societies – towards a 'Fortress Europe' increasingly insulated from asylum seekers and immigrants beyond the boundaries of the most prosperous states of the EU – backed by all kinds of reactionary social forces.) There is, of course, an obvious answer to this question. As Callinicos remarks: 'The fact that western big business has acquiesced over the past couple of decades in a marked tightening of immigration controls is itself "independent evidence" that these controls don't work against the interests of capital'.[170] So much for the 'autonomous imperatives' of the economic and political systems of late modernity!

The first part of Nigel Harris' argument also collapses on closer empirical inspection. There is little evidence of the remoteness of political and military struggles from economic and class interests or motives. It is, for one thing, something of a commonplace among historians of international relations 'that central to the Roosevelt administration's war aims was the construction of a global order in which US capital and commodities could flow freely'.[171] And it is equally well known that important sections of German capital regarded territorial expansion and the 'disciplining' of the working class at home as the long-term solution to the global economic crisis of the 1930s which hit Germany particularly hard. This is why leading capitalists sponsored Hitler's rise to power.[172]

Less well known, however, is that the primary war aim of the Japanese regime was to secure strategic control of East Asia, to force access to the raw materials and trading zones locked up by European imperialisms in the region, and to curtail the threat posed to Japanese exports by growing US economic dominance in China. State sponsored industrialisation in Japan had been initially motivated by the military threat posed by the USA. But then capitalist growth in Japan became endangered by the marginalisation of its commodities in parts of the world market crucial to its success. These and other economic pressures were the main stimulus to Japan's invasion of China, which then engendered yet more stringent pressures, which in turn motivated Japan's high-risk attack on the USA, the world's strongest imperial power.[173] Britain, by contrast, was motivated to enter the war primarily in order to preserve its colonies from younger imperialisms, which were major props for a recession-torn domestic economy.[174] Little surprise that the war did not encounter much resistance from private capital.

The same pattern has been depressingly true of most major conflicts in the years since the Second World War. The two most recent examples – the UN war against Iraq in 1990–1 and NATO's war against Serbia in 1999 – were unambiguously motivated by economic and strategic interests, not by the humanitarian and democratic ideals attributed to them, or by pursuit of 'power' for its own sake.[175] The Serbian war was about the playing out of the post Cold War role of NATO as guarantor of political stability in areas of strategic and material value to the western alliance.[176] Certainly pacification of the Balkans, in order to safeguard pipeline access to the enormous mineral reserves of the Caspian Sea, control of which is now seen as indispensable to capitalist growth in the twenty-first century, was a major goal of this NATO intervention.[177] The Gulf War was a simpler matter. This was about defending the oilfields of Kuwait and Saudi Arabia from a regime perceived as a possible threat to their pro-western ruling monarchies and the lucrative relations between these privileged elites and the major western transnational companies which own or control substantial assets in the region.[178]

Moreover, that the Korean War, and subsequent unprecedented high levels of military spending by the USA during the height of the Cold War, played a fundamental though perhaps unintended part in stabilising capitalist development (by engendering the permanent arms economy which supported the long post-war boom by easing the tendency towards the overaccumulation of capital and overproduction of commodities in the system's western heartlands) is also indisputable.[179] Aside from this, of course, it is surely fallacious to suggest, as Harris does, that US capital withstood the Vietnam War without any ill effects whatsoever. As Callinicos has observed, 'the inflation generated by the Vietnam War' and attendant 'financial disorders ... helped precipitate a small recession in 1970–1 and then the slump of 1974–5'. These economic constraints certainly played a part in 'persuading' the US government to withdraw from the conflict,[180] though the anti-war movement was of course equally efficacious in this regard.

Fourth, these empirical failings of 'state-centred' analysis are often compounded by conceptual errors. For example, having made the claim that the primary function of the state elite is to concentrate in its hands more power in order to 'reinforce the authority, political longevity, and social control of the state organisations', Skocpol goes on to specify the structural prerequisites which allow the state to achieve these goals.[181] Aside from her unremarkable insight that 'sheer sovereign integrity and the stable administrative control of a given territory are preconditions for any state's ability to implement policies',[182] Skocpol is prepared to admit that state autonomy has a definite economic basis and is always economically constrained. So, for instance, she argues that the capacity of states to act on their interests is dependent on whether they can draw upon powerful and diversified productive forces and the credit and financial reserves these engender.[183]

All of this is obvious enough, of course. But isn't this suggestive of a closer integration of interests between polity and economy than is indicated by the 'state-centred' approach? Isn't this suggestive of definite and fairly stringent limits to the degree of autonomy any state elite can achieve from propertied elites? After all, it follows from the logic of Skocpol's own account that most historical states (especially pre-capitalist ones) have enjoyed little real autonomy from class and economic relations, since their productive forces have been relatively undeveloped. And, of course, if states can better achieve their goals by virtue of a prosperous and diversified economic base, might not their dependence on this base allow those who control economic resources more leeway to bend political elites to their will?

Nigel Harris' recent work is also conceptually confused. As Callinicos rightly says, when Harris attempts to specify in concrete terms the autonomy of the state from capital his analysis quickly runs into contradictions and equivocations.[184]

> The role of the state is being … changed … from representing a national society and capital (the old corporatist 'social democratic' alliance of state, business and labour in Britain), to enforcing on the domestic economy and society the imperatives of a global economy; from promoting the interests of domestic capital to seeking to capture and keep a share of global output; from managing a relatively diversified and supposedly autonomous national economy to managing flows of goods and services which start and end far beyond the authority or even the knowledge of the state.[185]

But is this account really consistent with a view of state and capital as following 'parallel logics', as entering only into an 'alliance' of mutual convenience and benefit (albeit one which is now being undone by the internationalisation of production and finance and the growth of transnational corporations)? In fact, Harris' own argument, far from revealing the interaction of two separate structures of domination (polity and economy), instead is suggestive of something entirely different. This is of a 'shift of one form of subordination of the state to capital to another',[186] from the domination of the state by the imperatives and interests of a domestic economy and attendant capitalist class (autarkic state capitalism) to the domination of the state by the imperatives of a global economy and attendant international capitalist class (trans-state capitalism).

Fifth, research has shown that the state elites of contemporary capitalist societies are recruited almost entirely from the ranks of the propertied 'upper class', share common patterns of socialisation and education with those who are destined to become 'captains of industry', maintain close social networks (including ties of marriage) with fellow members of this class (and with no others), and often maintain business interests and connections even during their tenure as state officials.[187] This can hardly be seen as demonstrating a merely contingent relationship between state and capital, as is claimed by opponents of the 'instrumentalist' view of the state. Rather this is a structured relationship emergent from a long historical process whereby institutional mechanisms have been forged which ensure that the state elite responds appropriately to the structural pressures exerted by nationally and internationally based domestic capital with a minimum of friction.[188]

Little wonder, then, that top state administrators (and government ministers of whatever party) tend to identify the 'national interest' with securing conditions conducive to the competitiveness of domestic big capital on a local and international stage. How else explain this phenomenon other than in terms of the class cohesion of the economic and political elites of capitalist society? Certainly, an explanation of inter-state relations since the Second World War in these terms (i.e. in terms of the common class interests and enculturation of the political and economic elites of capitalist societies, as these are shaped by structural constraints imposed on the state by domestic capital and the global market) allow us a better purchase on this question than do abstract Weberian appeals to the 'will to power' or 'the madness or irrationality of people in power'.[189]

Finally, the neo-Weberian abstraction of state relations from class relations seems to derive much of its authority from a highly simplistic reading of the classical Marxist theory of the state, which is (falsely) held to grasp political institutions as a 'passive reflection' of the economy and defined entirely in terms of a domestic class structure.[190] This having been done, it is then an easy matter to refute a class analysis of the state by appealing to the self-evident fact that the interactions between states (and not simply the interactions between classes and capitals) are important in constraining or shaping the 'world political order'.

Yet, as Chris Harman rightly says, Marx's classical account of the state in *The Communist Manifesto* (in which he famously described it as 'a committee for managing the common affairs of the whole bourgeoisie')[191] was simply an attempt to draw out the class content of a *particular* form of state – namely the minimalist 'night-watchman' state of early Victorian England. His analysis here, like those of the classical political economists, mistakenly 'takes as given' the correspondence of this form of the state to a *developed* capitalist society in which the bourgeoisie has assumed complete mastery of the economy.

But this was not Marx's 'last word' on the problem of the interface between class relations and state relations. This is attested to by his careful analysis of 'Bonapartism' (the French imperial state of Napoleon I and Napoleon III), which for him had secured for itself a partial independence from the rival interests of the landowning and capitalist classes on the one hand, and from the workers and peasants on the other.[192] The state here was certainly not grasped by Marx as a mere tool of the economically dominant classes, as a 'passive superstructure' reflecting the economic interests of the propertied, nor as a mere 'effect' of the class struggle between propertied and propertyless.

Of equal significance, classical Marxists such as Lenin and Bukharin have sought to analyse state relations in the era of developed 'monopoly' capitalism, and in doing so have explicitly theorised 'imperialism' as a system of politico-military interactions between states, brought into being by the monopolisation and centralisation of production within national boundaries, and the resultant 'growing together' of economy and polity as 'state capitalism'.[193] This hardly adds up to a 'failure' on the part of Marxism to theorise 'state violence' or the 'global military order' (as is claimed by Giddens),[194] whatever one makes of the truth or falsity of the analysis on offer. Nor does it add up to a 'neglect' of inter-state relations in constraining the conduct and shaping the character of individual state apparatuses (as is claimed, for instance, by Nigel Harris).[195] In fact, far from portraying institutional state structures as a 'simple superstructure', as an appendage to capitalist relations of production, it is clear enough that classical Marxist scholars have instead grasped these as comprised of a nexus of political, cultural and economic relations, as simultaneously base and superstructure. 'So, for instance, "property rights" are judicial (part of the superstructure) but regulate the way exploitation takes place (part of the base)'.[196]

Enough has now been said about the weaknesses of anti-materialist 'state-centred' analysis. A second reason why the closeness of the 'functional' relationship between class interests and state interests is often obscured is simply that the latter does have an 'inherent tendency' towards *relative* autonomy from the former (the reverse side of the *partial* determination of state by economy). That is to say, the state does have 'a tendency to alienate itself from the society from which it was born':

> With the increase in the division of labour the state grows in importance as the organiser of social life. Its accumulating functions are no longer limited simply to representing the ruling class against the oppressed class and against the classes of other countries: it begins to concern itself with the economic and cultural interests of the society as a whole, though naturally this is a process which continues to be to the advantage of the ruling class as a whole. As the state grows more important, the state apparatus and the autonomy of movement of this apparatus also grow, and this has fundamental repercussions, both good and bad, on the economic basis. At this point the state has to insert its own needs (taxes, tariffs, etc.) directly into economic life, and in the process of doing this can sometimes harm the interests of the ruling class which it is trying to serve.[197]

The degree of autonomy of polity from the 'economically dominant class' obviously varies in different societal and historical contexts. This it does, crucially, in accordance with the balance of class forces:

> The absolute monarchies of the seventeenth and eighteenth centuries were strong because the power of the nobility and the bourgeoisie was evenly balanced, though even in this case the state cannot be said to have been independent of the relations of production. Absolutism was still based partly on feudal forces, whose political rights it upheld (even if in a somewhat reduced form) and whose economic existence it guaranteed by maintaining serfdom. On the other hand it had already begun to build on the growing bourgeoisie, representing the latter's economic interests by introducing the mercantilist policies which were needed for the development of modern industry. As soon as the bourgeoisie had established clear economic superiority this state was destroyed and gave way to another, which could express the bourgeoisie's economic domination in a political form. The bonapartism of the first and especially the second French empires, where bourgeoisie and proletariat had fought each other to a standstill, is another example of the relative autonomy of the state apparatus. Modern fascism, too, comes partly under this heading: an even balance of forces between capital and labour puts the petty bourgeois layers in political control, although they do not have any influence on the economic foundations of capitalism and are obliged to carry out policies in favour of the bourgeoisie, which is still the economically dominant class.[198]

As a rule, the relative autonomy of polity from the direct control of the ruling class acquires a consistently high form, and its most stable form, in a developed capitalist society. There are two reasons for this. First, the productive forces are sufficiently advanced here to support an independent 'unproductive' centralised administrative apparatus on a nationwide scale. Second, and more importantly, the structural configuration of capitalist relations of production (the total separation of the direct producers from access to the means of production) enables their routine reproduction by economic mechanisms without the continual intervention or threat of intervention of politico-military force in the class struggle. In Marx's words: 'The silent compulsion of economic relations sets the seal on the domination of the capitalist over the worker. Direct extra-economic force is still of course used, but only in exceptional cases'.[199] The fact that the capitalist state is not generally an integral part of the relations of production or economic exploitation in this sense (and especially not of the *laissez-faire* capitalism which existed in Victorian Britain) is what accounts for its establishment as a power *apart* from the economy, following its own relatively independent interests and historical development, whatever its role in intervening in the economy (domestic or otherwise) on behalf of capital or safeguarding the socio-political conditions in which capital can flourish both home and abroad.

Thus the very fact that the mode of production of capitalist society does allow a separation of its 'political' and 'economic' functions, ensures that a certain (though tightly circumscribed) space is opened up for a differentiation of interest between the state and capital to develop. The state elite does have a real interest in attempting to concentrate in its own hands a greater share of the total surplus value pumped out of the direct producers *against* capital. Further, because a major function of the state bureaucracy consists in overseeing and defending the overall political conditions of surplus-extraction of the national capital it represents, this can often mean that it finds itself in conflict with its 'own' bourgeoisie, for whom the military defence of some abstract 'world order' against uncooperative Third World states or anti-capitalist regimes often appears a less pressing concern than the protection of profit margins from an excessive burden of state expenditures (which cannot always be passed on to the workers).

Aside from this, of course, it is often the case that the state is forced into making concessions to a radicalised working class (or even to one which is not yet radicalised for tactical reasons). There is also plenty of scope for the state elite to bind itself to particular sections of capital at the expense of others (if these better service its interests or are perceived as especially conducive to overall national competitiveness). Nor are there any institutional barriers external to the state which might prevent the political executive from embarking upon policies which are disastrous from a capitalist point of view (e.g. embarking upon an economically debilitating war to legitimise an unpopular government). Finally, the 'relative autonomy' of the state from capitalist interests is also derived from the fact that certain of its functions are necessarily apolitical. Thus, whatever the class character or interests of the political elite, the role of the state in administering or overseeing a large-scale national community ensures that certain of its activities (e.g. upholding certain kinds of criminal law or traffic regulations such as the *Highway Code*) must be 'classless' in the sense that they are indispensable to the running of any industrialised urban society.

Yet (all of this having been said) it is important not to lose sight of the fact that there are definite limits to how far the 'autonomy' of the state from capital and class relations can go. This is because the capitalist class and the state elite are bound together by a relationship of structural interdependence from which neither can extricate themselves. On the one hand, as Chris Harman points out,

> [t]he limiting case for the state is that, even if it overrides the interests of particular capitalists, it cannot forget that its own revenues and its own ability to defend itself against other states depend, at the end of the day, on the continuation of capital accumulation. … Any state bureaucracy that fails to accomplish this is going to see the resources it needs for

> its own privileges and its own functioning dry up. ... Thus the Nazis could expropriate Thyssen, they could seize the wealth of Jewish capitalists, they could establish the horrific machinery of the death camps without it providing any appreciable benefit to German capital. They could even insist on continuing the war after it was clearly going to be lost and the interests of German capitalism would have been served by attempts at a negotiated peace. But they could only do all of these things so long a they ensured that capitalist exploitation took place on the most favourable terms for capital (state and private) and, therefore, that accumulation continued. The same applies to Peron, Nasser, the Ba'athists, the East European regimes and so on.

On the other hand,

> [t]he limiting case for the individual capital is that though it can, with considerable difficulty, uproot itself from one national state terrain and plant itself in another, it cannot operate for any length of time without having some state to do its will. It is too vulnerable to try to operate in a 'Wild West' situation in which there is no effective state, leaving it both prey to forces from below which might disrupt its normal rhythms of exploitation and to other capitals and their states. ... Productive capital cannot get a surplus unless the state ensures the a plentiful supply of 'free' labour with sufficient skills, and provides means of physical defence. It also requires that commodity capital ensures realisation of the surplus value and that money capital can provide the funds for further expanding production. Commodity capital cannot function effectively unless the state lays the basis for the operation of a stable national market and uses its influence to open up foreign markets.[200]

Thus it is this relationship of 'structural interdependence' between polity and economy in modern capitalism which 'sets the most fundamental limits on the "autonomy" of the state'. This mutual dependence does not prevent the economic and political elites from acting, up to a certain point, as if they are completely independent of each other.

> In particular, money capital and commodity capital can act as if they ha[ve] no dependence upon the geographically rooted means of production of industrial capital. In the same way, those who run the state can act, up to a certain point, as if their revenues d[o] not depend upon successful capitalist exploitation and accumulation. This is what happens when reformists, populists or even fascists get control of parts of the state structure and use them to carry through social change.[201]

Nonetheless, the 'structural dependence of the state on capital means that persisting in a policy which conflicts with the interests of capital will have negative consequences for the state, certainly in the long term, sometimes sooner'. There are a number of economic-class mechanisms which function to 'reign in' the state elite. The most obvious of these are, of course, capital flight, the 'investment strike', and speculative attacks on the currency. But there are other ways besides. 'If capitalists don't like a policy, they lobby against it. The informal networks linking them with the state bureaucracy, as well as the latter's economic dependence on capital, mean that more often than not they win out'.[202] Where all else fails, furthermore,

> the mutual interdependence of the different elements asserts itself in the most dramatic fashion, through crises – the sudden collapse of the system of credit, the sudden inability to sell the commodities, sudden balance of payments crises or even the threat of state bankruptcy.[203]

These economic constraints of the total system of commodity production are normally sufficient to force the state system into line with capitalist interests.

But this means that a class analysis of the state bureaucracy is altogether appropriate. For this can no longer be seen as a classless elite which is simply pressurised from without to do capital's bidding. And so, irrespective of the very real space which can open up between the goals and interests of the state elite and the economic elite, this 'structural interdependence' which binds them together ensures that they are invariably unified in opposition to the working class. In other words, since private capital and the state bureaucracy share a common objective relationship of economic exploitation with and against the proletariat (because both derive their revenue from a cut in the total surplus value left over after working-class consumption), they are compelled to close ranks against the workers in defence of capitalist relations of production. It is for this reason that Marxist analyses of power relations in capitalist society rightly stress (in opposition to the Weberian view of this matter) that economic and political elites are not different in kind, autonomous factors of 'stratification' (economic 'class' versus political 'ranking', etc.), but are rather distinct executive wings of a relatively unified propertied class of exploiters, whose internal differences of interest and antagonisms pale beside those which separate them from the direct producers.

Conclusion

In the foregoing I have attempted to accomplish two objectives. First, to articulate an account of structural properties which neither obliterates the voluntarism of human agency nor reduces it to the passive effect of socio-cultural hydraulics. Second, to outline and defend a materialist understanding of social systems – by means of a realist 'reconstruction' of Marx's base-superstructure model – which avoids the unacceptable extremes of monistic economic reductionism, on the one hand, and a pluralistic 'theory of factors', on the other. The purpose of my first argument is to make sense of the structural conditioning of human interaction without parting company from the view that people are alone responsible for structural statics or change. The purpose of my second argument is to theorise a hierarchical model of emergent structures, which can stand as a practical alternative to postmodern 'idealist reductionism' and neo-Weberian 'empiricism', and which is capable of supporting a history which grasps it as 'totality' and 'progress' (i.e. as an overall pattern of societal evolution and transformation governed by the dialectical interface between productive labour, class conflict and the contradictory economic structures within which these modes of agency are bounded).

My first argument works as follows. The differential positioning of interactants in emergent socio-economic structures ensures that their activity and consciousness is subject to structural conditioning. This does not mean that those irreducible needs and capacities (and hence objective interests in pursuing or exercising them) which pertain uniquely to human beings as organisms and subjects are negated. Structural conditioning does not work upon indeterminate material (upon which it can make what it will), for the simple reason that human beings are bearers of organismic and subjective properties which render social determination a non-starter. Subjects do not simply respond passively to external stimuli, in the manner of Pavlov's salivating dogs, because they are capable of abstracting themselves away from immediate reality and assessing the degree to which this is alienating or fulfilling of their aspirations and can be modified in accordance with their interests. Rather, structural conditioning functions by virtue of its role in distributing differential and normally antagonistic vested interests (in societal reproduction or reform and the appropriate social strategies which are required to achieve these ends) to agents who are differently placed, upon which they can normally be counted to act under pain of incurring punitive opportunity costs (declining living standards, etc.), hence imparting 'systemness' to their social interaction and 'directional guidance' to structural dynamics.

Such a schema in no way invalidates a conception of agents as 'sovereign artificers', nor a conception of society and history as dependent upon the powers and properties of human nature. Structural conditioning – the interface between involuntary placement, vested interests and attendant opportunity costs – works upon human agents by confronting them with an objective environment of finite cultural and material resources in which they have to act (and upon which they normally must draw in order to act) and by placing them in structured situations or 'situational logics' within this environment, which supply them with rational grounds or 'good reasons' for acting in accordance with structurally prescribed interests. This means that structural conditioning can function only by virtue of the organismic and subjective capacities of human agents, not in spite of them, or in opposition to them.

What is the relationship between the structural conditioning of human agency thus conceived and my account of Marx's structural sociology? I have interpreted Marx's base-superstructure distinction as specifying a hierarchical ordering of emergent social structures. Such structures have their 'ultimate genesis' in social labour to produce a livelihood from the physical environment, and they are reproduced or transformed only through the social agency of the living, though from the point of view of every living generation of agents they are always 'already made'.

Upon the 'basis' of the economic structures of material production and class exploitation arise a range of additional socio-cultural structures and ideological forms. Some of these structures are directly emergent from the economic base; others are directly emergent from those structures which rest immediately on the economic base and which have arisen to safeguard or challenge it. Those elements of the superstructure which develop directly out of and feed directly into material production and class exploitation (especially legal and politico-military structures and sometimes religious forms) function to *co*-determine with the 'economy' in various mixes further elaborations of ideological or aesthetic forms and non-productive socio-cultural relations. Those superstructural emergents which have their origins or locus in the activities of those agents situated in antecedent superstructural spheres (such as law from religious ideas and rationalist philosophy from the interface between religion, law and science) react back in turn upon their own 'causes' in anterior political or cultural structures, and upon the economic basis upon which all non-economic institutions, ideologies and practices are dependent 'in the final analysis'. Again, this occurs not through structural hydraulics, but through the generative mechanism of interest-governed class agency, as this is subject to directional guidance by virtue of the positioning of interactants in the relations of production *vis-à-vis* material and cultural resources.

According to this conception, the mode of production and class exploitation is 'basic' to society as a whole for three important reasons. First, because it provides 'conditions of possibility' for the existence of non-economic structures (the output of wealth to support structural differentiation over time) and sets limits and provides enablements for their subsequent development. Second, because class relations, centred on the uneven distribution of the means of production and subsistence, are the fundamental source of inequality in society, and hence of social malintegration (because of the conflicts of interest to which they give rise between the propertied and propertyless). Finally, because relations of production explain the content of those social and ideological structures which are closely related to the economic base (as expressions or articulations of the contradiction between these and the forces of production and of the conflict between exploiting and exploited classes), and the respective degrees of autonomy which are enjoyed by those cultural and other spheres which do not function to 'fix' or challenge the vested interests of the socially dominant class.

In the latter case, superstructural relations and ideologies are more or less 'determined' by or 'autonomous' of the economic base by virtue of the interest-governed social agency of the contending classes. Those institutions and ideologies which necessarily perform a key role in reproducing or legitimising relations of production (such as state relations and legal forms) are those which correspond most closely to the 'dominant side' of class relationships. This is for the obvious reason that propertied elites possess both vested interests in securing the domination of those institutions and cultural structures upon which the preservation of their wealth and power depends and the structural capacities (control of the means of wealth creation) to secure this domination.

The punitive opportunity costs of failing to translate economic domination into legal and politico-military domination, ensures in turn that propertied elites are subject to directional guidance to act in ways appropriate to their structurally determined vested interests. This means that there is a long-run tendency in any social system for relationships of relative compatibility or correspondence to be forged between relations of production and those elements of the superstructure which are 'functional' to their reproduction requirements. More generally, of course, the content of those superstructural relations and ideologies which express the contradictions of material life (between forces and relations of production) is the historical product of the ongoing dialectic of social conflict between the propertied and the propertyless (and sometimes between rival propertied elements), as this is shaped by the interplay between the respective situational logics, vested interests and corresponding opportunity costs (in acting in defence of these interests) of the contending classes.

Such is the complex nature of dialectical interaction between all the differentiated elements of any total social structure, that it is easy to forget altogether the 'social primacy' of the mode of production in the senses described in this chapter. The more developed the productive forces, the more elaborate and differentiated is the social structure which is supported by them, and the longer the chain of intermediary links which separate the 'higher' elements of the superstructure ('pure' ethics, art, theory, theology, philosophy, etc.) from their economic 'conditions of existence'. Indeed, precisely because the 'higher' elements of the superstructure are peripheral to the functioning of the relations of production, and therefore have the space to abstract themselves from the class struggle, it is unsurprising that these often enjoy a high degree of autonomy from 'economic conditions' or class interests.

But, despite the complexity of societal process, the explanatory primacy of the economic base remains, not simply because the mode of production and class exploitation is decisive in shaping the nature of those superstructural forms (especially political and legal structures) which are fundamental in fixing or stabilising an existing system of social relations, but because it is decisive also in shaping the systemic incompatibilities and social conflicts which can lead to the kinds of political agency which can bring about structural reform or transformation. By contrast, the greater the distance of superstructural emergents from the economic and material base, the less of a purchase they have on the real concerns and interests of human agents, and the less relevant they become for explaining the social agency which brings about societal change or its opposite.

Now, the purpose of Marx's structural sociology is to obtain an analytical purchase on the question of why and how societies or social systems are subject to processes of quantitative development interspersed by 'critical episodes' of qualitative transformation. His distinctions between forces and relations of production and between economic base and politico-ideological superstructure are crucial to an understanding of how this works. I have pointed out that forces of production are 'basic' to production relations by virtue of the capacity of the former to set limits on the range of the latter which are possible in any historical epoch. I have also argued that productive forces have an inherent (because transformative) tendency to develop under the impulse of objective human needs and interests, albeit needs and interests which are socially developed and culturally defined (under the auspices of advances in material production). The development of the productive forces at some point runs into limits imposed by existing relations of production (under which they had previously been at work) and by doing so places the latter under 'directional guidance' to undergo structural elaboration or transformation in a way which facilitates their further advance.

This argument is well made by Chris Harman:

> The history of society is the history of changes in the ways in which production takes place, each associated with changes in the relations between human beings immediately around the productive process. And these changes in turn exert a pressure on all the other social relations. … Expansion of material production is the cause, the social organisation of production the effect. … There is no mechanical principle which means that the expansion of material production – and with it changes in social relations – will automatically occur. But in any society there will be pressures in this direction at some point or other. … If, for instance, a band of hunter-gatherers adopts a means of radically increasing the food available to them (by, say, planting root vegetables for themselves instead of having to search for them) and of storing it for long periods of time (for instance, in earthenware pots) this necessarily changes their social relations with one another. Instead of continually moving, they have to stay in one spot until the crop can be harvested; if they are staying in one spot there is no longer any necessity for restriction on the number of children per woman; the crop becomes something which

> other bands of people can seize, so providing for the first time an incentive for warfare between rival bands.[204]

Not only at some point in any society are relations of production subject to directional guidance to undergo changes which unblock the development of the productive forces, but so too is the politico-ideological superstructure placed under this same pressure by the economic base (the forces and relations of production combined):

> Thus the first stirrings of capitalism in Europe generated pressures for a challenge to the Catholic Church which was both a major feudal landowner in its own right and provided ideological legitimation for the feudal order as a whole. The eventual outcome of these pressures was the Reformation of the 16th century and the emergence with Calvinism of a new form of Christianity favourable to the 'needs' of early capitalist accumulation. [Later on] ... the Industrial Revolution in Britain provided an impulse for the enfranchisement, first, of the industrial bourgeoisie and middle class, and then, of the industrial working-class (resulting in the Reform Acts of 1832, 1867 and 1884). [Later still] ... a change in the base – the massive rise in paid employment of women during the post-war economic boom – provided the impulse for a significant, though partial, change in the dominant social attitude towards women.[205]

Such structural pressures for social change (of the base upon the superstructure) do not, to reiterate a basic point, add up to structural laws which operate 'over the heads' of human agents. Instead these are a function of the social agency of a rising propertied class, or of the conflict between exploiting and exploited classes, as this is mediated by the interplay between involuntary placement, vested interests (in societal reform or replication) and attendant opportunity costs (which ensure that for the most part class agents find good reasons for acting in accordance with their structurally determined interests). Nor does the 'directional pressure' exerted by the base on the superstructure add up to a thesis of structural super-determinism (even if this is mediated through social agency) whereby economic 'causes' lead in monocausal fashion to societal 'effects'. In the historical examples cited above, for instance, 'none of the impulses were realised automatically or without bitter conflict, the outcome of which might have been different',[206] not least because 'conservative' elements of the superstructure (state and legal relations plus the political ideologies of the socially dominant class or classes) are mobilised to prevent the development of new forms of production and/or exploitation that challenge the status quo and the vested interests tied up in it, which have to be defeated politically and ideologically if a new form of society is to replace the old.

On the contrary, what is being proposed is this. First, that the key role of class relations in shaping access to allocative and authoritative resources, and in determining the conditions of life and vested interests of those differently placed, provides interactants with good reasons or pressing imperatives to engage in class struggle aimed at the preservation or reform of the existing structure of economic relations and those elements of the superstructure which have arisen or been modified to safeguard it. In other words, class struggle emergent from class structure is the primary form of *social* malintegration, which is a necessary though insufficient condition of structural change. Second, that such social malintegration (the conflict between classes) is brought to a head during 'critical episodes' in which *structural* malintegration (the fettering of productive forces by relations of production) generates an organic crisis, the historical result of which is not arbitrary but is bounded by 'economic necessity' (the level of development of material production and the kinds of class groupings and attendant class capacities this supports). This means that certain societal outcomes are objectively more likely than others (such as the long-standing decay of capitalism leading eventually to socialism rather than 'the common ruin of the contending classes' and attendant 'barbarism'), whereas others can be ruled out for certain (such as the development of capitalism out of the crisis of the tributary mode of production, or the development of socialism out of the crisis of feudalism).

Conclusion

In the foregoing I have sought to theorise the interface between the organismic, subjectivist, interactional and structural properties of social systems in a way which is consistent with a radicalised form of realist social theory: 'emergentist Marxism'. My purpose in so doing is twofold. First, sociological emergentism (and attendant methodological realism) is indispensable to constructing an anti-reductive understanding of the social world, which neither reduces human agents to social structures or processes of socialisation or enculturation, nor reduces social structures or social practices to human agents. Second, a 'materialistic' interpretation of socio-cultural emergentism allows the theorist to avoid the error of translating the realist thesis of the irreducibility of the distinct strata of human and social reality into an argument specifying the mutual *autonomy* of the 'ideal' and 'material' elements of society. So 'emergentist Marxism', a particular form of realist social theory, is not only antithetical to all forms of conflationary-reductionist social theory (whether holism, atomism or idealism in their various guises), but also provides the analyst with the conceptual and analytical tools to resist fashionable neo-Weberian and postmodern understandings of socio-cultural reality as simply a kaleidoscopic combinatory of heterogeneous structures or practices or 'power centres', none of which have any necessary connection or determinate relationship with each other.

The logic and structure of my argument can be briefly summarised as follows. First, I have sought to establish the relationship between philosophical realism and emergentist materialism, and the way in which the latter can both enrich the former and render defensible the central positions of Marxist philosophy and social theory (Chapter 1). I defend three claims here. First, that 'depth realism' is in fact a defensible anti-reductive form of ontological materialism (because validated by the activity and results of the various sciences) which is broadly consistent with Engels' dialectical materialism. Second, that methodological realism must be more explicitly 'dialectical' if it is to realise its rich potential for apprehending socio-cultural dynamics. Finally, that emergentist materialism, when translated into social science theory, renders defensible (indeed plausible) the central arguments of Marxism in anthropology and sociology: the explication of human beings, human consciousness and socio-cultural relations in terms of the historical interface between the 'structuralist' and 'activist' dimensions of the forces and relations of production.

The remainder of my thesis is an elaboration and defence of these core propositions. My first task has been to theorise the properties and powers which pertain to human agents as organisms, subjects and interactants (social agents and institutional actors) which are precisely responsible for structural-systemic elaboration or reproduction. Chapter 2 is concerned with the 'microstructures' of human society and history: human nature and its emergent properties. My argument is that Marx's 'labour theory' of species-being furnishes us with a simultaneously naturalistic and social account of individuals as subjects, and with the most basic explanation of social order and social change (societal organisation and societal transformation presupposing properties and powers of mind and self irreducible to the imprint of society; societal change presupposing objective species-needs and interests which 'found' the social struggles of human agents). Chapter 3 is concerned with analysing the 'interaction order' which is emergent from the 'micro' level of the organismic and subjectivist capacities and needs of human agents, yet overdetermined by the 'macro' level of emergent socio-cultural relations. My argument is that this 'interaction order' is the linchpin connecting individuals with the structural properties of social systems.

From this perspective, human agents are the bearers of a determinate range of biologically based needs and capacities, and are furthermore in possession of 'subjective emergents', by virtue of which they have secured for themselves a relative autonomy from their physical and social environments, including the capacity to remake these in accordance with their needs and interests. This means that an adequate understanding of human social interaction is, before everything else, an *interest*-explanation, not an explanation in terms of the 'functional imperatives' of an abstract social system. Individuals have basic needs (both physical and psychological) by virtue of their membership of a particular biological species. They therefore have human interests in ensuring that these needs are met by whatever social means are to hand. Yet human needs and interests are not reducible simply to a 'biological substratum', definable in terms of access to those material necessaries (of food, clothing and shelter, etc.) which ensure human survival. On the contrary, human needs and interests are those which ensure the physical and psychological well-being of the subject, and this well-being is always defined by cultural standards, which are themselves determined objectively by the level of development of material production and social labour, and the degree of welfare and self-autonomy this allows individuals to reasonably expect from the societies to which they belong.

But I have said that (aside from possessing objective needs and interests by virtue of the historical interface between biology, social labour and physical nature) human agents also possess the species-capacities of mind, self, intentionality, rationality, etc., to articulate these needs and interests and act consciously in accordance with them. This being the case, where human agents find themselves situated in social relations rooted in economic exploitation and political domination, by virtue of which they are denied the freedom and life-chances of others better placed, or the consumption which the output of their own labour merits, they will feel these social relations to be unjust and oppressive, and will seek to resist or reform or even overturn them. In doing so they will encounter resistance from those elite groupings in society who have vested interests in the status quo by virtue of their control of allocative and authoritative resources. It is this 'dialectic of control', between those agential collectivities who have vested interests in societal replication and those who have vested interests in societal change, which provides history with much of its dynamic, as Marx rightly insists.

Now, elite groupings will tend to be the beneficiaries of life-chances and degrees of autonomy much above the cultural average. So much so in fact, that it is defensible to view the privileges they enjoy as constituting a 'surplus' over and above their objective human needs (as these are defined by productive force development and the average standards of living this can support). This means that the vested social interests of elite groupings are constituted by those institutional means (appropriate to their structural positioning) by which they meet their objective human needs, *and* by which they defend or enhance their sectoral advantages (which are also a function of their positioning in emergent social relations, and which are invariably won at the expense of the life-chances of subordinate groupings). By contrast, the vested social interests of subordinate groupings are comprised of those institutional means by which they pursue or further their objective socially developed human needs and capacities *without remainder*, their 'vested' interest in human emancipation from the tyranny of 'artificial scarcity' being determined by their specific propertyless status in society. In the former case, vested social interests correspond to privileged life-chances, to the beneficiaries of mechanisms of class exploitation by which the life-chances of the many are subordinated to service those of the few. In the latter case, vested social interests correspond to universal needs, and are comprised of those social practices necessary to ensure these needs are met.

This provides an ethical basis for championing the struggles of the oppressed and exploited against their oppressors and exploiters (a naturalistic principle of justice). Social relations which are capable of sustaining a certain reasonable standard of living for all (given a relatively egalitarian distribution of allocative resources), and which objectively allow the possibility of a more even distribution of authoritative resources (in the sense of not endangering the stable reproduction of society within its material means), but which fail to do so because an elite stratum has monopolised effective political power plus a cut of the social product above the cultural median, are morally reprehensible. Such social relations are morally reprehensible because they stand in contradiction to the maximum realisation of human needs and capacities which is here possible to achieve.

All of this brings me to the arguments contained in Chapter 4. I have said that the positioning of agents in emergent structures (and in specific contexts or environments within emergent structures) ensures their social conduct is subject to a range of constraints, impulses and enablements. The significance of structure is that it comprises a social and material integument, historically predating the interaction of human agents, which shapes their subsequent activity by immersing them in stratified social relations which determine their respective access to material and cultural resources, and which define their objective social interests relative to other agents. This does not mean that the psycho-organic powers and properties which pertain uniquely to human agents and their social interaction are negated or subsumed under social practices or processes of enculturation. The social agency of individuals is still the mechanism of structural elaboration and/or reproduction, and agents are still sovereign artificers, who act relatively voluntaristically (within a range of socio-cultural possibilities) on the basis of needs and interests which are irreducible to the imprint of society. Instead, structural conditioning, defined here as the interplay between involuntary placement, vested interests and attendant opportunity costs, impinges upon agents by virtue of the fact they are situated in 'positions' in social relations which furnish them with rational motives (the defence or pursuit of improved life-chances) for acting in accordance with their structurally defined interests.

Yet there can be no doubt that it is the 'situational logics' and attached agential interests determined by the positioning of interactants in class relations, which have explanatory primacy in shaping their socio-political consciousness and agency. This is because class positions within emergent relations of production are decisive in determining the access of agents to authoritative and allocative resources in societies past and present. This renders meaningful the Marxist thesis that the economic structure of a society not only provides 'conditions of existence' for non-economic structures and practices, but also 'determines' its politico-ideological superstructure and decisively shapes the social conflicts which give rise to epochal societal change.

There are two basic reasons for this. First, the mode of production can now be plausibly seen as fixing the fundamental axis of social inequality, and hence as constituting the primary source of social (and system) malintegration in most historical societies. Second, because class interests and capacities are crucial in explaining the socio-political agency of interactants, it follows that there is a long-run tendency in any social system for superstructural emergents (and especially legal and political relations) to 'correspond' to the contradictions internal to relations of production, and especially to structures of class domination.

I conclude that 'emergentist Marxism' offers an account of societal development and/or transformation which is logically and conceptually defensible. This is rooted in the dialectical interface between particular kinds of structural and interactional mechanisms – namely between forces and relations of production, base and superstructure, social labour and class conflict. The only interesting question which remains is this: how adequate is emergentist Marxism to the task of meeting the criteria of scientificity and empirical progress famously specified by philosopher of science Imre Lakatos? Lakatos argued that a 'progressive' research programme is characterised by its capacity for theoretical development and renewal (on the basis of its core conceptual positions), its capacity to resist falsification, and its capacity to predict novel facts. Assessing the validity of historical materialism's claim for 'scientificity' *vis-à-vis* its major rivals in social theory and sociology is, I contend, the outstanding remaining task of Marxist analysis.

Notes

Introduction

1 M. S. Archer, *Realist Social Theory: The Morphogenetic Approach*, Cambridge, Cambridge University Press, 1995, p. 14.
2 *ibid.*, p. 247.
3 *ibid.*, pp. 93–134.
4 *ibid.*, pp. 135–61.
5 N. Mouzelis, *Sociological Theory: What Went Wrong?*, London, Routledge, 1995, p. 122.
6 P. Cohen, *Modern Social Theory*, London, Heinemann, 1968, p. 93.

1 Critical realism and Marxism

1 K. Marx, *Grundrisse*, Harmondsworth, Penguin, 1973, p. 100.
2 *ibid.*
3 A. Sayer, *Method in Social Science: A Realist Approach*, 2nd edn, London, Routledge, 1992, p. 87.
4 A. Wood, *Karl Marx*, London, Routledge and Kegan Paul, 1981, p. 219.
5 A. Callinicos, 'The secret of the dialectic', *International Socialism*, 1998, 2:78, p. 94.
6 G. W. F. Hegel, *The Phenomenology of Spirit*, Oxford, Oxford University Press, 1977, p. 11.
7 P. Murray, *Marx's Theory of Scientific Knowledge*, Atlantic Highlands NJ, Humanities Press, 1988, p. xiv.
8 P. Gasper, 'Marxism and science', *International Socialism*, 1998, 2:79, p. 142.
9 *ibid.*, p. 143.
10 *ibid.*, p. 142.
11 K. Marx, *Capital*, vol. 1, Harmondsworth, Penguin, 1976, p. 103.
12 Callinicos, 1998, *op. cit.*, p. 94; J. Rees, *The Algebra of Revolution: The Dialectic and the Classical Marxist Tradition*, London, Routledge, 1998, pp. 50–2.
13 G. W. F. Hegel, *The Science of Logic*, vol. 2, London, Allen and Unwin, 1966, p. 67.
14 Hegel cites the excellent example of the negation of a bud as it bursts forth into a blossom, and of the blossom as it is transformed into fruit, to demonstrate this point. For him this shows that forms 'are not just distinguished from one another … [but] also supplant one another as mutually incompatible' and yet, despite this, remain 'moments of an organic unity … which alone constitutes the life of the whole' (Hegel, 1977, *op. cit.*, p. 2).
15 Rees, 1998, *op. cit.*, p. 46.

16 'The concept of "concrete objects" does not merely concern "whatever exists" but draws attention to the fact that objects are usually constituted by a combination of diverse elements or forces' (Sayer, 1992, *op. cit.*, p. 87).

17 Gasper, 1998, *op. cit.*, p. 142.

18 K. Marx and F. Engels, *Collected Works*, vol. 25, London, Lawrence and Wishart, 1987, p. 24.

19 See esp. P. Anderson, 'Class struggle in the Ancient World', *History Workshop*, 1983, 16, p. 68; P. Anderson, *Passages from Antiquity to Feudalism*, London, New Left Books, 1979; G. Bois, *The Crisis of Feudalism*, Cambridge, Cambridge University Press, 1982; G. E. M. de Ste Croix, *The Class Struggle in the Ancient Greek World*, London, Duckworth, 1981, pp. 226–59; C. Harman, 'The Transition from Feudalism to Capitalism', *International Socialism*, 1989, 2:45.

20 Rees, 1998, *op. cit.*, p. 7.

21 Marx and Engels, 1987, *op. cit.*, p. 495.

22 This is Andrew Collier's definition of Bhaskar's philosophical realism (A. Collier, *Critical Realism: An Introduction to Roy Bhaskar's Philosophy*, London, Verso, 1994, esp. pp. 42–50).

23 Such as a materialist understanding of causality *in* nature conjoined with an idealist understanding of the 'origins' *of* nature.

24 P. Davies, *God and the New Physics*, Harmondsworth, Penguin, 1983, p. ix; P. Davies, *Other Worlds*, London, Allen Lane, 1982; S. Hawking, *A Brief History of Time*, London, Bantam, 1989, p. 175; I. Prigogine and I. Stengers, *Order out of Chaos*, London, Heinemann, 1988, p. 313; I. Stewart, *Does God Play Dice? The Mathematics of Chaos*, Oxford, Blackwell, 1989. Such views were also shared by the 'founders' of modern physics – Newton and Einstein.

25 K. Marx and F. Engels, *On Religion*, New York, Schocken Books, 1977, pp. 295–8.

26 This, for instance, is Giddens' view. His definition of structure as 'rules and resources' is supposed to capture the simultaneously ideational and material contexts of interaction.

27 So it is that sociobiologists, such as Wilson and Dawkins, end up invoking a 'free will' which allows us to subordinate our genetic imperatives to moral or ethical concerns (R. Dawkins, *The Selfish Gene*, Oxford, Oxford University Press, 1976; C. J. Lumsden and E. O. Wilson, *Genes, Mind and Culture*, Cambridge MA, Harvard University Press, 1981). They are forced into taking this step because they do not wish to lend support to the idea that deviants or lawbreakers are victims of their biology, a position which their own reductionist philosophy logically requires them to take. Yet 'free will', if it is to mean anything, must refer to mind-states which are somehow 'autonomous' of brain-states and of the interface between these and the material environment. This being the case, where else, other than from a cosmic super-subject, can this 'mind stuff' be derived?

28 Social idealism, for instance, appears to be logically dependent on subjective idealism, because material structures or circumstances can be deemed inefficacious in shaping socio-cultural conduct and outcomes only where these are 'mind-dependent' in the sense of being denied the autonomous power to constrain or condition the products of human consciousness. Social idealism, on the other hand, is not logically dependent upon the stronger version of objective idealism, because the former, unlike the latter, does not necessarily deny the reality of matter or the dependence of human cognition on matter. Nonetheless, there is a close affinity between the two sets of views for the simple reason that it is more plausible to decentre 'material factors' in a causal explanation of society and history if these can be seen as ultimately illusory, mere expressions of the consciousness of a cosmic super-subject, or if the ultimate

dependence of mind upon matter can be called into question. After all, if the material world is the product of 'free will', why cannot those material beings made in God's image and accordingly given a 'free will' of their own follow the lead of their maker and put 'consciousness in charge'?

The relationship between the stronger version of objective idealism and subjective idealism is also one of close affinity rather than logical necessity. Again, the reason for this is that the latter need not deny the reality of matter, nor the dependence of human consciousness on matter, merely its capacity to shape or influence the products of human consciousness, though the philosopher has an easier time asserting the autonomy of the human subject from material determinations if the contrary is upheld. Finally, the same relationship of affinity rather than logical necessity holds true between the weaker form of objective idealism and both subjective and social idealism. Subjective and social idealists may hold that the world is created by God or they may not. For it is possible to assert that history is driven by ideas or that matter is 'indeterminate' until structured by thought without asserting the reality of God. But as a matter of record most have done so, again because positing the primacy of 'consciousness' over 'conditions', or of social consciousness over social structure, is given a plausibility which would be lacking in its absence. After all, if human agents are subject to various objective laws (of physics, chemistry, biology and social structure), the role of these laws in shaping consciousness and history can be reasonably denied only if they can be rendered subordinate to 'spirit', which is plausible only if the ultimate 'autonomy' of mind from matter is upheld.

29 Collier, 1994, *op. cit.*, p. 4.

30 A. Collier, 'Materialism and explanation in the human sciences', in J. Mepham and D.-H. Ruben (eds) *Issues in Marxist Philosophy*, vol. 2, Atlantic Highlands NJ, Humanities Press, 1979, pp. 36–8. The relationship between ontological materialism and explanatory materialism is one of logical necessity, or so it seems to me. The reason for this is that ontological materialism is logically supportive of an epistemological position which does not simply assert the *externality* of the objects of knowledge, their autonomy from the knowing subject, but also their capacity to condition or shape the manner of their appropriation by the knowing subject. This means that the consciousness and agency of individuals must always be explained in terms of a material referent (physical and social circumstances). Ontological materialism asserts the determination of 'mind' and 'will' by 'matter'; explanatory materialism is a refinement of this position – asserting the determination of the products and projects of mind (i.e. social action) by the material structures of nature, human nature and society combined.

31 F. Engels, *Anti-Dühring*, London, Lawrence and Wishart, 1969; F. Engels, *The Dialectics of Nature*, Moscow, Progress Publishers, 1954. The term 'dialectical materialism' was coined not by Engels but by the Marxists of the Second International, most of whom do not seem to have understood his philosophy very well. Nonetheless it is as reasonable a title of Engels' ontological approach as any, and for this reason I have retained it.

32 'Critical naturalism' is the term by which Andrew Collier describes his own and Bhaskar's social ontology (Collier, 1994, *op. cit.*, esp. pp. 237–61).

33 Andrew Collier, to whom I owe this useful distinction between vertical and horizontal causality in social analysis, appears to endorse the first but not the second aspect of my argument (A. Collier, *Scientific Realism and Socialist Thought*, Hemel Hempstead, Harvester Wheatsheaf, 1989, pp. 58–61). His argument is that historical materialism is defensible only as a thesis of vertical determination (of superstructure by base). But I cannot see how this under-

standing of Marxism can support a materialist theory of *history* (or *historical* materialism) as opposed to a materialist theory of *social structure* (or *sociological* materialism).

34 R. Bhaskar, 'Philosophy and scientific realism', in M. S. Archer, R. Bhaskar, A. Collier, A. T. Lawson and A. Norrie, (eds) *Critical Realism: Essential Readings*, London, Routledge, 1998, pp. 19, 23–4.
35 R. Bhaskar, *A Realist Theory of Science*, 2nd edn, Brighton, Harvester Press, 1978, p. 29.
36 Bhaskar, 'Philosophy', Archer *et al.*, 1998, *op. cit.*, p. 25.
37 R. Bhaskar, *Scientific Realism and Human Emancipation*, London, Verso, 1986, p. 35.
38 Collier, 1994, *op. cit.*, pp. 32–7.
39 This is the Humean interpretation of natural necessity endorsed by empirical realists.
40 Bhaskar, R., 'Philosophy', Archer *et. al.*, 1998, *op. cit.*, p. 25.
41 *ibid.*
42 Collier, 1994, *op. cit.*, pp. 36–7.
43 *ibid.*, pp. 44–5.
44 Though for an alternative view see D.-H. Ruben, *Marxism and Materialism*, Hassocks, Harvester Press, 1977, pp. 100–2, 128–33. Ruben also argues, rightly in this case, that philosophy must base itself on the results or knowledges of the empirical sciences, not simply on its activity (*ibid.*, pp. 102–5).
45 Or, in the case of human beings, of psychological laws by social *and* biological laws.
46 D. C. Dennett, *Darwin's Dangerous Idea: Evolution and the Meaning of Life*, London, Allen Lane, 1996, pp. 181–3. Dennett distinguishes 'reductionism, which is a good thing, from *greedy reductionism*, which is not'. For him 'a proper reductionistic explanation of … phenomena would leave them still standing, but just demystified, unified, placed on more secure foundations'. Since by 'greedy reductionism' Dennett means to denote a position which denies 'the existence of real levels, real complexities, real phenomena', it is clear that his meaning here corresponds to the realist concept of 'reductionism'.
47 R. Rorty, *Philosophy and the Mirror of Nature*, Oxford, Blackwell, 1980, p. 354.
48 R. Bhaskar, *Philosophy and the Idea of Freedom*, Oxford, Blackwell, 1991, p. 48.
49 Collier, 1994, *op. cit.*, p. 46.
50 A. Callinicos, 'Darwin, materialism and evolution', *International Socialism*, 1996, 2:71, p. 107.
51 S. Rose, R. C. Lewontin and L. J. Kamin, *Not in our Genes: Biology, Ideology and Human Nature*, Harmondsworth, Penguin, 1984, pp. 277–8.
52 Collier, 1994, *op. cit.*, p. 109.
53 Bhaskar, 1978, *op. cit.*, p. 119.
54 Collier, 1994, *op. cit.*, pp. 107, 131.
55 *ibid.*, p. 110.
56 Bhaskar, 1978, *op. cit.*, p. 115.
57 Sayer, 1992, *op. cit.*, p. 119.
58 *ibid.*, p. 105.
59 *ibid.*, p. 119.
60 Rose *et al.*, 1984, p. 286.
61 R. Bhaskar, *The Possibility of Naturalism*, 2nd edn, Hemel Hempstead, Harvester Wheatsheaf, 1989, p. 98.
62 T. Benton, 'Natural science and cultural struggle: Engels and the philosophy of the natural sciences', in Mepham and Ruben, 1979, *op. cit.*, p. 122.
63 Engels, 1969, *op. cit.*, p. 83.
64 *ibid.*, p. 442.

65 Benton, 'Natural science', in Mepham and Ruben, 1979, *op. cit.*, pp. 121 and 125.
66 *ibid.*, p. 126.
67 S. J. Gould, *Wonderful Life*, Harmondsworth, Penguin, 1989, pp. 49–50, 289.
68 K. Marx and F. Engels, *Selected Works*, London, Lawrence and Wishart, 1973, vol. 3, pp. 339, 362–3.
69 Benton, 'Natural science', in Mepham and Ruben, 1979, *op. cit.*, pp. 122.
70 *ibid.*, p.124.
71 *ibid.*, pp. 124, 128.
72 *ibid.*, p. 123.
73 *ibid.*, p. 125.
74 *ibid.*, 124.
75 *ibid.*
76 Teleological views of history are those which attribute goals or purposes to developmental processes which are immanent from their genesis and towards the fulfilment of which they inevitably gravitate. Developmental theory, as such, is not necessarily teleological.
77 Dennett, 1996, *op. cit.*, pp. 41, 65, 69, 76, 205, 308, 343.
78 Nobel-prize winning chemist Melvin Calvin, quoted in P. N. Siegel, *The Meek and the Militant: Religion and Power Across the World*, London, Zed Books, 1986, p. 11.
79 Marx and Engels, 1987, *op. cit.*, p. 124.
80 *ibid.*, pp. 12–13. Or, as Engels puts it elsewhere,

> [i]n every field of science, in natural as in historical science, one must proceed from the given facts ... the interconnections are not to be built into the facts but to be discovered in them, and when discovered to be verified as far as possible by experiment.
>
> (*ibid.*, pp. 342–3)

81 *ibid.*, p. 132.
82 F. Engels, *Ludwig Feuerbach and the End of Classical German Philosophy*, Peking, Foreign Languages Press, 1976, pp. 45–6.
83 Rees, 1998, *op. cit.*, p. 286.
84 Marx and Engels, 1987, *op. cit.*, p. 121.
85 D. Blackie, 'Revolution in science', *International Socialism*, 1989, 2:42.
86 T. S. Kuhn, *The Structure of Scientific Revolutions*, 2nd edn, Chicago, University of Chicago Press, 1970; P. K. Feyerabend, *Against Method*, London, New Left Books, 1975; P. K. Feyerabend, *Science in a Free Society*, London, New Left Books, 1978.
87 Perhaps the most important recent example of this is provided by the work of the 'left Darwinians' (i.e. Steven Rose, Richard Lewontin and Richard Levins) in microbiology and evolutionary ecology. A less recent, though still contemporary example, is provided by the contribution of scientists in the former USSR to quantum theory and relativity, following the relaxation of state ideological controls on scientific enterprise after Stalin. The historian of science Loren R. Graham has pointed out that dialectical materialism equipped Soviet scientists with the philosophical *orientation* to 'arrive at views which won them international recognition among their foreign colleagues' (L. R. Graham, *Science and Philosophy in the Soviet Union*, New York, Knopf, 1972, p. 6).
88 Engels, 1954, *op. cit.*, pp. 83–91.
89 P. Pomper (ed.) *Trotsky's Notebooks 1933–1935: Writings on Lenin, Dialectics and Evolutionism*, New York, Columbia University Press, 1986, p. 88.

90 Where 'metaphysics' is defined as a 'speculative' or 'descriptive' ontology of nature which founds the physical sciences instead of being based upon them.
91 This is especially clear in the sciences of eco-biology, the 'new physics' of relativity and quantum mechanics, and the 'sciences of complexity'. See esp. R. Lewontin and R. Levins, *The Dialectical Biologist*, Cambridge MA, Harvard University Press, 1985; S. Rose, *Lifelines*, London, Allen Lane, 1997; P. McGarr, 'Order out of chaos', *International Socialism*, 1990, 2:48, pp. 148–55; P. McGarr, 1994, *op. cit.*, pp. 156–76.
92 Engels, 1976, *op. cit.*, p. 40.
93 After all, Engels at once proceeds to argue that the laws are 'different in their expression insofar as the human mind can apply them consciously, while in nature ... these laws assert themselves unconsciously, in the form of external necessity' (*ibid.*).
94 Callinicos, 1998, *op. cit.*, p. 100.
95 Rees, 1998, *op. cit.*, p. 286.
96 Callinicos, 1998, *op. cit.*, p. 100.
97 Chapter 2, pp. 84–5, 127–32, Chapter 3, pp. 185–8, 194–9.
98 Chapter 2, pp. 71–89, Chapter 3, pp. 183–4, 188–92.
99 S. Timpanaro, *On Materialism*, London, New Left Books, 1975, pp. 44–5.
100 *ibid.*, pp. 34, 45.
101 *ibid.*, p. 45.
102 In fact, the mechanisms of human biology and the physical world are better seen as being 'constitutive' of individuals and socio-cultural relations, and as giving rise to both 'passive' and 'active' human experience. By contrast, stressing the 'passive role of experience' in shaping individuals and social interaction can give sustenance to a 'materialist pessimism'. For a detailed articulation of this argument and sympathetic critique of Timpanaro, see esp. R. Williams, *Problems in Materialism and Culture*, London, Verso, 1980, pp. 106–16.
103 Chapter 2, pp. 71–89. Chapter 3, pp. 188–95.
104 Chapter 2, pp. 116–18, 119–21, 126–36.
105 From Engels' speech at the graveside of Marx. See K. Marx and F. Engels, *Selected Works*, London, Lawrence and Wishart, 1968, p. 430.
106 Collier, 'Materialism', in Mepham and Ruben, 1979, *op. cit.*, p. 43.
107 Marx, 1976, *op. cit.*, p. 102. A similar argument is made by Engels: 'We comprehend the ideas in our heads materialistically again – as reflections of real things instead of regarding the real things as reflections of this or that stage of the absolute idea' (Engels, 1976, *op. cit.*, p. 40).
108 J. Rees, 'Engels' Marxism', *International Socialism*, 1994, 2:65, p. 74.
109 Engels, 1976, *op. cit.*, p. 55.
110 F. Engels, *Selected Correspondence*, Moscow, Progress Publishers, 1975, p. 457.
111 Engels, 1969, *op. cit.*, p. 55.
112 A. Labriola, *Essays on the Materialistic Conception of History*, New York, Monthly Review Press, 1966, p. 155.
113 K. Marx, *The Economic and Philosophic Manuscripts of 1844*, London, Lawrence and Wishart, 1959, p. 67.
114 K. Marx and F. Engels, *Collected Works*, vol. 5, London, Lawrence and Wishart, 1975, p. 36.
115 *ibid.*, p. 37.
116 F. Engels, 'The part played by labour in the transition from ape to man', in Engels, 1954, *op. cit.*, pp. 228–32, 234, 237.
117 C. Harman, 'Engels and the origins of human society', *International Socialism*, 1994, 2:65, p. 85.
118 B. Trigger, 'Comment on Tobias' "Piltdown: the Case against Keith" ', *Current Anthropology*, 1992, vol. 33, no. 3, p. 275.

119 R. Leakey, *The Making of Mankind*, London, Book Club Associates, 1981, p. 56.
120 Most notably, of course, of Raymond Dart's discovery in the 1950s of the remains of a bipedal ape in East Africa.
121 Harman, 1994, *op. cit.*, p. 86.
122 Leakey, 1981, *op. cit.*, p. 48.
123 Quoted in *ibid.*, p. 52.
124 Quoted in R. Leakey and R. Lewin, 1993, *Origins Reconsidered*, London, Abacus, p. 91.
125 *ibid.*
126 David Pilbeam, quoted in R. Leakey, 1981, *op. cit.*, p. 52.
127 Leakey and Lewin, 1993, *op. cit.*, p. 164.
128 *ibid.*, p. 165.
129 *ibid.*, p. 166.
130 *ibid.*, pp. 166, 172. This is the argument of neurophysiologist Bob Martin.
131 *ibid.*, pp. 166–7, 168, 172.
132 *ibid.*, p. 198.
133 Leakey, 1981, *op. cit.*, p. 139
134 For useful expositions of Isaac's views, see R. J. Blumenschine, 'Breakfast at Olorgesailie', *Journal of Human Evolution*, 1991, vol. 21, no. 4; J. M. Sept, 'Was there no place like home?', *Current Anthropology*, 1992, vol. 32, no. 2.
135 Leakey and Lewin, 1993, *op. cit.*, pp. 304–5.
136 Cited in *ibid.*, p. 249.
137 *ibid.*, p. 259.
138 Leakey, 1981, *op. cit.*, pp. 138–9.
139 Harman, 1994, *op. cit.*, p. 95.
140 Postmodern idealism, as in other of the human sciences, has obtained a foothold in archaeology and paleaoanthropology in recent years, though here a marginal one. Thus Lewis Binford, Stephen Jay Gould, Adam Kuper and others argue that culture and language arose abrubtly about 25,000 to 35,000 years ago with the emergence of *homo sapiens* as part of a 'human revolution'. Such views have virtually no empirical backing and have been subject to damaging critiques. For the more effective of these, see R. A. Foley, *The Origins of Human Behaviour*, London, Unwin Hyman, 1991, p. 383; P. Graves, 'New models and metaphors for the Neanderthal debate', *Current Anthropology*, 1991, vol. 32, no. 5, pp. 519–21; Harman, 1994, 'Origins', *op. cit.*, pp. 96–102; Leakey and Lewin, 1993, *op. cit.*, pp. 185–99; C. Stringer, 'Human evolution and biological adaptation in the Pleistocene', in R. A. Foley (ed.) *Hominid Evolution and Community Ethnology*, London, Academic Press, 1984, p. 64.
141 Harman, 1994, *op. cit.*, p. 95.
142 C. Woolfson, 1982, *The Labour Theory of Culture: A Re-examination of Engels' Theory of Human Origins*, London, Routledge and Kegan Paul, 1982, p. 3.
143 Timpanaro, 1975, *op. cit.*, pp. 40–1, 43–52.
144 Chapter 4, pp. 236–70.
145 *ibid.*, pp. 217–18, 232–5.
146 Labriola, 1966, *op. cit.*, p. 20.
147 *ibid.*, p. 217.
148 Timpanaro, 1975, *op. cit.*, pp. 48–52.
149 This dilemma has recently been posed by Andrew Collier (Collier, 1989, *op. cit.*, pp. 54–5). But it is a more longstanding objection of postmodernists to Marxism.
150 F. Engels, 'Letter to Joseph Bloch', in F. Engels, *Letters on Historical Materialism, 1890–94*, Moscow, Progress Publishers, 1980, p. 10.
151 F. Engels, 'Letter to Conrad Schmidt', in K. Marx, F. Engels and V. I. Lenin, *On Historical Materialism*, Moscow, Progress Publishers, 1972, p. 299.

152 M. A. Coulson and C. Riddell, *Approaching Sociology: A Critical Introduction*, London, Routledge and Kegan Paul, 1970, p. 81.
153 K. Marx and F. Engels, *The Communist Manifesto*, Harmondsworth, Penguin, 1967, p. 79.
154 As Rosa Luxemburg once famously put it.
155 A point made by Engels himself when specifying the relationship between polity and economy in capitalist society ('Letter to Schmidt', in Marx *et al.*, 1972, *op. cit.*, p. 299).
156 C. Harman, 'Base and superstructure', *International Socialism*, 1986, 2:32, p. 15.

2 Organisms, subjects and society

1 K. Marx, *The Economic and Philosophical Manuscripts of 1844*, London, Lawrence and Wishart, 1959, p. 67.
2 *ibid.*, p. 98.
3 K. Marx and F. Engels, *Selected Works*, vol. 3, Moscow, Progress Publishers, 1973, p. 13.
4 K. Marx and F. Engels, *The German Ideology*, London, Lawrence and Wishart, 1970, p. 42.
5 *ibid.*, p. 121.
6 *ibid.*, p. 47.
7 *ibid.*, p. 122.
8 *ibid.*, p. 64.
9 N. Geras, *Marx and Human Nature: Refutation of a Legend*, London, Verso, 1983.
10 J. Elster, *Making Sense of Marx*, Cambridge, Cambridge University Press, 1985, pp. 64–6.
11 See Geras, 1983, *op. cit.*, pp. 61–2, 69–73, 83–6.
12 Marx, 1959, *op. cit.*, p. 68.
13 Marx and Engels, 1970, *op. cit.*, p. 42 (my emphasis).
14 K. Marx and F. Engels, *Collected Works*, vol. 3, London, Lawrence and Wishart, 1975, p. 333.
15 Marx, 1959, *op. cit.*, p. 69.
16 K. Marx, *Grundrisse*, Harmondsworth, Penguin, 1973, p. 83.
17 *ibid.*, p. 84.
18 A. Callinicos, *The Revolutionary Ideas of Karl Marx*, London, Bookmarks, 1983, p. 68.
19 For useful summaries of the modern materialist theory of human origins and evolution, see J. R. Durant (ed.) *Human Origins*, Oxford, Clarendon Press, 1989; R. A. Foley (ed.) *The Origins of Human Behaviour*, London, Unwin Hyman, 1991; R. A. Foley (ed.) *Hominid Evolution and Community Ethnology: Prehistorical Human Adaptation in Biological Perspective*, London, Academic Press, 1984; P. B. Hammond, *Physical Anthropology and Archaeology*, New York, Macmillan, 1976; J. Kingdon, *Self-Made Man and His Undoing*, London, Simon and Schuster, 1993; R. Leakey and R. Lewin, *Origins: What New Discoveries Reveal about the Emergence of Our Species and its Possible Future*, London, Macdonald and Janes, 1977; R. Leakey and R. Lewin, *Origins Reconsidered*, London, Abacus, 1993; C. Renfrew (ed.) *The Explanation of Cultural Change: Models in Pre-history*, London, Duckworth, 1973; C. Woolfson, *The Labour Theory of Culture: A Re-Examination of Engels' Theory of Human Origins*, London, Routledge and Kegan Paul, 1982.
20 N. M. Tanner, *On Becoming Human*, Cambridge, Cambridge University Press, 1981, p. 155.
21 J. Rawls, *A Theory of Justice*, Oxford, Clarendon Press, 1971.

22 J. Sandel, *Liberalism and the Limits of Justice*, Cambridge, Cambridge University Press, 1982, p. 53.
23 *ibid.*, p. 64.
24 *ibid.*, p. 150.
25 I am grateful to Andrew Collier for this insight.
26 See G. A. Cohen, 'Reconsidering historical materialism', in J. R. Pennock and J. W. Chapman (eds) *Marxism: Nomos XXVI*, New York, New York University Press, 1983, p. 233.
27 L. Doyle and R. Harris, *Empiricism, Explanation and Rationality: An Introduction to the Philosophy of Social Science*, London, Routledge and Kegan Paul, 1986, pp. 142–55.
28 Marx and Engels, 1970, *op. cit.*, p. 51.
29 Quoted in R. Leakey, *The Making of Mankind*, London, Book Club Associates, 1981, pp. 141–2 (my emphasis).
30 That human consciousness is necessarily social, and that language is socially dependent, is certainly Marx's own view. In his words:

> The 'mind' is from the start afflicted with the curse of being 'burdened' with matter, which here makes its appearance in the form of agitated layers of air, sounds, in short, of language. Language is as old as consciousness, language is practical, real consciousness that exists for other men as well, and only therefore does it exist for me; language, like consciousness, only arises from the need, the necessity of intercourse with other men. … Consciousness is, therefore, from the very beginning a social product, and remains so as long as men exist at all.
>
> (Marx and Engels, 1970, *op. cit.*, pp. 50–1)

31 Leakey, 1981, *op. cit.*, pp. 140–2.
32 S. Rose, *The Conscious Brain*, Harmondsworth, Penguin, 1976, p. 173.
33 Marx and Engels, 1970, *op. cit.*, p. 48. For Marx, 'species-being' is in part definable as 'my needs … my own nature, this totality of needs and drives' (Marx, 1973, *op. cit.*, p. 245).
34 K. Marx, *Capital*, vol. 1, Harmondsworth, Penguin, 1976, pp. 275, 277, 341, 375–6, 621; K. Marx, *Capital*, vol. 3, Progress Publishers, Moscow, 1962, pp. 826, 837, 854. Here Marx describes these basic material needs as both biological and social imperatives. The former are described variously as 'natural needs', 'physical needs', the need for a 'healthy maintenance of the body', including the need for 'healthy relations between the sexes'; the latter are described as being conditioned by the 'level of civilisation'.
35 Marx, 1962, *op. cit.*, p. 800; K. Marx, *Theories of Surplus Value*, vol. 2, Progress Publishers, Moscow, 1970, pp. 117–18; Marx, 1973, *op. cit.*, p. 488.
36 Marx and Engels, 1975, *op. cit.*, p. 217; K. Marx and F. Engels, *Collected Works*, vol. 5, London, Lawrence and Wishart, 1976, p. 437.
37 Marx describes this variously as all round development of *individuals*, free development of individuals, 'the means of cultivating [one's] gifts in all directions', the need for 'the free play of the vital forces of [the] body and … mind', and provision of 'scope for the development of man's faculties' (Marx and Engels, 1976, *op. cit.*, pp. 255, 439, 78; Marx, 1976, *op. cit.*, pp. 375, 460, 772; K. Marx, *Theories of Surplus Value*, vol. 3, Moscow, Progress Publishers, 1972, p. 256).
38 Geras, 1983, *op. cit.*, p. 83.
39 Marx describes this as the need for 'space, light, air and protection against the dangerous or the unhealthy concomitants of the production process'. Without

this protection, the 'five senses pay the penalty' (Marx, 1962, *op. cit.*, p. 86; Marx, 1976, *op. cit.*, pp. 586, 591).

40 Geras, 1983, *op. cit.*, pp. 72–3; A. Heller, *The Theory of Need in Marx*, London, Tavistock, 1976, pp. 23–5, 44–8, 75–8, 96–9, 123–6.

41 The universal existence in human society of such norms as 'reciprocal altruism', 'distributive justice' and 'fairness' has been noted even by ardent defenders of methodological individualism. George Homans, for example, was prepared to acknowledge their salience in human history, although his theoretical interests and political values led him to attempt to colonise them for utilitarianism (see G. Homans, *Social Behaviour: Its Elementary Forms*, London, Routledge and Kegan Paul, 1964).

42 T. B. Bottomore (ed.) *Karl Marx: Early Writings*, New York, International Publishers, 1964, pp. 127, 148.

43 J. Elster, *Explaining Technical Change*, Cambridge, Cambridge University Press, 1983a, pp. 74 and 87–88; J. Elster, *Sour Grapes*, Cambridge, Cambridge University Press, 1983b, ch. 1.

44 J. Elster, *The Multiple Self*, Cambridge, Cambridge University Press, 1986.

45 E. O. Wilson, *Sociobiology: The New Synthesis*, Cambridge MA, Harvard University Press, 1975, p. 4. See also E. O. Wilson quoted in R. Trigg, *The Shaping of Man: Philosophical Aspects of Sociobiology*, Oxford, Blackwell, 1982, p. 110.

46 E. O. Wilson, *On Human Nature*, Cambridge MA, Harvard University Press, 1978, p. 172.

47 S. Rose, R. C. Lewontin and L. J. Kamin, *Not in Our Genes: Biology, Ideology and Human Nature*, Harmondsworth, Penguin, 1984, p. 244.

48 Wilson, 1975, *op. cit.*, p. 4.

49 R. Dawkins, *The Selfish Gene*, Oxford, Oxford University Press, 1976, p. v.

50 Rose *et. al.*, 1984, *op. cit.*, p. 245.

51 R. Dart, 'The predatory transition from ape to man', *International Anthropological and Linguistic Review*, 1953, vol. 1, no. 4.

52 R. Ardrey, *African Genesis*, London, Collins, 1967; R. Ardrey, *The Social Contract*, London, Collins, 1970; R. Ardrey, *The Territorial Imperative*, London, Collins, 1976.

53 Quoted in Leakey, 1981, *op. cit.*, p. 221.

54 K. Lorenz, *On Aggression*, London, Methuen, 1966.

55 As two opponents of this view put the argument (M. Wohlpoff and A. Thorne, 'The case against Eve', *New Scientist*, 22 June 1991).

56 Leakey, 1981, *op. cit.*, pp. 17–20, 65–6, 70, 73; Rose *et al.*, 1984, *op. cit.*, p. 230.

57 C. Stringer, '*Homo sapiens*: single or multiple origin?', in Durant, 1989, *op. cit.*, p. 77; P. Graves, 'New models and metaphors for the Neanderthal debate', *Current Anthropology*, 1991, vol. 32. no. 5, p. 521. See also E. Zubrow, quoted in Leakey and Lewin, 1993, *op. cit.*, pp. 234–5.

58 See for example R. Benedict, *Patterns of Culture*, London, Routledge and Kegan Paul, 1964; M. G. Bicchieri (ed.) *Hunters and Gatherers Today*, New York, Holt, Reinhart and Winston, 1972; G. V. Childe, *Man Makes Himself*, London, Watts, 1956; G. V. Childe, *Social Evolution*, London, Watts, 1963; S. Diamond, *In Search of the Primitive: A Critique of Civilisation*, New Brunswick NJ, Transaction Press, 1974; E. Gellner, *Plough, Sword and Book: The Structure of Human History*, London, Routledge, 1991; E. Friedl, *Men and Women: The Anthropologists' View*, London, Holt, Reinart and Winston, 1975; T. Ingold, D. Riches and A. Woodburn, *Hunters and Gatherers*, vol. 1, New York, Berg Publishers, 1991; E. Leacock, *Myths of Male Dominance*, New York, Monthly Review Press, 1981; R. Lee, *The !Kung San: Men, Women and Work in a Foraging Society*, Cam-

bridge, Cambridge University Press, 1979; W. Lloyd-Warner, *A Black Civilisation*, New York, Random House, 1964; B. Malinowski (ed.) *Argonauts of the Western Pacific*, London, Routledge and Kegan Paul, 1970; J. V. S. Megaw, *Hunter Gatherers and the First Farmers Beyond Europe*, New Jersey, Leicester University Press, 1977; E. Pritchard and M. Fortes, *African Political Systems*, Oxford, Oxford University Press, 1961; M. Sahlins, *Stone Age Economics*, Chicago, Aldine, 1976; C. Schrire (ed.) *Past and Present in Hunter Gatherer Studies*, New York, Academic Press, 1984; C. Turnbull, *The Forest People*, New York, Chatto and Windus, 1962.

59 Quoted in Leakey, 1981, *op. cit.*, p. 97.

60 *ibid.*, p. 98.

61 See C. Harman, 'Engels and the origins of human society', *International Socialism*, 2:65, 1994, pp. 104–12, for a useful summary of recent anthropological research which sheds light on the nature of 'primitive communism'.

62 Friedl, 1975, *op. cit.*, p. 136; Leacock, 1981, *op. cit.*, pp. 139–40; Lee, 1979, *op. cit.*, p. 118; Lee, in Leakey, 1981, *op. cit.*, p. 107.

63 Lee, 1979, *op. cit.*, pp. 244, 343–5, 336–8.

64 Wilson, 1975, *op. cit.*, p. 574.

65 *ibid.*, pp. 572, 575.

66 Leakey, 1981, *op. cit.*, p. 97.

67 Harman, 1994, *op. cit.*, p. 112.

68 My claim that human nature predisposes or acclimatises individuals for life in egalitarian social relations and towards altruistic behaviour would doubtless be treated as contentious by many who would accept that human beings are naturally cooperative and sociable creatures. Yet a perfectly reasonable natural selection argument can be made which infers altruism and egalitarianism from the historical interface between self-conscious 'cooperative man' and the social and physical circumstances of our hominid forebears.

Such an explanation takes as its starting point the economic benefits of social cooperation in ensuring the 'reproductive fitness' of humanity's anthropoid ancestors. As we have seen, given the elementary sociality of the hominids, in specific environmental circumstances (the retreat of the rain forest and its replacement by more demanding savannah-type terrain), natural selection operated here in the direction of intelligence, social learning, and economic cooperation. One important consequence of this 'evolutionary ratchet' being set in motion was the acquisition by human beings of self-consciousness and language, which corresponded with the transition from simpler forms of scavenger-forager social relations to more complex hunter-gather modes of societal organisation. In these socio-economic and physical conditions, egalitarian values (and hence practices of reciprocal altruism and distributive justice) became indispensable to the 'survival value' or reproductive success of the human species and individual genotype. This is because hunter-gatherer modes of subsistence were incapable of generating the economic surpluses which would sustain an unegalitarian distribution and consumption of allocative goods amongst the community or band. Since the scavenger-forager and hunter-gatherer ways of life, which characterised human existence throughout the 2.5 million year formative epoch of modern *homo sapiens*, were highly functional in terms of ensuring the 'reproductive fitness' of the 'Darwinian phenotypes', and since these modes of environmental adaptation could be reproduced only by means of a food-sharing strategy, it is quite acceptable to suppose that natural selection operated here not only in the direction of enhanced sociality and intellect, but also towards a greater intensity and quality of sociality associated with reciprocated altruism and egalitarian living.

Interestingly, this argument is accepted by Hayek, one of the leading gurus of the New Right. In his view, thousands of years of primitive communism have produced 'lamentable' and 'dangerous' 'long-submerged innate instincts' and 'primordial emotions' towards socialism, leading the mass of people to desire 'a just distribution', in which 'organised power is used to allocate to each what he deserves', to 'pursue perceived desirable common objectives', and 'to do good to known people' (Hayek, quoted in Gellner, 1991, *op. cit.*, p. 22). Accordingly, the task of the responsible state, according to Hayek, is to resist these pressures with every ideological and political means available in the interests of economic rationality.

69 R. Lee, 'Reflections on primitive communism', in T. Ingold *et al.*, 1991, *op. cit.*, pp. 268, 262.
70 Quoted in Leakey, 1981, *op. cit.*, p. 242.
71 Harman, 1994, *op. cit.*, pp. 111–12.
72 The point has been made that 'man and chimpanzee are more closely related than horse and donkey, cat and lion, or dog and fox' (S. I. Washburn and R. More, 'Only once', Hammond, 1976, *op. cit.*, p. 18.
73 Wilson, *op. cit.*, pp. 551–2.
74 *ibid.*, p. 551
75 E. O. Wilson and C. J. Lumsden, *Genes, Mind and Culture: The Co-evolutionary Process*, Cambridge MA, Harvard University Press, 1981, pp. 354, 355–6.
76 Harman, 1994, *op. cit.*, p. 88.
77 *ibid.*
78 *ibid.*, p. 89.
79 *ibid.*, pp. 89–90.
80 Leakey, 1981, *op. cit.*, p. 240.
81 Harman, 1994, *op. cit.*, pp. 106–12; Leakey, 1981, *op. cit.*, pp. 99–109.
82 See Harman, 1994, *op. cit.*, pp. 107–9; Leakey, 1981, *op. cit.*, pp. 98–9; Leakey and Lewin, 1993, *op. cit.*, pp. 46–7, 141–2, 177–82, 184–9.
83 M. S. Archer, *Realist Social Theory: The Morphogenetic Approach*, Cambridge: Cambridge University Press, 1995, p. 288.
84 Marx and Engels, 1970, *op. cit.*, p. 109.
85 C. Taylor, 'What is human agency?', in T. Mischel (ed.) *The Self: Psychological and Philosophical Issues*, Oxford, Blackwell, 1977.
86 *ibid.*, pp. 103–4.
87 *ibid.*, pp. 107, 114.
88 Callinicos, 1987, *op. cit.*, p. 118.
89 A. K. Sen, 'Rational fools', in A. K. Sen (ed.) *Choice, Welfare and Measurement*, Oxford, Blackwell, 1982, pp. 89–92, 99, 100–1, 103.
90 Scott, 1995, *op. cit.*, p. 87.
91 Callinicos, 1987, *op. cit.*, p. 119.
92 It should go without saying, for instance, that if 'Prisoner A' undergoing interrogation believes that his or her confederate ('Prisoner B') is *trustworthy*, and consequently will not 'crack under pressure', the former will have *rational* motives for refusing to 'grass up' the latter, knowing that the 'worst case' scenario will not be the maximum gaol sentence for either of them. A breach of trust by Prisoner A, on the other hand, although it might facilitate for him or her the minimum gaol sentence, equally likely might encourage a reciprocation by Prisoner B, and hence the maximum gaol sentence for both. Where prisoners believe each other to be trustworthy, a *breach* of trust by either party is the high-risk strategy, and thus the less rational course of action.
93 Sen, 1982, *op. cit.*, pp. 89–92.
94 M. Abrahamson, *Sociological Theory*, Berkeley, University of California Press, 1981, pp. 179–80.

95 For example, I have suggested that utilitarianism cannot explain how the capitalist economy and state-run public services (e.g. education, health and welfare) could continue to function at all, given its simple datum that individuals generally act socially in order to maximise or 'satisfice' rewards and forego costs. For it is undoubtedly the case that these would quickly collapse, were it not for millions of acts of co-operation and self-sacrifice by workers beyond the call of duty or employment contract, for which no monetary or symbolic reward is expected or forthcoming. Talk of 'reciprocal debts', payable at a later date, will not always suffice in these circumstances. This is because those individuals who offer a 'helping hand' to others do not always (or even normally) have any inkling that they may in the future require assistance in return, or that those they have helped in the past will be in a position to 'pay their debts' at a later date. To make this point is not, of course, to deny that there is an important and necessary instrumental dimension to human motivation and social interaction, nor to minimise its importance (especially in capitalist society). It is, rather, to refute the claim of utilitarianism that instrumentally rational social action is the most significant feature of society and hence the key explanatory concept in social analysis. The fact that the 'limiting conditions' introduced by contemporary utilitarians to insulate the concept of instrumental rationality from rational criticism are the *norm* rather than the *exception* of social life precisely undermines their treatment of these as a mere 'imperfection' in an otherwise uncontaminated theoretical perspective. The capacity of human persons to feel and express trust, sympathy, solidarity, loyalty and altruism, as normative and affectual emergents of humanity's co-operative, egalitarian and self-conscious modes of biological adaptation to the environment, simply cannot be reduced to any anterior or primitive psychological motivational state, least of all one which assumes universal human self-interest..

96 I. Craib, *Modern Social Theory*, 2nd edn, Hemel Hempstead, Harvester Wheatsheaf, 1992, p. 78.

97 J. Elster, *The Cement of Society: A Study of Social Order*, Cambridge, Cambridge University Press, 1989a, p. 98.

98 J. Elster, *Nuts and Bolts for the Social Sciences*, Cambridge, Cambridge University Press, 1989b, pp. 119, 123.

99 G. Homans, 'Bringing Men Back In', *American Sociological Review*, 1964, 29, pp. 809–18.

100 J. S. Coleman, 'Foundations for a theory of collective decisions', *American Journal of Sociology*, 1966, 71, pp. 615–27; P. Blau, *Exchange and Power in Social Life*, New York, Wiley, 1964, *op. cit.*, pp. 75–9.

101 A. Giddens, *Sociology*, Cambridge, Polity Press, 1990, pp. 32, 60, 86.

102 C. Cooley, *Social Organisation*, New York, Schocken, 1909; C. Cooley, *Human Nature and the Social Order*, New York, Charles Scribners and Sons, 1922.

103 H. S. Becker, *Outsiders: Studies in the Sociology of Deviance*, New York, Free Press, 1963; E. M. Lemert, *Human Deviance, Social Problems and Social Control*, 2nd edn, Englewood Cliffs NJ, Prentice-Hall, 1972.

104 Abrahamson, 1981, *op. cit.*, pp. 15, 16–17, 19.

105 G. H. Mead, 'The mechanisms of social consciousness', *Journal of Philosophy*, 1919, 9, pp. 402–5; G. H. Mead, *Mind, Self and Society*, Chicago, University of Chicago Press, 1934.

106 *ibid.*, pp. 154, 169, 270.

107 *ibid.*, p. 169.

108 R. Gottlieb, *Marxism: Origins, Betrayal, Rebirth*, London, Routledge, 1992, p. 193.

109 Giddens, 1990, *op. cit.*, pp. 75–6.

110 A. Giddens, *Modernity and Self-Identity*, Cambridge, Polity Press, 1991, p. 51.
111 Archer, 1995, *op. cit.*, p. 122.
112 Giddens, 1991, *op. cit.*, p. 45.
113 *ibid.*, pp. 38, 42.
114 Gottlieb, 1992, *op. cit.*, p. 195.
115 M. Foucault, *Power/Knowledge*, Brighton, Harvester Press, 1980, pp. 73–4.
116 *ibid.*, p. 90.
117 M. Foucault, *La Volonté de Savoir*, Paris, Editions de Minuit, 1976, pp. 125–6.
118 *ibid.*, p. 126.
119 M. Foucault, 'The subject and power', in H. L. Dreyfuss and P. Rabinow, *Michel Foucault: Beyond Structuralism and Hermeneutics*, Brighton, Harvester Press, 1982, pp. 208–21.
120 *ibid.*, p. 221.
121 M. Foucault, *L'Usage des Plaisirs*, Paris, Editions du Seuil, 1984, pp. 16–17.
122 Abrahamson, 1981, *op. cit.*, p. 16.
123 *ibid.*, p. 10.
124 Mead, cited in Abrahamson, 1981, *op. cit.*, pp. 11–12.
125 *ibid.*, p. 12.
126 D. Lee and H. Newby, *The Problem of Sociology*, London, Unwin Hyman, 1983, pp. 317–18.
127 Giddens, 1991, *op. cit.*, p. 51.
128 *ibid.*, p. 42.
129 E. Goffman, *The Presentation of Self in Everyday Life*, London, Allen Lane, 1969.
130 *ibid.*, p. 87.
131 E. Goffman, *Asylums: Essays on the Social Situation of Mental Patients and Other Inmates*, New York, Doubleday, 1961.
132 Giddens, 1991, *op. cit.*, pp. 42–53.
133 *ibid.*, p. 53.
134 Archer, 1995, *op. cit.*, p. 126.
135 Giddens, 1991, *op. cit.*, p. 55.
136 Archer, 1995, *op. cit.*, p. 122.
137 Chapter 3, pp. 188–90, 191–2, 196–201.
138 Giddens, 1991, *op. cit.*, p. 51.
139 Archer, 1995, *op. cit.*, p. 123.
140 *ibid.*
141 *ibid.*
142 *ibid.*
143 Giddens, 1991, *op. cit.*, p. 38.
144 Archer, 1995, *op. cit.*, p. 122.
145 *ibid.*, p. 124.
146 Giddens, 1991, *op. cit.*, p. 45.
147 Archer, 1995, *op. cit.*, p. 125.
148 *ibid.*, p. 126.
149 *ibid.*
150 *ibid.*
151 J. Shotter, 'The duality of structure and intentionality in an ecological psychology', *Journal for the Theory of Social Behaviour*, 1983, 13, pp. 39, 19–20.
152 Archer, 1995, *op. cit.*, p. 127.
153 As, for instance, the wealthy textile magnate Morozov did prior to the 1905 revolution in Russia. Morozov was an important source of funding for the Bolsheviks during the period in which the party was illegal and forced to operate underground. Tragically, he committed suicide after the 1905 defeat.
154 Archer, 1995, *op. cit.*, pp. 128–9.
155 *ibid.*, p. 129.

156 *ibid.*
157 A. Giddens, *The Constitution of Society: Outline of the Theory of Structuration*, Cambridge, Polity Press, 1984, pp. 77–81.
158 N. Thrift, 'Bear and mouse or bear and tree? Anthony Giddens' reconstitution of social theory', *Sociology*, 1985, 19, pp. 339–53.
159 M. Bertilsson, 'The theory of structuration: prospects and problems', *Acta Sociologica*, 1984, 27, p. 344.
160 I. Craib, *Anthony Giddens*, London, Routledge, 1992, pp. 167–9.
161 *ibid.*, p. 171.
162 *ibid.*, pp. 169–71
163 Giddens, 1984, *op. cit.*, pp. 79–81.
164 Richard Leakey, quoted in C. Harman, *How Marxism Works*, London, Bookmarks, 1986, p. 19.
165 Anthony Giddens refers to these as 'cultural universals'. These include 'grammatically complex language', 'some recognisable form of family system', 'the institution of marriage', 'some form of incest prohibition', 'the existence of art, dancing, bodily adornment, games, gift-taking, jokes and rules of hygiene' (Giddens, 1990, *op. cit.*, pp. 39–40). See also J. Freidl, *The Human Portrait: Introduction to Cultural Anthropology*, Englewood Cliffs NJ, Prentice-Hall, 1981; P. G. Heibert, *Cultural Anthropology*, Philadelphia, Lippincott, 1976; G. P. Murdock, 'The common denominator of cultures', in R. Linton (ed.) *The Science of Man in a World of Crisis*, New York, Columbia University Press, 1945.

3 Subjects, actors and agents

1 M. Weber, *Economy and Society*, vol. 2, New York, Bedminster Press, 1968.
2 See S. Clarke, *Marx, Marginalism and Modern Sociology*, 2nd edn, London, Macmillan, 1991, pp. 197–229, for a useful critique of Weber's interpretative methodology.
3 G. MacDonald and P. Pettit, *Semantics and Social Science*, London, Routledge and Kegan Paul, 1981. See also B. Davidson, *Essays on Actions and Events*, Oxford, Clarendon Press, 1979; D. C. Dennet, *Brainstorms*, Brighton, Harvester Press, 1978.
4 MacDonald and Pettit, 1981, *op. cit.*; B. Davidson, *Inquiries in Truth and Interpretation*, Oxford, Clarendon Press, 1984.
5 L. Wittgenstein, *Remarks on the Foundations of Mathematics*, Oxford, Blackwell, 1978, p. 39; L. Wittgenstein, *Philosophical Investigations*, Oxford, Blackwell, 1968, p. 206.
6 D. Wiggins, *Sameness and Substance*, Oxford, Blackwell, 1980, pp. 222–3.
7 J. Elster, *The Cement of Society: A Study of Social Order*, Cambridge, Cambridge University Press, 1989a; J. Elster, *Nuts and Bolts For the Social Sciences*, Cambridge, Cambridge University Press, 1989b; J. Elster, *Solomic Judgements*, Cambridge, Cambridge University Press, 1989c.
8 J. S. Coleman, *The Foundations of Social Theory*, Cambridge MA, Belknap, 1990.
9 N. Mouzelis, *Sociological Theory: What Went Wrong?*, London, Routledge, 1995, p. 37.
10 A. Callinicos, *Making History: Agency, Structure and Change in Social Theory*, Cambridge, Polity Press, 1987, p. 122.
11 A. Giddens, *Central Problems in Social Theory*, London, Macmillan, 1979, p. 189.
12 Callinicos, 1987, *op. cit.*, p. 123. See also R. A. Dahl, 'A critique of the ruling elite model', in J. Urry and J. Wakeford (eds) *Power in Britain*, London, Heinemann, 1973; R. A. Dahl, *Who Governs?*, New Haven CT, Yale University

Press, 1961; A. M. Rose, *The Power Structure: Political Process in an American City*, New York, Open University Press, 1967.

13 Callinicos, 1987, *op. cit.*, pp. 124–5. See also W. E. Connolly, *The Terms of Political Discourse*, Oxford, Robertson, 1983, pp. 44–6; J. Elster, *Making Sense of Marx*, Cambridge, Cambridge University Press, 1986, p. 349; A. Levine, *Arguing for Socialism*, London, Verso, 1984, pp. 109–10.

14 Callinicos, 1987, *op. cit.*, p. 123.

15 P. Bachrach and M. S. Baratz, 'Two faces of power', in R. Bell (ed.) *Political Power*, New York, Wiley, 1969; S. Lukes, *Power: A Radical View*, London, Macmillan, 1974.

16 As Callinicos points out, these and other problems with the orthodox conception of interests, have encouraged many modern social theorists to abandon the category altogether as an explanatory concept (Callinicos, 1987, *op. cit.*, p. 126). This view, for example, is forcefully put by G. Therborn, *The Ideology of Power and the Power of Ideology*, London, Verso, 1980.

17 It is, after all, rather absurd to believe otherwise, given the current distribution of wealth in Britain. Thus the British working class today (approximately 75 per cent of the adult population) own a mere 20 per cent of the total wealth of society. The bottom 50 per cent of the British population (the manual working class and dependants) own just 8 per cent of national wealth. By contrast, the top 5 per cent own half and the top 25 per cent own 80 per cent of all wealth. See *Social Trends*, 21, London, HMSO, 1991, p. 96.

18 R. Miliband, *The State in Capitalist Society*, London, Quartet, 1973, pp. 24, 42, 67–73.

19 For a useful discussion of 'structural capacities', see E. O. Wright, *Class, Crisis and the State*, London, New Left Books, 1978, pp. 99–101. See also Callinicos, 1987, *op. cit.*, pp. 86–91, 132–3, 184–7, 235–6.

20 L. German, *A Question of Class*, London, Bookmarks, 1996, pp. 7–20, 21–61.

21 Mouzelis, 1995, *op. cit.*, pp. 37–38.

22 Coleman, 1990, *op. cit.*, pp, 29, 32, 243.

23 As Mouzelis puts it (1995, *op. cit.*, p. 38). See Elster, 1989a, *op. cit.*, p. 15.

24 Mouzelis, 1995, *op. cit.*, p. 37.

25 Elster, 1989a, *op. cit.*, p. 100.

26 Mouzelis, 1995, *op. cit.*, p. 39.

27 Elster, 1989b, *op. cit.*, p. 76.

28 See my discussion of this in Chapter 2 (pp. 87, 108–9, 291 n41, 292 n68).

29 See those texts cited in Chapter 2 (pp. 291–2 n58).

30 M. Weber, 1961, *General Economic History*, London, Collier-Macmillan, 1961, pp. 207, 275–8, 352–4.

31 Mouzelis, 1995, *op. cit.*, p. 39.

32 *ibid.*

33 M. S. Archer, *Realist Social Theory: The Morphogenetic Approach*, Cambridge, Cambridge University Press, 1995, pp. 254–7.

34 *ibid.*, p. 259.

35 P. Anderson, *Arguments within English Marxism*, London, New Left Books, 1980, p. 19.

36 Archer, 1995, *op. cit.*, p. 258.

37 Anderson, *op. cit.*, p. 20.

38 But this does not mean that the other distinctions I have made in the category of 'interaction' are not important. For example, the distinction between collective and individual social agency is necessary to grasp the way in which the agential circumstances of persons can result in both individualistic and group responses to external pressures.

39 Archer, 1995, *op. cit.*, p. 258.

40 *ibid.*, p. 259.
41 *ibid.*, p. 260.
42 *ibid.*
43 *ibid.*, p. 260–1.
44 *ibid.*, p. 261.
45 See esp. C. Wickham, 'The uniqueness of the East', *Journal of Peasant Studies*, 1985, 12, 2, 3.
46 Archer, 1995 *op. cit.*, p. 262.
47 *ibid.*
48 *ibid.*, p. 263.
49 *ibid.*
50 A. Farrell, *Crime, Class and Corruption: the Politics of the Police*, London, Bookmarks, 1992, pp. 48–63.
51 A. T. Scull, *Decarceration: Community Treatment and the Deviant*, Englewood Cliffs NJ, Prentice-Hall, 1977, pp. 16, 25–33.
52 V. A. C. Gatrell, *The Hanging Tree: Execution and the English People 1760–1868*, Oxford, Oxford University Press, 1994; P. Linebaugh, *The London Hanged: Crime and Civil Society in Eighteenth Century England*, Harmondsworth, Penguin, 1993.
53 D. Fraser, *The Evolution of the Welfare State*, London, Macmillan, 1973, pp. 42–8; L. J. Hammond and B. Hammond, *The Labourer 1760–1832*, London, Alan Sutton, 1995; E. J. Hobsbawm, *Industry and Empire*, Harmondsworth, Penguin, 1969, pp. 86, 100–2, 229; E. J. Hobsbawm, *The Age of Revolution 1789–1848*, London, Cardinal, 1973, pp. 66, 188, 203, 242; M. O'Brien, 'The bloody birth of capitalism', *International Socialism*, 1996a, 2:70, pp. 120–6; E. P. Thompson, *The Making of the English Working Class*, London, Pelican, 1963, pp. 90, 147, 165, 199, 217, 234, 237–43, 245, 247, 249, 256–7, 262–4, 271, 283, 294–6, 311–12, 321, 334–5, 379–80, 546–65, 575, 595–8, 835, 904–5.
54 *ibid.*, pp. 67, 92, 176, 198, 201, 211, 229, 253–5, 266, 284–5, 313, 321, 325–6, 333, 387, 400, 428, 437–40, 458, 469, 482–3, 529, 533, 537–45, 563, 569–70, 593–4, 598–659, 703–14, 732–3, 784–8, 800–6, 858, 875–6, 904, 905, 908–13. For an excellent account of the Luddite movement, see Hammond and Hammond, 1995, *op. cit.*, pp. 259–304. See also: O'Brien, 1996a, *op. cit.*, pp. 129–32. For outstanding histories of the Chartist movement, see M. O'Brien, *'Perish the Privileged Orders': A Socialist History of the Chartist Movement*, London, Redwords, 1996b; D. Thompson, *The Chartists*, Hounslow, Temple, 1989.
55 Fraser, 1973, *op. cit.*, pp. 12, 15–30; I. Gough, *The Political Economy of the Welfare State*, London, Macmillan, 1979, p. 55; A. Rogers, 'Back to the workhouse?', *International Socialism*, 1993, 2:59, pp. 7–8; J. Dearlove, and P. Saunders, *An Introduction to British Politics: Analysing a Capitalist Democracy*, Cambridge, Polity Press, 1984, pp. 304–5; Fraser, 1973, *op. cit.*, pp. 15–26.
56 This does not mean that the organised working class did not embark on fierce and large-scale struggles against the state and capital during this period. This was especially true of the period of the 'New Unionism' at the close of the nineteenth century, during the 'Great Unrest' of 1912, again in 1918-19 in the immediate aftermath of the Bolshevik revolution, and during the General Strike of 1926. Nor am I saying that the working class were lacking in the objective (institutional) and subjective (ideological) capacities to force through a radical reform of capitalism or even the replacement of capitalism with socialism during these periods of unrest. Rather, due to poor quality, politically confused and conservative leadership, the appropriate class capacities were not applied consistently, and class energies and struggles were dissipated and defeated.

57 J. Clarke, A. Cochrane and C. Smart, *Ideologies of Welfare: From Dreams to Disillusion*, London, Hutchinson, 1987, pp. 20–3; Dearlove and Saunders, 1984, *op. cit.*, pp. 305–6; B. B. Gilbert, *The Evolution of National Insurance in Britain: The Evolution of the Welfare State*, London, Michael Joseph, 1966, pp. 24–8, 32–9, 59–61, 67–8, 72–3, 75–80, 81–7, 90–4, 101, 107, 152; N. Ginsberg, *Class, Capital and Social Policy*, London, Macmillan, 1979, pp. 8–13; Hay, J., *The Origins of the Liberal Welfare Reforms 1906–14*, London, Macmillan, 1975; E. J. Hobsbawm, *The Age of Empire 1875–1914*, London, Weidenfeld and Nicolson, 1987, pp. 101–3; M. Langan and B. Schwarz (eds) *Crises in the British State 1880–1930*, London, Hutchinson, 1985, pp. 20–22, 23, 24, 53, 69–71, 74–5, 80–126, 227, 229, 261, 266–7, 269; Rogers, 1993, *op. cit.*, pp. 10–12; G. Stedman-Jones, *Outcast London: A Study in the Relationship between Classes in Victorian Society*, Harmondsworth, Penguin, 1971, pp. 246–7, 251–3, 254–61, 265–70, 271–7, 331–3, 334–6.

58 Dearlove and Saunders, 1984, *op. cit.*, p. 304; Fraser, 1973, *op. cit.*, pp. 59, 70–1, 75; Rogers, 1993, *op. cit.*, p. 9.

59 Dearlove and Saunders, 1984, *op. cit.*, p. 304; Gilbert, 1966, *op. cit.*, pp. 98–101, 107, 111; Langan and Schwarz, 1985, *op. cit.*, pp. 74–5, 256–73.

60 N. McCord, 'Ratepayers and social policy', in P. Thane (ed.) *The Origins of British Social Policy*, London, Croom Helm, 1978, pp. 21–36; J. R. Hay, 'Employers' attitudes to social policy and the concept of social control', *ibid.*, pp. 107–26.

61 Gilbert, 1966, *op. cit.*, pp. 221–2; Langan and Schwarz, 1985, *op. cit.*, pp. 111–12; Thane, 1978, *op. cit.*, p. 140.

62 Gilbert, 1966, *op. cit.*, pp. 269–77; Langan and Schwarz, 1985, *op. cit.*, p. 75.

63 Gilbert, 1966, *op. cit.*, pp. 111,114–15, 222; P. Thane, 'Non-contributory versus insurance pensions 1878–1908', in Thane, 1978, *op. cit.*, pp. 84–104.

64 Dearlove and Saunders, 1984, *op. cit.*, p. 305; Fraser, 1973, *op. cit.*, pp. 79, 86; Langan and Schwarz, 1985, *op. cit.*, p. 267–9.

65 T. Cliff and D. Gluckstein, *The Labour Party: A Marxist History*, 2nd edn, London, Bookmarks, 1996, pp. 8–22, 23–54, 98–104, 151–65; R. Miliband, *Parliamentary Socialism: A Study in the Politics of Labour*, 2nd edn, London, Merlin, 1972, pp. 17–24, 98, 101–3, 108, 161–3; K. O. Morgan, *The Age of Lloyd-George: The Liberal Party and British Politics 1890–1929*, London, Weidenfeld and Nicolson, 1971, pp. 38–57.

66 By acclimatising working-class opinion to the language and aspirations of democratic (political and economic) participation in society. 'Individual Chartists went on to play a vital role in working class radical politics as councillors and publishers, in agitation for reform' as well as 'in the organisation of the early trade unions' (O'Brien, 1996b, *op. cit.*, pp. 107–8).

67 D. Blackie, *Socialism and the Labour Party*, London, Bookmarks, 1991, pp. 15–18; Cliff and Gluckstein, 1996, *op. cit.*, pp. 223–7; Gough, 1979, *op. cit.*, pp. 66, 69–71.

68 Cliff and Gluckstein, 1996, *op. cit.*, pp. 210–17, 220–24. See also: Dearlove and Saunders, 1985, *op. cit.*, pp. 270–6; V. George and P. Wilding, *Ideology and Social Welfare*, London, Routledge and Kegan Paul, 1985, ch. 3; Ginsberg, 1979, *op. cit.*, p. 34; K. Schott, 'The rise of Keynesian economics: Britain 1940–64', in D. Held (ed.) *States and Societies*, Oxford, Open University Press, 1983.

69 Cliff and Gluckstein, 1996, *op. cit.*, pp. 236–7; Dearlove and Saunders, 1984, *op. cit.*, pp. 42–48, 57, 64, 93, 221, 272–86; R. Mishra, *The Welfare State in Crisis: Social Thought and Social Change*, Brighton, Harvester Wheatsheaf, 1984, pp. 1–29.

70 For a summary of these attacks on the welfare state, see Clarke *et. al.*, 1987, *op. cit.*, pp. 189–97; S. Clegg, 'Thatcher and the welfare state', *International Socialism*, 1989, 2:44, pp. 59–99; Dearlove and Saunders, 1984, *op. cit.*, pp. 286–94, 311–13, 321–31; P. Lee and C. Raban, *Welfare Theory and Social Policy*, London, Sage, 1988, pp. 220–8; Mishra, 1984, *op. cit.*, pp. 46–53; Rogers, 1993, *op. cit.*, pp. 17–35; N. Timmins, *The Five Giants: A Biography of the Welfare State*, London, Fontana, 1996, pp. 369–494. For useful accounts of the welfare ideology of the New Right, see Clarke *et al.*, 1987, *op. cit.*, pp. 131–45; Dearlove and Saunders, 1984, *op. cit.*, pp. 321–7; George and Wilding, 1985, *op. cit.*, pp. 19–44; Mishra, 1984, *op. cit.*, pp. 26–46. For an excellent account of the impact of the New Right in government in the USA, see J. K. Galbraith, *The Culture of Contentment*, Harmondsworth, Penguin, 1993.

71 For excellent documentaries of Labour's gradual abandonment of labourism in favour of what is to all intents and purposes the politics of the New Right seasoned with 'One Nation Toryism' (and dressed up in vague talk of 'New Labour'), see A. Callinicos, *New Labour or Socialism?*, London, Bookmarks, 1996a; A. Callinicos, 'Betrayal and discontent: Labour under Blair', *International Socialism*, 1996b, 2:72; Cliff and Gluckstein, 1996, *op. cit.*, pp. 347–81, 389–429; P. Foot, 'When will the Blair bubble burst?', *International Socialism*, 1995, 2:67; C. Harman, 'From Bernstein to Blair: one hundred years of revisionism', *International Socialism*, 1995, 2:67.

72 Cliff and Gluckstein, 1996, *op. cit.*, pp. 94–105, 133–7,188–92; Miliband, 1972, *op. cit.*, pp. 93–120, 152–92. It was this ideological stance which partly explains why the Labour Party and TUC so disgracefully 'sold out' the General Strike of 1926, despite mass support by the rank and file for its continuance (see T. Cliff and D. Gluckstein, *Marxism and Trade Union Struggle: the General Strike of 1926*, London, Bookmarks, 1986, pp. 185–254, 266–82, 285–97). Equally lamentably, it was the Labour leadership's craven endorsement of neoclassical economic orthodoxy (together with the worst assumptions of bourgeois morality) which explains why MacDonald's governments of 1924 and 1929–31 refused to take any steps to reduce unemployment or to alleviate its material impact upon the workless and their families, and also continued to implement Tory measures (such as the 'Genuinely Seeking Work Test') which disqualified millions of the unemployed from desperately needed relief and stigmatised them as 'malingerers' (see esp. A. Deacon, 'Concession and coercion: the politics of unemployment insurance in the twenties', in A. Briggs and J. Saville (eds) *Essays in Labour History 1918–1939*, London, Croom Helm, 1977, pp. 9–35).

73 Cliff and Gluckstein, 1996, *op. cit.*, pp. 347–50, 356–9, 372–4.

74 For a full explanation of why the current crisis of capitalism (characterised as it is by increasingly deep and protracted slumps interspersed by weak and short-lived upturns) is likely to persist indefinitely, see A. Callinicos, *The Revolutionary Ideas of Karl Marx*, London, Bookmarks, 1983, pp. 185–92; C. Harman, *Explaining the Crisis: A Marxist Reappraisal*, London, Bookmarks, 1984, pp. 75–122, 122–55; C. Harman, *The Economics of the Madhouse: Capitalism and the Market Today*, London, Bookmarks, 1995, pp. 32–45, 51–62, 65–85; C. Harman, 'Where is capitalism going?' (parts 1 and 2) *International Socialism*, 1993, 2:58, 2:60. For useful discussions of how the crisis of capitalism is paralleled by a crisis of orthodox economics, see C. Harman, 'The crisis of bourgeois economics', *International Socialism*, 1996, 2:70; P. Ormerod, *The Death of Economics*, London, Faber, 1995. Concerning the future of public welfare in the contemporary economic climate, Clauss Offe appears to have hit the nail on the head when he remarks that modern capitalism can neither live with nor with-

out the welfare state (C. Offe, *Contradictions of the Welfare State*, London, Hutchinson, 1984).

75 T. Cliff, 'Prospects for socialists', *International Socialism*, 1992, 2:55, p. 69.

76 T. Cliff, *Lenin, 1893–1914: Building the Party*, London, Bookmarks, 1986, pp. 228–35; S. Wright, *The Making of the Revolution*, London, Bookmarks, 1984, pp. 5–8.

77 C. Barker (ed.) *Revolutionary Rehearsals*, Bookmarks, London, 1982 (chs on France and Portugal); C. Harman, *The Fire Last Time: 1968 and After*, London, Bookmarks, 1988, pp. 85–121, 277–312; C. Doyle, *France 1968: Month of Revolution*, London, Fortress, 1988.

78 Barker, 1982, *op. cit.* (chs on Chile and China); C. Harman, *Germany: The Lost Revolution 1918–23*, London, Bookmarks, 1982; R. Sewell, *Germany: From Revolution to Counter-Revolution*, London, Fortress, 1988; P. Marshall, *Revolution and Counter-Revolution in Iran*, London, Bookmarks, 1988.

79 S. Hall, 'The great moving right show', in S. Hall and M. Jacques (eds) *The Politics of Thatcherism*, London, Lawrence and Wishart, 1983.

80 Cliff and Gluckstein, 1996, *op. cit.*, pp. 345–88.

81 V. I. Lenin, *What is to be Done?*, Peking, Foreign Languages Press, 1973. Lenin's claim here was that the workers could acquire spontaneously only a reformist outlook ('trade union consciousness'). Consequently the role of the socialist party was to 'bring socialism to the workers' from without. This position was formally abandoned by Lenin in his *State and Revolution*.

82 T. Cliff, *Lenin, 1914–17: All Power to the Soviets*, London, Bookmarks, 1985, pp. 140–69, 258–71, 315–26, 335–80; T. Cliff, *Lenin, 1917–23: The Revolution Besieged*, London, Bookmarks, 1987, pp. 367–93; C. Harman, 'Party and class', in T. Cliff, D. Hallas, C. Harman and L. Trotsky, *Party and Class*, London, Bookmarks, 1996, pp. 23–33; P. Le Blanc, *Lenin and the Revolutionary Party*, Oxford, Blackwell, 1993; M. Liebman, *Leninism Under Lenin*, London, Merlin, 1985, pp. 25–52, 84–96, 162–89, 190–209; J. Molyneux, *Marxism and the Party*, London, Bookmarks, 1978, pp. 36–50, 69–84, 93–5, 96–115.

83 The former scenario characterised the ill-fated German revolution of 1923. After failing to exploit earlier revolutionary situations (because of poor tactics and organisation), the Communist Party consequently squandered the support of the working class and, isolated, was crushed by the forces of the German state (see Harman, 1982, *op. cit.*, pp. 264–302). The latter scenario characterised the earlier German revolution of 1919–20 (the 'Spartakist Days' of January 1919 and the 'March Action' of 1920), where the workers rose up spontaneously without a coherent insurrectionary strategy and against the advice of the Bolsheviks and most KPD leaders (*ibid.*, pp. 163–96, 192–221). Such was also the fate of the Portuguese revolution of 1973–4, the Iranian revolution of 1979 (see Barker, 1982, *op. cit.*), and of course the 1905 revolution in Russia (Wright, 1984, *op. cit.*, pp. 5–8).

84 Archer, 1995, *op. cit.*, pp. 259, 260, 262.

85 As was the case, for example, in Britain immediately prior to the Chartist movement of the 1830s and 1840s (see O'Brien, 1996b, *op. cit.*, pp. 7–16).

86 For example, the formation of the Labour Party ('out of the bowels of the TUC') occurred in the aftermath of the 'Great Unrest' of the 1880s and early 1890s. See Cliff and Gluckstein, 1996, *op. cit.*, pp. 5–23.

87 Again, another obvious example of this process was the rapid growth of the Bolshevik Party in the wake of the February 1917 revolution in Russia. Within a period of months the party was transformed from a small 'sect' to a mass party capable of organising and leading the October insurrection (see Cliff, 1985, *op. cit.*, pp. 97–139, 140–69, 258–71, 335–80).

88 This is especially the case where corporate political agents of the propertyless absurdly attempt to reconcile the interests of those they purportedly represent with the interests of powerful propertied elites. Until recently this was the project of the Labour Party in Britain. For a useful survey of the dismal record of reformism and labourism in office in the postwar years, see I. Birchall, *Bailing out the System: Reformist Socialism in Western Europe 1945–85*, London, Bookmarks, 1986.
89 D. Hallas, 'Towards a revolutionary socialist party', in Cliff *et al.*, 1996, *op. cit.*, pp. 38–55. See also Molyneux, 1978, *op. cit.*, pp. 162–9.
90 Perhaps the most sophisticated version of 'role theory', which attempts (ultimately unsuccessfully) to overcome cultural determinism, is to be found in the work of Martin Hollis. See esp. M. Hollis, *Models of Man: Philosophical Thoughts on Social Action*, Cambridge, Cambridge University Press, 1977; M. Hollis, *The Cunning of Reason*, Cambridge, Cambridge University Press, 1988.
91 J. Scott, *Sociological Theory: Contemporary Debates*, Aldershot, Edward Elgar, 1995, p. 116.
92 Mouzelis, 1995, *op. cit.*, p. 16.
93 Or 'methodological situationalism', as one of its leading exponents, Randall Collins, describes it (R. Collins, 'On the micro foundations of macro sociology', *American Journal of Sociology*, 1981, vol. 86, p. 988). Mouzelis rightly points out that

> the theoretical stance of social action theory is not so very different from that of methodological individualism. Just as the latter, in its more extreme form, reduces macro phenomena to a heap of isolated individuals, so methodological situationalism reduces them to an assembly of encounters. In the first case the monad is the individual, in the second the micro encounter.
>
> (Mouzelis, 1995, *op. cit.*, p. 22)

94 P. Berger and T. Luckmann, *The Social Construction of Reality*, London, Allen Lane, 1967, p. 127.
95 Mouzelis, 1995, *op. cit.*, p. 16.
96 Collins, 1981, *op. cit.*, p. 988.
97 Mouzelis, 1995, *op. cit.*, p. 21.
98 P. Berger and H. Kellner, 'Marriage and the construction of reality', in H. P. Drietzel (ed.) *Recent Sociology*, vol. 2, New York, Collier-Macmillan, 1970, pp. 62–3.
99 Berger and Luckmann, 1967, *op. cit.*, p. 103.
100 R. Watson, 'Reasons as causes of action', unpublished sociology Ph.D. thesis, University of Warwick Central Library, 1992, p. 375.
101 Archer, 1995, *op. cit.*, p. 278.
102 *ibid.*, p. 277.
103 *ibid.*
104 *ibid.*
105 *ibid.*
106 *ibid.*, p. 278.
107 F. Saussure, *Course in General Linguistics*, London, Fontana, 1974, p. 112.
108 J. Molyneux, 'The politically correct controversy', *International Socialism*, 1994, 2:61, p. 60.
109 Archer, 1995, *op. cit.*, pp. 285–6.
110 Molyneux, 1994, *op. cit.*, p. 59.
111 Which is, of course, a function of the rise of science and machine technology. It seems reasonable to believe that the enormous productive power of modern

capitalist societies is itself illustrative of a greater objective human control over and penetration of the physical environment, which is in turn persuasive evidence of a deepening practical human knowledge of nature.

112 Dennett, 1978, *op. cit.*; D. C. Dennett, *Consciousness Explained*, London, Viking, 1993; D. C. Dennett, *Darwin's Dangerous Idea: Evolution and the Meaning of Life*, London, Allen Lane, 1996.

113 As Alex Callinicos accurately summarises his approach (A. Callinicos, 'Darwin, materialism and evolution', *International Socialism*, 1996c, 2:71, p. 101). My analysis of Dennett's contribution to the contemporary materialist philosophy of mind owes much to this outstanding review of his work.

114 *ibid.*

115 This does not mean that Dennett endorses the view that the human mind is simply 'the program that runs on your brain's computer'. In fact he is careful to distinguish the ways in which minds and computers differ. Uppermost among these is the way in which human minds (unlike computer brains) are brought into direct contact with nature by specialised sensory equipment mediated by organismic needs and capacities. Another is his recognition that '[t]here is a big difference between a ... computer's serial architecture and the parallel architecture of the brain' (Dennett, 1993, *op. cit.*, p. 215). Dennett's point is simply to illustrate that both computers and minds are 'virtual machines', composite structures arranged hierarchically. 'A virtual machine is what you get when you impose a particular pattern of rules ... on all that plasticity' (*ibid.*, p. 211).

116 In *Consciousness Explained*, Dennett describes these sub-systems (homunculi) as 'units with particular circumscribed competences' (1993, *op. cit.*, pp. 261–2).

117 Dennet, 1996, *op. cit.*, p. 206.

118 Callinicos, 1996c, *op. cit.*, p. 101.

119 Dennett, 1993, *op. cit.*, p. 228.

120 *ibid.*, pp. 29, 108.

121 *ibid.*, pp. 228, 108, 111, 215.

122 *ibid.*, pp 108, 111, 214.

123 Callinicos, 1996c, *op. cit.*, p. 102.

124 Dennett, 1996, *op. cit.*, pp. 205–6.

125 *ibid.*, pp. 41, 343.

126 Callinicos, 1996c, *op. cit.*, pp. 104–5. As Dennett puts it: '[b]efore intentionality can be *fully fledged*, it must first go through an awkward, ugly, featherless pseudo-intentionality' (Dennett, 1996, *op. cit.*, p. 205.

127 *ibid.*, p. 76.

128 *ibid.*, p. 65.

129 Archer, 1995, *op. cit.*, pp. 281–2.

130 *ibid.*, p. 284.

131 E. Durkheim, *The Elementary Forms of Religious Life*, London, Allen and Unwin, 1976, p. 138.

132 Archer, 1995, *op. cit.*, p. 286.

133 I. Craib, *Modern Social Theory*, 2nd edn, Hemel Hempstead, Harvester Wheatsheaf, 1992, p. 180.

134 Archer, 1995, *op. cit.*, pp. 283–4.

135 R. Leakey and R. Lewin, *Origins Reconsidered*, London, Abacus, 1993, p. 300.

136 *ibid.*, pp. 298–300. Another measure of self-awareness in non-human primates, which has been developed by psychologist Gordon Gallup, is the 'mirror test'. Leakey and Lewin explain: 'The goal of Gallup's mirror test is to determine whether an animal is able to recognise the reflection as its own self instead of just another individual. The test is simplicity itself. It involves first familiarizing the animal with the mirror, then marking the animal's head with a red

spot. If the animal touches the spot after looking at its reflection anew, then ... the animal does indeed recognise the image as its own.' (Leakey and Lewin,1992, *op. cit.*, p. 298). Gallup concludes: 'The first time we tried it [the mirror test] with chimps, it worked. ... These data would seem to qualify as the first experimental demonstration of self-concept in a non-human form' (*ibid.*). Since Gallup's experiments 'many higher primates have been given the test, and so far only two have shown positive results: the chimpanzee, as in the original study, and the orangutan'. However, as Leakey and Lewin point out, 'some observers claim to have seen self-directed behaviour by gorillas in front of mirrors, which they take to indicate the presence of a sense of self in these animals' (*ibid.*, pp. 298–9).

137 *ibid.*, p. 244.

138 Cited in A. Giddens, *Sociology*, Cambridge, Polity Press, 1990, p. 40.

139 Primatologist Sheelagh Savage-Rumbaugh, cited in Leakey and Lewin, 1993, *op. cit.*, p. 244.

140 Archer, 1995, *op. cit.*, p. 286. As Nehemas puts it: 'Because it is organised coherently, the body provides the common ground that allows conflicting thoughts, desires, and actions to be grouped together as features of a single subject' (A. Nehemas, *Nietzsche: Life as Literature*, Cambridge MA, Harvard University Press, 1985, p. 181).

141 Archer, 1995, *op. cit.*, p. 288.

142 *ibid.*, p. 289.

143 *ibid.*, p. 290.

144 *ibid.*

145 *ibid.*, p. 290–1.

146 *ibid.*, p. 291.

147 *ibid.*, p. 124–5.

148 *ibid.*, p. 257.

149 See for example: J. H. Goldthorpe, *The Affluent Worker in the Class Structure*, Cambridge, Cambridge University Press, 1969, pp. 56–8, 64–8, 69–70, 77–8, 80–2, 90–2, 98–103, 121–3, 150–1, 153–4, 181–5, 189–90.

150 G. Almond, 'The German resistance movement', *Current History*, 1946, 10, pp. 409–527; L. Dawidowicz, *The War Against the Jews*, London, Allen Lane, 1987, pp. 191–2; M. Marrus, *The Holocaust in History*, London, Pelican, 1987, p. 91; A. Merson, *Communist Resistance in Nazi Germany*, London, Lawrence and Wishart, 1985; D. Peukart, *Inside Nazi Germany: Conformity, Opposition and Racism in Everyday Life*, London, Batsford, 1987; H. D. Leuner, *When Compassion was a Crime: Germany's Silent Heroes*, London, Wolff, 1966.

4 Structure, power and conflict

1 M. A. Coulson and C. Riddell, *Approaching Sociology*, London, Routledge and Kegan Paul, 1970, p. 43.

2 M. Weber, *The Protestant Ethic and the Spirit of Capitalism*, London, Unwin University Books, 1930; M. Weber, *The Theory of Social and Economic Organisation*, Glencoe IL, Free Press, 1947; M. Weber, *From Max Weber: Essays in Sociology*, London, Routledge and Kegan Paul, 1948; M. Weber, *General Economic History*, New York, Collier Books, 1961.

3 A. Callinicos, *Making History: Agency, Structure and Change in Social Theory*, Cambridge, Polity Press, 1987, p. 39.

4 *ibid.*

5 E. Durkheim, *The Rules of Sociological Method*, London, Macmillan, 1982, pp. 50–1.

6 E. O. Wright, *Class Structure and Income Distribution*, New York, Academic Press, 1979.
7 Coulson and Riddell, 1970, *op. cit.*, p. 51.
8 *ibid.*, p. 44.
9 *ibid.*, pp. 43–4.
10 *ibid.*, p. 44.
11 M. S. Archer, *Realist Social Theory: The Morphogenetic Approach*, Cambridge, Cambridge University Press, 1995, p. 196 (italics removed).
12 *ibid.*, p. 201.
13 *ibid.*, pp. 201–8.
14 *ibid.*, p. 201.
15 *ibid.*
16 *ibid.*, p. 202.
17 *ibid.*, p. 203.
18 *ibid.*
19 *ibid.*, p. 205.
20 *ibid.*
21 *ibid.*, p. 206.
22 *ibid.*, p. 208.
23 J. Rees, 'The class struggle under New Labour', *International Socialism*, 1997, 2:75, pp. 3–23.
24 Or rather see the labour-process as an integral part of the forces of production. See for instance K. Marx, *Capital*, vol. 1, Harmondsworth, Penguin, 1976, ch. 7.
25 K. Marx, *A Contribution to the Critique of Political Economy*, London, Lawrence and Wishart, 1970, pp. 20–1.
26 K. Marx, *The Eighteenth Brumaire of Louis Bonaparte*, Moscow, Progress Publishers, 1954, p. 12.
27 G. A. Cohen, *Karl Marx's Theory of History: A Defence*, Oxford, Clarendon Press, 1978.
28 R. Brenner, 'Agrarian class structure and economic development in pre-industrial Europe', *Past and Present*, 1976, 70; R. Brenner, 'The origins of capitalist development: a critique of neo-Smithian Marxism', *New Left Review*, 1977, 104; R. Brenner, 'The agrarian roots of European capitalism', *Past and Present*, 1982, 97; R. Brenner, 'The social basis of economic development', in J. Roemer (ed.) *Analytical Marxism*, Cambridge, Cambridge University Press, 1987; A. Callinicos, *Is there a Future for Marxism?*, London, Macmillan, pp. 146–7; A. Callinicos, *Marxism and Philosophy*, Oxford, Oxford University Press, 1983a, pp. 110–13; A. Callinicos, 'A comment on Chris Harman's "Base and Superstructure" ', *International Socialism*, 1986, 2:34, pp. 122–5.
29 S. Clarke, 'Althusser's Marxism', in S. Clarke, V. J. Seidler, K. McDonnell, K. Robins and T. Lovell (eds) *One Dimensional Marxism: Althusser and the Politics of Culture*, London, Allison and Busby, 1980, p. 20.
30 A. Callinicos, *The Revolutionary Ideas of Karl Marx*, London, Bookmarks, 1983b, pp. 83–4.
31 K. Marx, *Capital*, vol. 3, Moscow, Progress Publishers, 1962, p. 791.
32 Marx, 1976, *op. cit.*, p. 287.
33 It is this which renders meaningful Marx's claim that the contradiction between forces and relations of production shapes the class conflicts which provide history with its dynamic.
34 Callinicos, 1987, *op. cit.*, p. 50.
35 Marx, 1976, *op. cit.*, pp. 344–5.
36 G. E. M. de Ste Croix, *The Class Struggle in the Ancient Greek World*, London, Duckworth, 1981, pp. 43–4.

37 Wright, 1979, *op. cit.*, p. 22.
38 J. Elster, *Making Sense of Marx*, Cambridge, Cambridge University Press, 1985, pp. 257–8.
39 K. Marx, *Grundrisse*, Harmondsworth, Penguin, 1973, p. 414.
40 Callinicos, 1987, *op. cit.*, p. 50.
41 *ibid.*
42 Marx, 1973, *op. cit.*, pp. 651 and 657.
43 Callinicos, 1987, *op. cit.*, p. 52.
44 *ibid.*
45 E. Laclau and C. Mouffe, *Hegemony and Socialist Strategy*, London, Verso, 1985, pp. 77–8.
46 J. Elster, *An Introduction to Karl Marx*, Cambridge, Cambridge University Press, 1986, pp. 105–6.
47 T. Spybey, *Social Change, Development and Dependency*, Cambridge, Polity Press, 1992, p. 15.
48 Marx, 1976, *op. cit.*, p. 286.
49 K. Marx, *The Poverty of Philosophy*, Peking, Foreign Languages Press, 1978, p. 103.
50 Marx, 1962, *op. cit.*, p. 791.
51 Marx, 1976, *op. cit.*, p. 325.
52 C. Harman, 'Base and superstructure', *International Socialism*, 1986, 2:32, p. 19.
53 Callinicos, 1983a, *op. cit.*, pp. 112–13.
54 G. A. Cohen, 'Forces and relations of production', in Roemer, 1987, *op. cit.*, pp. 13–14.
55 Callinicos, 1983a, *op. cit.*, p. 112.
56 Marx, 1962, *op. cit.*, p. 791.
57 Cohen, 1978, *op. cit.*, p. 98.
58 S. Clarke, *Marx, Marginalism and Modern Sociology*, 2nd edn, London, Macmillan, 1991.
59 K. Marx and F. Engels, *Collected Works*, vol. 5, London, Lawrence and Wishart, 1975, p. 43.
60 Marx, 1970, *op. cit.*, p. 20.
61 Marx, 1962, *op. cit.*, p. 791.
62 See especially Engels, in Marx and Engels, 1975, *op. cit.*, pp. 348–9.
63 J. Molyneux, 'Is Marxism deterministic?', *International Socialism*, 1995, 2:68, p. 52.
64 *ibid.*, p. 64.
65 L. Trotsky, *The Struggle Against Fascism in Germany*, New York, Pathfinder Press, 1971, p. 137.
66 Marx, 1970, *op. cit.*, p. 21.
67 Chapter 1, pp. 62–3.
68 Cohen, 'Forces', in Roemer, 1987, *op. cit.*, p. 14.
69 Marx, 1954, *op. cit.*, pp. 40–1.
70 K. Marx and F. Engels, *The German Ideology*, London, Lawrence and Wishart, 1970, p. 42.
71 F. Engels, 'Letter to Borgius', in F. Engels, *Letters on Historical Materialism 1890–94*, Moscow, Progress Publishers, 1980, p. 26.
72 Callinicos, 1987, *op. cit.*, p. 41.
73 This drift has affected even those Marxists who reject the voluntarism of the New Left and the economic determinism of Stalinised historical materialism. Colin Barker, for instance, asks: 'Is base and superstructure such a necessary distinction?'. He thinks not, because this 'is not a metaphor that Marx uses much in *Capital*, the mature version of his Critique of Political Economy' (C. Barker, 'A comment on Harman's "Base and superstructure" ', *International*

Socialism, 1986, 2:34, p. 119). Yet Marx *does* use the base-superstructure model in *Capital*, as Barker acknowledges. Indeed, this 'metaphor' is precisely what justifies Marx's analytical focus here on the mode of production and the 'economic law of motion of modern society'. Elsewhere, of course, Marx describes the base-superstructure model as the 'guiding principle' of his studies (Marx, 1970, *op. cit.*, p. 20).

74 P. Binns, 'What are the tasks of Marxism in philosophy?', *International Socialism*, 1982, 2:17, pp. 99–101.

75 This seems to be what Ellen Wood is driving at when she argues that 'the formula concerning the contradiction between forces of production and relations of production' is a 'law of capitalist development' but not of pre-capitalist class formations (E. M. Wood, 'Marxism and the course of history', *New Left Review*, 1984, 147, p. 102).

76 D. Lee and H. Newby, *The Problem of Sociology*, London, Unwin Hyman, pp. 115–18. In fact, the distinction between 'materialists' and 'humanists' in neo-Marxism is less clear-cut than Lee and Newby imply (*ibid.*, p. 118). Though the humanists were hostile to the base-superstructure model, scientific Marxists (such as Althusser and Poulantzas) tended to theoretically undermine it also. Althusser, for instance, presented a theory of structural 'autonomisation' (which divided society into a number of distinct 'regions' – the economic, political, cultural, etc. – each of which followed their own logics of development), denied that economics were 'dominant' in pre-capitalist societies, and asserted that even in capitalism the 'lonely hour of the final [economic] instance never comes'. In practice this was a dualistic-pluralistic conception of society and social change, not a materialist understanding at all.

77 *ibid.*, p.117.

78 M. Weber, *The Methodology of the Social Sciences*, Glencoe IL, Free Press, 1949, pp. 68–9.

79 E. Acton, *Rethinking the Russian Revolution*, London, Edward Arnold, 1990, p. 2.

80 Spybey, *op. cit.*, pp. 16–17.

81 Marx, 1970, *op. cit.*, pp. 20–1.

82 Marx and Engels, 1970, *op. cit.*, p. 48.

83 Molyneux, 1995, *op. cit.*, p. 55.

84 R. Gottlieb, *Marxism: Origins, Betrayal, Rebirth*, London, Routledge, 1992, pp. 12–13.

85 Harman, 1986, *op. cit.*, p. 10.

86 F. Engels, 'Letter to Borgius', in Engels, 1980, *op. cit.*, p. 26.

87 As far as I am aware there are no figures examining the distribution of property and wealth by ethnicity. I have arrived at the figures cited in the text by the following statistical means. First, I examined data revealing the class composition of black and white populations (T. Jones, *Britain's Ethnic Minorities*, London, Policy Studies Institute, 1993). This showed that 21 per cent of the black and 27 per cent of the white adult population are members of the PM or employer classes (and so 79 per cent and 73 per cent of the black and white populations respectively are members of the working class). Second, I examined the distribution of wealth by class. Roughly speaking, the employer and PM classes (about 27 per cent of the population according to Jones' figures) own 79 per cent of national wealth, whereas the working class (73 per cent of the population) owns just 21 per cent (see n94 below). Third, I examined data revealing the relative sizes of the black and white populations, and used these to calculate the social composition and distribution of the class structure by ethnicity. Since ethnic minorities constitute about 6 per cent of the population, it is reasonable to surmise that these make up about 1.25 per cent of the

membership of the PM and employer classes, and about 4.75 per cent of the membership of the working class. Fourth, I then assumed (for the sake of argument) that the effects of race discrimination would ensure that the top 10 per cent of property owners (who control about 50 per cent of the total wealth) are exclusively white and that the black working class is composed entirely of semi-skilled and unskilled manual workers (being located therefore in the lower 50 per cent of the population who together own just 8 per cent of national wealth), both of these assumptions most likely leading to a significant *overestimation* of the impact of racism as a factor of stratification determining the distribution of property. On this basis, I was able to calculate that the black PM and employer classes own a minimum of 1.3 per cent (approximately) of property compared to 77.7 per cent for members of the white PM and employer classes, whereas the black working class own just 0.7 per cent of property compared to 19.3 per cent for members of the white working class. This means that ethnic minorities (6 per cent of the population) own roughly 2 per cent of national wealth whereas whites (94 per cent of the population) own 98 per cent.

88 J. Westergaard and H. Resler, *Class in a Capitalist Society*, Harmondsworth, Penguin, 1976, p. 114.

89 Jones, *op. cit.*, p. 99.

90 G. Routh, *Occupation and Pay in Great Britain 1906–79*, London, Macmillan, 1980, p. 4.

91 *Employment Gazette*, July 1994, p. 255.

92 V. Bogdanor, *Women at the Top*, London, Hansard, 1990; A. Giddens, *Sociology*, 3rd edn, Cambridge, Polity Press, 1997, pp. 319–20; K. Grint, *The Sociology of Work*, Cambridge, Polity Press, 1994; S. Lie and V. O'Leary, *Storming the Tower: Women in the Academic World*, London, Kogan Page, 1990. See also *Lloyds Bank Economic Bulletin*, July 1988.

93 N. Abercrombie and A. Warde, *Contemporary British Society*, Cambridge, Polity Press, 1988, pp. 210, 255.

94 *Social Trends*, 21, London, HMSO, 1991, p. 95. These figures exclude pension fund holdings and the value of houses.

95 See n87 above.

96 Routh, 1980, *op. cit.*, p. 127.

97 *New Earnings Survey*, London, HMSO, 1984, part A, tables 10, 11.

98 Abercrombie and Warde, 1988, *op. cit.*, p. 255.

99 D. Glass, *Social Mobility in Britain*, London, Routledge and Kegan Paul, 1954, p. 183.

100 J. Goldthorpe, C. Llewellyn and G. Payne, *Social Mobility and Class Structure in Modern Britain*, Oxford, Clarendon Press, 1980, pp. 44, 48. In fact, Goldthorpe and his co-authors do not estimate the total percentage of sons from manual working class backgrounds who have 'made it' into the PM and employer classes, instead basing their calculations on the percentages of sons from specific occupational bands (unskilled and skilled workers, etc.) who have done so. I have arrived at the figure cited in the text for total male working class mobility by combining Goldthorpe's occupational categories. In doing so I have assumed for the sake of convenience that the respective sizes of the skilled working class and the unskilled and semi-skilled working class are equivalent. That this is not the case does not damage my argument in the least (there being more unskilled and semi-skilled male workers than skilled workers). This is because the differences in mobility rates for sons of skilled manual workers, on the one hand, and for sons of semi-skilled and unskilled workers, on the other hand, are not sufficient to significantly affect the total calculation

of intergenerational working-class mobility I have derived from Goldthorpe's statistics.

101 G. Marshall, D. Rose, H. Newby and C. Vogler, *Social Class in Modern Britain*, London, Unwin Hyman, 1988.

102 *ibid.*, p. 77. Again, I have reconstructed Marshall's data to calculate the mobility rates for the male offspring of manual workers as a whole, not for specific occupational bands. In doing so I have followed the same procedure as specified above for Goldthorpe (see n100 above).

103 Goldthorpe *et al.*, 1980, *op. cit.*, pp. 44, 48; Marshall *et al.*, 1988, *op. cit.*, p. 77.

104 These calculations are based on Goldthorpe's and Marshall's data (*ibid.*).

105 See A. Giddens and P. Stanworth, 'An economic elite: a demographic profile of company chairmen', in A. Giddens and P. Stanworth, (eds) *Elites and Power in British Society*, Cambridge, Cambridge University Press, 1974.

106 Marshall *et. al.*, 1988, *op. cit.*, p. 77.

107 *ibid.*

108 *Social Trends 24*, London, HMSO, 1994, p. 50.

109 *ibid.*

110 Jones, *op. cit.*, p. 46.

111 That is, Afro-Caribbean blacks. Lord Swann, *Education For All: A Brief Guide*, London, HMSO, 1985, ch. 3, tables 2, 4, 7.

112 *Social Trends 24*, 1994, *op. cit.*, p. 52.

113 *ibid.*

114 *General Household Survey of 1990–1*, London, HMSO, 1993, table 10.14, p. 218; *Social Trends 23*, London, HMSO, 1993, table 3.26, p. 48.

115 *Social Trends 24*, 1994, *op. cit.*, p. 47; *Social Trends 23*, 1993, *op. cit.*, p. 48.

116 *Social Trends 24*, 1994, *op. cit.*, pp. 47, 52.

117 *ibid.*, p. 47; Jones, *op. cit.*, pp. 31–2, 33, 42, 44.

118 Jones, *op. cit.*, p. 46; *General Household Survey of 1990–1*, 1993, *op. cit.*, table 10.4, p. 214.

119 Abercrombie and Warde, 1988, *op. cit.*, p. 355.

120 *General Household Survey of 1990–1*, 1993, *op. cit.*, p. 204.

121 Jones, *op. cit.*, p. 44.

122 *Social Trends 24*, 1994, *op. cit.*, p. 47.

123 *ibid.*, p. 52.

124 *General Household Survey of 1990–1*, 1993, *op. cit.*, p. 208.

125 K. Marx and F. Engels, *The Communist Manifesto*, Harmondsworth, Penguin, 1967, p. 79.

126 For example, by considering the so-called 'race riot' which occurred in Los Angeles in the spring of 1992. My reason for so doing is simply that one would most expect to discover evidence of the primacy of ethnic divisions in shaping social conflict in this context. Indeed, the absence of any such evidence, if this is what close analysis reveals, must surely call into question the views of those who hold that racial divisions are more fundamental forms of inequality (and hence of social antagonisms) than class divisions in contemporary capitalist societies (and especially in the USA).

So what explains the agency of those involved (whether as participants or as agents of law and order) in the LA riot? The common view is that this was a spontaneous uprising against 'white authority' by alienated black, Asian and Hispanic youth in response to institutionalised race discrimination in all areas of life, including and especially the racist conduct of the police. Certainly this perspective contains a nugget of truth. The immediate stimulus of the riot was the acquittal by a white jury of four white police officers who had been caught out on camera beating up an unarmed black motorist. Thousands of black and Latino youth had recently been arrested on trivial charges during 'Operation

Hammer', a vast paramilitary police incursion into the LA ghetto (M. Davis, *City of Quartz: Excavating the Future in Los Angeles*, London, Verso, 1990, ch. 5). Most of the rioters were from ethnic minorities. They were predominantly young. They were (and of course are) the victims of race discrimination. And racism is an important factor of stratification in the USA by virtue of which ethnic minorities (and especially Latinos and blacks) are more likely than whites to be unemployed or located in the lowest-paid jobs or over-represented as victims of crime or police victimisation (A. Hacker, *Two Nations*, New York, Charles Scribners Sons, 1993).

Nonetheless, a racial explanation of the LA riot is inadequate. Why? First, like the inner city riots which rocked the UK in the summer of 1981 – also dubbed 'race riots' despite the fact that 67 per cent of those arrested were white (D. Hiro, *Black British White British: A History of Race Relations in Britain*, 2nd edn, London, Grafton, 1992, p. 90) – 'the rebellion was *multi-ethnic* in character' (A. Callinicos, *Race and Class*, London, Bookmarks, 1993, p. 53), involving the cooperation of whites and non-whites in pillaging shops, destroying property, setting up barricades and fighting the police.

> Willie Brown, a leading black California Democrat and the speaker of the state assembly, acknowledged that 'the violence was not contained in the inner city: it spread to outlying and upscale neighbourhoods. ... For the first time in American history, many of the demonstrations, and much of the violence and crime, especially the looting, was multi-racial – blacks, whites, Hispanics and Asians were all involved.' Of the first 5,000 people arrested in the riot 52 per cent were Latinos, 10 per cent were whites, and only 38 per cent were blacks.
>
> (Callinicos, 1993, *op. cit.*, p. 53)

Second, the underlying cause of the rebellion was to be found in the combined impact of 'Reaganomics' (a particular economic strategy of the Reagan and Bush administrations to boost the profitability of US capital by systematically redistributing 'wealth and income [from poor to rich], leaving real wages to fall') and the deep recession 'which set in 1990 ... hitting the sometime boom economy of California particularly hard' (Callinicos, 1993, *op. cit.*, p. 53), upon the ghettoised working class. Again, there is a clear parallel here with the UK riots of 1981, the roots of which lay in the deflationary attacks on welfare rights and retrogressive tax policies of the Wilson-Callaghan and Thatcher governments, and the recessions of the mid-1970s and early 1980s, which plunged millions of urban proletarians into unemployment and poverty (C. Harman, 'The riots of 1981', *International Socialism*, 1981, 2:14, pp. 15–19).

Finally, the central conflict which unfolded during the course of the rebellion was not one which pitted (largely) ethnic minority rioters against white agents of 'law and order' and the local white petty bourgeoisie. On the contrary, it was essentially a class conflict, which pitted the urban poor against local multi-ethnic shopkeepers (who were perceived – rightly or wrongly – as profiteers exploiting the poverty of their customers) and PMC whites and blacks in key authority positions in the LA state apparatus. That class and not race was the key antagonism of the LA rebellion was thus starkly revealed by the fact that middle-class blacks in key managerial-administrative positions in US society played a leading role in quashing it and were sometimes as vociferous as their white colleagues in their moralistic condemnation of the 'criminals' who took part (Callinicos, 1993, *op. cit.*, pp. 53–4; M. Davis, 'The rebellion that rocked a superpower', in L. German and R. Hoveman, (eds) *A Socialist Review*, Bookmarks, London, 1998, pp. 271–3). For them there was no question of 'ethnic issues' (the plight of ghettoised immigrant minorities) getting in the way of naked class self-interest (the 'united front' with bourgeois whites in defence of property and 'law and order'). Clearly, the political thinking and agency of these PMC blacks entailed the subordination of racial to class allegiances during a 'critical episode' where these were forced into conflict. This immediate 'closing of ranks' of leading black and white members of the US power structure in opposition to and condemnation of the LA rioters, and the dishonourable role of leading blacks in suppressing the rebellion by force, was, I contend, an entirely predictable chain of events, on the grounds that class relations were (and are) here fundamental in determining the life-chances and hence vested interests of interactants.

127 My distinction here is between those modes of class agency which are necessary to emancipate workers from political subordination and economic exploitation (i.e. revolutionary class conflict aimed at the socialist reconstruction of society) and those modes of class agency which are necessary to alleviate or ameliorate the material situation of the workers within capitalist society (i.e. voting for reformist parties and trade union action in defence of wages and conditions of work).

128 P. Alexander, *Racism, Resistance and Revolution*, London, Bookmarks, 1987, pp. 81–7, 96–111; T. Cliff, *Class Struggle and Women's Liberation*, London, Bookmarks, 1984, pp. 161–2, 189–95; L. German, 'The rise and fall of the Women's Movement', *International Socialism*, 1987, 2:37, pp. 21–2; K. Ovenden, *Malcolm X: Black Nationalism and Socialism*, London, Bookmarks, 1992, pp. 53–9; A. Shawki, 'Black liberation and socialism in the United States', *International Socialism*, 1990, 2:47, pp. 76–88.

129 German, 1987, *op. cit.*, pp. 11, 36–44.

130 S. Field, *The Attitudes of Ethnic Minorities*, London, HMSO, 1984.

131 C. Brown, *Black and White in Britain: Policy Studies Institute Report*, London, Gower, 1985, p. 282.

132 R. Jowell, L. Brook and B. Taylor (eds) *British Social Attitudes: The 9th Annual Report*, Aldershot, Dartmouth Publishers, 1992, pp. 183, 185.

133 W. Bennett, 'How we mixed and matched', *Socialist Worker*, 5 September 1998.

134 Cliff, 1984, *op. cit.*, p. 10.

135 M. Eichler, *The Double Standard: A Feminist Critique of Feminist Social Science*, London, Croom Helm, 1980.

136 Alexander, 1987, *op. cit.*, pp. 81–7; Cliff, 1984, *op. cit.*, pp. 161–5, 172, 192; German, 1987, *op. cit.*, pp. 8–10; M. Marable, 'Beyond racial identity politics', *Race and Class*, 1993, 35:1, p. 121; Ovenden, 1992, *op. cit.*, pp. 64–5; S. Rowbotham and L. Segal, *Beyond the Fragments: Feminism and the Making of Socialism*, London, Merlin, 1979, p. 45; Shawki, 1990, *op. cit.*, pp. 94–5; A. Sivandan, 'All that melts into air is solid', *Race and Class*, 1990, 31:3; S. Smith, 'Mistaken identity; or can identity politics liberate the oppressed?, *International Socialism*, 1994, 2:62, pp. 9–11, 22–4.

137 Who would doubt, for instance, that feminism has become transformed since the early 1970s into a means of occupational self-advancement for a handful of privileged women, especially in academia, journalism and local government? Certainly this process of integration of former women's rights activists into prestigious role-positions in major institutions has been accompanied by their gradual abandonment of socialistic politics and of a class analysis of society, for which (as we have seen) patriarchy theory has provided theoretical legitimation. Indeed, the politics of contemporary feminism are more often than not *explicitly* anti-working class and anti-socialist. Former 'Eurocommunist' Beatrix Campbell, for instance, once claimed (in the middle of a hospital strike whose victory would have benefited the wage packets of many thousands of women as

well as men) that trade unions were part of the 'patriarchal system' by which men oppress women, before going on to dismiss strikes as an outmoded macho 'dispute practice' left over from a bygone era (*Guardian*, 9 August 1982). Elsewhere Campbell recommended that free collective bargaining be replaced by a redistribution of income from male to female workers (as if the former were responsible for the low wages of the latter!), a policy which if enacted would undoubtedly have served to lower the consumption of the working class as a whole, not least because it would have sowed the seeds of greater factionalism in the working class, and done so without dismantling the sexual division of labour from which gender inequalities are derived (B. Campbell, 'Work to rule', *Red Flag*, 1978, no. 14; B. Campbell and A. Coote, *Sweet Freedom: The Struggle for Women's Liberation*, London, Picador, 1982).

This drift into union-bashing and left-baiting is extremely pronounced in the modern feminist 'movement', often being predicated on the baseless assumption that the trade union campaign for the 'family wage' in the nineteenth century was a plot hatched by male workers and male employers to confine women to the domestic sphere and reduce them to domestic servitude (see esp. H. Hartmann, 'The unhappy marriage of Marxism and feminism', *Capital and Class*, 1979, no. 8, for an elaboration of the feminist argument; L. German, *Sex, Class and Socialism*, London, Bookmarks, 1989, pp. 31–6, 74–5, provides an effective critique of the Hartmann thesis). Such reactionary politics were of course especially lamentable and unhelpful during a period (the 1980s) in which the working class and trade union movement was taking a terrible battering from the state and capital. Yet they were (and are) entirely consistent with the class interests of bourgeois women, particularly during a period of downturn in the class struggle. After all, the class basis of bourgeois feminism grants its allegiants definite class interests in and class capacities for the *reproduction*, not transformation, of existing structures of economic power and privilege, which themselves depend in part on the subordination of women within the family unit (L. German, 'Theories of patriarchy', *International Socialism*, 1981, 2:12, pp. 45–7; German, 1989, *op. cit.*, pp. 61–79). So much so, in fact, that many women in positions of power and authority in capitalist society, many of whom would doubtless claim to be feminists or influenced by feminism, appear oblivious to the fact they actively reproduce social practices which reinforce ideas of 'women's proper place' – such as the employment of working-class women in domestic service (M. Barrett and M. McIntosh, *The Anti-Social Family*, London, Verso, 1982, pp. 144–5; C. Epstein, *Woman's Place*, Berkeley and London, University of California Press, 1970, p. 138; German, 1989, *op. cit.*, p. 78) – or which reduce the life-chances of the most powerless and downtrodden of women (a striking recent example of this being Harriet Harman's decision to cut welfare benefits to single parents, supported by all but one of New Labour's women MPs), and for reasons entirely explainable in terms of class interests.

The class basis of 'black politics' in the USA is equally clear. The 1980s and 1990s have seen concerted efforts by consecutive administrations of both main parties, to secure the profitability of US capital by means of a retrogressive taxation policy and swingeing reductions in public spending. This, together with the recessions of the 1980s and early 1990s, plus an especially aggressive employers offensive (which has succeeded in reducing real average wages and widening the gap between white and black wages), has ensured that the living conditions of the huge majority of non-white minorities have radically worsened and are now scarcely any better than in the mid-1960s, resulting among other things (for blacks) in a falling rate of enrolment in colleges and universities, declining life-expectancy, rising crime and unemployment, and subordination to a much higher degree of state racism and police victimisation (Alexander, 1987, *op. cit.*, p. 98; Ovenden, 1992, *op. cit.*, pp. 65–8; Smith, 1992, *op. cit.*, pp. 18–20).

By contrast, whereas the living standards of most blacks have deteriorated sharply over the past twenty years, those of a tiny minority of blacks have increased sharply (M. Marable, *Race, Reform and Rebellion: The Second Reconstruction*, 2nd edn, Jackson and London, University Press of Mississippi, 1991, p. 151; M. Marable, 'Black America in search of itself', *The Progressive*, November 1991, p. 22). In the meantime, the number of elected black officials has gone through the roof, from a mere 100 in 1966 to over 7,000 today (Ovenden, 1992, *op. cit.*, p. 66), of whom more than 200 are mayors. Many other blacks hold key authority positions in the US power structure – including Clarence Thomas (Supreme Court Judge) and General Colin Powell (recently chairman of the US Joint Chiefs of Staff). These PMC blacks have all benefited from the affirmative action programmes of the 1960s won by the civil rights movement. But all are integrated into state structures which have systematically attacked the civil liberties and life-chances of proletarian whites and blacks. Indeed, specific black state officials have been to the forefront of the offensive against the working class and ghettoised minorities. The following examples should make this clear. Colin Powell sent the federal troops into LA which put down the riot of 1992 (Callinicos, 1993, *op. cit.*, p. 53). LA police chief Willie Williams and Mayor Tom Bradley have played a leading role in the vicious repression (including mass deportations) which has been meted out upon the black and Latino poor of the city in revenge for the riot (Davis, 'Rebellion', in German and Hoveman, 1998, *op. cit.*, pp. 271–2). Clarence Thomas has been to the forefront of the campaign against affirmative action (Ovenden, 1992, *op. cit.*, p. 68). Douglas Wilder (governor of Virginia) has proudly boasted of his lack of involvement in any civil rights demonstration, and has made clear his support for the death penalty (despite the fact that economic subordination and racism combined ensure that 50 per cent of America's prison population are blacks) and for anti-trade union legislation (Ovenden, 1992, *op. cit.*, p. 68).

138 E. Laclau and C. Mouffe, 'Post-Marxism without apologies', *New Left Review*, 1987, 166, p. 49.

139 J. Rees, 'Engels' Marxism', *International Socialism*, 1994, 2:65, p. 71.

140 de Ste Croix, 1981, *op. cit.*, pp. 427–38.

141 Marx, 1970, *op. cit.*, p. 21.

142 Molyneux, 1995, *op. cit.*, p. 55.

143 *ibid.*

144 *ibid.*

145 F. Jakubowski, *Ideology and Superstructure in Historical Materialism*, 2nd edn, London, Pluto Press, 1990. p. 38.

146 Jakubowski, 1990, *op. cit.*, p. 41.

147 F. Engels, *The Origin of the Family, Private Property and the State*, New York, International Publishers, 1942, p. 155.

148 N. Harris, 'A comment on *National Liberation*', *International Socialism*, 1991, 2:53, p. 82.

149 A. Giddens, *A Contemporary Critique of Historical Materialism,* vol. 1, London, Macmillan, 1981; N. Harris, *National Liberation*, London, I.B. Tauris, 1990; M. Mann, *The Sources of Social Power*, vol. 1, Cambridge, Cambridge University Press, 1986; T. Skocpol, *States and Social Revolutions: A Comparative Analysis of France, Russia and China*, Cambridge, Cambridge University Press, 1979; E. P. Thompson, *Exterminism and the Cold War*, London, Verso, 1982.

150 Harris, 1991, *op. cit.*, pp. 83–4.

151 A. Giddens, *The Consequences of Modernity*, Cambridge, Polity Press, 1990; E. P. Thompson, 'Exterminism reviewed', in E. P. Thompson, *The Heavy Dancers*, London, Merlin, 1985.

152 R. Miliband, 'Class analysis', in A. Giddens and J. Turner (eds) *Social Theory Today*, Cambridge, Polity Press, 1987, p. 339. See also R. Miliband, *Divided Societies: Class Struggle in Contemporary Capitalism*, Oxford, Oxford University Press, 1989, pp. 167–202.

153 R. J. Barnet and R. E. Muller, *Global Reach: The Power of the Multinational Corporation*, New York, Simon and Schuster, 1974; A. Callinicos, 'Marxism and imperialism today', *International Socialism*, 1991, 2:50, pp. 16–26; A. Callinicos, 'Imperialism, capitalism and the state today', *International Socialism*, 1987, 2:35, pp. 79–84; E. Galeano, *The Open Veins of Latin America: Five Centuries of the Pillage of a Continent*, New York, Monthly Review Press, 1973; C. Harman, *Explaining the Crisis: A Marxist Reappraisal*, London, Bookmarks, 1984, pp. 84–90; N. Harris, *India-China: Underdevelopment and Revolution*, New Delhi, Vikas Publishing House, 1974; N. Harris, 'Imperialism today', in N. Harris and J. Palmer, *World Crisis: Essays in Revolutionary Socialism*, London, Hutchinson, 1971; T. Hayter, *The Creation of World Poverty*, London, Pluto Press, 1981; T. Hayter and C. Watson, *Aid: Rhetoric and Reality*, London, Pluto Press, 1985; A. M. M. Hoogvelt, *The Third World in Global Development*, London, Macmillan, 1982; H. Magdoff, *Imperialism: from the Colonial Age to the Present*, New York, Monthly Review Press, 1978; R. Owen and B. Sutcliffe (eds) *Studies in the Theory of Imperialism*, London, Longman, 1972, pp. 144–70, 171–94, 312–30; J. Petras and M. Morley, *US Hegemony under Siege: Class, Politics and Development in Latin America*, London, Verso, 1990, pp. 197–8, 201; J. Rees, 'The new imperialism', *International Socialism*, 1990, 2:48, pp. 53–7; D. Seers (ed.) *Dependency Theory: a Critical Reassessment*, London, Frances Pinter, 1981.

154 N. Bukharin, *Imperialism and World Economy*, London, Merlin, 1972; Callinicos, 1991, *op. cit.*, pp. 5–9; E. J. Hobsbawm, *The Age of Empire*, London, Weidenfeld and Nicolson, 1987, pp. 45–6, 56–83; V. I. Lenin, *Imperialism: the Highest Stage of Capitalism*, Peking, Foreign Languages Press, 1965.

155 T. Skocpol, 'Bringing the state back in: strategies of analysis in current research', in P. Evans, D. Rueschemeyer and T. Skocpol (eds) *Bringing the State Back In*, Cambridge, Cambridge University Press, 1985.

156 *ibid.*, p. 11.

157 Chapter 3, pp. 61–9.

158 Skocpol, 1979, *op. cit.*, pp. 51–67.

159 *ibid.*, pp. 60–7.

160 J. Rees (ed.) *Marxism and the Great French Revolution*, London, Bookmarks, 1989, pp. 24–8.

161 *ibid.*, pp. 16–19, 21–2, 28–33.

162 Skocpol, 1979, *op. cit.*, p. 110.

163 *ibid.*, p. 47.

164 Harris, 1991, *op. cit.*, p. 83.

165 *ibid.*, pp. 83–4.

166 *ibid.*, p. 87. See also Harris, 1990, *op. cit.*, pp. 262–5.

167 A. Callinicos, 'Capitalism and the state system', *International Socialism*, 1992, 2:54, p. 137.

168 Harris, 1990, *op. cit.*, p. 278–81; Harris, 1991, *op. cit.*, pp. 79–86. See also N. Harris, *The New Untouchables: Immigration and the New World Order*, London, I.B. Tauris, 1995, pp. 216–17, 224–8.

169 Harris, 1991, *op. cit.*, p. 87.

170 Callinicos, 1992, *op. cit.*, p. 137. For effective critiques of Harris' disassociation of immigration controls from capitalist interests, see also A. Callinicos, 'The end of nationalism?', *International Socialism*, 1991, 2:51, pp. 63–4; P. Morgan, 'Capitalism without frontiers?', *International Socialism*, 1997, 2:74, pp. 96–9.
171 Callinicos, 1992, *op. cit.*, p. 136.
172 D. Guerin, *Fascism and Big Business*, New York, Pathfinder Press, 1973.
173 Initially the high tariffs imposed on Japanese imports to the USA in 1930 (at a time when the Japanese economy was mired in recession). In response to Japan's invasion of China, the USA imposed an informal trade embargo, followed by a blockade, which in effect cut Japan off from 66 per cent of its oil supply, and threatened the country's economic survival (C. Bambery, 'Was the Second World War a war for democracy?', *International Socialism*, 1995, 2:67, pp. 70–1).
174 E. Mandel, *The Meaning of the Second World War*, London, Verso, 1986, pp. 24, 29.
175 A. Callinicos *et al.*, 'Why we say no to NATO's war', *Socialist Review*, May 1999, no. 230, pp. 3–20.
176 M. Haynes, 'Theses on the Balkan War', *International Socialism*, 1999, 2:83, pp. 90–6.
177 J. Rees, 'NATO and the new imperialism', *Socialist Review*, June, 1999, no. 231, pp. 17–19.
178 V. Brittain (ed.) *The Gulf Between Us: The Gulf War and Beyond*, London, Virago, 1991.
179 M. Kidron, *A Permanent Arms Economy*, London, Bookmarks, 1989. See also Harman, 1984, *op. cit.*, esp. pp. 75–122.
180 Callinicos, 1992, *op. cit.*, p. 136.
181 Skocpol, 1985, *op. cit.*, pp. 15–17
182 *ibid.*, p. 16
183 *ibid.*, pp. 16–17.
184 Callinicos, 1992, *op. cit.*, p. 134.
185 Harris, 1991, *op. cit.*, p. 80.
186 Callinicos, 1992, *op. cit.*, p. 134.
187 T. B. Bottomore and R. T. Brym, *The Capitalist Class: An International Study*, London, Harvester Wheatsheaf, 1989; D. Boyd, *Elites and their Education*, Windsor, NFER, 1973; S. Clegg, P. Boreham and G. Dow, *Class, Politics and the Economy*, London, Routledge and Kegan Paul, 1986; B. Criddle, 'Candidates', in D. Butler and D. Kavanagh (eds) *The British General Election of 1987*, London, Macmillan, 1988; G. W. Domhoff, *Who Rules America?*, Englewod Cliffs NJ, Prentice-Hall, 1967; G. W. F. Domhoff, *The Higher Circles: The Governing Class in America*, New York, Vintage, 1971; A. Giddens, 'An anatomy of the British ruling class', *New Society*, 4 October 1979; F. Longstreth, 'The city, industry and the state', in C. Crouch (ed.) *State and Economy in Contemporary Capitalism*, London, Croom Helm, 1979; T. Lupton and S. Wilson, 'The social background and connections of top decision makers', in J. Urry and J. Wakeford (eds) *Power in Britain*, London, Heinemann, 1973; R. Miliband, *The State in Capitalist Society*, London, Quartet, 1973; C. B. Otley, 'Militarism and the social affiliations of the British army elite', in C. van Doorn (ed.) *Armed Forces and Society*, the Hague, Mouton, 1968; J. Scott, *The Upper Classes: Property and Privilege in Britain*, London, Macmillan, 1979; J. Scott, *Corporations, Classes and Capitalism*, London, Hutchinson, 1985; J. Scott, 'The British upper class', in D. Coates, G. Johnson and R. Bush (eds) *A Socialist Anatomy of Britain*, Cambridge, Polity Press, 1985; J. Scott, *Who Rules Britain?*, Cambridge, Polity Press, 1991; Stanworth and Giddens, 1974, *op. cit.*; Westergaard and Resler, 1976, *op. cit.*; C. W. Mills, *The Power Elite*, Oxford, Oxford University Press, 1956.

188 C. Harman, 'The state and capital today', *International Socialism*, 1991, 2:51, pp. 10–14.
189 R. Miliband, 'Class analysis', in A. Giddens and J. Turner (eds) *Social Theory Today*, Cambridge, Polity Press, 1987, p. 340.
190 Theda Skocpol, for instance, takes Marxism to task for endorsing an economistic and 'class-centred' analysis of the state:

> At the theoretical level, virtually all neo-Marxist writers on the state have retained deeply embedded society-centred assumptions, not allowing themselves to doubt that, at base, states are inherently shaped by classes or class struggles and function to preserve and expand modes of production.
>
> (Skocpol, 1985, *op. cit.*, p. 5)

By contrast, Skocpol sees 'state-centred' power relations on a global scale as being crucial in shaping class structures and class agency within the individual nation-state. In fairness to Skocpol and other 'state-centred' theorists, it should be noted that some of the blame for this vulgarisation of the Marxist theory of the state must be laid at the door of certain neo-Marxists. For example, as Harman says, both Miliband and Poulantzas, in their famous debate of the 1970s, treated the state as purely superstructural to a domestic capitalist economy and class structure (Harman, 1991, *op. cit.*, p. 4). Yet the same error was not made by Marx, nor by Lenin, Bukharin, Hilferding, or more contemporary analysts of state- and trans-state capitalism – such as Cliff, Harman and Kidron. For these theorists, domestic class structures are shaped by competitive inter-state relations in the global economy, as well as by local elites and the ups and downs of domestic class struggle. Nor are states seen by them as simple superstructures. Skocpol and other 'state-centred' theorists cannot afford to admit this, however, because doing so would blunt their claim to be offering an analysis of the state which goes beyond the 'economic reductionism' of Marxism. The result is a failure to engage seriously with Marxist accounts of the 'relative autonomy' of the state (Skocpol, 1979, *op. cit.* pp. 26–7).
191 Marx and Engels, 1967, *op. cit.*, p. 82.
192 Marx, 1954, *op. cit.*
193 Bukharin, 1972, *op. cit.*; Lenin, 1965, *op. cit.*
194 Giddens, 1981, *op. cit.*, pp. 3, 250.
195 Harris, 1991, *op. cit.*, pp. 82–6.
196 Harman, 1986, *op. cit.*, p. 14.
197 Jakubowski, 1990, *op. cit.*, p. 42.
198 *ibid.*, pp. 42–3.
199 Marx, 1976, *op. cit.*, p. 899.
200 Harman, 1991, *op. cit.*, pp. 15, 18, 19.
201 *ibid.*, pp. 18, 19.
202 Callinicos, 1992, *op. cit.*, p. 137.
203 Harman, 1991, *op. cit.*, pp. 19–20. This point is made explicitly by Engels. In his words:

> The reaction of the state power upon economic development can be of three kinds: it can run in the same direction, and then development is more rapid; it can oppose the line of development, in which case … [the state] will go to pieces in the long run … or it can prevent the economic development from proceeding along certain lines, and prescribe other lines. This case ultimately resolves itself to one of the two previous ones.
>
> (F. Engels, 'Letter to Schmidt', in Engels, 1980, *op. cit.*, p. 16)

The abandonment of Keynesian reformism as state policy by all major western governments in the late 1970s and 1980s, in response to the global recessions and increasing internationalisation-integration of production, finance and trade of these years, in favour of deregulation, deflation, privatisation and the 'war on welfare', provides a striking recent demonstration of Engels' argument. In this case, the 'law of motion' of the world economy (in its trans-state monopoly 'stage' of development) has ultimately forced the state system into line with the interests and imperatives of an increasingly internationalised capitalist class. These same pressures have, of course, broken apart the old Stalinist states of Eastern Europe (A. Callinicos, *The Revenge of History: Marxism and the East European Revolutions*, Cambridge, Polity Press, 1991), and are increasingly undermining the social-democratic corporatist state structures of Germany and Scandinavia (A. Callinicos, 'Crisis and class struggle in Europe today', *International Socialism*, 1994, 2:63; A. Callinicos, 'Europe – the mounting crisis', *International Socialism*, 1997, 2:75; C. Harman, *The Economics of the Madhouse: Capitalism and the Market Today*, London, Bookmarks, 1996, pp. 94–7).

204 Harman, 1986, *op. cit.*, pp. 12, 20.

205 Molyneux, 1995, *op. cit.*, p. 55.

206 *ibid.*

Index